The Development
of Corporate Capitalism
in Kenya
1918–77

Nicola Swainson

Visiting Lecturer in Politics
University of California, Los Angeles

UNIVERSITY OF CALIFORNIA PRESS

BERKELEY AND LOS ANGELES

University of California Press
Berkeley and Los Angeles, California

ISBN 0–520–03988–2
ISBN 0–520–04019–8 pbk.
Library of Congress Catalog Card No. 79–65768

This book was set in 10/11 pt Times
by Bishopsgate Press Ltd., London
and printed in Great Britain
by Whitstable Litho Ltd, Whitstable, Kent

For Tita

Contents

PART II

PART III

List of Tables

List of Appendices to Chapter 6

Acknowledgements

I would like to thank all those who helped make possible the work that went into this book. I am indebted to the Social Science Research Council (UK) for funding the first part of the research. Most of the writing was done while I was teaching at the University of Dar es Salaam. The revisions of the manuscript were completed while I was a Killam Research Fellow at Dalhousie University. Stimulating discussions at these places have been most helpful.

In Kenya, many individuals, institutions and private firms offered their time, facilities and information, for which I am most grateful. In particular I would like to thank the staff of the Registrar General's Department who had me under their feet for many months, also the Kenya National Archives, the Institute for Development Studies (Nairobi), the Statistics Division of the Treasury, the East African Newspaper Cuttings Library and the Macmillan Library.

Unfortunately it is not possible to list all those individuals who have contributed so much to my work over the past four years. For his continual support and encouragement throughout the course of this project, I must extend my special thanks to Mike Cowen. The thorough comments on the manuscript by Colin Leys were extremely helpful at the writing-up stage. Henry Bernstein also made useful comments on an earlier draft. Critical discussions with many other people have contributed a great deal to my work. Some of these are: Apollo Njonjo, Scott MacWilliam, James Mayall, Martin Godfrey, Max Collande, Yash Tandon, Anna-Maria Gentili, Mahmood Mamdani, Michael Lofchie and David Rosenberg.

Finally I must express sincere appreciation of the tolerance of those friends who provided support of different kinds during the course of my research and writing. Without the help of those acknowledged above and many others, this book would have been impossible.

Abbreviations

BBL	Brooke Bond Leibig Ltd
CDC	Colonial Development Corporation
(*after 1960*)	Commonwealth Development Corporation
CO	Colonial Office (London)
COTU	Confederation of Trade Unions
EATGA	East African Tea Growers' Association
ICDC	Industrial and Commercial Development Corporation
IDC	Industrial Development Corporation
ITA	International Tea Agreements
ITC	International Tea Committee
JEAB	Joint East Africa Board
KAM	Kenya Association of Manufacturers
KANU	Kenya African National Union
KAU	Kenya African Union
KNTC	Kenya National Trading Corporation
KPU	Kenya People's Union
KTDA	Kenya Tea Development Authority
LEGCO	Legislative Council
MCI	Ministry of Commerce and Industry
MNC	Multinational Corporation
SCDA	Special Crops Development Authority
SCI	Secretary for Commerce and Industry

Libraries and Publishers

CUP	Cambridge University Press
DN	*Daily Nation*
EALB	East African Literature Bureau
EAPH	East African Publishing House
EAS	*East African Standard* Newspapers
HMSO	Her Majesty's Stationery Office
IDS, Nairobi	Institute of Development Studies, Nairobi
KNA	*Kenya National Archives* (Nairobi)

ML	Macmillan Library (Nairobi)
MRP	Monthly Review Press (New York City)
NLB	New Left Books (London)
NLR	*New Left Review*
OUP	Oxford University Press
RAPE	*Review of African Political Economy*

INTRODUCTION
The State and Economy in Kenya
1918–77

What is important is that capitalism cannot exist and develop without constantly expanding the sphere of its domination, without colonising new countries and drawing old non-capitalist countries into the whirlpool of the world economy . . . the spasmodic character of economic development, the rapid transformation of the methods of production, the disappearance of all forms of personal dependence and patriarchism in relationships, the mobility of the population, the influence of the big industrial centres . . . all lead to a profound change in the character of the producers. (V.I. Lenin, *The Development of Capitalism in Russia*, Progress Publishers, Moscow, 1974, pp. 604–5).

This book is concerned to examine the underlying mechanisms of capitalist development in Kenya during the colonial and post-colonial periods. Within this broad framework, the main focus is on patterns of corporate accumulation in the economy. The study is not, however, confined to a bird's-eye view of multinational corporations in Kenya, but it rather seeks to explain the *political* conditions which underlie particular periods of capitalist development. Before proceeding to an overview of 'capital and the state' in the three different historical periods under consideration, it is necessary to locate our discussion within the context of the current debates on *international firms* and *underdevelopment*.

Multinational firms in the twentieth century were an outgrowth of the monopoly phase of capitalism which was marked by the *concentration* of capital on a world scale. Indeed, in the period covered by this study (1918–77), there has been a historical shift in the form of foreign investment from portfolio to direct investment carried out by large, centralized multinational corporations. This change was most clearly evident after the Second World War as the larger firms in the capitalist metropoles gradually absorbed the weaker ones and large, vertically integrated corporations emerged.

1

In the academic literature on foreign investment it is possible to identify both critical and supportive views.[1]

In the view of bourgeois economic theory it is assumed that market mechanisms will operate in order to develop a rational international division of labour, which will optimize the world's productive resources. According to this argument, nation states should not interfere with the 'good of mankind'. A more moderate version of this position is expressed in the work of Vernon, Dunning and Rolfe.[2] Their basic framework is cast in the same mould (neo-classical trade and welfare theory), but it emphasizes the need to manage the operations of the multinational corporation (MNC) in the 'national interest', by political means if necessary. The corporations in this view are seen as offering to host countries a package deal of skills, technology and finance which can be evaluated in terms of economic welfare. Under this scheme, the political and economic aspects of foreign investment are considered to be separate. For instance, in a discussion of nationalist objections to MNCs, Rolfe states: 'here politics and human feeling rather than economics are involved: economic benefits and political or emotional costs are difficult to compare, they are denominated in a different coin'.[3]

There is considerable diversity within the camp that is *critical* of foreign investment, and it is often difficult to distinguish between the radical, Marxist or neo-Marxist interpretations of multinational corporations. An orthodox Marxist view would seek to outline the contradictory nature of the capitalist world economy at the same time as recognizing the historically progressive role of capitalism in developing the means of production and breaking down outmoded social formations. Such a position usually stresses the *class* nature of capital and the state.

For instance, Lenin, at the turn of the twentieth century, wrote: 'recognition of the progressiveness of this role is quite compatible with the full recognition of the negative and dark sides of capitalism . . . which are inevitably inherent in capitalism.'[4]

The theoretical writings on *imperialism* and the export of capital trace their origins to different aspects of Marx's picture of capitalism. The word 'imperialism' did not appear in the writings of Marx and Engels, but came into usage in England during the 1860s and 1870s to describe the views of those who wished to strengthen the links between

1. For a variety of views on international firms see H. Radice (ed.), *International Firms and Modern Imperialism*, Penguin, Harmondsworth, 1975.

2. For instance, J. Dunning, *Studies in International Investment*, Allen & Unwin, London, 1970, and S. Rolfe and W. Damm, *The International Corporation*, Praeger, New York, 1970.

3. Rolfe and Damm, op. cit.

4 V. I. Lenin, *The Development of Capitalism in Russia*, Progress Publishers, Moscow, 1974, p. 602.

Britain and the empire.[5] The Marxists of the early twentieth century (primarily Lenin, Bukharin, Hilferding and Rosa Luxemburg), began to analyse imperialism in terms of the export of capital from the advanced capitalist metropoles to the less-developed regions. They were primarily concerned to understand the laws of capital accumulation which had given rise to the new trends of capital exports overseas and to explain these in the political context of the class struggles in the home countries. Unfortunately, there is no space here to analyse the different theories of imperialism.

Since the Second World War, Marxist writers seeking to explain the causes of economic underdevelopment have developed a 'radical' theory that is critical of foreign investment. The most important of these underdevelopment theorists since the 1950s are Paul Baran, Gunder Frank, Wallerstein and Samir Amin. These 'radical' interpretations of underdevelopment will be considered in the context of our discussion of 'the state and economy' in post-colonial Kenya.

Before embarking on an overview of capitalism in Kenya during three historical periods, it is necessary to define some of the concepts that will be employed.

A *social formation* here is taken to mean the determinate mode of production and its specific conditions of existence, which include also ideological and political factors. Unfortunately, the Marxist theory of *the state* is not well developed and there have been few attempts to apply the theory to post-colonial states. *The Communist Manifesto* was the starting point for Marx's theory of the state; here the modern state was characterized as being a 'committee for managing the common affairs of the whole bourgeoisie'. The capitalist state, by this view, was perceived as the product of the growing division of society into the appropriators of surplus value who own the means of production (the bourgeoisie) and those whose labour is exploited (the proletariat). The *state* form arose from the increasing autonomy of the government machinery from the class society. When it came to applying this theory to concrete political situations, such as the 1848 Revolution in France, Marx found it necessary to evolve a more sophisticated notion of the state and classes. In his discussion of class struggles in France,[6] Marx tried to distinguish a wider variety of classes and class fractions than the basic bourgeoisie/proletariat division. France at that time, like many African countries today, had not developed fully capitalist relations of production, and Marx found it necessary to distinguish between the landowners, self-employed peasants, financial bourgeoisie,

5. Refer to M. Barratt Brown, 'A critique of Marxist theories of imperialism', in R. Owen and R. Sutcliffe (eds.), *Studies in the Theory of Imperialism*, Longman, London, 1972.

6. Karl Marx, *The Revolutions of 1848 and Surveys from Exile*, ed. D. Fernbach, Penguin and NLB, London, 1973.

industrial bourgeoisie, petty bourgeoisie and industrial proletariat. The *petty bourgeoisie* were an amorphous category found between the bourgeoisie and the proletariat and they included small property-owners, traders, low-level bureaucrats and peasants working in their own enterprises.

In his writings on France, Marx identified not one *ruling class*, but rather a ruling bloc composed of a plurality of classes or fractions of classes, where *one* fraction was politically dominant. The actual state *machinery* was conceived of as a repressive apparatus which enabled the ruling class simultaneously to effect its domination over the working class and to ensure conditions of surplus-value production. The apparatuses of the capitalist state include the police, judiciary, prisons, army, and so on. Furthermore, the state has the ideological functions (through education, propaganda, etc.) which also serve the prevailing system of capital reproduction.

The advanced capitalist state in the twentieth century has taken on a high degree of *autonomy* with regard to civil society. Althusser has attempted to give theoretical recognition to the specificity of *political* forces and issues. He claims that the political level is relatively auton-omous, in that it exists within the boundaries set by the global mode of production.[7] Even though the political structure represents social clas-ses which exist at the economic level, these are considered to be more than a simple reflection. There is invariably a discrepancy between the classes at the level of the economic and the forces represented in politics.

Nicos Poulantzas has taken this position further: 'the fact that the structures of the whole are determined in the last instance by the economic does not mean that the economic *always* holds the dominant role in that structure. The unity constituted by the structure in domi-nance implies that every mode of production has a dominant level or instance.'[8] Critics have accused Poulantzas of ending up by determin-ing classes at the economic level, despite the assertions of relative autonomy. Indeed, his overtly schematic way of analysing classes in advanced capitalism does tend to gloss over the relationship between the class fraction that retains state power and the dominant social classes. However, the most positive aspect of Poulantzas's work on the state has been his diversion away from the notion that the state is crudely an *instrument* of the ruling class,[9] back to the idea of the state as an *objective* relation. Indeed, the relationship between the political

---

7 Louis Althusser, *Essays in Self-Criticism*, NLB, London, 1976.

8 N. Poulantzas, *Political Power and Social Classes*, NLB, London, 1973, pp. 13–15. For two critiques of Poulantzas, see E. Laclau, *Economy and Society*, vol. iv, 1975, and Paul Hirst, 'Economic classes and politics', in Alan Hunt (ed.), *Class and Class Structure*, Lawrence & Wishart, London, 1977.

9 This has been a common position among the European revisionist communist parties, such as the French CP.

and economic in Marxist theory is highly controversial. The whole question of identifying social classes is in danger of becoming an academic exercise, whereas Marx stressed that such problems could only be resolved in the arena of class struggles.

It is important for our analysis of capitalism in Kenya to reiterate a fundamental proposition that the *production and exchange* of things is the basis of all social structures. In every society that has appeared in history, 'the manner in which wealth is distributed and society is divided into classes is dependent on what is produced, how it is produced and how the products are exchanged'.[10]

Therefore, what distinguishes different *social classes* is their relation to the labour process, and class relations under capitalism are necessarily *contradictory*.

Although this book is not a treatise on capital and class[11] in Kenya, it does seek to show the way in which changes in the economy are mediated by politics. For each historical period, the aim is to outline the nature of the social formation in terms of the ownership and control of capital, forms of surplus appropriation and the character of state intervention.

The Interwar Period 1918–39

Kenya's links with western capitalism were forged from the late nineteenth century during a period when the world market was dominated by a few industrial giants such as Britain, France and Germany. Having been under the control of the British East African Company in the last decades of the nineteenth century, Kenya became a protectorate under Britain in 1895 and a Crown colony in 1920. By the early twentieth century, the autonomy of pre-colonial modes of production was being broken down by the agents of western capitalism, as East Africa was linked to the centres of metropolitan accumulation. Commodity production for the world market developed gradually on peasant farms and European estates. From the outset of British rule, a European settler class was established in Kenya and with the development of a market economy, other forms of production became subjected to the needs of *capital*.

It has been illustrated convincingly elsewhere that Britain's accumulation from the seventeenth century onwards was intimately bound up with the exploitation of the colonies.[12] The East African territories in

---

10 F. Engels, *Anti-Dühring*, Progress Publishers, Moscow, 1975, p. 303.

11 The short discussion of the state and classes has been schematic, due to the problems associated with placing my own discussion of corporate accumulation in the context of the wider political economy.

12 See Tom Nairn, 'The decline of the British state', *NLR*, nos 101–2, April 1977.

the first part of the twentieth century offered no great mineral wealth as in the case of Northern Rhodesia and South Africa. Nevertheless, by the 1920s, the East African territories (Uganda in particular) were providing raw materials and foodstuffs for the imperial market at the same time as offering outlets for British investment.

The *colonial state* in several respects existed under very different conditions from the classic model of a bourgeois state. The administration in Kenya, for instance, during the interwar years represented a condensation of both *internal and external* class forces. This administration was compelled to operate in several distinct spheres: it connected the metropolis to the colony at the same time as mediating between internal classes. The main concern here is briefly to shed some light on the class balance within the colonial state in Kenya and assess the form and effects of state intervention.

A group of European farmers had been encouraged to settle in Kenya from 1900 onwards, in order to grow agricultural products which would help finance the Uganda Railway. By the early 1920s, the number of Europeans in Kenya had reached about 20 000 compared with 3 million African inhabitants, and these settlers were to exercise a degree of influence out of all proportion to their numbers. Estate capital was prevalent in Kenya before 1939, and this category included the larger settler farmers and foreign estate companies. However, the *resident* section of estate capital was the *dominant* political force within the administration.[13]

By the time that Kenya became a Crown colony in 1920, settler farmers constituted a group whose interests were bound up with *internal* accumulation. The difference between a settler farmer like Lord Delamere and a large British plantation company was that the ownership and control of the latter lay outside of the social formation. The dominant settler farmers were intent on controlling the means of production and exchange within Kenya and they expected full support from the administration to this end. In this respect the settler bourgeoisie in Kenya was involved in a process of primitive accumulation of capital, a phase which has some aspects in common with the current phase of indigenous capitalism.

From 1922 onwards it was intended that a dual policy of African and European agricultural production should prevail in Kenya. The metropolitan government at that time asserted the doctrine of 'native paramountcy' which in theory protected indigenous interests in the colony. Metropolitan policy towards Kenya was fraught with contradictions from the outset. For instance, it encouraged dual forms of

---

13 For a most enlightening discussion of the colonial state in Kenya, see J. Lonsdale, 'The growth and transformation of the colonial state in Kenya', 1929–1952, mimeo., Cambridge, October 1977, and J. Lonsdale and B. Berman, *Accumulation and Control: The Colonial State in Kenya, 1888–1929*, ASAUK Conference, 1978.

agricultural production, peasant-households and estates, which competed directly with each other for labour. One of the chief functions of
the Kenyan administration from the early period of European settlement had been to ensure a *labour supply* to the estates. By means of
taxation and forced labour before 1925, Africans were compelled to
either sell their labour to the European farmers or to cultivate cash
crops for the market. The settlers were determined to force Africans
into the labour market. Elspeth Huxley, a prominent exponent of the
settler cause, articulated this demand: 'the government has an obliga-
tion to see that the fit adult African male does in fact enter the labour
market in sufficient numbers to build up the country's strength'.[14]

A paradox existed in that the state was required to force as many
Africans as possible on to the settler estates, despite the fact that it
relied heavily in the early years on the revenue raised from African-
grown cash crops. For instance in 1913, products of African origin
furnished about three-quarters of the country's export earnings![15] The
coexistence of African and settler agriculture presented political as
well as economic problems to the colonial administration. It was hard
to perpetuate the myth of racial supremacy in the face of the true
statistics on African agriculture. African agriculture was intended to
be *complementary* to, but never competitive with, settler enterprise.

On the other hand, the foreign estates, although benefiting immediately from the ensured labour supplies, cared little from where or how
they acquired their commodities. In the long run, both estate and
merchant firms were just as willing to develop a sector of peasant
production as long as they could retain control over the distribution of
that commodity. Therein lay an incipient conflict with metropolitan
capital, for the settlers could not tolerate the large-scale development
of an African farming class, as it might compete with their own enterprise and undermine their political monopoly.

During the interwar years, these material contradictions were mani-
fested in the conflicts between the Kenyan and metropolitan
administrations. That the settlers opposed any attempts at metropolitan political direction did not concern the latter unduly as long as the
colony balanced its budgets and the supply of primary products was
forthcoming. Conflicts between colony and metropolis tended to arise
in times of financial crisis. In the late 1920s when the government was
required to set up a Land Bank to solve problems of indebtedness
faced by the smaller settlers, metropolitan reservations were expressed
with regard to settler supremacy in Kenya.

Another clash between the 'settler state' and the Colonial Office in
Britain occurred with regard to the interpretation of *trusteeship* for the
native peoples. The settler political leaders maintained that the trans-

---

14 E. Huxley, *The Settlers of Kenya*, Greenwood, Connecticut, 1975 edn, p. 47.
15 Lonsdale and Berman, op. cit.

ient officials of the metropolitan government should respect the supreme right of the settler minority to exercise the responsibilities of trusteeship.[16] This led to continual disputes over the rights of Africans and Asians in Kenya to political representation in the colony. Before the Second World War the European minority in Kenya were able to assert exclusive political authority and effectively resist any pressure from the indigenous people for the devolution of their power. However, the settler class should not be thought of as monolithic, and there were indeed struggles between different fractions of settler capital, which were arbitrated by the administration.[17] At the political level, however, it was necessary for them to maintain a degree of political unity in the face of potential threats to their hegemony from the indigenous population.

In 1923, when the metropolitan government declared that the interests of the native peoples were to be paramount in British territories, settler designs for self-government along the lines of Southern Rhodesia (in 1921) were quashed. Nevertheless, they succeeded in asserting their political hegemony through existing colonial structures. The state *apparatus* in Kenya was staffed by metropolitan officials, but during the 1920s the settlers were able to increase their formal and informal powers in the following ways:

(1) through their elected representatives in the Legislative Council (LEGCO), which enabled them to exert control over financial matters;

(2) through a devolution of power to the local district councils, which gave the settlers the formal powers to allocate regional resources;

(3) the connection between government departments and producer boards (such as maize and dairy) was formalized.[18]

Consequently the dominant fraction of settler capital (the large estate farmers) were able to determine the distribution of surplus in Kenya, a process which was unmediated by democratic representation of the indigenous peoples.[19]

Brett[20] has correctly portrayed the settlers in Kenya as the first 'economic nationalists' of the region, in that they were intent on promoting domestic accumulation under protected conditions. Before 1939 the Kenyan administration had quite a high degree of autonomy in promoting internal accumulation in that it could raise loans inde-

---

16 For further details see Huxley, op. cit., ch. 8.

17 For instance the Cost of Living Commission in 1929 exhibited the different interests of the white petty bourgeoisie and the farmers.

18 Lonsdale and Berman, op. cit.

19 The local native councils, established in the mid-1920s, were designed to co-opt nationalist opposition to the colonial government.

20 E. A. Brett, *Colonialism and Underdevelopment, the Politics of Economic Change, 1919–1939*, Heinemann, London, 1973.

pendently and make most of the major decisions concerning the allocation of government revenue. It is no accident that the settlers considered the British government as a hindrance rather than a help, with its *laissez-faire* colonial policies.

The highly protective nature of government support to the settlers and the investment in the means of production (land and infrastructure) before the war served to develop the productive forces more thoroughly in Kenya Colony than in the other two East African territories. The level of investment was higher in Kenya and, despite the drain of some capital outside the country through the estate and trading firms based in England, a larger proportion of the surplus was utilized internally.

The failure to develop an industrial base in Kenya before 1939 related to the limited size of the internal market, and the shortage of money capital from either government or private sources. Nevertheless, by 1945 enough surplus had been accumulated from agricultural production to stimulate the expansion of capital into manufacturing industry.

At the political level during this period it was necessary for the local administration in Kenya to maintain a balance between contending settler fractions, foreign capital and indigenous class forces. The maintenance of a broad 'united front' of European supremacy was crucial in terms of maintaining the colonial system.

The subtle balance of internal and external classes was finally to be torn asunder by the nationalist challenge in the 1950s.

The Postwar Period 1945–63

In this period the forms of ownership and control of capital began to undergo a long-term shift in favour of international capital, which was accompanied by a relative decline in settler production in the colony. This change was reflected at the level of the state by an increasing degree of metropolitan direction within the Kenyan administration.

The changing role of Britain in the world economy after 1945, in the face of American supremacy, led to a fundamental reorganization of the home economy which was followed by an adjustment in colonial policy. New forms of *finance* capital became intimately linked with the interventionist state in Britain. The fusion of banking and productive capitals outlined by Lenin in his work on 'imperialism'[21] became increasingly apparent after 1945 as the world economy came to be dominated by large multinational corporations which were absorbing

---

21 V. I. Lenin, *Imperialism, the Highest Stage of Capitalism*, Progress Publishers, Moscow, 1974.

smaller units of capital. To conceptualize finance capital accurately is problematic and raises some theoretical questions which cannot be dealt with here.[22] Nevertheless it is clear that finance capital in this period became more than merely the 'book-keeper' of productive capital.

In any event, finance capital came to be closely integrated with government policy after the war. The predominant feature in postwar Kenya was the massive investment of state financial agencies in *African cash-crop agriculture*. This was effected by extending loan capital and providing link-ups with technical expertise for agricultural and industrial projects which were not initially attractive to private capital. This policy was implemented under the auspices of the *Swynnerton Plan of 1954* which was aimed at developing indigenous agriculture for the world market. The new government development programmes were able to break the competitive opposition which had previously existed between estate and household commodity production and to integrate the two under the aegis of *international capital*. Multinational firms were closely linked with government plans to develop cash crops such as pyrethrum and tea.[23] Through its participation in the administration of these schemes, international capital was able to influence the quantity and quality of production, at the same time as acting as a medium of distribution for the world market. This illustrates the way in which international capital can extract surplus value from any labour process.

Of course these changes in Kenya's structure of production necessitated the destruction of the racial boundaries surrounding production. The inflow of foreign capital into Kenya after 1945 coincided with a large increase in domestic savings in the colony. Capitalist relations were extended and larger numbers of Africans entered the labour market in both agricultural and industrial production. Larger numbers of workers and peasants were being subjected to capital either directly (in the factories and estates) or indirectly (through peasant cash-crop production).

The metropolitan state increased its level of aid to the colony and this was largely directed to welfare and education services, thus providing the prerequisites for the intervention of private capital.

During the postwar years in Kenya, the role of the colonial administration was substantially changed with regard to the type of state intervention and the dominant class interests. This period can be characterized as being a *transitional* one in terms of political domi-

---

22 M. P. Cowen and K. Kinyanjui, 'Capital and class in Kenya', mimeo., IDS, Nairobi, 1977, p. 23. In footnote 21 of the preface, the authors draw attention to the weakness of theory surrounding finance capital and the potential problems associated with the law of value.

23 These crops were dominated by Mitchell Cotts and Brooke Bond respectively.

nance. The postwar administration was more closely under metropolitan control, although it became increasingly hard to arbitrate between contending class forces of settler, indigenous and foreign elements.

The new development plans for African agriculture and the close integration of British finance capital with state policy after 1945 required a break in settler monopolies over production and distribution in Kenya. The new metropolitan direction to raise productivity involved the encouragement of an African middle class, which would hopefully stabilize the political scene and pre-empt a more radical nationalism. Some degree of African participation was allowed in the agricultural boards, although this attempt to incorporate African nationalism within a political system still dominated by whites was doomed to failure.

Furthermore, by the late 1950s the metropolitan government was attempting to pressure the Europeans into acceptance of a multiracial society. Indeed, during this period many of the larger farmers and European businessmen had realized that their political future lay in a compromise with African nationalism.[24] However, the bulk of the smaller settlers had everything to lose from a nationalist settlement.

In material terms, settler capital was in relative decline after the war and settler enterprises were being rapidly absorbed by Asian and foreign firms. Output from European farms was dropping as a percentage of the total GNP. Paradoxically, it was during the early 1950s, in the face of a violent threat to their political hegemony, that settler cohesion was at its peak. During the war and postwar years in Kenya, the numbers of white officials had swelled in the Kenyan administration. This apparent increase in settler political power[25] was illusory and the proliferation of committees and boards in Kenya from the war years onwards proved to be a medium of metropolitan control. The ultimate defeat of settler aspirations to self-government occurred in the early 1950s when the metropolitan government brought the colony under direct military control in order to crush the Mau Mau movement. This British military intervention served to restore civil order and confirmed a rising suspicion amongst the settlers that final political authority rested with the metropolitan government. Indeed, the logic of metropolitan control led to the nationalist settlement of the early 1960s, which was the final death blow to settler supremacy.

The political crisis in Kenya during the 1950s was indicative of the state's failure to maintain the balance between contending class interests. Without a radical restructuring of political representation, the

---

24 For a fascinating account of the transformation of the 'progressive' settler wing into an alliance with African nationalists, see M. Blundell, *So Rough a Wind*, Weidenfeld & Nicolson, London, 1964.

25 This is detailed in G. Bennett, *Kenya, a Political History: The Colonial Period*, OUP, London, 1963.

state was incapable of incorporating or neutralizing nationalist demands. The moderate nationalist organizations, such as Kenya African Union (KAU), had completely failed to break the settler hold over production and distribution in the colony. These contradictions could not be worked out within the framework of settler supremacy, and it was only after the violent assault on the state by Mau Mau that plans for immediate political representation for Africans were brought to the top of the agenda.

The civil unrest and the fight for political dominance in Kenya during this period were finally arbitrated by the metropolitan power. This 'transitional' period was to give way to the hegemony of the indigenous bourgeoisie in the 1960s. Nevertheless, during the postwar period, the actual forms of state intervention in the colonial economy were indicative of a closer integration of the area into the world market.

Post-Colonial Kenya 1963–77

RADICAL THEORY

Before analysing Kenya's social formation after independence, it is important to set the argument in the context of current debates on the impact of foreign capital on the 'peripheral' countries. This is particularly relevant in so far as the discussion here takes issue with some aspects of the 'radical' interpretations of underdevelopment.

The existing treatments of East African political economy have been strongly influenced by the work of Gunder Frank[26] and the Latin American *dependency school*. The source of underdevelopment theory can be traced back to the Economic Commission for Latin America (ECLA), which in the 1940s and 1950s began to articulate a nationalist attack on the negative effects of foreign investment in Latin American countries. The logic of its position was to recommend the redirection of foreign investment into import-substitution industries inside the peripheral countries, which would hopefully cut down on the 'surplus drain' to the metropolis via the traditional-export sector. By the 1960s it was clear that this 'self-centred' model of development had failed to produce the desired effect, so that a new radical version of dependency emerged. Gunder Frank became the best-known exponent of the left wing of the 'structural-dependency school' in Latin America,[27] and he attacked the rationality of an import-substitution

---

26 A. Gunder Frank, *Capitalism and Underdevelopment in Latin America, MRP*, New York, 1969.

27 For a good account of the origins of underdevelopment theory, see P. J. O'Brien, 'A critique of Latin American theories of dependency', in I. Oxaal, T. Barnett and D. Booth (eds.), *Beyond the Sociology of Development*, Routledge & Kegan Paul, London, 1975.

policy which still involved a high degree of foreign investment resulting in balance-of-payments deficits. He supported the position of the Latin American Solidarity Organization in 1967 that, due to the heavy dependence of Latin American countries on foreign capital, the local bourgeoisies were incapable of acting independently. Frank's view that underdevelopment could only be understood as part of the world economic system was not new. His basic proposition was that the centre countries were responsible for the drain of surplus from the peripheries, which denied the latter any prospect of internal accumulation. He maintained that it was the satellite status of poor countries in the global capitalist system that generated underdevelopment and, therefore, the weaker the ties of the periphery to the centre, the greater the possibility of local development. The dependency theorists of the 1960s certainly broke from the stagnation of orthodox development theory, which maintained that all countries were working from an original state of underdevelopment through various stages of growth to reach the paradigm of western capitalism. Critics on the left took as their starting point the reverse position: that underdevelopment was the *product* of capitalist penetration. More recently, substantial controversy has arisen amongst Marxists over the problematic of underdevelopment theory itself.[28]

The major flaw in the 'radical' interpretation of underdevelopment lies in its *conceptualization of capitalism*,[29] a problem most clearly demonstrated in the works of Frank, Wallerstein and Samir Amin. Wallerstein and Frank[30] in particular maintain that the world market was capitalist from its very inception. The radicals' periodization of capital is completely lacking and the colonial world is assumed to be capitalist from the sixteenth century with the Spanish conquests of Latin America. By this token, the whole history of colonialism is seen as being a totality of production relations where capitalist enterprises subjugated peasant labour. The problem with such formulations is that they equate capitalism with a *trade*-based division of labour, where the dynamics of accumulation are assumed to operate through the imperatives of *exchange* rather than *production*.

Samir Amin[31] has transposed dependency theory to the study of Africa. He postulates that there is a fundamental *difference* between the model of capital accumulation characteristic of a *self-centred system* and that of a *peripheral system*. Centre capitalism is defined as

28 See an excellent review of these debates in Colin Leys, 'Underdevelopment and dependency, some critical notes', *Journal of Contemporary Asia*, vol. 1, 1977.

29 See Henry Bernstein, 'Sociology of underdevelopment vs sociology of development?', mimeo., University of Dar es Salaam, 1977.

30 I. Wallerstein, *The Modern World System*, MRP, New York, 1974, and Gunder Frank, op. cit.

31 S. Amin, 'Accumulation and development: a theoretical model', *RAPE*, no. 1, 1974, and S. Amin, *Unequal Development*, Harvester, Hassocks, Sussex, 1976.

being autonomous and self-centred in its development, with a high degree of integration between capital-goods sectors (Dept I) and consumer-goods sectors (Dept II). He argues that such contradictions as do exist in the metropolitan countries, namely, the overproduction of the consumer-goods sectors, are solved by means of an extension of markets into the peripheries. His work on unequal development[32] seems to contain a fundamental contradiction in that it characterizes capitalist development as being both autonomous and integrated and yet structurally dependent on the periphery. This would seem to contradict his own recognition that at the present stage of imperialism most capital exports take place between advanced countries, rather than between centres and peripheries.

The analysis of the underdevelopment theorists which has been briefly sketched here has a common element, in that from their view of capitalism, *socialism* emerges as a *policy alternative* for the national bourgeoisie rather than being the product of a class struggle. The logic of such arguments of 'structural dependency' of the peripheries on centre countries is to deny the importance of internal class struggles and substitute the notion of exploitation by countries rather than by classes.

THEORIES OF POST-COLONIAL STATES

If theories of the capitalist state during the present phase of imperialism are unsatisfactory, then those concerning post-colonial states are even more so. Robin Murray[33] has brought into question the analytical primacy of the *nation state* and the relationship of political and economic organization, in the context of the rising power of the multinational corporations. He maintains that although the level of state intervention in advanced capitalist economies has intensified since the Second World War, the functions of the state as an instrument of capitalism are increasingly being enacted through bodies *other* than the nation state. For instance, the sheer size and integration of international firms since 1945 means that they are performing many functions previously carried out by the state. This means that in the poorer countries, large multinationals make control by the nation state difficult if not impossible. Therefore, the logic of the internationalization of capital through the agency of multinationals is the decreasing independence of *national* economies.

Murray's internationalization thesis has been subjected to criticism by Bill Warren. He argues to the contrary that the special conditions of 'late capitalism' have required nation states to supervise and direct their economies to a point where their power has been enhanced not

---

32 For an interesting review of *Unequal Development*, see Bernstein, op. cit.

33 Robin Murray, 'The internationalisation of capital and the nation state', in H. Radice (ed.), op. cit., and Bill Warren, 'How international is capital?'

diminished. The only solution to the continual crises of capitalism in the twentieth century has been the *strengthening* of the nation state *vis-à-vis* international capital. Warren makes a valid point to support his contentions: that inter-imperialist rivalry is an illustration of the national basis of capital accumulation. Most writers on the post-colonial state would concur with Murray's position on the declining importance of the nation state in the context of the economic dominance of international capital. The internationalization of capital certainly does raise important questions with regard to the efficacy of the nation state, which will arise in our discussion of post-colonial Kenya. The problem with the Warren/Murray juxtaposition is that it does not adequately periodize capital and the state, due to the general level of the discussion. These issues can only be worked out through concrete studies of particular social formations. The 'national question' is a problematic one for both metropolitan and developing countries alike.

There has been considerable and inconclusive debate as to whether *post-colonial states* are any more or less autonomous than their western counterparts. The discussion on the specificity of post-colonial states was initiated by Hamza Alavi[34] in his work on Pakistan and Bangladesh. He claimed that newly independent countries inherited a state apparatus that had been 'overdeveloped' during the colonial period, in order that it could subordinate domestic classes and mediate between indigenous and foreign interests. 'The essential problem about the state in post-colonial societies stems from the fact that it was not established by an ascendant native bourgeosie but instead a foreign imperialist bourgeoisie.'[35] Colin Leys[36] has correctly pointed out that, in most cases, the large-scale extension in the state apparatuses occurred after formal independence. In any event, it is not clear where the concept of 'overdeveloped' post-colonial states really leads us.

Most writers on the left have identified the *metropolitan bourgeoisie* as the dominant class force within the post-colonial states. John Saul has confirmed Fanon's original statement about the dependent nature of the indigenous elites in newly independent African countries: 'the national middle class discovers its historic mission: that of an intermediary . . . it consists prosaically, of being the transmission line between the nation and capitalism, rampant though camouflaged, which today puts on the masque of neo-colonialism'.[37]

Saul maintains that this intermediary class is not even a 'national middle class' but is a petty bourgeoisie of small traders and bureau-

34 H. Alavi, 'The post-colonial state: Pakistan and Bangladesh', *NLR*, no. 74, 1972.
35 ibid.
36 Colin Leys, 'The overdeveloped post colonial state: a re-evaluation', *RAPE*, no. 5, April 1976.
37 Franz Fanon, quoted in J. Saul, 'The unsteady state: Uganda, Obote and General Amin', *RAPE*, no. 5, April 1976.

crats. Several other interpretations[38] of East African political economy
have reached a similar conclusion with regard to the role of indigenous
classes. Von Freyhold, for instance, considers that 'unless the governing class actually determines the process of economic reproduction in
the country, it cannot be called a ruling class however large its formal
powers may be'. Although she concedes that the model of particular
states varies according to the specific circumstances, such as the
development of productive forces, balance of power, and so on, she
concludes that 'the actual dynamic of economic and social development is determined by the metropolitan bourgeoisie, irrespective of
the form in which it intervenes'.[39] Colin Leys, in his examination of the
post-colonial state, also concurred with this view: 'at all events in post
colonial societies in Africa, there can be little doubt that the dominant
class force is still the foreign bourgeoisie'.[40]

My own study would support the contention that East Africa was
integrated into the world market through the force of colonial capitalism. To maintain, as do many of the above writers on the post-colonial
state, that the metropolitan bourgeoisie is the dominant class force is
acceptable at the economic level. Unfortunately it is not difficult to
move from these assumptions to a position which takes it for granted
that *every* instance in the 'neo-colony' is dictated by the metropolitan
bourgeoisie. Under this schema it becomes impossible to distinguish
the specificity of each social formation. How, for instance, can one
distinguish between the different patterns of accumulation and state
forms in post-colonial Kenya and Tanzania? Simply to identify
economic dependence on the metropole as the determinant factor in
social relations is to bypass the relative autonomy of politics and ignore
the particular characteristics of internal class formation.

POST-COLONIAL KENYA

The section on post-colonial Kenya on pages 173–82 shows how an
embryonic African bourgeoisie began to emerge from the 1920s
onwards, based on new forms of commodity production and the employment of wage labour. The 1950s marked the decline of settler
power which portended the ultimate victory of the nationalist movement. By the early 1960s, the stage was set for the transition to
independence under the hegemony of the indigenous bourgeoisie. The
indigenous bourgeoisie proceeded to use state power to further their
control over the means of production, at the same time purging any
radical elements within the ruling party, KANU.

---

38 I. Shivji, *Class Struggles in Tanzania*, Heinemann, London, 1976, and M. von
Freyhold, 'The post-colonial state and its Tanzanian version', *RAPE*, no. 8, 1977.
39 ibid.
40 Leys, 1976, op. cit.

The problem with regard to the previous views of 'neo-colonial' states in East Africa is that they assume that the local bourgeoisies are impotent intermediaries for foreign capital destined to remain at the level of small-scale trade. Leys, for instance, in his original work on Kenya, confirmed Fanon's dictum that 'this native bourgeoisie will realise with its mouth watering that it lacks something essential to the bourgeoisie: money'.[41] Leys also assumed at that time that there would be a minimal investment of indigenous capital in production, due to the apparently small size of domestic enterprises compared with foreign firms in the early 1970s. The importance of capitalist development in the 1970s, in my view, lies not in the relative size of enterprises, but rather the *process* of accumulation.

The indigenous bourgeoisie in Kenya have used the state to support their investment, first in large-scale agriculture and then in manufacturing. The post-colonial state has also acted to ensure the conditions of capital reproduction in general by ensuring civil order and repressing the labour movement, which has obviously been to the advantage of both local and foreign capitalists.

The extension of internal accumulation has been accompanied by an increased penetration of foreign capital in the Kenyan manufacturing sector. The investment of foreign firms in manufacturing during the 1960s and 1970s was partly in response to global conditions of accumulation which in general have given rise to a massive export of productive capital. This shift in emphasis of foreign capital away from the traditional plantation sectors into manufacturing has also been a response to pressure from indigenous capitalists who have made land their exclusive preserve since independence. The Capital Issues Committee, established in 1971, epitomized the development of more stringent nationalist controls over the economy.

Capital accumulation in Kenya has exhibited two contradictory trends in the post-colonial period: *nationalism and internationalism*. Since 1970 there has been a trend of government investment in all the major sectors of the economy and this has been accompanied by the expansion of domestic capital into manufacturing. Industrial development has taken place during the 1970s through the *partnership* form of joint ventures between local and foreign capital. In theory, therefore, the government has created the mechanisms to control the conditions under which foreign firms invest in Kenya, although in practice multinational firms are able (through patents and technical agreements) to take advantage of their technological monopoly. The susceptibility of the state apparatus to political corruption has tended to contradict the strength of Kenya's controls on foreign capital in the post-colonial period.

---

41 Colin Leys, *Underdevelopment in Kenya, the Political Economy of Neo-Colonialism*, Heinemann, London, 1975, p. 149.

The development of an indigenous manufacturing sector during the 1970s has been the logical outcome of the conversion of merchant into productive capital at a certain stage of accumulation. In some instances, foreign capital has been threatened by competition from new local enterprises and in other projects, local and foreign partners collaborate. Where domestic and foreign capital compete, the state will invariably (as in the case of tea) act in support of national capital.

Nevertheless, by the mid-1970s, the development of an 'economic nationalist' ideology was quite advanced within the Kenyan bureaucracy and this was reflected in the high-level political struggles over the conditions of foreign investment. There has been considerable conflict within the state apparatus between those with ultimate political power[42] to support their private accumulation, and those lacking such political strength. This has been played out by the constant attacks by the media and some politicians on 'corruption'[43] in high office.

Writers such as Langdon and Godfrey have characterized the relationship between the Kenyan state and foreign capital as being a 'symbiotic one'.[44] They claim that the state acts to integrate local and foreign capital. Indeed, the heavy dependence of the domestic bourgeoisie in Kenya on state support in this period has been portrayed as an indication of the inherent weakness of indigenous capitalism. The problem with this formulation is that it assumes capitalist relations to be static. It is rather maintained here that, throughout the history of capitalism, domestic bourgeoisies have relied extensively on state support at an early stage of accumulation.[45] The capitalist state during this time invariably supports local capitalists in the face of foreign competition (by the provision of tariffs, incentives, subsidies, and so on).

---

42 In the period from 1963 to 1978 when President Kenyatta died, the family of the President would come under this category.

43 These kind of attacks have been made throughout the independence period by the petty bourgeoisie opposition.

44 M. Godfrey and S. Langdon, 'Partners in underdevelopment, the transnationalization thesis in a Kenya context', *Journal of Commonwealth and Comparative Politics*, vol. 14, no. 1, 1976.

45 Germany in the nineteenth century, for example.

PART I

CHAPTER 1

The State and Economy in Kenya Colony 1918–39

Chapter 1 intends to show the forms of ownership and control over the means of production in the light of the mediation of the colonial state. Through the case studies and examination of corporate growth patterns, the intention is to illustrate the contradictions between the settler drive towards internal accumulation and the imperatives of metropolitan capital.

The section on the colonial state in Kenya, pages 21–6, examines the relationship between the 'settler' state and Britain, in the context of their conflicting interests. The structure of the economy is then outlined in order to illustrate the predominantly agrarian base and the level of state support required to ensure the existence of settler enterprise. There follows a consideration of the role of finance capital as the 'book-keeper' of productive capital. This shows the way in which finance capital links up metropolitan money supplies with colonial production.

The part on trade and tariffs, pages 40–7, explores the colony's trading links with the world market in the context of Britain's relative decline as the dominant trading partner. The final section, pages 48–57, examines the different types of corporate expansion in Kenya during the interwar years, by using company statistics. This illustrates some of the features of colonial capitalism, such as the strong overlap between class and race. It is hoped that the details of this section will provide a background for the later themes of capitalist development in Kenya.

The Colonial State in Kenya

From the nineteenth century, East Africa was linked to the world market through the agency of British colonialism. Kenya was declared a protectorate under the British Crown in 1895 and converted into a Crown colony in 1920. European settlers had originally been encour-

21

aged to settle in Kenya by the metropolitan government which was concerned to cover the costs of the Uganda Railway which had been completed in 1902. The formation of a Crown colony in 1920 was the official sanction of settler dominance in Kenya.[1]   From the outset of British colonial rule there emerged a policy of simple *primary production*. Indeed, the main thrust behind British imperial expansion in the late nineteenth and early twentieth centuries was to develop and control sources of strategic raw materials.[2] However, the actual process of colonization in East Africa was relatively haphazard and dependent on political factors, such as competition between the European powers. An official British policy on colonial development evolved gradually and was largely pragmatic in the early years. Following the logic of *laissez-faire* capitalism, Lord Milner commented in the early 1920s that there was a greater scope for *complementary* development in the dependent empire than in the dominions, because the former was less 'advanced'. A senior Colonial Office official in 1924 commented: 'I am convinced that nationally the most remunerative expenditure we can incur is in the development of markets which would be complementary and not competitive. Africa fulfils this condition to a peculiar degree, and it is at the same time a great potential source of supply for raw materials.'[3]

This view of colonial economies being complementary to the metropolis was pervasive by the 1920s. Nevertheless, in Kenya the metropolitan government played a minimal role in economic development after the construction of the Uganda Railway (1898–1902). The initial metropolitan 'grants in aid' were aimed at the development of basic infrastructure, such as ports and railways, which would facilitate the export of foodcrops and raw materials. Of course the provision of loans for railway development by the metropolitan government would serve to stimulate the production of British goods for colonial markets. By the end of the 1920s, government investment in East African infrastructure had been considerable: almost 1300 miles of new railway track were opened and five deep-water berths were built at Mombasa between 1920 and 1932.[4] However, it soon became clear that Britain expected the Kenyan administration to become 'self-sufficient' in terms of revenue for economic expansion.

---

1 For a fascinating account of settler politics in the early colonial period, see W. McGregor Ross, *Kenya From Within*, Cass, 1968 edn (orig. edn 1927).

2 More details on Britain's need for strategic raw materials between 1880 and 1930 can be found in R. D. Wolff, *Britain and Kenya, 1870–1930*, TransAfrica Publishers, Nairobi, 1974, ch. I.

3 Colonial Office files (1924), quoted in G. Oates, 'The Colonial Office, Kenya and development, 1929–45', Cambridge History Conference, 1975, p. 2.

4 E. A. Brett, *Colonialism and Underdevelopment in East Africa, the Politics of Economic Change, 1919–39*, Heinemann, London, 1973, p. 142. This is the best work on British colonial policy in East Africa before 1939.

The small amount of British aid to Kenya under the *Colonial Development and Welfare Act* of 1929 was an anachronism. It was hoped that this Act would alleviate Britain's unemployment problem by stimulating exports to the colonial territories. It was designed to provide funds for the territories which would, in the first place, service the interest on loans raised by the colonial governments that gave contracts to British firms. The CDA was in general aimed at encouraging the construction of railways in order to promote trade with Britain. However, by 1936, the total of such 'grants in aid' to British territories in Africa had only reached £270 000,[5] the maximum going to Kenya being £100 000 in that year. In fact the scheme assumed that the bulk of expenditure on infrastructure and services would be paid for by revenue generated *within* the colonial economy itself.

The CDA never fulfilled even the limited intentions of the British government, owing to the collapse of international commodity markets by 1929. The onset of the depression and credit restrictions in England made it impossible for colonial governments to raise loans. By 1930 a policy of *retrenchment* was in full swing in the colonies. The Lord Privy Seal in 1931 suggested that, in order to assist the United Kingdom, colonies receiving grants in aid should make all economies possible: 'in those better placed, no loans should be raised if possible, since every loan raised will necessarily put a fresh strain on the structure of British credit'.[6] It is not surprising that between 1929 and 1935 Kenya received only £181 000 under the CDA, which had a negligible effect on economic development.[7]

Therefore, the development of infrastructure between the wars was largely financed by revenue raised within Kenya from the native population. For instance, the hut and poll tax, together with a smaller amount of customs duties, constituted 60–80 per cent of the colonies' revenue. During the 1920s in Kenya there was substantial expenditure on infrastructure. Including cross-payments with regard to the railway administration, expenditure in Kenya Colony rose from £1 909 051 in 1922 to £3 114 912 in 1930. Kenya's public debt in 1936 was equal to £17 580 000, £17 200 000 of which was incurred between 1921 and 1933, but of which 75 per cent was for railways and harbours.[8] As revenues dropped in the 1930s, interest became a heavier burden on the local administration. It is clear that the administration in Kenya had minimal support from the metropolitan government during this period.

Indeed, there was a constant battle between the Colonial Office and the Kenyan administration concerning the extent to which the latter

5 Lord W. Hailey, *An African Survey*, OUP, London, 1956 edn, p. 1323.
6 In Oates, op. cit., p. 2.
7 Brett, op. cit., p. 137.
8 Oates, op. cit., p. 5.

was shoring up settler agriculture. The Colonial Office were of the opinion that the levels of both settler and African agricultural production were too low to merit the large amount of assistance and protection offered by the local administration. A Colonial Office note in 1935 expressed reserve about the viability of the settler economy in Kenya:

> The whole policy of Kenya requires review with the general end of tapering off the bounties and protection on the parasitical crops and so stopping them becoming a burden on the real economic industries of the country.[9]

Pursuing the 'free enterprise' position the Colonial Office continually complained of the extent of the Kenya government's intervention in the economy, particularly when it came to subsidizing maize production and investment in collective marketing facilities. Sir John Cambell, the financial advisor to the Secretary of State, noted on this issue:

> the root of the problem seems to be political . . . the constitutional position is such that the settlers' interests are over-represented by the sheer nature of things. Under the existing conditions, the policy of the country is constantly bent towards the furtherance of their interests. As a body they are neither easy to deal with nor far seeing. The Government has not in practice a free hand as regards native interests . . . ever since I came here I have seen how political exigencies have forced the government time and again to do things it was reluctant to do and which would have been better left undone.[10]

Lugard's dictum of native paramountcy had been taken up generally as the principle under which Britain should administer the 'protected' territories. In theory this involved granting precedence to indigenous populations. In the case of Kenya the doctrine was bypassed in favour of settler predominance. Although there were different fractions of settler capital, the local administration in Kenya sought to preserve the monopoly of services and protection for the settlers over the native population. Colonial Office concern with education and welfare of the 'African communities' was ignored by the settler administration, and this created considerable tension with the Colonial Office. Any Colonial Office legislation that hit at settler predominance over the native populations was strongly rejected.

Income tax was a case in point. In Kenya the whole financial policy of the colony up to 1930 was founded on the principle that Africans should provide the bulk of the tax revenue, while the Europeans benefited most substantially from the services provided. In 1920, the

9 Colonial Office Report 852/13/19201.
10 Colonial Office Minute, CO 852/12/15201.

Colonial Office took action and demanded that if the Kenya government wished to proceed with the elevation of native tax, it must impose new taxation specifically upon the Indians and Europeans. Upon investigation it became clear that the native population was being overtaxed while the European population was paying no direct income tax at all. The efforts of the metropolitan state to impose income tax on the European community in Kenya began in 1920 when the Income Tax Ordinance was passed through LEGCO, the *Legislative Council*. This Tax Bill had been instigated in response to strong Colonial Office pressure while preparing the 1922 budget for the colony. A prominent settler leader of the time, Lord Delamere, heading the New League (which represented the large European farmers in Kenya), pushed to repeal the Income Tax Ordinance.[11] In 1922 Delamere moved a resolution in LEGCO that the Income Tax Ordinance of 1920 should be repealed and increased import duties be substituted for tax on the settlers. The Kenya government accordingly made representations to the Secretary of State in Britain that the tax was unpopular and the Colonial Office were pressured into sanctioning the repeal of the Income Tax Bill in 1922. This successful resistance of an income-tax provision for Europeans was a double victory for the large-scale settlers in that direct taxation on Europeans had been averted and protective duties were imposed on foodstuffs. The latter covered items such as wheat, sugar and tea, which were consumed largely by Africans. This principle of protection for settler agriculture was reaffirmed by the *Kenya Tariff Committee* of 1929.[12]

By 1933, in the context of retrenchment in Britain and its colonies, the Colonial Office began to exert renewed pressure on the Kenyan administration to impose a form of income tax on the European population. Finally an income-tax provision was passed in 1936, after a change of governorship in the colony.[13] The difficulties of imposing such legislation indicated the immense political power of the large settler farmers. Indeed, between the wars, there was a constant dispute between Kenya Colony and the metropolis on the question of political control. In the early 1930s, Lord Delamere had actually resigned his seat in LEGCO on the grounds that the secretary of state in Britain had more real and complete control of government in Kenya than the elected members. Indeed the settler barons would have preferred total autonomy from the metropolitan government if it had been possible.

The most serious conflict between the Kenyan administration and its settler clients came in 1923 with the 'Indian Question'. The Wood–Winterton agreement was summarized in a government White Paper

11 McGregor Ross, op. cit., pp. 155–9.
12 Details to be found in the *Report of the Kenya Tariff Committee*, Govt Printer, Nairobi, May 1929, ML.
13 McGregor Ross, op. cit., p. 155.

of 1922; the most important proposal was that the Indian community in Kenya should have a form of electoral representation in LEGCO[14] and in the municipalities. It also asserted that there should be no segregation (either commercial or residential) along racial lines. The settler political associations were in open revolt during 1923 and there were rumours of a *coup d'état* to impose settler self-government. The settlers sent representations to London over a two-year period and finally the proposals for Indian representation were abandoned by the Colonial Office. These examples make it clear that the dominant settlers in Kenya before 1939 had ultimate control over the means of representation.

BRITISH POLICY AND INDUSTRIAL DEVELOPMENT IN KENYA

The period under consideration here (1918–39) marks the twilight of Britain's free-trade imperialism. The first stage of British colonialism in East Africa from the 1890s was concerned with the extraction of raw materials and foodstuffs. The imperial interest in primary production was accompanied by the assumption that the colonial territories would provide 'captive markets' for the products of British industry. During this time it is not surprising that the Colonial Office were indifferent and often hostile to colonial attempts to develop manufacturing industry. The work of the so-called development agencies before 1939 illustrates the general unwillingness on the part of the British government to encourage colonial industries. The Empire Marketing Board, for instance, gave no assistance to any forms of manufacturing and limited itself to the marketing of colonial food and raw materials. The Colonial Development Advisory Committee in theory placed no limit on its spheres of activity, but in practice it totally ignored the industrial sector. By 1939, it had allocated just under £8 million to the colonies, of which only £151 000 was for industrial projects. Of this amount, only £23 000 or 0·3 per cent of the total allocations had been disbursed.[15]

Clearly, the colonial territories were considered as markets for British industrial goods and the development of colonial manufacturing represented a threat to British products in the home market. The destruction of the Indian textile industry during the eighteenth century had no parallel in terms of scale in nineteenth- and twentieth-century East Africa. However, it is the case that the pre-capitalist craft production of textiles and pottery that did exist was effectively wiped out by the competition of British industrial goods from the late nineteenth century onwards. The textile industry in Kenya during the interwar

14 It was suggested that the Indians have only 10 per cent of their electoral roll, but the settlers were terrified of even a small degree of devolution of their political power. See ibid., pp. 375–85.
15 Brett, op. cit., p. 268.

period is an example of a branch of manufacturing that was blocked off until after 1945 because of the strength of the metropolitan textiles interests. It has been estimated[16] that in Kenya the 'technological threshold' for textile manufacture was reached as early as 1925, when the colony imported some 29 million square yards of cotton piece goods. The repeated attempts of Asian capitalists before 1939 to establish textile plants in Kenya (and Tanganyika) were consistently vetoed by the Colonial Office acting under pressure from the powerful British textile manufacturers. However, given the highly protective nature of the Kenyan administration in the interwar period, it is a consideration that if settler capital had been involved in the textile industry, metropolitan interests would have been defied. It is no coincidence that the two attempts by the Colonial Office directly to undermine colonial industries occurred in Uganda and Tanganyika and *not* in Kenya. The first of these projects was a *match factory* which had been set up by a Japanese firm in the 1920s to make matches from local timber.[17]

The *Joint East Africa Board,* a collection of individuals with business interests in the colonies, sent representatives to the Colonial Office to the effect that such a factory in Tanganyika would diminish import-duty revenues of all three East African territories. The loss of revenues was hardly relevant, particularly since Kenya had just protected two local industries (beer and tobacco) by increasing the import tariff at the same time as imposing an excise duty on local production for revenue purposes. The essence of the problem was that the JEAB, representing British industrial capital as a whole, did not want a precedent established in the colonies which might support the further development of local industries. Accordingly, the Colonial Office instructed the local administration to impose an excise duty on local production which would cancel out the protective effects of the existing import-revenue duty. The match factory under such prohibitive conditions was to collapse in a few years, as it could not compete with the imported equivalents.

Another important example of the way in which colonial industries were blocked was in the case of *sisal twine* in Tanganyika. This industry was set up by a British firm in the early 1930s to manufacture sisal products of different kinds for the export market. The imperial preference system of trade relationships, established in response to the depression by the Ottawa Agreements[18] in 1932 between Britain and

---

16 In R. Eglin, 'The oligopolistic structure and competitive characteristics of direct foreign investment in Kenya's manufacturing sector', revised in R. Kaplinsky (ed.), *Readings on the Multinational Corporation in Kenya*, OUP, East Africa, 1978.

17 The cases of the match and sisal-twine factories were first cited in Brett, op. cit.

18 The Ottawa Agreements also applied to dominion status territories (such as Canada and Australia) and these wanted to build up their own import-substitution industries.

its colonies, was intended to guarantee colonial producers 'free access' to British and colonial markets. However, when the question of colonial industries exporting their *manufactured* goods to Britain arose, it became clear that the preference system functioned only selectively and in favour of metropolitan industrial capital.

The sisal-twine factory in East Africa was a test case, as a letter from the Secretary of State for the Colonies to the Governor of Tanganyika in 1943 showed:

> The Secretary of State has received very vigorous complaints from the binder twine manufacturers in this country about the importation of binder twine from Tanganyika. While the actual amount is not large, only about 500 tons out of a total consumption of about 10,000 tons per annum, the manufacturers complain that the arrival of the twine in this country and its offer at prices substantially below their own is threatening to undermine the whole structure of the industry . . . the home market is the only secure market which the manufacturers enjoy and it is only in that market that they can make any profit at all . . . the Secretary of State cannot but admit that the complaint of the manufacturers is a reasonable one. The agreement by which the rope manufacturers have undertaken to foster the use of colonial sisal in this country and elsewhere is of the greatest importance to the colonial sisal producers and they could not possibly countenance any action which would alienate the sympathies of the rope manufacturers.[19]

This represented a clear threat to the colonial producers of twine: if they did not cease their exports to metropolitan markets, then stern measures would be invoked against them. The Tanganyikan twine-manufacturing company refused to agree to restrict its exports to Britain, so that a prohibitive tariff was invoked in 1934 on a whole range of articles from the colonial territories, including sisal twine. These moves forced the sisal company to negotiate with the Twine and Net Makers' Federation and agree to raise its prices on the condition of it being allowed entry to the British market. Under these punitive conditions the Tanganyikan company ceased operating in 1938. It is important to note that this company was owned by a British sisal manufacturer. This shows that although individual capitals in some instances set out to establish production plants in the colonies, the overall position of industrial capital was expressed through Colonial Office policy. During the debate that followed the demise of the Tanganyikan enterprise, the splits between different fractions of Brit-

---

19 The details of this conflict and the official correspondence between the Colonial Office and the Tanganyikan twine company are to be found in *Prohibitive Duties on Colonial Products*, a Colonial Office pamphlet, 1934, ML.

ish capital illustrated the complexity of the whole issue of colonial industrialization.

In 1938 Cunliffe-Lister, the Secretary of State for the Colonies, was asked to explain the untimely demise of the twine industry in Tanganyika by some members of the Joint East Africa Board who had been involved in the scheme. In defence of the imperial government's action, Lister denied that 'all goods manufactured by native labour within the colonial empire would be debarred from Britain', but he stressed that 'the great interest of the colonies is to secure markets for their primary products'[20] and in this connection he underlined the importance of the complementary preferences which covered primary exports to Britain and British manufactured exports back to the colonies. The basis of the position of the imperial government in the case of colonial industries which competed directly with British products was asserted in the conclusion of his speech:

> It is only in comparatively few cases that a conflict of interests arises, and in such cases I hope that the realisation of the importance of the general policy will lead to satisfactory agreements (as in the case of the cordage company).[21]

In other words, the interest of capital as a whole was being asserted over that of individual capitals. The secretary of state was right in claiming that such conflicts rarely arose, but their possibility could not be excluded.

The members of the Tanganyika Legislative Council (representing the small group of settlers in that territory) did not find metropolitan explanations satisfactory. One of them commented on the decision taken to impose a tariff against Tanganyikan twine products entering Britain:

> If we are to accept it as a hard and fast rule that no industry can be allowed to establish itself without having to pay the full cost of Customs Protection as it exists in this country today, we can never hope to establish local industry in this country and what will our position be in the future if we allow this to happen?[22]

These examples illustrate the general position of the metropolitan government towards industrialization in the colonial territories in the interwar period. The metropolitan government actively supported individual British processing projects in only two instances, namely a flax mill in Tanganyika and a beef-processing plant in Kenya. In 1934, the international meat processing and distributing firm Liebigs

---

20 ibid.
21 ibid.
22 ibid.

Limited (of the UK) proposed to the Kenya government the establishment of a plant to process canned and preserved meat both for the local market and for export. The active role of the state in this project reflected the closeness of the local colonial administration and the settlers. The government in Kenya not only undertook to provide loan capital for the construction of the plant at Athi River, but also guaranteed the factory a consistent throughput of cattle by introducing compulsory purchasing legislation on local African cattleholders.

This project had two functions for the local colonial state: first, it would provide the settlers with a reliable outlet for their chilled beef exports (with lower grades of cattle being used for canning) and, secondly, the administration could reduce the number of cattle in the WaKamba herds. As the government was concerned with overgrazing of the Ukambani, the forcible destocking of this area could be justified. In fact, the move to forcibly purchase their cattle was met with strong resistance from the larger cattle-owners. These obstructing tactics on the part of Kamba served to hold up the operation of the factory for several years.[23] Nevertheless, the importance of this project is the unusually active role of the administration in supporting an industrial enterprise. It is significant that this project was complementary to settler agriculture. Indeed, many more food and raw-materials processing plants were established in Kenya during this period than in Tanganyika or Uganda. This can only be explained by the 'economic nationalist' policies pursued by the local administration in response to settler demands.

For instance, during the 1930s, the Kenyan Farmers' Association (KFA) kept up constant pressure on the East African section of the London Chamber of Commerce to liberalize imperial policy towards colonial industrialization. In 1936, the Colonial Office responded to such pressure by announcing that 'there is no law by which the Colonial Office can prohibit industries'.[24]

It can be concluded that the metropolitan government played a minimal role in Kenya's early economic development. Indeed there was continuing conflict during this period between the 'internal' and 'external' elements of Kenya's colonial settlement. In the era of *laissez-faire* capitalism, the Colonial Office objected to the high level of support granted by the local administration to the settlers. This age of Kenya's relative autonomy from the metropolis was nearing an end in the context of changing conditions in the world market. For a period during the war, metropolitan and settler aims coincided in that both sought to develop agricultural *and* industrial self-sufficiency within the colony. Even by 1939 the managing director of Smith Mackenzie (one

---

23 *KNA*, CS/23.
24 'East Africa and Rhodesia', debate of the London Chamber of Commerce, 25 January 1940, Foreign Office Library, London.

of the largest British merchant houses operating in East Africa) claimed that 'the opinion in England on secondary industry in the colonies is altering to the better'.[25] By 1940 there was accordingly a change in Board of Trade and Treasury policy which was now in favour of British participation in industrial development overseas. In 1943, it was pointed out in the Colonial Office; 'businessmen in East Africa are perfectly well aware that in the self governing colony of Northern Rhodesia, considerable strides have been made in secondary industries, e.g. cement manufacture. That East Africa is behind in this respect is apt to be attributed, rightly or wrongly, to Downing St. control, and is likely to encourage aspirations of local autonomy . . . it is politically desirable that we do all we can to alter this impression.'[26]

The large settlers for their part had always pushed for the establishment of industries in Kenya in order to strengthen their own material base. After the *Colonial Development and Welfare Act*[27] of 1940, metropolitan funds for industry were forthcoming. The following extract from the *East African Standard* in 1943 illustrates the temporary convergence of settler and metropolitan aims: 'development of industry offers to East Africa opportunities to strengthen the foundations of white settlement by making a place for the skilled worker and master craftsman . . . in Britain it is now recognised that the Dominions will want a new kind of settler . . . the opportunities for planned industrial development along modern lines are progressively increasing openings for European workers of the best type.[28]

It will be shown later that the change in British policy towards colonial industrialization was in response to a long-term decline in its competitiveness on the world market. Settler hopes that the new postwar industrial plans would strengthen their position were not to be fulfilled and international capital was to undermine the basis of white supremacy.

Structure of the Economy and Finance Capital

ECONOMY

This part will examine the structure of the Kenyan economy in the interwar period which will illustrate more fully the basis of settler supremacy. The foundations of primitive accumulation in the early colonial period were land and agriculture. It has been seen that the state played an extensive role in supporting agricultural development through the provision of infrastructure, and labour supplies. The

---

25 Brett, op. cit., p. 279.
26 CO Minute 852 (1943), in Oates, op. cit., p. 8.
27 This superseded the CDWA of 1929.
28 *EAS*, 6 December 1943.

TABLE 1a   *African Labour Force 1920–31*

Year	Average Labour Units Per Month on European Farms
1920	53 709
1921	67 388
1922	61 649
1923	70 957
1924	87 092
1925	78 527
1926	84 611
1927	102 074
1928	114 320
1929	110 697
1930	125 885
1931	120 210

Source: Agricultural census and annual reports, quoted in M. R. Dilley, *British Policy Towards Kenya Colony*, 2nd edn, Cass, London, 1966, p. 235.

TABLE 1b   *Number of Registered Labourers 1923–42*

Year		Kenya's Population (m.)
1923	129 296	
1928	152 122	
1929	160 076	4·0
1930	157 359	
1931	141 085	
1932	132 089	
1933	141 085	4·2
1942	179 085	4·7

Source: Native Affairs Department, annual reports, in R. M. A. van Zwanenberg, *Colonial Capitalism and Labour in Kenya, 1919–1939*, EALB, Nairobi, 1975, p. 74.

institution of hut and poll taxes served a twofold purpose: it raised revenue and it forced a proportion of the African population into wage labour. The state further regulated and controlled the movement of labour through the kipande system (a labour record card).

McGregor Ross, the well-known Fabian critic of the colonial regime in Kenya, observed in 1928 that 'the native population was regarded simply and solely as a labour force for the planters and farmers, who in 1917 numbered 1,011'.[29] Although the African population during this time was not fully proletarianized and divorced from the means of production (land), by the mid-1920s it has been estimated that more than half the able-bodied men in the two largest agricultural tribes (the Kikuyu and the Luo) were working on European farms.[30] Table 1a shows how the average labour units per month on European farms more than doubled between 1920 and 1931. The quite rapid entry of Africans into the labour market reflected the effectiveness of state policy. This early period of colonial capitalism has been characterized by its 'despotic' relations of production.[31] However, by the mid-1920s, the system of forced labour operated through the African chiefs had more or less given way to economic constraints. The imposition of a money economy through taxation was more effective in the long run than brute force[32] in terms of encouraging Africans into the labour market.

Both the foreign-owned estates and settler farms were equally dependent on state support to ensure adequate labour supplies. However, the settlers had internal accumulation interests to maintain and foreign capital was more flexible. The colonial state, acting to ensure settler predominance, took measures to confine African agricultural production within limits that would complement but not compete with European agriculture. Before 1920, most of Kenya's export revenue was raised from African produce, although by the mid-1920s the flow of labour to European estates had caused a shortage of labour in the reserves. African agricultural production for the market and internal consumption was carried on in a fairly traditional way and there were few innovations in techniques. Official encouragement was limited to the subsistence sector, which would subsidize estate agriculture by providing foodstuffs. The 1920s, therefore, was a period of relative stagnation for African agriculture. There was no increase in the value of commodities from African areas between 1922 and 1938, although the quantity certainly increased. The main items marketed from the African reserves during this time were live animals, hides and skins,

---

29 McGregor Ross, op. cit., p. 102.

30 Norman Leys, *Kenya*, Hogarth Press, London, 1924, p. 179.

31 M. von Freyhold, 'On colonial modes of production', mimeo., University of Dar es Salaam, 1977.

32 For details of forced labour, see McGregor Ross, op. cit., ch. VI.

TABLE 2   *Value of Exports from African Areas in Kenya 1922–38 (£000s)*

1922	1924	1926	1928	1930	1932	1934	1936	1938
175	480	472	484	404	275	301	474	488

Source: Agriculture Dept, annual reports, in Heyer, op. cit., p. 9.

TABLE 3   *Export Commodities as Percentages of the Value of Total Domestic Exports – Kenya*

	1913 %	1923 %	1932 %
From European settler areas:			
Coffee	3	32	53
Sisal	0	15	8
Sodium Carbonate	0	9	8
Tea	0	0	1
Gold Bullion	0	0	3
Dairy Products	2	0	2
Sugar	0	0	1
Subtotal	5	56	76
From African areas:			
Hides and Skins	21	8	5
Wattle, Bark, etc.	0	0	4
Raw Cotton	3	0	0
Subtotal	24	8	9
From both areas:			
Maize	13	16	5
Miscellaneous	58	20	10
Subtotal	71	36	15
TOTAL EXPORTS	100	100	100

Source: GB CP CO, 'Report of the Commission appointed to enquire into and report on the financial position and system of taxation of Kenya', Colonial Office Paper No. 116, p. 8, from Wolff, op. cit., p. 137.

maize, cotton, groundnuts, sim sim and copra.[33] It has been estimated that African subsistence agriculture in 1929 accounted for 60 per cent of Kenya's GNP.[34] It was an uncomfortable reality for the settlers that the African farmers were subsidizing their production indirectly.

By the 1930s the picture changed and as the demand for labour on the European estates slackened, so the strength of European arguments against increasing African production were reduced. In the 1930s African areas got more staff and the development of food and famine-reserve crops intensified. During this period there was a substantial growth in marketed output from the African areas and in 1933 the ban on coffee-growing in the reserves was lifted for experimental plots. Nevertheless, the new crops encouraged by the administration during the 1930s were primarily aimed at the export market and they included tobacco, cashews and wattle.

The actual choice of crops in Kenya Colony was the result of a balance between central government promptings and suitability of climate and cultivation in the areas of European settlement. It is no coincidence that exports from the colony were soon dominated by a few crops. For instance, from the 1920s coffee, sisal and maize constituted 47 per cent of total exports from Kenya and this had risen to 72 per cent by 1930.[35] Cotton became a major cash crop in the Protectorate of Uganda, although the settlers in Kenya abandoned the crop when the returns were too low.

In the first three decades of European settlement the nature of settler agriculture was precarious and many farmers were ruined by bad planning, blight and fluctuating international prices for commodities. For instance, in Kericho district between 1919 and 1920 there was widespread planting of flax in response to a world boom. In the next year the price fell and many farmers were ruined. The whole framework of settler production would never have survived had it not been for extensive state support. The local administration provided extensive infrastructure to the settler farming areas: roads, water, extension services and compensation in the event of failure. This heavy investment in infrastructure at an early stage was to pay off by 1939, by which time a thorough basis had been laid for the expansion of capitalist production. Table 4 illustrates the sectors of capital formation and it is significant that during the 1920s, the highest proportion of capital formation (44 per cent) was in the public sector. The Railways and Harbours Administration was a major borrower and investor in the 1920s. It is evident from estimates that the largest proportion of private fixed-asset formation was in European agriculture.[36]

33 For further details, see J. Heyer, *A Survey of Agricultural Development in the Small Farm Areas of Kenya since the 1920s*, IDS, Nairobi, working paper no. 194, 1974.

34 H. W. Ord, 'The Kenya economy as a whole, 1929–1952', mimeo., Edinburgh, 1976, p. 11.

35 Wolff, op. cit., p. 80.

36 Ord, op. cit.

TABLE 4   *Kenya Gross Capital Formation 1923–39*

	1923–29 £m.	%	1930–39 £m.	%
Railways and Harbours	10·6	30·6	3·5	11·4
Other Public Sectors	5·6	13·3	9·2	30·0
Non-African Agriculture	n.a.	n.a.		
Other Private Sectors	19·4	56·1	18·0	58·6
TOTAL	35·6	100·0	30·7	100·0

Source: Ord, op. cit.

The settlers had complete control over the marketing and distribution of agricultural products, although British trading firms exported
the commodities to Europe. Through their marketing organizations
and the Kenya Farmers' Association (KFA), the settlers imposed a
monopoly over the internal distribution of commodities. These marketing organizations were dominated by the large estate farmers, but
they served as a means of protecting the weaker sections of the settler
farmers by guaranteeing prices for commodities.

An indication of the gradual expansion of commodity relations in
Kenya before 1939 is the extent of consumption among the local
population. Although the bulk of agricultural production was directed
towards the export market, the extended circulation of consumer
goods was a mark of the advance of a monetary economy. Table 5

TABLE 5   *Consumption in East Africa of Excisable Commodities
in 1937*

	Kenya	Uganda	Tanganyika
Tobacco (manuf. lb)	—	735 563	102 491
Cigarettes (lb)	—	569 209	90 487
Beer (gallons)	131 733	—	33 284
Sugar (tons)	13 663	22 591	533
Tea (lb)	1 951 565	274 236	137 855
Exports from:			
Tobacco (lb)	—	2 935	741
Cigarettes (lb)	—	259 292	—
Sugar (tons)	2 601	6 069	2 864
Tea (lb)	8 931 016	154 158	215 152

Source: Dept of Overseas Trade report, 1937–8.

shows how the internal consumption of export commodities such as tea, tobacco and coffee gradually rose along with the expansion in production. For instance, in 1937, about one-eighth of the internal tea production of Kenya was consumed within the territory. There was also considerable interchange of commodities such as tobacco, tea and sugar between the three East African countries. The consumption of commodities was accelerated rapidly after the Second World War, with the rise of money incomes and increase in wage employment.[37]

FINANCE CAPITAL

The traditional role of commercial banks is to lubricate the flow of money capital into productive enterprise. After the linking up of East Africa with the world market from the 1890s it is not surprising to find the entry of *commercial banks*. The entry of British banks came in the wake of expansion of trade in East Africa. One of the first commercial banks to be established in East Africa was the National Bank of India (later to become Grindlays Bank), which was a British bank with extensive operations in India. Like most exchange banks, the Bank of India concentrated on financing external trade. This became the bank's main function in East Africa and it represented a typical pattern of all the British banks operating in the area at that time.

The entry of the National Bank of India was soon followed by Barclays Bank (then Barclays Dominion, Colonial and Overseas) and by the Standard Bank of South Africa, now the Standard Bank.[38] All these banks initially established their offices in connection with the financing of trade in commodities. The development of export crops in East Africa, such as coffee, hides and ivory from both the settler estates and African smallholder agriculture, directly linked these economies with world commodity markets. This flow of commodities from East Africa to the metropoles was facilitated by the services of these commercial banks. As capitalism expanded in Kenya, the function of the banks was extended in scale to provide credit (derived from British funds) for the financing, collection and export of primary commodities and the distribution of the imports of British consumer goods. The function of the banks was, therefore, to link up production areas with the world market. The functions of these three commercial banks in East Africa expanded further to cover deposit banking as well as commodity financing.

When the settler economy had recovered from the depression after

37 The GNP per head (monetary) at 1948 prices rose from £3·5 in 1939 to £10·2 in 1948; Ord, op. cit.

38 A good descriptive account of banking in East Africa is to be found in W. T. Newlyn, *Money in an African Context*, OUP, Nairobi, 1967, ch. 4.

the 1930s, these banks collected deposits in excess of what they were able to utilize in East Africa. This surplus was then sent to Britain. However, in the first stage of colonization between the 1910s and the mid-1930s, the commercial banks would only finance[39] those individuals who had large enough fixed security (in terms of land and other assets). Many of the smaller settler farmers, due to the precarious nature of their enterprises, were not able to find the exacting security requirements in order to qualify for a commercial loan. The restriction of loans to the better-off farmers can be illustrated by the fact that in 1938 the total of deposits was less than £4 million.[40] There was a considerable potential for expansion *if* opportunities for local lending were to open up; this expansion was not to take place until after the Second World War.

From 1933 to 1935, Kenya had a positive balance of payments and, in general, the colony from 1934 to the end of the Second World War exported more than it imported with the result that the banks acquired even larger reserves. By 1945, the banks held a reserve ratio of 88 per cent which represented an enormous potential for capitalist expansion in subsequent years. The willingness of banks to lend after the war with the rapid expansion of the economy soon reversed the proportions between local and external use of bank funds.

The erratic development of settler capitalism in the prewar period itself determined the limited use of credit in the economy. From the outset, the bulk of settler farmers in Kenya had problems in raising security for both long- and short-term loans. Usually the role of the commercial banks was confined to the provision of short-term loans to finance crops in advance. Longer-term loans were provided through mortgages from the merchant and commercial banks in England.[41] The Hall Report (Report of the Agricultural Commission, 1929) emphasized the inadequacy of credit facilities offered to the settler farming community:

> there is a pressing need for further credit facilities and we recommend that the government institute a specific enquiry into the means whereby such facilities may be most safely and economically provided.[42]

Up to 1929, the credit structure had developed without any state support and many of the settler farmers had borne a high level of debt which had not been helped by the fall in producer prices in 1929.

It was the economic depression which was to further worsen the

---

39 Through the provision of long- and short-term loans.

40 Newlyn, op. cit., p. 47.

41 Branches of merchant banks operating in Kenya from the 1920s onwards included Arbuthnot & Lathan, Jardine & Matheson.

42 R. van Zwanenberg, *Colonial Capitalism and Labour in Kenya, 1919–39*, EALB, Nairobi, 1975, p. 17.

position of European farmers in Kenya. During the 1920s, speculation had raised land prices beyond their productive capacity, after a rise in commodity prices on the world market. Credit granted by the commercial banks had been assessed on the basis of land price and not productive capacity, and when prices fell, the debtors could not repay their loans to the commercial banks.

The Banks progressively curtailed the credit facilities previously granted and in some cases discouraged them. Private loans and mortgages became more difficult to obtain. Those merchants who continued to extend advances on the security of crops did so on a restricted basis.[43]

The price of land collapsed and in order to preserve the settler economy the government was at last forced to intervene. A precarious level of indebtedness set in from 1930 and the European maize-growers were hit hard. Between 1931 and 1934, the price of coffee fell by around 20 per cent f.o.r. and this drop was lower than that in maize. By 1930 the capital debt of the colony had reached just under £17 million, £13 million of which was from loans raised by the Uganda Railway. During the depression the repayment of interest on the Kenya debt remained constant and at the same time cash earned by exports from Kenya decreased sharply. Visible export values dropped from £3·4 million in 1930 to £1·9 million in 1934. The metropolitan government had for some time considered that the level of capital investment in infrastructure was proceeding faster than was warranted by production levels. Nevertheless the central government was forced to act to save the settler economy and in 1931, after years of pressure from the small settler farmers for financial assistance, a *Land Bank* was formed. The commercial banks had always rejected any form of government intervention while commodity prices were buoyant. However, when prices fell, most commercial banks stopped loans and supported the formation of a government bank. The capital for the new Land Bank was raised on the London market by means of a government guarantee and capital was lent to settler farmers in Kenya at a lower rate of interest than that offered by commercial banks.

The *Agricultural Advances Ordinance* of 1930 provided statutory means to set up a Central Board to assess the problems of indebted farmers and in 1934 the Land Bank took over the administration of the scheme. The state was now reluctantly forced into an interventionist role. The changes in the structure of financial facilities in the colony by the 1930s illustrate the way in which the state is compelled to support weak capitalist producers in time of crisis. Sir E. Grigg, the Governor of Kenya Colony, commented in 1931 on the role of the state in relation to private banks:

---

43 ibid.

the end of private enterprises is for many reasons now in sight and the state must definitely step in if not only farming is to prosper but the financial stability of both the Colonial Government and the Railway is to be assured. The economic position of the Colony as a whole turns on this necessity. In Kenya, hitherto, settlement has been entirely haphazard . . . but the banking system of Kenya has been carried far beyond the normal range of operation of a commercial bank . . . the banks take the view that further financing of farming on the present basis is *not* within their proper duties.[44]

A large proportion of the bank's finances were used to buy out creditors and by 1938 the bank had lent £834 489 to farmers and £328 148 had been dispensed for the purpose of discharging existing mortgages.[45] Approximately £1 million had been raised through the Land Bank from colonial surplus balances to support ailing sections of the European farming community in Kenya.

Before 1939, capitalist relations of production had developed considerably in the colony. However the racial boundaries that surrounded production were inimical to the further advancement of the capitalist mode of production. Indigenous capitalism in prewar Kenya had not been stifled; indeed, the development of commodity production in some areas was threatening to capture potential labour destined for the European estates. However it was not until the mid-1950s that the settler monopoly of production and distribution was to be broken by a combination of circumstances which included the hostility of international capital to racial boundaries and the political organization of indigenous capitalism. However volatile the fortune of colonial capitalism was before the war, the intensive state support given to the implanted estate capital provided the basis for the postwar expansion of capitalism.

Trade and Tariffs in the Colony

Other forms of state support to European agriculture were import protection and export incentives. A discussion of the colony's tariff structures is followed by an examination of Kenya's trading links with the world market.

TARIFFS

Prior to 1922, import duties in Kenya and the other two East African territories were limited in scope and designed to raise revenue without having any protective intent. However, the larger estate farmers in the

---

44 ibid., pp. 25–6.
45 ibid., p. 26.

colony, whose livelihood depended on the export of agricultural products as well as on the home market, clearly found that tariffs against
imported foodstuffs were an essential protection. It has been shown
that the larger estate producers, such as Lord Delamere, exerted a
strong influence over the direction of policy of the colonial administration in Kenya. It is not surprising that in 1922 the *Bowring Committee*,
which had been set up to evaluate the need for protective tariffs in the
colony, deliberately adopted the principle of fostering 'suitable industries' as a foundation of economic policy.[46]

The main aim of the Committee's recommendations was to encourage local production for export in order to stimulate the agricultural
industry as a whole and 'to improve the economic position of the
colony by developing local resources so as to render unnecessary the
importation of foodstuffs and other articles which could be produced
locally'.[47] It was decided that each branch of the agricultural industry
would be given substantial import protection for a period of seven
years, after which time its effectiveness would be reconsidered.

Thus, in 1922, a whole series of new import duties were imposed on
specific and general items: beer, for instance, had a duty imposed of 2s
per imperial gallon; cheese and butter, a duty of 1s per lb; grain wheat
had a duty of 5s per 100 lb and ground wheat, 6s per 100 lb. In
addition, manufactured goods were subject to an *ad valorem* tax of
10–30 per cent on three main groups of items.

The structure of duties established in 1922 was to remain unchanged
until 1930. In 1924, a *Cost of Living Commission* was set up to monitor
price increases in the colony. This was in response to considerable
pressure from the white petty bourgeoisie (traders, professionals and
self-employed) who, by the mid-1920s, were feeling 'the squeeze' of
the increased prices of consumption items on their standard of living.[48]
This Cost of Living Commission reported early in 1929 and in
response the *Kenya Tariff Committee* was set up in the same year to
review the systems of tariffs in the colony. All the recommendations of
the Kenya Tariff Committee were accepted by LEGCO in 1930.

The aim of the new tariff structures was to strike a balance between
the dominant settler farmers and the bulk of European consumers in
the colony. The intention was to protect certain local industries more
specifically than before and to reduce duties on some items which were
consumed by Europeans. Thus, the existing system of classification by
rates was abandoned in favour of classification by *commodities* and all
ad valorem groups were converted into duties for specific items.[49] The

---

46 *Report of the Kenya Tariff Committee*, May 1929, p. 3.
47 ibid., p. 2.
48 For further information on the Cost of Living Commission and a real wage/prices
index from 1924 to 1972 see J. R. Newman and M. P. Cowen, 'Real wages in Central
Kenya', mimeo., Nairobi, 1975.
49 Tariff Committee, op. cit., p. 18.

principle of suspended duties was also introduced on some items in order that the three East African governments could more easily adjust the common system of duties to their own requirements. There was a general move of tariff rates downwards which was in response to the European consumers who had instigated the Cost of Living Commission.

There was a reduction in rates of duty on imported sugar, reduced from 12s per 100 lb to 6s per 100 lb, on cotton piece goods, reduced from 40 cents per lb to 30 cents per lb; and on cement, where the *ad valorem* duty was reduced by 10 per cent. The most drastic reduction was on wheat (on the grain) and wheat flour, which were reduced from 5s per 100 lb to 3s and from 6s per 100 lb to 3s respectively.[50] These changes were certainly of assistance to the bulk of the white consumers (Africans consumed mainly maize flour rather than wheat), but what effect did they have on the Kenyan wheat industry? The Committee officially concluded that the reduction of duties on this commodity would 'have no effect on importations of wheat for milling in up-country mills . . . also no harm to the industry will be caused by a reduction in the duty to be levied on wheat on the grain, to the normal rate on foodstuffs'.[51] Only two local industries were directly protected in the 1929 report: beer was given an extra 50 cents duty in addition to the 2s per imperial gallon imposed in 1922, and the tea duty was raised from 45 cents to 50 cents per lb.

It would seem from examining the changes in the tariff structure in 1930 that the white consumers of the colony were taking precedence over the principle of protecting local farming produce. This was most certainly *not* the case, due to the existence of highly protective *railway rates* for local produce. The Tariff Committee reviewed the existing railway rates and agreed to support the continuance of the system and the further extension of differential rates between country produce and import traffic. These railway rates provided an important medium of protection for local industries, enhanced the effects of protective duties and rendered the imported item consistently more expensive than the local equivalent.[52]

The tariff structure established in 1930 was designed to balance the interests of different fractions of the settler class and favourable railway rates counterbalanced reductions of import tariffs on certain food items.

---

50 Information on tariff details are to be found in the Blue Books for Kenya Colony, ML.

51 Tariff Committee, op. cit., p. 19.

52 All the European members of the Tariff Committee agreed that the railway rates should be retained and extended further. It is significant that the only members to dissent from this conclusion were the Asian members, who represented the small traders with interests opposite to those of the farmers.

TRADE IN THE COLONY

The *Ottawa Agreements* of 1932 established a system of imperial preference between Britain and her colonies, which enabled colonial goods to enter Britain at a lower rate than those from other areas. A mitigating factor for Kenya during the slump in commodity prices was that under the terms of the *Congo Basin Treaty*, the East African territories were unable to discriminate against consumer goods of Japanese manufacture. These cheap consumer goods became available in East Africa at such low prices as to maintain the real value of money wages even though they were reduced absolutely.[53] In order to highlight some of the main aspects of national competition for East African markets, Kenya's trading patterns will be considered.

IMPORTS

Britain's position in relation to other principal sources of supply is traced over a period of twenty years from 1927 to 1947 in Table 7. At first sight it appears that the share of Britain and the empire in Kenya and Uganda's imports[54] remains consistently higher than the 'other foreign' group. Also Britain was the largest single importer at that time.

These figures in aggregate are, however, misleading, for not only is the absolute British share of total 'empire' imports into East Africa *static,* but more important, if imports on government account (i.e. imports of bullion, specie and trans-shipment goods) are disregarded, the share of private British business to the colony was not 39 per cent in 1937 but 9·8 per cent leaving Japan as the largest single supplier of goods to Kenya in that year with 18·4 per cent of the total.[55]

Before the Second World War the other foreign suppliers, notably Japan, were seriously challenging British and empire predominance in East African markets. In fact, the war called a halt to this trend by temporarily eliminating two of Britain's competitors, Japan and Germany, from the East African market. Indeed the *Report on the Economic and Commercial Conditions in British East Africa, 1937–1938* went so far as to assert that 'apart from machinery, competition from Japan is now experienced in most lines for which East

---

53 For further details of the Congo Basin Treaties see C. C. Wrigley, 'Kenya: the patterns of economic life, 1902–45', in V. Harlow, E. M. Chilver and A. Smith (Eds), *The History of East Africa*, vol. 2, Clarendon Press, Oxford, 1965.

54 Newman and Cowen, op. cit., p. 6, bear out this point.

55 The annual trade accounts do not contain a table of imports into Kenya and Uganda, *excluding* the government account from the British total. In fact this point might have been overlooked if it were not for the publication *Economic and Commercial Conditions in British East Africa, 1937–1938*, Dept of Overseas Trade, ML.

TABLE 6   *Sources of Major Imports of Glassware into Kenya and Uganda in 1936 and 1937*

	1936 (£)	%	1937 (£)	%
UK	7 339	25	8 573	22
Belgium	1 644	6	2 519	6
Germany	3 889	13	5 883	15
Japan	13 314	45	17 145	44
TOTAL	29 126		38 943	

Source: Colonial trade accounts.

Africa affords a market'.[56] An indication of this rapid transition of Japan from a small supplier in the early 1920s to the largest single importer into Kenya and Uganda can be illustrated by its dominance of the cotton piece goods markets. Japan moved from having an 18 per cent share in Kenya's and Uganda's markets for cotton fabrics in 1925 to controlling 70 per cent of these markets, largely displacing Britain, India and Holland as the former suppliers of this product. By 1937, therefore, apart from exporting large quantities of cotton and silk piece goods to the East African market at competitive prices, Japan was also supplying cement, clothes, boots, shoes and enamelware. Japan had, of course, achieved this penetration of the East African markets by undercutting the established suppliers such as Britain. An example of such tactics can be found in the following comparative costs for production of china and porcelain and ceramic tiles:

China and porcelain:	UK	101s (average c.i.f. per cwt)
	Japan	20s (average c.i.f. per 1 000)
Ceramic tiles:	UK	225s (average c.i.f. per 1 000)
	Japan	69s (average c.i.f. per 1 000)

In glassware also Japan predominated, having ousted Britain as the main supplier of this product by the 1920s (see Table 6).

This threat to British and empire hold over the East African markets from Japan did not go unobserved in Britain. In 1928, Ormsby-Gore, the Secretary of State for the Colonies, was being closely questioned in the House of Commons about Japanese trade with the East African colonies. Mr Hannon (Conservative) asked the Secretary of State for the Colonies whether the government was aware that an economic commission appointed by the Japanese government had recently visi-

56 ibid.

TABLE 7a   *Imports into Kenya and Uganda 1927–47 by Countries of Origin (%)*

	1927	1928	1929	1930	1931	1932	1933	1934	1935	1947
GB & N. Ireland	38·3	34·6	37·0	44·3	44·5	39·3	38·3	37·6	37·0	39·7
British Possessions	25·6	27·6	23·1	20·4	18·6	24·1	15·1	23·3	22·0	28·2
Total British Empire	63·9	62·2	60·1	64·7	63·1	63·4	63·4	60·9	59·0	67·9
Belgium	1·4	1·3	1·5	1·0	1·4	1·6	1·8	1·7	1·9	3·6
Dutch E. Indies	2·4	2·2	3·3	3·6	2·6	3·4	1·8	1·7	1·4	1·4
Germany	4·6	4·4	4·6	3·4	3·2	2·6	3·1	3·5	4·4	—
Holland	4·9	5·4	5·1	4·0	4·3	3·9	3·4	1·4	0·9	1·4
Japan	4·1	4·5	5·7	3·3	8·6	11·0	12·9	15·0	15·2	0·7
USA	10·8	11·3	12·0	10·3	19·0	5·3	4·3	6·1	7·6	14·9
Persia	2·1	2·4	1·6	2·0	1·9	2·5	2·9	4·1	4·3	5·5
Foreign (other)	5·8	6·3	6·1	7·7	5·9	6·1	6·4	5·6	5·3	7·4
GRAND TOTAL FOREIGN	36·0	37·8	39·9	35·3	36·9	36·6	36·6	39·1	41·0	34·9

Source: Colonial trade accounts.

ted Kenya and Uganda with the object of extending Japanese trade in the area and furthermore,

> having regard to the loan commitment of this country to Kenya and Uganda, whether he will devise measures to safeguard British export trade to British East Africa against the competition of Japan and other countries?

Ormsby-Gore replied in the affirmative to the first part of the question, but when it came to protection he asserted the imperial government's policy at the time:

> HM Government are anxious to foster British export trade to the territories concerned – and would welcome suggestions. But it would be inconsistent with existing international obligations to extend any preferential treatment to goods of British origin imported into these territories.[57]

Hence the principle of free trade was asserted once again. Any change towards a protectionist policy favouring British goods entering the colony would have abrogated the Congo Basin Treaties.

Another country to take a large proportion of the East African import trade from 1925 to 1937 was America, which was in fact ahead of Japan until it was ousted as the largest single non-empire trading

57 Article, 'Buy British', in *EAS*, 14 January 1928.

TABLE 7b   *Total Imports into Kenya and Uganda (£s)*

1927	1929	1931	1933	1935
781 611	8 920 579	5 092 665	4 898 722	6 641 135

Source: Annual trade accounts for Kenya and Uganda.

partner in 1931. Table 7 shows the way in which the war was temporarily to destroy Japan's threat to Britain's hold on the East African market and how the USA was able to replace Japan as the major non-empire supplier after 1945. The USA was mainly involved with supplying technical and engineering goods to the East African market: motor vehicles, oil, petrol, kerosene and tyres. These articles were in direct competition with similar goods imported by British firms, whereas the Japanese challenge affected goods not only from Britain but also from other empire sources such as India, particularly in the area of low-cost enamelware and cotton goods.

EXPORTS

The three East African territories were oriented towards primary production for export before the Second World War. Table 8 shows the principal exports from Kenya Colony in 1937. The largest proportion of these commodities were exported to the metropolis, as shown in Table 9. However, it is clear that Britain's position as the major destination of East Africa's exports was slowly declining by the 1930s. The non-empire 'foreign' group takes a small but increasing proportion of the exports of Kenya and Uganda. While the share of the empire increased during this period, that of Britain declined abso-

TABLE 8   *Principal Exports from Kenya Colony in 1937*

	£	%
Coffee	732 263	18·8
Sisal	673 719	17·3
Tea	466 872	12·0
Gold	415 967	10·7
Maize	198 832	5·1
Hides	196 071	5·0
Sodium Carbonate	187 429	5·0
Skins	104 289	3·0
TOTAL EXPORTS	3 888 320	

Source: Overseas Economic Survey, 1937.

TABLE 9   *Direction of Exports from Kenya and Uganda 1923–33 (%)*

	1923	1925	1927	1929	1931	1933
United Kingdom	47·1	56·4	47·4	36·9	36·6	35·6
British Possessions	36·7	27·8	23·2	35·2	41·1	42·3
Total British and Empire	83·8	84·2	70·6	72·1	77·7	77·9
Others: Belgium	4·9	3·5	5·0	6·2	4·9	3·0
Japan	1·7	2·1	11·2	10·6	3·3	7·9
USA	2·2	1·3	1·4	2·3	4·6	1·6
Total Others	16·2	15·8	29·4	27·9	22·3	22·1
TOTAL %	100	100	100	100	100	100

Source: Colonial trade accounts for 1933.

lutely. It is significant that once again Japan was the largest non-empire receiver of East African exports, although its percentage of total trade remained small, at 8 per cent in 1933.

It was no surprise that in 1928 some Labour members in the British Parliament queried the expenditure on East African cotton-growing made by the Empire Cotton Growing Association, on the grounds that Britain was subsidizing Japanese competitors. For instance, in the first nine months of 1927, one-quarter of the cotton exported from Mombasa was consigned to Japan.[58] They went on to suggest that Japanese freighters were carrying East African cotton free of charge, being subsidized by the Japanese government. The president of the Board of Trade agreed that the reason for Japan's good fortune in the East African cotton market was that its freight rates were lower than those of Britain.

Britain's free-trade practice during the interwar years meant that its manufactured goods were required to face increasingly tough competition in colonial markets from other industrial countries such as Japan and the USA. The interests of European consumers in Kenya were in no way served by supporting imperial goods in preference to those from Japan. Although the larger settler farmers fostered a system of protection for their food and beverage industries, the overall interests of the settler economy were served by the continued flow of cheap-wage goods such as cloth. The ultimate response of many British firms to this competition after the Second World War was to go behind the tariff wall and actually manufacture goods within the colony.

58 Article, 'Japanese competition for East African cotton', *EAS*, 31 March 1928.

Company Formation in Kenya 1907–45

The earlier discussion has illustrated that the basis of accumulation in Kenya was agricultural production. Here the intention is to analyse the specific nature of *corporate* accumulation during the interwar years. This aspect of capitalist development in Kenya sets the stage for a more detailed consideration in the next chapter of patterns of foreign investment.

The analysis of company formation in Kenya is divided into two parts, the first from 1907 to 1922 and the second from 1922 to 1945. These divisions are important in that they reflect both a change in the pattern of company formation (which after 1922 is more extensive) and also a significant change in company law.[59]

COMPANY FORMATION 1907–22

In the first phase of settler capitalism, business formations and land were largely controlled by the politically dominant fraction of the settler class. This group of individuals, although small in number, had a powerful influence over state policy which was invariably bent to support their own accumulation.

The most striking feature of the first period of company formation in Kenya is the *instability* of such investments and the interlocking nature of ownership.[60] The average lifespan of the first thirty-five public companies to form in Kenya was only nine years, with five of them surviving for less than one year.[61] The concentration of assets of these firms amongst such a small number of individuals can be shown by the extent of their personal holdings. Lord Delamere, one of the most prominent settler barons,[62] owned a share in the capital of three of these companies: Unga Ltd, Nyama Ltd and *The Times of East Africa* (the latter being an important organ of settler politics). Nyama was a cattle ranch and Unga was a grain-milling concern. Delamere's position as part of the large farming group and prominent politician was reflected in his business formations.

The infamous Captain E. S. Grogan, another settler politician who was principally a timber concessionaire and property speculator, had

---

59 In 1922, the Indian Companies Act which had been operative in the territory was changed to the British Companies Act. This was an attempt to accommodate the expanding scale of company formation in Kenya.

60 There is a strong parallel here with the patterns of company formation in the post-colonial period, undertaken by the indigenous bourgeoisie. See Chapter 5.

61 All this information on early company formation was obtained from the first register of public companies in the Registrar General's Dept in Nairobi.

62 Lord Delamere was member of LEGCO for the Rift Valley, and a member of a multitude of government committees.

shareholdings in a total of six out of these thirty-five companies. Most of these companies were owned jointly with other members of his family, notably his wife and his brother. These six companies were concerned with the exploitation of land and property speculation, and they included Kilindini Habour and Wharf Company, Upper Nairobi Township and Estate Company, Masailand Trust Corporation, Ndimu, Miti and Kenani Fibrelands.[63]

The control of Kilindini Harbour and Wharf Company became controversial and illustrated the political strength of the larger settlers when it came to manipulating the state to their own advantage. The company had been set up in 1906 by Captain Grogan along with his wife and another settler, W. Hunter, with the Grogan family having the controlling interest. Grogan had been unofficially granted 50 acres of land abutting on Kilindini Harbour in Mombasa, which was not confirmed until 1918. Here he had constructed a small timber wharf, equipped with overhead transport gear for unloading cargoes from ships. There was strong pressure on the administration from elements of the settler group to purchase the wharf. They resented the fact that an essential service was controlled by an individual rather than by the state. Finally, after four years of negotiation, Grogan agreed to sell the wharf and 50 acres of adjoining land to the government at a price of K£350 000 in 1925. This 'package' included the wharf which had been valued at £37,000 in 1920 and 50 acres of land which had been leased to Grogan at a nominal rent, with some properties, in all a total of 146 acres. Despite having paid an exorbitant price for the wharf and the land, the government was not able to enjoy the use of the wharf for some years as it had been privately leased by Grogan to another wharfage company. The lease continued to operate to the exclusion of the new owner, the government. Furthermore, within six months of purchase, the wharf began to show signs of collapse. This is an example of speculation that suceeds only if the individual has close connections with the bureaucracy. Both Grogan and Delamere were prominent on a number of committees and boards, responsible for policy-making in the colony.[64]

Hunter, a company secretary (and Grogan's brother-in-law), had shareholdings in nine companies, several of which overlapped with Grogan. These firms, including the Upper Nairobi Township Company, were mainly in the areas of property and farming. Similarly, W. Fletcher, a law clerk in Nairobi, had shares in eleven companies. These firms were in land, property and farming, the only exception being the Nairobi Motor Transport Company. Fletcher was also involved in Lord Delamere's company, Nyama Ltd, a meat firm. His companies

---

63 Kenani Fibrelands was a sisal estate and Miti Ltd a timber company; the others were concerned with land and property development.
64 Further details in McGregor Ross, op. cit., pp. 159 and 162.

also overlapped with Grogan. For instance, the joint subscribers to the Masailand Trust Corporation were Grogan, Allsopp and Fletcher. The Mackinnon Brothers owned two firms in this group which were concerned with land development: the Nairobi Prospecting and Acquiring Syndicate (1907) and Mackinnon Bros Ltd (1911). These two were established in the import/export trade.

If these settlers had not engaged in full-time farming they were invariably in some kind of profession which they used as a base for their accumulation. These professions were diverse and included accountants, solicitors, jewellers, engineers and architects. A common feature of this early phase of primitive accumulation is the combination of *ownership and management* in these firms.[65] Other characteristics of these early companies are that the areas of investment are limited in scope and directed towards concerns that will reproduce capital quickly. In other words this period of accumulation was highly *speculative*, in that corruption and rapid buying and selling made for an unstable pattern of early company formation. For instance, out of a total of thirty-five public firms, twenty-five were involved in land, property development and agriculture, with the remainder in trading or small-scale servicing such as printing, repair work and newspapers.

Another aspect of this initial stage of capital formation is the scarcity of investment in manufacturing enterprise which requires larger amounts of capital. Capital begins to expand into small processing and basic manufacturing during the next period of company formation after 1922. The only exception in the earlier period was the Mombasa Electric Light and Power Company formed in 1908 to generate electric power in Mombasa, the first town in East Africa to have electric light. The company was notable in other respects for it was unusually a partnership between Asian and European shareholders; Messrs Esmailjee Jivanjee & Company held 70 per cent and a local town councillor, Udall, held the remaining 30 per cent. In 1924 this company was to be incorporated as a public company, East African Power & Lighting. This new formation included the recruitment of foreign technical expertise in the form of Power Securities Corporation and Balfour Beatty, who acted as the company's management and technical consultants until 1970.

All of the first thirty-five public companies to form in Kenya are now extinct, although several, as in the case of EAPL, have been reconstituted in a different form. Unga, originally Lord Delamere's preserve, was reconstituted several times and from 1928 onwards it was controlled by the Kenya Farmers' Association (KFA), which was dominated by the larger estate farmers.[66] For instance, the Co-operative Society

---

65 This tendency of overlap between the professions and private business is observed in the discussion of indigenous capital in Chapter 5.

66 Unga Ltd is still in existence and is part of a larger conglomerate, Mercat Ltd, which is now the dominant firm in the bread and grain-milling industry.

of BEA went into liquidation only nine months after its formation in 1907 due to indebtedness.

The Nairobi Printing and Publishing Company collapsed in a similar fashion in the year of its formation, in 1904. *The Times of East Africa*, a newspaper controlled by Lord Delamere, lasted from 1905 to 1908 when it was re-formed. The absence of Asian capital in the public-company sector was not altogether surprising, for their operations were not yet on a large enough scale to form public firms as their commercial activities around the turn of the century were confined to business partnership forms. The two exceptions in this group were the Mombasa Electric Light Company and the Indian Trading Association, registered in 1904, which went into liquidation in 1910.

The pattern of early formation of settler companies in Kenya Colony exhibits certain features common to most preliminary stages of accumulation. These features can be summarized as general instability, limited range of enterprises often of a speculative nature and interlocking personnel, both in terms of management and shareholding.

COMPANY FORMATION 1922–45

Number and Size of Companies   In the first period of company formation (1907–22), the unstable characteristics have been stressed. Conversely, the interwar period is characterized by a greater degree of stability and by an increase in the number of companies; a process accompanied by an expansion in the size and activities of both local and foreign firms. It is predictable that after two decades of commodity production and capitalist circulation in the colony, companies would expand in absolute numbers and survive over a longer period. Table 10 shows the number of firms on the register of the Registrar General and those struck off each year between 1927 and 1945. A consistent trend

TABLE 10   *Companies on the Register and Those Struck off*

Date	Cos on the Register	Cos Struck off	Struck off as % of Total
1927	289	19	6·6
1930	399	37	9·3
1933	472	30	6·4
1936	593	29	5·0
1939	641	25	4·0
1942	679	18	2·6
1945	811	16	2·0

Source: Annual reports of the Registrar General.

TABLE 11a   *Sample of Private Companies Registered between 1922 and 1945 by Enterprise and Ownership*

	European	Foreign	Asian	Total No.	Total %
1 Agricultural Production and Ancillary Services	8	3	5	16	19
2 Food and Beverages, Manuf. of Chemicals, Clothes and Textiles	1	1	5	7	8
3 General Engineering and Mining	1	—	—	1	1
4 Transport	—	2	2	4	5
5 Investment and Finance	1	—	2	3	4
6 Real Estate, Property, Building and Construction	6	1	6	13	15
7 Import/Export	1	2	12	15	18
8 Wholesale/Retail (incl. Catering and Printing)	1	7	18	26	30
TOTAL COMPANIES	19	16	50	85	100

TABLE 11b   *Sample of Public Companies 1922–45*

	European	Foreign	Asian	Total No.
1 Agricultural Production and Ancillary Services	3	1	—	4
2 Food and Beverages, Manuf. of Chemicals, Clothes and Textiles	3	2	—	5
3 General Engineering and Mining	2	3	—	5
4 Transport	—	1	—	1
5 Investment and Finance	—	—	1	1
6 Real Estate, Property, Building and Construction	2	—	—	2
7 Import/Export	1	—	--	1
8 Wholesale/Retail (incl. Catering and Printing)	2	1	—	3
TOTAL COMPANIES	13	8	1	22

Source: (a) Private companies sample, 1922–45, one-third list sample.
(b) Public companies sample, one-quarter sample, both conducted 1974–5, Registrar General of Companies.

of expansion is exhibited in the total number of companies on the register, with a corresponding decline in those struck off over the period between 1927 and 1945. (The year in which most companies failed was 1930, and this relates to the worldwide depression.)

Private Companies The growing level of company formation was accompanied by an expansion in the size and range of activities of these firms. Out of a one-third list sample of companies registering between 1922 and 1945, the average paid-up[67] capital for the eighty-five firms was £97 065. This average covers a wide range of firm sizes, with a standard deviation of £22 457. Some companies have a small paid-up capital as in the case of Cobb Ltd, a firm of planters with an equity of £499. Some of them were larger, such as the East African Tanning and Extract Company (a British firm manufacturing wattle extract), which had a paid-up capital of £800 000 in 1937.

This sample of eighty-five private companies in Kenya indicates the different areas of investment. Table 11a divides the sample firms into activity groupings according to race. Racial categories were used under both the colonial and post-colonial company classification systems, and in the first case it reflects the prevailing ideology of European supremacy.[68] The largest category of all communities together is that of wholesale and retail (30 per cent), import/export (18 per cent), building, construction and real estate (15 per cent). From the sample, *European* firms predominate in the area of agriculture, which was exclusively a settler preserve. The next largest sector in which European firms predominated was property and real estate. There appear to be few European firms in manufacturing. This can be explained by the fact that the settlers in most cases processed their commodities collectively through state-sponsored bodies such as the Kenya Farmers' Association, Kenya Co-operative Creameries and the Kenya Planters' Union. Co-operative marketing organizations such as these were the best way of ensuring the survival of the settler economy.[69] However in the smaller number of large public companies, during the same period, Europeans took quite a substantial interest in the processing of primary products.

The regulations against land holdings in the most productive areas of Kenya which applied to 'non-Europeans' ensured that Asian[70] partici-

---

67 Paid-up capital is not an ideal measure of firm size, but the only one available in Kenya for private firms.

68 The continuation of racial categories in the Registrar General's Dept after 1963 reflected the ideology of Africanization.

69 Van Zwanenberg, op. cit., shows how precarious was the foundation of settler agriculture.

70 In 1915, the *Crown Lands Ordinance* empowered the governor to veto land transactions between races. Even in 1908, Lord Elgin had noted 'as a matter of administrative convenience, grants of land in the upland areas should not be made to Indians'.

pation in agricultural production was minimal. From the sample, it is clear that Asian merchant capital was channelled mainly into trade and services, the largest single category being the import/export trade, followed by wholesale/retail and services. There was a considerable increase in the rate of Asian company formation before the Second World War. Furthermore, Asian partnerships formed an overwhelming proportion of those firms registered under the Business Partnership Act.[71] For instance, in 1949 they constituted 90 per cent of these businesses, although by 1955 this proportion had dropped to 75 per cent, African firms having filled the gap by this time. (African enterprises do not really feature in company or business partnerships until after the Second World War, when in 1946 twenty-four companies were formed.)

However, it is significant that in the earlier years of company formation, these Asian business partnerships were largely confined to wholesale and retail trade. Any enterprise that needed to raise large sums of local capital could do so more effectively through the vehicle of a joint-stock company. It is clear from this sample that Asian merchant capital was not to expand in any significant way into manufacturing until after the Second World War. Nevertheless, some Asian firms had moved into primary processing even before 1939, the most important forms of enterprise being oil-milling and cotton-ginning in both Kenya and Uganda. The merchant capital accumulated by this class before 1945 was to provide the basis for their move into industrial production after the war. Leys identified this class as a merchant capitalist class which was poised to become an industrial bourgeoisie of the classical type.[72] After the war large industrial empires grew up out of the merchant capital accumulated during the 1920s and 1930s in Kenya and Uganda, such as those of the Madvhanis, the Manjis, the Khimasias and the Chandarias. However, this potential 'industrial bourgeoisie' was never able to consolidate its position in any of the three East African countries, for reasons that will be outlined later.

The inherent weakness of settler capital was evident when it came to withstanding competition from Asian and foreign firms, and this is shown by its failure to move into industry either before or after the Second World War. This reflects the weakness of settler capitalism in terms of management limitations and size of enterprises. The family mode of operation in Asian enterprises rendered them more competitive than settler enterprises. It is not surprising that immediately after

---

71 The *Partnership Act* enabled only two partners to participate in business which was not protected by limited liability, which meant that any debts incurred by the business could fall personally on the partners. These conditions meant that larger-scale enterprises would become limited liability companies, partnerships being confined to small enterprises.

72 Colin Leys, *Underdevelopment in Kenya, the Political Economy of Neo-Colonialism*, Heinemann, London, 1975, p. 38.

TABLE 12   *Changing Ownership of Eight Private Firms*

	Year Reg.	Business	Date	Transfer From	Transfer To
1	1922	Drapers	1945	J. Stephens	M. Desai & Sons
2	1924	Cotton ginning	1945	G. Small	Kassim *et al*.
3	1928	Merchants and Jewellers	1943	Lewison	Patels
4	1928	Property	1930	Keith	Singh *et al*.
5	1930	Printing	1945	Balabanoff	Keshavji *et al*.
6	1933	Dairymen	1955	J. K. Watson	Patels
7	1941	Catering	1945	L. Holden	K. S. Jamal
8	1945	Merchants	1950	Morgan	Patel *et al*.

Source: Private companies sample, 1922–45.

the Second World War, between 1945 and 1950, a large number of local settler firms were absorbed either by Asian firms or by foreign-based operations.[73] Despite the limited numbers in the 1922–45 sample of firms, there is an unmistakable tendency for Asian firms to take over European enterprises. The eight companies in Table 12 fall into this category.

Public Companies   To make this analysis complete it is necessary to examine also public-company formation during the same period, 1922–45. This was covered by a one-quarter list sample of all public companies forming between these dates. There are fewer public companies in Kenya than there are private, and public companies are usually larger in terms of asset and equity size than their private counterparts. To give some indication of the comparative size difference between the two types of company, the average capital per company in each of the samples was calculated. From eighty-five private companies, the average paid-up capital per company was £97 065 (with a standard deviation of £22 457), whereas the average equity for the twenty-two public companies was £396 083 (standard deviation £20 908).[74] The public and private companies, therefore, being derived from a *different* population of companies, exhibit different characteristics, with the private firms showing a slightly higher variation from the mean.

The different composition of the samples in Table 13 clearly shows that the Asian group form the largest proportion (59 per cent) of the private companies, while in the public group European and foreign

73 This point is also made in Eglin, op. cit., p. 16.

74 A two-tailed T-test showed that the difference between the two values of deflated paid-up capital is significant at the 1 per cent level (*t* = 15·47); deflated by real-wage index of Cowen and Newman, op. cit.

TABLE 13   *Constitution of Samples, Private and Public Companies*[75]

Private Companies			Public Companies		
Racial Group	No. of Cos	%	Racial Group	No. of Cos	%
Asian	50	59	Asian	2	9
Foreign	14	16	Foreign	9	41
European	21	25	European	11	50
TOTAL	85	100	TOTAL	22	100

firms predominate together with 91 per cent of the companies. Whereas the private Asian firms are concentrated in the area of trading with small capital requirements, the European and foreign groups of public companies are mainly situated within the areas of manufacturing, general engineering and mining. European firms from the public companies sample were dominant in the areas of agriculture and agricultural processing. The manufacturing group contains five companies, three of which are local European firms. These firms are all significantly concerned with processing primary products, whereas the two foreign firms in the group are engaged in non-agricultural manufacturing. The limited numbers of firms in the industrial sector before the Second World War will also be stressed in the next part on international capital.

Foreign Branch Firms   In addition to those foreign firms registered in Kenya Colony in the form of public or private firms, there are also a number of firms classified as 'foreign' branches.[76] These firms cannot raise capital within Kenya but are merely branches or offices of the foreign parent company. The foreign banks, for instance, are registered in this form, for example, the Standard & National and Grindlays. During the interwar period, a high proportion of these foreign firms invested in mining enterprises. In 1937 alone, nine new foreign mining companies were registered. These moves were in response to the so-called 'Kakamaga Gold Rush', which attracted both foreign and local capital in a series of highly speculative ventures.

Local mining companies also mushroomed between 1929 and 1934. Most of them, such as the Nyanza Goldfields (1933) and the Kenya Mining Investment Limited (1933), only survived for a brief spell

---

75 These racial groups are derived from the nationality of the majority (over 50 per cent) of the firm's share capital. Before 1945 there were very few 'inter-racial' partnerships, so this method is quite an accurate assessment of ownership.

76 These foreign branch companies are registered under Section 206 of the *Companies Act (Kenya)* and they are exempt from filing any financial or shareholding details; they cannot raise capital inside Kenya.

before collapsing under a mountain of debt. This speculative enter-prise attracted both local and foreign capital alike.

Conclusion

By showing the extent of company growth and the ownership patterns during the interwar period in Kenya, it has been possible to highlight several aspects of capitalist development. The overall features are that company formation was largely in the area of agricultural production, ancillary services and primary processing. It is suggested that capitalist expansion in Kenya was limited in terms of the partial integration of the mass of the population into the wage labour force and the racial barriers that surrounded production. The consequent limitations on the size of the internal market meant that the economy remained fundamentally agrarian, and secondary industry was not developed until the Second World War. However, the concentration of capital within the agricultural sector did give rise to some basic forms of primary processing, largely for the local market.

It is clear that, by 1939, Asian merchant capital dominated the sphere of retail trade, while settler and foreign firms remained largely within the area of plantations and import/export trade.

CHAPTER 2

International Capital in Kenya before 1945

This chapter will illustrate the nature and extent of the penetration of foreign capital into East Africa before the Second World War. During this period, international firms invested in estate agriculture, primary processing, trading and mineral exploitation. Unfortunately, there is little reliable statistical information on the exact quantity and composition of foreign investment before 1945. However, through samples conducted on the firms that registered in Kenya during this time, it has been possible to identify the most significant companies in terms of the size of their operations.[1]

These foreign firms have been divided into three main groups, according to the *type* of investment: estates and primary processing, trading, and manufacturing and mineral extraction. First, these groups are considered in general and then a case study is developed from each one. There is naturally some overlap of activities within the three groupings, but in general the investments fall into one of three main areas. As the aim is to show the *tendencies* behind certain forms of corporate expansion, we have not adhered strictly to time boundaries, although the analysis concentrates on the interwar period. One of the aims of such an approach has been to show the historical movement of capital from trade into production in response to competitive conditions on the world market.[2] For instance, the merchant companies in this sample of firms usually expanded into production of the commodities in which they traded.

---

1 Most firms during this time were not required to register balance sheets in Kenya, and the only information available to the company researcher is *issued* capital. The table listing major foreign investments up to 1945 gives the average size of some foreign firms by issued capital. Foreign firms tended to be larger than local ones although fewer in number. Refer to tables in Chapter 1.

2 G. Kay, *Development and Underdevelopment, a Marxist Analysis*, Macmillan, London, 1975. See, for example, Chapter 5.

International Capital

The preceding examination of the settler economy and patterns of corporate growth have illustrated the uneven expansion of the capitalist mode of production in the colony. Initially, the area offered limited internal markets for commodities and the bulk of agricultural products were grown for export. It is not surprising, therefore, that the enterprises formed during this period were limited to the processing of primary products such as cotton, coffee, tea and sisal. Factory production in all of the three East African territories was not significant before 1945. The manufacture of items of consumption was on a small scale and designed to serve a small European and Asian group and a rising number of wage-earning Africans. The products manufactured in Kenya before the Second World War include sisal twine, flour, fats, dairy products, sugar, soap, beer, jams, tobacco, cigarettes and mineral waters. Nevertheless, the home production of these articles had only in a few cases ousted the imported equivalent by 1939.[3] The East African territories remained dependent on manufactured goods imported mainly from Britain during the interwar years. At this point it is appropriate to consider the investment of British merchant firms in Kenya during the first decades of the twentieth century.

TRADING COMPANIES

British trading and shipping firms quickly recognized the potential offered by new and expanding markets in East Africa. The firm with the oldest links with East Africa was the shipping and trading firm Smith Mackenzie, which had opened a branch in Zanzibar in the early nineteenth century. Other trading firms which extended their operations to Kenya by the early 1900s included Baumann & Company, Gibson & Company, Leslie & Anderson, the British East African Corporation (BEAC) and Mitchell Cotts. These firms were all involved in exporting primary produce from Kenya and selling imported manufactured goods on the internal market. By the 1930s, in terms of the value of goods which they handled, A. Baumann and Mitchell Cotts were probably the largest. What was the background to their intervention in East Africa?

Mitchell Cotts was a leading South African merchant and shipping organization: shipping and coaling were the two main activities of the company at the time of entry into East Africa in 1926.[4] The firm established its first shipping branch in Mombasa in 1926, extended to

---

3 This contention is borne out by the colonial trade accounts for the interwar years. The consumption of meat and dairy products, for instance, was almost entirely from local sources.

4 The move of Mitchell Cotts into East Africa was part of an overall drive to extend its area of operation from South Africa along the Indian Ocean shipping routes.

Nairobi in 1927 and Kitale in 1928. By 1932, it had established itself as the sole contractor for the supply of South African coal to the Kenya and Uganda railways and supplied over 100 000 tons in 1932.[5] The tactic of each of these firms was to establish a monopoly over one particular commodity or group of commodities. Mitchell Cotts rapidly established its pre-eminence in the import and export trade in several commodities, its main import into East Africa being coal during the 1920s and 1930s.

The primary exports over which it had gained a secure hold by 1930 were wheat and maize. It managed through skilful manoeuvring to obtain the sole agency for the export of agricultural products (wheat, maize, butter, cheese, etc.) of the Kenya Farmers' Association (KFA). There is evidence that in this capacity Mitchell Cotts handled no less than 95 per cent of the wheat crop. The nature of this control over exports was extensive, as this extract from the company's annual report of 1932 shows:

> we handle exclusively their [KFA] exports of grain from the time it is received on to the time it is sold in London. The commission on this to London alone from 1928–1932 accounted for about £10,000. In cases where ships are chartered, this naturally bring us agency fees and bunker orders, and in turn this assists our coal bunkering operations. London also earns buying commission on all KFA's wants.[6]

Mitchell Cotts was also involved in the coffee trade in Kenya and set up coffee and maize mills at Kitale in 1928. As far as the import trade was concerned, the company held a wide variety of agencies for manufactured goods, such as the weighing machines of Messrs Pooley & Sons and products of the California Spray Chemical Corporation, which provided insecticides for the coffee-growers in East Africa. In 1933, Mitchell Cotts East Africa was incorporated as a wholly owned subsidiary of Mitchell Cotts & Company which by this time had its head office in London.

In 1936 the company added sisal to its list of primary products for export and in that year it purchased an existing settler sisal estate and processing plant at Ruiru. In 1933 it also acquired Simpson & Whitelaw, a local settler firm of grain and seed merchants.[7] Thus the Mitchell Cotts group in East Africa consolidated through expansion of its own enterprises and through purchase of existing local firms already involved in primary processing.

---

5 Report by H. Hamilton, a general manager of Mitchell Cotts Company in the 1920s, on the company's business in East Africa (in Mitchell Cotts company records for 1932, Cotts House, Nairobi).

6 Mitchell Cotts records, op. cit.

7 *Kenya Weekly News*, Show Supplement, 1952, ML.

The interests of the Mitchell Cotts group in primary production were enhanced further after the war when it moved on a large scale into pyrethrum processing, acting as the marketing agents for the parastatal growing authority. In 1950, it bought out a settler tea company, Mekong Estates, which became known as the Nandi Tea Estates Ltd. Despite the expansion in its range of activities in Kenya before the war, the company still relied for the bulk of its revenue on coaling, shipping and freight carriage.

The British East Africa Corporation (BEA Ltd) was one of the oldest established trading companies in East Africa and it was to merge with the Mitchell Cotts empire after 1945. The BEA was incorporated in England in 1906 by a syndicate with interests in the East African territories. From the outset it acted as agent for, and was closely associated with, the Cotton Growing Association, who wanted to encourage the cultivation of cotton in order to ensure supplies of raw materials to British manufacturers of cotton fabrics. This agency was the foundation of the BEA company in East Africa, and lasted from 1906 to 1914 when some differences arose between the BEA and the Association over the method of financing cotton purchased by the Corporation.[8] However, by 1914, the BEA company was well acquainted with conditions in the East African market and had invested directly in primary production of a wide range of commodities. It owned or managed estates cultivating sisal and wattle and operated oil mills and cotton ginneries. It also held many agencies for the import and distribution of manufactured goods into East Africa. In 1939 the firm was completely reorganized and registration transferred to Kenya. In 1946, all the primary processing and trading agencies of the BEA group were acquired by the Mitchell Cotts Company, as part of its postwar consolidation drive.

Smith Mackenzie was set up in 1909 and was another large shipping agency, concerned with warehousing and shipping worldwide, and import/export trade. The company's development was so similar to the preceding two trading firms that there will not be any detailed discussion of its activities.

Gailey & Roberts differs from the other trading firms in that it was not directly concerned with the export of primary commodities. It was rather a specialized importing agency for agricultural machinery. Gailey & Roberts is different from the others in that it was originally a local firm established by settlers, and was later taken over by a branch of international capital. The firm was established by James Gailey and D. O. Roberts who had been surveyors employed by the Uganda Railway Corporation in the early 1900s. They quickly recognized the early need of the settler farmers for tools and equipment, James Gailey

---

8 Annual reports of the British Cotton Growers' Association, 1907–14; Mitchell Cotts records.

was reported to have said: 'If Delamere persuades the settlers to take up land here they will need ploughs, spades, buckets, nails and building materials.'[9] It was in response to the demand for such items of equipment and servicing that they set up an engineering workshop in Nairobi in 1904–5. Before the First World War they enlarged the existing workshop and acquired another settler company, the Nairobi Engineering Company Ltd. Gailey & Roberts concentrated on offering technical services after sales, which involved the engagement of technical staff as well as the import of necessary equipment. During the years between the formation of the company and 1930, the bulk of the firm's work was in supplying machinery to farmers, but it also secured contracts to equip whole factories in Kenya and Uganda with machinery.

The company grew rapidly and by the mid-1930s it needed more capital for expansion. One of its chief suppliers of agricultural and engineering equipment from Britain, the United Africa Company,[10] took over 100 per cent of the share capital on the death of the partners. This Unilever subsidiary had thus managed to gain a direct stake in a most important service ancillary to agriculture in Kenya. The takeover by UAC of this potentially important servicing industry, even before 1945, illustrates the precarious nature of settler capitalism in terms of its failure to ensure supplies of money capital for expansion and the small size of its operation.

After infusions of loan capital and technical expertise from UAC, the company expanded rapidly. By 1938, one year after the UAC takeover, the firm's turnover in Kenya alone totalled £373 750 and the goods imported on the company's account consisted of 4 per cent of the total imports into Kenya and Uganda. The firm also set up branches in Tanganyika and Uganda. By 1952, with the total import bill in Kenya of over £100 million, the turnover of Gailey & Roberts had increased to over £2·5 million and by 1960 the firm had reached an annual turnover of over £5 million.[11] All the trading firms investing in East Africa before the war exhibited common characteristics. However, most of these firms (with the exception of Gailey & Roberts, which originally dealt in agricultural machinery) soon invested directly in productive activities such as sisal cultivation and processing of coffee and tea. The competition amongst these firms was so intense that they were left with no option but to produce the commodity which they exported.[12] The case studies elaborate on these tendencies.

---

9 See 'The history of Gailey & Roberts in Kenya', *EAS*, 15 March 1954.

10 The United Africa Corporation was a trading subsidiary of the British Unilever Company and it set up a branch in Kenya during the 1920s.

11 This information is from the *EAS* article, op. cit.

12 Hence the purchase of cotton and sisal estates by the Tanganyika Cotton Company (TANCOT) in the 1930s and Mitchell Cotts's purchase of a large settler-owned sisal estate in 1936.

ESTATES AND PRIMARY PROCESSING

These firms were usually concerned with exploiting one particular commodity in which they had a global interest. Table 14a shows the major firms in this group before 1945, and all of them except the sisal company both cultivated *and* processed agricultural commodities. The establishment of manufacturing or processing units was in all cases preceded by a trading branch through which the firms exported primary commodities to Europe such as tea, meat products, sisal and tobacco leaf. Trading firms usually set up processing plants in response to conditions of *international competition* in that commodity. So the decision to invest was never limited to local market considerations, but rather was incorporated in the global strategy of the firms.

The *British Imperial Tobacco Company* (BAT), one of the major cigarette and tobacco manufacturers in the world, in 1907 established a trading branch in East Africa to distribute tobacco products to the local market. During this time it encouraged the cultivation of tobacco in Uganda in order to export the raw material to Britain for processing. However, it became imperative to process the tobacco within the area in order to defend its markets from the competition of other tobacco firms like Rothmans.[13] Accordingly, in 1934 the *East African Tobacco Company* constructed its first factory in Uganda to process tobacco and cigarettes for the expanding local market. Tobacco was not manufactured in Kenya until 1954, because the size of the Kenyan crop did not merit the construction of a factory and the market there could be supplied from the Ugandan plant.

Tea was another example of an 'import-substitution' industry which was developed by Brooke Bond for the export market and to keep competitors at bay from the internal tea market. The case study will examine these trends in the tea industry in some detail.

The manufacture of *beer* was initially undertaken by some small settler firms and the largest was formed in 1922 as East African Breweries. During the 1930s, a British brewing concern, Ind Coope, took a share in the enterprise and provided management assistance until the late 1960s. The only foreign firm to benefit from any state assistance during this period was the Liebigs meat factory. This firm, which already had extensive investments in the Rhodesian meat industry, wanted to develop another producing area for expanding European markets. Thanks to early government support in the 1930s, the firm was able to exert a monopoly over meat production and marketing in both Tanzania and Kenya until the late 1960s, when it was taken over by the respective state corporations.

Another example of a primary commodity which was developed

---

13 BAT's subsidiary in Kenya, the East African Tobacco Company, took over Rothmans' marketing organization in Kenya in 1967 after a bitter two years of competition.

TABLE 14a   *Principal Foreign-Based Firms in Kenya before 1945*

Year	Firm	Business	Country of Origin/ Parent
Estates and Primary Processing:			
1906	British East Africa Co.	Exporters of primary produce, manuf. agents	BEA, Mitchell Cotts (after 1945)
1907	East African Tobacco Co.	Trading and growing tobacco products	British Imperial Tobacco Co. (UK) (later British American Tobacco Co.)
1922	East African Breweries	Beer manuf.	Ind Coope Ltd (UK)
1924	African Highlands Produce Co.	Tea manuf.	James Finlay (UK)
1931	Anglo-French Sisal Co.	Sisal-growing	Anglo–French Sisal Co. (Paris)
1924	Kenya Tea Co.	Tea- and coffee-processing	Brooke Bond (UK)
1932	East African Tanning & Extract Co.	Wattle bark and extract manuf.	1 Natal Tanning & Extract Co. 2 Forestal Land & Timber (UK)
1935	East African Meat Co.	Meat-processing	Liebigs (UK) (1969 Brooke Bond, Liebig)
Trading:			
1920	Bird & Co. Africa Ltd	Merchants, transport shipping, warehousing	Bird & Co. (UK)
1920	Gibson & Co.	Manuf. agents, export of primary produce	Gibson & Co. (UK)
1924	Gailey & Roberts	Import and servicing of machinery	United Africa Co. (Unilever Ltd, UK)
1934	Holland Africa Line	Shipping agents and warehousing	Holland Africa Line (Holland)
Manufacture and Minerals:			
1911	Magadi Soda Co.	Soda extraction and processing	1 East African Syndicate 2 Imperial Chemicals Inc. (ICI) UK
1922	East African Power	Power generation	Balfour Beatty (UK) and Power Securities (UK)
1933	East African Portland Cement	Cement-processing, clinker-grinding	Associated Portland Cement (UK)

Source: Registrar General of Companies, Kenya.

TABLE 14b   *Size of Some Foreign Firms by Paid-up Capital*

Firm	Issued Capital 1930 (£)	Issued Capital 1945 (£)
1 East African Breweries	2 085	70 637
Kenya Tea Co. (Brooke Bond)	50 000	150 000
East African Tanning & Extract Co.	60 000	477 201
East African Sisal Estates	10 000	20 000
2 Gailey & Roberts	133 142	146 692
British East Africa Co.	n.a.	47 410
3 Magadi Soda Co.	597 141	796 260
East African Power & Lighting	570 000	4 213 333
East African Portland Cement Co.	35 000	70 000
Total (available) Issued Share Capital	1 457 368	5 991 533
Average Capital Per Company	182 171	665 729

Source: Registrar General of Companies, Kenya. This was constituted from a one-quarter list sample of public firms registering in Kenya.

initially by merchant capital for sale on the world market and then taken over by industrial capital was *wattle*. The *Forestal Land and Timber Company* in the 1930s took over the largest wattle-growing areas in Kenya in a drive to consolidate its hold over the conditions of wattle production on a world level. The case study on Baumann will show a prolonged struggle between the firm which was exporting wattle bark and Forestal which was by 1940 to enforce its hegemony over all the stages of wattle production in Kenya.[14]

In the estates sector there were also several sisal plantations which exported raw sisal to European manufacturers of sisal twine, such as the Anglo–French Sisal Company and the East African Sisal Estates. The latter firm was taken over by Mitchell Cotts in 1936.

The above examples of primary processing firms illustrate a general trend: that the direct investment in production stemmed from the competitive conditions existing in the global production of those commodities.

14 For a fuller exposition, see M. P. Cowen, 'Wattle production in the Central Province', mimeo., Nairobi, 1975, later a PhD thesis for Cambridge University.

MANUFACTURING AND MINERALS[15]

It is clear that manufacturing in East Africa before 1945 was limited to the processing of raw materials and agricultural products. However, the only significant mineral to be exploited in Kenya before 1945 was *soda ash*. By the 1920s one of the world's largest deposits of soda ash at Magadi was under the control of a British consortium, the Imperial Chemical Company (ICI). This will be fully discussed in the case study on the Magadi Soda Company.

The generation of *power* was the only capital-intensive activity outside the agricultural sector. Power was an essential service for the expansion of production in the colonial territories. As early as 1906, the Mombasa Electric Light & Power Company was formed by Esmailjee Jivanjee of Mombasa in partnership with some European engineers. Power facilities were first installed in Nairobi in 1907 with a hydroelectric station at Ruiru.

Nairobi grew so fast that soon additional installations (two steam generators) were constructed at Parklands. Lack of capital for further developments prompted the formation of a London board of this company, which was reconstituted as the *East African Power and Lighting Company* in 1922. During 1929, licences were obtained by the EAPL to purchase the Tanganyika Electric Supply Company, which provided power to Dar es Salaam and other areas. The first power installations in Uganda were constructed by the company in 1938.

After 1924 the company became associated with Power Securities Ltd and Balfour Beatty and Company, and these two British companies provided the technical assistance and management services for EAPL in Kenya until 1970 when the firm was nationalized.[16] Balfour Beatty and Power Securities were linked through directorship and shareholding and had been involved in colonial supply undertakings since the beginning of the twentieth century. Due to the specialized nature of power generation, this partnership was able to maintain a monopoly over power supplies in all the East African countries until the 1960s.

An intermediate industrial process in the form of a cement-grinding mill was established by the Tunnel Cement Company of the UK and Associated Portland Cement in 1933.[17] This import-substitution exercise was an attempt to raise the level of profit on the commodity. For the British distributors and suppliers of cement to East Africa found that transport costs for such a bulky commodity were prohibitive.

---

15 Manufacturing and minerals are placed together as both involve large-scale investments *outside* the agricultural sector.

16 See 'East African Power and Lighting Company', *EAS*, 5 May 1965.

17 The main cement distributors, Smith Mackenzie, Baumann and the African Mercantile Company, each took a £20 000 share in the venture. From an interview with Eric Baumann in Nairobi, June 1975.

However, clinker (the raw material for cement-making) could be carried as ballast on ships at a lower rate than fully processed cement. Due to lack of government support and a small market, the partnership did not construct a full cement plant until the 1950s.

From the foregoing discussion it is clear that before the Second World War, foreign investment was mainly located in the spheres of commodity trading and estates. Apart from some primary processing, the extent of interest in manufacturing was limited, as the scale of primitive accumulation restricted the demand for consumer goods until after the Second World War.

Case Studies: Introduction

Three case studies of foreign firms have been selected from each of the three major activity groups.[18] They were chosen as they each illustrate a certain pattern of corporate expansion in different areas of production. One tendency present in all three is the need of capital at a particular stage to control the conditions of production and distribution of certain commodities.

The first case on the trading company of A. Baumann emphasizes the competitive conditions surrounding commodity trade which eventually compelled that firm to invest directly in production. The second study of the Magadi Soda Company identifies the international conditions of production that dictated the move of this conglomerate to control the East African source of supply of soda ash from the 1920s onwards. Soda-ash exploitation is an example of a capital-intensive extractive industry, the products of which are exclusively designed for the export market.

The Brooke Bond study is longer than the other two and examines the evolution of a major export industry which was developed along the plantation form. The focus is on the attempts of Brooke Bond and the other dominant tea firms to control the conditions of tea production in a way that conformed with their global requirements. In this study it is possible to illustrate the clash between local and foreign interests, a theme which is continued in the post-colonial state. During the period under consideration, Brooke Bond was able to effect a monopoly over the internal tea market.

Case Study: A. Baumann & Company, Trading

A. Baumann, originally a small family firm at the turn of the twentieth century, emerged as one of the most important commodity trading

---

18 The actual choice of firms within the three activity groups was dependent on the availability of information.

firms in the East African territories. During the 1930s it dominated the trade in East Africa's most important commodities, for instance, groundnuts in Tanganyika, wattle bark in Kenya, coffee and cotton in Uganda.

This company's development demonstrates the conditions under which merchant capital is compelled to invest in production. In 1899, Alfred Baumann bought an existing hides and skins firm, Schweder & Company. This firm was reconstituted as A. Baumann & Company in London and it continued to deal in hides and skins obtained from India and South Africa.[19]

By 1918, the increasing concentration of capital and formation of cartels in Europe meant that manufacturers were making direct contacts with the suppliers of commodities overseas, and the middleman was being rendered redundant. One solution for the small Baumann firm was for the company to expand into all aspects of the commodity: to become supplier, transporter and also the marketing agent. Baumann, therefore, decided to expand its business in a primary producing area. Accordingly, in 1926, Baumann and a Belgian partner formed a partnership in Kenya and opened a branch in Mombasa. The East African operation prospered and was soon expanded when branch offices were opened in Dar es Salaam (1928) and Kampala (1931).

COMPETITION FOR CONTROL OF COMMODITIES

From the late 1920s, when the company began its operations in East Africa, the Baumann partnership was mainly concerned with importing a range of manufactured goods from Britain such as textiles, cement, building materials and equipment, in return for the export of East African primary products such as oil seeds, coffee, wattle bark, groundnuts, maize, mangrove bark, chillies and beeswax. Most of these primary products were purchased from Asian traders who brought the goods to Mombasa from the up-country markets, but in some commodities there was a necessity for the company to become directly involved in production.

The two largest items of export from Uganda dealt with by the company in the 1930s were coffee and oil seed. This trade was not 'captured' lightly and Baumann's came to control the trade in these commodities after a period of bitter competition with other British-based trading companies.

By the 1930s Uganda was producing considerable quantities of *coffee* grown by African farmers who had been encouraged by the administration since the early 1920s. In 1931, Gibson & Company, another primary exporting firm in East Africa, was urged by the Director of Agriculture to set up a processing plant for the coffee crop.

19 Interview with Eric Baumann, Nairobi, June 1975.

TABLE 15   *Exports of Coffee from Uganda*

Year	Weight (cwt)	Value (£)
1927	43 578	170 568
1932	87 007	223 162
1933	100 444	210 638
1937	257 938	420 483

Source: Colonial trade accounts, 1926–37.

At that time Gibson & Company and Jamal Ramji & Company set up coffee mills independently to handle the crop of approximately 10 000 tons of raw coffee. Coffee production increased rapidly and the Gibson Company required an infusion of capital for the construction of new coffee plants and a general expansion of its operations. It accordingly approached another East African exporting firm, Leslie & Anderson, to provide the loan capital, but after this company had turned down Gibson's request, A. Baumann & Company stepped in and agreed to finance the construction of new coffee mills in Uganda. This act enabled the company to out-manoeuvre one of its main competitors in Uganda, Leslie & Anderson, and to give the company a greater degree of control over the production of this commodity. Baumann, in co-operation with the Gibson Company, thus came to dominate the trade in Uganda for about twenty-five years. Some idea of the quantity involved can be estimated from the Ugandan coffee exports.[20] Table 15 shows a rapid expansion in coffee exports[21] which more than doubled between 1933 and 1937. The table gives some indication of the scale of the trade under Baumann's control.

Coffee was certainly Baumann's most important commodity in the 1930s, but it was not the only one. Next in importance was *cotton seed*, which was sent in raw form to British oil manufacturers. In the 1920s Leslie & Anderson, Baumann's largest competitor in East Africa, was the sole supplier of Uganda cotton seed to J. Bibes of Liverpool, who used the seed to manufacture animal feed. Bibes was not entirely satisfied with the buying arrangement by weight as the oil content of the seed varied. So Baumann's London office seized the opportunity to offer a more favourable purchasing contract based on the oil content of the seed and Bibes accepted the offer. Baumann's then came to an

20 The Baumann Company was one of the three companies which controlled the largest proportion of Uganda's coffee trade in the 1930s. It obtained (along with Jamal Ramji & Company and the Old East Africa Trading Company) exclusive licences under the Native Produce Marketing Ordinance for the purchase and curing of Robusta coffee throughout Buganda. The details are found in M. Mamdani, *Politics and Class Formation in Uganda*, Heinemann, London, 1976, pp. 106–7.

21 Most exports of coffee from Uganda prior to 1930 were in raw form.

agreement with Leslie & Anderson to share the East African cotton seed market and export the seed exclusively to the largest British manufacturers of animal feed: Bibes and Unilever. The trade was considerable and amounted to about 90 000 tons of oil per annum. The slump gave a further boost to Baumann's control over the cotton seed trade, as the price of seed offered to the ginning companies was so low that Baumann's was able to hold large stocks until the prices improved.[22]

In the 1920s, the logical commodity for the Baumann Company to go into was the trade in *wattle bark*, given the company's previous connections with tanneries of hides and skins. Before 1932, Baumann's purchased wattle bark mainly from Asian merchants, exported it to Europe and sold it to European manufacturers of extract. Baumann's, as a source of merchant capital, represented a threat to industrial capital by undermining Forestal's control over supplies of wattle bark. The Forestal Land and Timber Company came to control wattle extract factories in Kenya in the early 1930s as part of a global drive to control the conditions of production in this commodity. Since 1926, Baumann & Company had been diverting supplies of wattle bark to Forestal's European competitors in extract manufacture. When Forestal moved into Kenya in the early 1930s in order to establish extract factories and absorb this wattle bark supply, Baumann's changed its tactics and decided to export extract instead of wattle bark. Forestal's chief competitor in Kenya for the manufacture of wattle bark into extract was the Asian firm Premchand Raichand, and Baumann's was to champion the cause of this local capital in order to perpetuate its own share in the wattle trade.[23]

Forestal hoped to control the commodity in Kenya by forcing Premchand Raichand, the other manufacturer, into some agreement that would establish a joint share of the market to favour the international company. Baumann's was strongly opposed to any kind of agreement between local and international capital which would exclude it. Therefore Baumann's maintained that:

> Forestal's moves to readjust proportions of supplies of wattle bark, to limit the issuing of manufacturing licences, to fix minimum export prices of bark and extract, and maximum purchasing prices, would push Premchand Raichand into a position in which they will have to seek the active help of the Kenya Government to avoid being squeezed out of existence.[24]

---

22 All these details are from the interview with E. Baumann; unfortunately there is little company information before 1945 since the firm operated as a partnership in Kenya before that time.

23 Cowen (1975), op. cit., pp. 38–40.

24 ibid., p. 38.

However, Baumann's vigorous attempts to reorient the terms of the voluntary agreement between Forestal and Premchand Raichand failed due to the political pressure that Forestal was able to exert on the Colonial Office in London. Baumann's strongly objected to the terms reached under which the duopsony would operate, and maintained that only the state could 'wrench the agreement from the clutch of a demon'.[25] But when it came to wielding power at the level of the imperial government, Forestal was in a stronger position than the Baumann Company, and the latter was gradually eliminated from the wattle trade in East Africa. It so happened that the decline in Baumann's interest in wattle after the Second World War coincided with a fall in the price of extract and the advent of synthetic tanning materials. To a trading firm with such a wide range of interests, the loss of one commodity could be compensated for in other areas.

BAUMANN: POSTWAR DIVERSIFICATION

After the war, due to high company taxation in Britain, all of the assets of A. Baumann & Company were transferred to East Africa and the firm was incorporated as a public company on the Nairobi Stock Exchange. Another reason behind the local incorporation was to expand into new areas, away from commodity trading.

In 1948, the company received an infusion of capital from Steel Brothers (UK), who took 25 per cent of Baumann's share capital in East Africa. Steel Brothers was a British-based multinational which had been involved with teak and rice production in Asia. Changing political circumstances on that continent had given rise to the desire of the firm to find an alternative outlet for investment. The company expanded rapidly to become a huge conglomerate by 1975 with a wide range of interests and in 1973 it absorbed Baumann East Africa.

It has been stressed that before the Second World War, Baumann's interests were confined to importing manufactured goods and exporting primary products. The only exception to this had been its investment in the cement grinding mill in 1933, which was intimately linked to its trading interest in the commodity. In the 1930s Baumann's became the sole distributor in Kenya of cement produced by the East African Portland Cement Company.[26]

Another of Baumann's importing agencies was that of Leyland Paints products from Britain. There were problems for distributors of paints in East Africa, as large stocks were needed to cater for consumer demand. Competition was fierce for rather limited prewar markets, so that after 1950 negotiations began between Baumann and Leyland Paints about the possibility of setting up a plant to manufacture paint in

25 ibid.
26 The East African market was divided between the three firms and the other two cement distributors in East Africa supplied Uganda and Tanganyika.

Kenya. The original plan was postponed until 1956 due to the out-break of the Emergency, but in that year a factory was constructed in Nairobi as a fifty/fifty partnership between the Leyland Paint Company (UK) and Baumann's, with the former providing management and technical expertise. This only forestalled the other competitors for a couple of years, and between 1958 and 1960 Sadolins and Robbialac set up other paint-manufacturing plants in Kenya.

Baumann's were also the agents for the products of Hall Thermotank (J. D. Hall) in East Africa, and after 1945 they jointly established an assembly plant and engineering workshop in Kenya. However, Baumann's was to sell its interest in the project in 1968. During the 1950s, Baumann's continued its moves towards *diversification*. By 1954 it had taken over Milmet estates, consisting of 170 acres of coffee and a beef cattle ranch, from some settlers. Also in the 1950s the company took a 50 per cent share in the Kenyan subsidiary of Jardine & Matheson, the tea merchants. This partnership in the 1970s still purchased East African tea for the export market. Baumann's completed its diversification drive in 1965 with the acquisition of ABC Foods, an ailing settler enterprise which manufactured animal feeds.

Baumann's had finally managed to gain access to the shipping and freight business when it acquired its old rival, Leslie & Anderson, and its subsidiary, Wafco Ltd, in 1965. Its interests in East Africa covered food distribution agencies, warehousing and shipping, and Baumann's had been competing with its steamship agencies since the 1930s.

By the 1970s, therefore, Baumann's in East Africa was composed of a whole gamut of different enterprises in both primary and industrial production. With the exception of coffee, its interest in primary commodities had waned by the 1960s. In 1970, Baumann's had the remainder of its share capital purchased by Steel Brothers of the UK. This conglomerate owned subsidiaries in over thirty countries and in a wide variety of concerns ranging from housing construction to commodity trading and insurance.

The Baumann case shows how a merchant firm was pressured by competition into investing directly in production. Finally, the firm was absorbed into a larger industrial combine after 1945 when the concentration of capital was a dominant global tendency.

Case Study: The Magadi Soda Company, Minerals

In this study on soda-ash production in Kenya, the intention is to show how the needs of a British industrial firm were served by expansion into a producing area in order to control the source of that commodity. It is necessary to locate this discussion in the context of the global conditions of production which led to concentration of capital within this branch.

ORIGINS OF MAGADI

Lake Magadi was first surveyed in 1900 by Rhodesian prospectors.[27] In 1902 the concession was sold to a mining engineer, who in turn sold the rights to the East African Syndicate, a London-based operation which had interests in land speculation. A full scientific expedition to the Magadi Soda Lake was not made until 1903, when the surveyors reported: 'reckoning 20 square miles of deposit at a thickness of 4 inches, this represents over four million tons of raw soda'.[28] The soda samples were sent to London for testing and the percentage of soda content was estimated at around 68 per cent, which by international standards was commercially viable.

In 1904, a lease for the Magadi concession was drawn up between the government of the protectorate and the East African Syndicate for a period of twenty years. This covered 89 square miles, which included the lake together with the lands on the shores of the lake. The royalty payment by the lessee to the government was fixed at 5 per cent of the net profits made on the extraction and marketing of soda. The EA Syndicate was reconstituted in 1906 as the 'East Africa Soda and Railway Company'.[29] The draft prospectus proposed a calcinating plant at the junction of the branch line with the Uganda Railway. It was intended that the firm would form a subsidiary in Britain to manufacture soda crystals and caustic soda under the guidance of a British chemical firm, Chance Hunt of the UK. In 1908 the syndicate sought financial assistance from the UK government to develop Magadi, but its efforts were not successful. In 1910, the syndicate was wound up and the deposits remained untapped.

The *Magadi Soda Company* was launched in 1911, underwritten by Marcus Samuel & Company and the Central Mining and Investment Corporation, with a capital of £1 312 000. M. Samuel was the selling agents for soda products worldwide. Clearly the first task of the new company was to establish contact between Magadi and the coast, before any exploitation of soda resources could begin. Plans were drawn up to construct a 91-mile railway to join the Uganda Railway, in addition to a water pipeline from the Ngong Hills to Magadi, which was situated in an arid zone. The branch line was to be constructed and financed by the company and then handed over to the government, and leased from it at a rate of 5s per year. The line would be maintained by the Uganda Railway administration, which undertook to provide rolling stock sufficient to carry 160 000 tons of soda per year. Profits on the branch line would be divided equally between the Uganda Railway administration and the lessees. Royalty payment to the gov-

---

27 There is some evidence of pre-colonial trade in Magadi salt, but this has not been explored here.
28 See 'Magadi sets the pattern for Kenya', *EAS*, 27 January 1961.
29 ibid.

ernment by the company was readjusted to 21s per ton of raw soda sold from Magadi and if used for commercial purposes only 3s per ton of soda or soda products.[30]

The case of Magadi Soda illustrates the relative indifference of government policy when it came to providing infrastructure for industrial projects. The metropolitan government had raised loans for the construction of the Uganda Railway, but that was the extent of its commitment to private enterprise. The Kenyan administration, although it did not assist Magadi in constructing a branch line, did provide the company with generous land grants, to the extent of 2900 acres in a Maasai reserve.[31]

In the initial prospectus, the underwriters of the firm, M. Samuel & Company, guaranteed sales of 'good quality' Magadi soda for the first five years. It was estimated that a profit of at least 20s per ton could be expected. The estimated expenditure on infrastructure for the project amounted to £950 000, which left £300 000 for working capital.[32]

However, the importance of Magadi to the British partnership (consisting of Samuel & Company, The British Aluminium Company and the remnants of the East African Syndicate) was to keep this soda deposit out of the hands of their competitors. Firms involved in soda processing were constantly on the look-out for new sources of raw soda as markets in the Far East and Europe were expanding rapidly. Wartime conditions halted the construction of the firm's soda plants in Britain.

THE INTERWAR YEARS: COMPETITION

Production at Magadi, despite the efforts of the parent company, ground to a halt during the First World War. This was due to technical problems experienced by the new plant and also to the difficulties associated with shipping the commodity to European markets.

In the meantime, a scheme was mounted for the reconstruction of the Magadi company. The firm's chief competitor in the world soda market, Brunner Mond, expressed an interest in taking over the firm. This move was opposed and the Secretary of State for the Colonies, Thomas, prevented Brunner Mond from gaining control of Magadi at this time. The Colonial Office were opposed to the formation of a cartel by Brunner Mond which would secure a virtual monopoly of soda-ash trade in the Far East. They were also concerned that Brunner Mond, if it gained control of the Kenyan soda deposits, might not develop them fully. The CO, acting partly in response to pressure from the Kenyan administration, refused to accept Brunner Mond's plans to meet the Magadi Soda Company's liabilities.

30 M. F. Hill, *The Story of Magadi*, ICI, England, 1960.
31 The colonial state did not protect 'infant industries' until after 1945.
32 Hill, op. cit., p. 20.

By the end of 1918, the existing company was facing financial crisis, railway costs had exceeded the estimates and the company's working capital was exhausted. Thus it was imperative either to raise more capital or to close the plant down. By 1922 the company was finally on the verge of collapse, for currency conversion in East Africa meant that the company's costs were arbitrarily inflated, a blow to a company dependent on exports.[33] During 1920 the output fell to 12 000 tons and further losses seemed inevitable.

From 1920 onwards the export trade in soda ash showed a marked increase due mainly to expanding Japanese sales.[34] Nevertheless, Magadi Soda encountered severe competition from European manufactured alkalis and specifically with the products of Brunner Mond. The chairman of Brunner Mond had rejected several proposals by Magadi for controlling competition in the soda-ash market. Despite its production difficulties, in 1921, the Magadi Soda Company's selling agents in Japan had formed a subsidiary to deal with the increased volume of trade in Kenyan soda ash. Thus Brunner Mond's markets in the Far East were being seriously threatened by Magadi Soda.

However, despite the bright prospects for Magadi Soda production on the world market, the company was unable to raise the capital required to finance expansion and in 1923 the directors gave notice that it was impractical to carry on business. Their initial failure to gain control of the Magadi Soda Company did not deter the Brunner Mond Company. In July 1924 they sent a technical mission to the Magadi site to report on every aspect of production. This group undertook to lobby the Kenyan administration and on their return to England reported that the governor now seemed well disposed towards the company and anxious to help. The Kenyan administration had by this time reached the conclusion that it was better to accept the terms of a monopoly producer than lose revenue through the lack of development of Magadi deposits. Brunner Mond, therefore, was finally given permission to buy out the share capital of the former Magadi Soda Company in 1925 and another company was constituted in London.

MONOPOLY CONDITIONS AND AMALGAMATION OF CHEMICAL FIRMS

From 1925, Brunner Mond was able to reinforce the ailing enterprise at Magadi with its technical and commercial knowledge of the soda business. Brunner Mond had finally achieved its objective of absorbing its chief competitor in the soda trade, and now Magadi Soda was marketed in co-operation with Brunner Mond's own ammonium soda

---

33 For further details of the significance of currency conversion in East Africa, see MacGregor Ross, op. cit., chs 1 and 2.

34 In 1918, Lever Brothers were buying raw soda at £5 per ton at Kilindini and they were linked through shareholding with Brunner Mond.

TABLE 16   *National Shares of Soda Exports from Kenya Colony*

Year	Destination	Quantity (tons)	% of Total	Exports of Soda Ash (tons)
1923	Britain	3 932	12	n.a.
1923	Japan	15 619	49	31 762
1925	Japan	38 126	79	48 306
1927	Japan	44 500	79	56 421
1936	Japan	22 400	48	46 549

Source: Colonial trade accounts, 1923–36.

products. Steps were taken to integrate Magadi's production with its global organization and a programme of capital expenditure was immediately started at the Magadi plant.

Having traced the absorption of Magadi's production into one of the world's largest soda conglomerates, we shall now briefly explore the conditions in the chemical industry which gave rise to further amalgamation of firms and concentration of production.

In 1914, Britain had been dependent on Germany for many fine chemicals, dyes and dyestuffs and wartime conditions encouraged British chemical firms to remedy this imbalance. It was in response to competition from the two great chemical combinations, I. G. Farbenindustrie A. G. in Germany and Allied du Pont in America, that British chemical firms were compelled to unite. In 1926, after six months of negotiation, four great British chemical enterprises, (Brunner Mond & Company,[35] Nobel Industries Ltd, the United Alkali Company and the British Dyestuffs Corporation) amalgamated to form *Imperial Chemical Industries* Ltd (ICI).

In December 1926, therefore, the giant ICI corporation registered with an issued capital of £57 million and Sir Alfred Mond (chairman of Brunner Mond) became the new chairman. Thus the Magadi Soda Company became an offshoot of one of Britain's largest industrial combines.[36]

MAGADI UNDER ICI

From 1925 the Magadi Soda Company was under the control of a highly sophisticated chemical firm, which proceeded to reorganize Kenyan production in accordance with its global standards of production. ICI started a sales promotion scheme for Magadi soda ash, for its

---

35 Brunner Mond had begun to manufacture nitrates in 1914.
36 Hill, op. cit., pp. 80–90.

high quality had meant that outlets were limited to specialized markets.[37]

Despite the infusion of capital from the ICI parent company, the project did not fare well. The company secretary of ICI in 1929 came to a depressing conclusion: 'an indefinite prolongation of present methods of soda ash production would yield little, if any, regular profit . . . Magadi is approaching a serious turning point'.[38] By 1930 output had fallen to 44 479 tons, which was less than the figure for 1927. The years of depression had hit the company hard; in 1930 Kenya's domestic exports were valued at £3 422 571 and by 1934 they had fallen to £1 909 876. ICI had considered that the methods of production at Magadi were unsatisfactory and since 1925 they had been experimenting with a new bicarbonation process for purifying soda ash.

Thus ICI, in the face of competition on the world market, was faced with three alternatives: it could install a purification process at Magadi which would be initially expensive, it could manufacture caustic soda in Japan or it could simply close the Magadi plant. The parent company decided that the company should carry on, as competitors might take over the Magadi plant if it were abandoned. The first option was decided on and the company embarked on a campaign to cut costs of production at the same time as introducing a new process. In 1933, a gas plant was installed instead of oil fuel, and a new calcination plant built.[39] This saved on costs although it involved the use of more labour. In 1933, £5000 was also allocated for the production of rough salt for the local market.[40] Despite these improvements in production techniques, the parent company in 1939 announced grim prospects for the Magadi plant; 'we have reached the conclusion that the Magadi enterprise, while still possessing a restricted value, can no longer be regarded as capable of providing an adequate reward for the capital which has proved necessary for its development'.[41]

However, world market forces were to boost the fortunes of the Magadi soda plant during the Second World War. With supplies from Europe cut off, the Magadi company was able to expand its exports to India, South Africa, Australia and South America. The patterns of trade developed during the war years have continued into the 1960s and 1970s.[42] From 1941 onwards, production at Magadi increased

37 During the 1920s Japan took the largest proportion of Magadi soda.

38 AGM report, 1929, ICI.

39 The new process increased the output at Magadi, as it reduced the calcination time and costs of raw soda. The cost of making soda fell from 41s per ton in 1930 to 24s per ton in 1936.

40 In the 1970s Magadi still supplies most of Kenya's domestic demand for rough grades of salt, although a small amount is exported.

41 Magadi Soda Company, AGM, 1939.

42 Exports to South Africa were terminated by the Kenya government after independence in 1963.

TABLE 17 *Annual Returns for the Magadi Soda Company 1926–70*

Year	Issued Capital	Net Assets	Net Profit (post tax)
1926	597 141	1 108 102	(35 497) loss
1930	597 141	1 131 701	(17 249) loss
1940	737 095	1 084 728	17 203
1950	796 260	1 379 459	186 540
1960	977 754	1 514 028	366 558
1970	2 727 933	3 289 341	410 957

Source: Annual company returns, Registrar General's Dept. ;

rapidly to meet expanding demand, and by 1945, over 6000 tons of soda ash and 15 000 tons of salt were produced. From this point onwards the demand for high-quality soda for industrial uses has not faltered. During the 1970s sales from Magadi were restricted, not by the plant's capacity, but rather by the inability of the railway to cope with the volume of traffic to the port at Mombasa. Between 1939 and 1961, shipments from Magadi totalled more than 2 million tons and the exports by 1961 exceeded 150 000 tons per annum, representing approximately 5 per cent of Kenyan domestic exports.

Between 1929 and 1960, capital expenditure at Magadi amounted to £2 116 601, and of this 94 per cent was spent between 1945 and 1960.[43] These years witness a marked improvement in processing techniques and by the 1960s the plant had specialized in the production of one single grade of soda (90 per cent Na_2Co_3). A summary of the company's balance sheets since 1926 (Table 17) illustrates the rapid growth of the company after the Second World War.

Only a corporation with centralized structure and large resources was able to take advantage of the Magadi soda plant after such a long period of market instability. This analysis has shown how one international firm found it advantageous to keep a source of raw material under its control even when the project was not immediately profitable.

Case Study: Brooke Bond in Kenya, Estates and Primary Processing

In the final case study, the concern is to show the way in which one particular firm, Brooke Bond, was able to assert its predominance over the conditions of production and distribution of tea in Kenya.

43 Annual reports of the Magadi Soda Company.

THE ENTRY OF INTERNATIONAL FIRMS

In the 1920s tea-drinking was a luxury confined to a small European and Asian minority in East Africa. The tea trade in East Africa was likely to remain small unless the African population was initiated into the habit of tea-drinking. This was equally unlikely so long as the product remained relatively expensive; by the 1920s an import duty of 45 cents per lb was being levied on tea.

During this time there were several British tea merchants competing with each other in the East African markets. The largest of these were Brooke Bond and Liptons; among the less important ones was the Twinings Tea Company. In 1916 Brooke Bond had appointed a selling agent in Nairobi to market its teas in East Africa. By 1922 a formal branch of Brooke Bond was set up in order to challenge Lipton's virtual monopoly over tea imports into the region.[44]

Tea at this time was marketed in two different forms, one in bulk via Asian wholesalers and the other in packets. The former was aimed chiefly at the African market, which existed mainly in Zanzibar and the coastal regions of East Africa. However, the two largest importing firms, Brooke Bond and Liptons, dealt mainly in packeted teas which came directly from Ceylon and India. Indeed by the mid-1920s around 99 per cent of East African tea imports were derived from India and Ceylon.

The trade in bulk teas was largely in the hands of Indian wholesalers, who imported directly from the country of origin. Twinings had also entered the market, and in 1922 made a short-lived attempt to challenge Brooke Bond and Lipton's hold over the tea-import trade. Despite the relatively small market, there was strong competition for a share in the potentially larger cake. For instance in 1924, Brooke Bond sales in East Africa constituted approximately 50 per cent of the total amount of tea imported into the East African territories and Zanzibar (around 1 million lb). For instance, the closing sales of Brooke Bond in 1925 were 650 000 lb, or 60 per cent of total tea imports, with a ratio of 70 per cent in packets and 30 per cent in bulk.[45]

TEA PRODUCTION IN EAST AFRICA

By 1920 Brooke Bond had only recently invested in tea estates in addition to its traditional tea-marketing concerns. Between 1900 and 1914, Brooke Bond had even set up tea-blending centres in India and Ceylon in order to be freed from the caprice of London markets. Brooke Bond invested directly in tea production in 1919, when the

---

44 See G. Pollard (an employee of Brooke Bond in the 1930s), 'A brief history of the East African branch of Brooke Bond & Co (India) Ltd', from the Brook Bond Company files at Kericho.
45 ibid.

first estate was purchased in Assam. After that time a number of existing tea estates were absorbed by the company, which had also established a large tea distribution network in India after the First World War.[46]

As the market for tea in East Africa was small, those engaged in the trade experienced strong competition. From Brooke Bond's point of view, this state of affairs coincided with a desire to diversify sources of production from India, where the political climate in the early 1920s was perceived as unstable. The most significant motive behind the decision to invest in tea estates in East Africa was, of course, the *export market*, and by producing tea in East Africa, it would also be possible to compete more effectively with the other British tea-trading firms.

Tea is primarily an export crop and the planting programmes of all the main producers were based on the assumption of finding a profitable market on the London auctions. These were the two main motives for the move of the two largest producing companies, James Finlay and Brooke Bond, into Kenya: *to capture the local market and develop alternative producing areas*. Both of these objectives were to be realized by Brooke Bond by 1938.

This was the background to the acquisition of 1000 acres at Limuru in 1924 by the Brooke Bond Company.[47] At the same time the company made an arrangement with a number of local tea farmers, to buy their tea and process it in a central Brooke Bond factory at Mabroukie. Farmers in Kericho had also been experimenting with tea-growing since 1910. An agent of one of the James Finlay companies arrived in Kenya in 1925 at the same time as the Brooke Bond representative, to discover that 25 000 acres of BEADOC (British East Africa Disabled Officers Corporation) land in Kericho was for sale, as the scheme had failed.[48] Despite the risk involved, 20 000 acres was purchased by the James Finlay group (the largest tea-growers in the world both in 1924 and at the present). The land was purchased from the government for a paltry £60 and a yearly rental on a 999-year lease of £200, and the James Finlay Company formed a private firm registered in the United Kingdom, known as *African Highlands Produce Company Ltd*. Brooke Bond purchased the remaining portion (5000 acres), and formed a private company known as the *Kenya Tea Company Ltd*.

Brooke Bond gradually advanced its acreage by absorbing small

---

46 D. Wainwright, *Brooke Bond, a Hundred Years*, Brooke Bond Ltd, London, 1969, pp. 29–31.

47 The information on land acquisition by Brooke Bond and African Highlands was obtained from the Land Registry in Nairobi.

48 The BEADOC organization was formed after the First World War in order to assist the settlement of ex-army officers. The scheme was a total failure largely due to undercapitalization and inexperience of the settlers. Having unsuccessfully attempted to cultivate both flax and coffee in the Kericho district, the corporation was forced to sell its land in order to pay off debts.

planters' plots. Thus by 1926, tea development in Kenya was effected by two large foreign companies, two locally owned public companies (Buret and Jamji) and ten small private planters. By the outbreak of the war, the last had been reduced to five from ten, and the total acreage under tea cultivation in Kenya had risen from 382 in 1924 to 12 662 in 1934. Between the same years, tea production in Kenya rose from 1341 lb to 4 024 722 lb and exports from nil to 2 476 900 lb in 1934. Brooke Bond and African Highlands Produce Company, therefore, held the largest proportion of mature tea acreage before and after the Second World War. Unfortunately I do not have the precise acreage for Brooke Bond in the 1930s, although in 1934 African Highlands held 5032 acres of tea in Kenya and the total area under tea for that year was 12 662.[49] From the Land Registry's accounts it seems likely that Brooke Bond at this time had approximately the same acreage as African Highlands at around 5000; the balance of 2662 acres or so being held by another foreign company, the Nandi Tea estates, and the two local firms, Buret and Jamji. By 1943, the local firms had slightly increased their share of Kenyan tea acreage and a memo from the Department of Agriculture to the International Tea Committee in November 1943 stated that the proportion of tea acreage held by non-residents and residents in the colony was 70 per cent and 30 per cent respectively.[50] As Brooke Bond and African Highlands dominated the non-resident group, it is reasonable to estimate that their percentage of total tea acreage in Kenya (which was 15 656 acres just before the end of the Second World War) was somewhere between 65 and 70 per cent; which would leave these two foreign companies with approximately 11 000 acres between them in that year.

By 1955 there were seventy-five licensed tea-holders in Kenya, fifty-four in Uganda and twenty-five estates in Tanganyika. The size of holdings ranged from 10 000 acres to less than 500 acres. By 1958, Brooke Bond had 3000 hectares of mature tea at Kericho, having absorbed the Jamji estate after the Second World War, in 1946. Brooke Bond's consolidation of tea lands in the Kericho district was completed in 1971, with the acquisition of the only remaining large, local tea estate, the Buret Tea Company.[51]

Of all the tea companies in East Africa after 1924, Brooke Bond was the only one with an established distribution network in Kenya. Brooke Bond's policy in the years after 1924 was to make the local

---

49 Information on acreage and production for the African Highlands Company was obtained from its headquarters at Kericho. The Brooke Bond Company did not, unfortunately, have figures before the Second World War.

50 *KNA*, Tea file, November 1943.

51 By 1955, Brooke Bond had invested a total of £6 million in the tea industry in East Africa. The information in this paragraph came from interviews held with Brooke Bond in February 1974 at Kericho headquarters.

market its primary concern. Unfortunately for all the tea-growers in East Africa, their production came on to the market just at the onset of the depression, when the London prices fell below those obtained on the local market. Therefore the larger estates, such as African Highlands and Brooke Bond, who would normally have exported their tea, turned to the local market as the most profitable outlet and in 1928 a period of intense competition began in response to these conditions. This cut-throat competition was having the effect of cutting the East African price level down to the London auction equivalent, which caused concern among the directors of the parent companies in Britain. In 1931, the government unexpectedly imposed a tea excise duty of 10 cents per lb, but competition was so hot that none dared to pass on the increase to the consumer in East Africa. Therefore, the thoughts of the large companies turned to devising a more durable form of *sales co-operation* on the local market.

In 1933, with the onset of the International Tea Restriction Scheme, Brooke Bond took the opportunity to exercise a determined bid for oligopolistic price leadership and gradually raised its prices. The other producers followed suit, although Brooke Bond's share of the market never fell below 50 per cent. However, by 1935, the prices on the world tea market had improved, as London auction prices rose, thus relieving the pressure on the large tea companies to unload on the local market.[52]

Kenya had not been included in the International Tea Agreement of 1933, but when the scheme came up for renewal, it was expected that East Africa would be included as it was anticipated that production would have increased faster than local consumption and producers would be increasingly forced to export. It became imperative to work out a sales agreement before that time. The general form that such a scheme would take was clear: a quota share of the local market for each company, based on production and acreage, with an administrative body to run the scheme. However, the conflict of interests between the producers was to delay the conclusion of the agreement for three years.

The negotiations during the years were exclusively between the two largest tea-growers, both subsidiaries of British-based firms. Brooke Bond wanted to become agents for the co-operative marketing organization, thereby retaining control over detailed sales policy; for any proportionate share-out of the internal market on the basis of production would mean this firm sacrificing about 40 per cent of its marketing share. Brooke Bond might have defended its hold on the internal market by pushing out the smaller producers, due to its superior sales organization, but it would not be so easy to dislodge the African

---

52 These details are from M. D. MacWilliam, 'The East African tea industry 1920–1956'. M.Phil. thesis, Nuffield College, Oxford, 1958, pp. 84–8.

Highlands Produce Company, with its strong overseas backing. There were, therefore, compelling reasons for Brooke Bond either to enter into a joint selling agreement or to forsake restrictions on exports. The pressures for a local agreement were overwhelming, as Brooke Bond's global organization favoured international sales restrictions.

However, the James Finlay subsidiary wanted a fully owned producer's organization and a neutral trademark. These provisions meant that Brooke Bond would have to relinquish its dominant hold over tea distribution in East Africa.

Finally, after discussions in London during 1937, James Finlay prepared a memo outlining the scheme for co-operative selling of tea, which accepted all the points which Brooke Bond had originally pressed for. This change of heart had been instigated by altered world conditions of tea production. Previously, the main incentive for a joint selling scheme was the international export restrictions to be imposed on the firms operating in Kenya, which would make the local market an important sales priority. When East Africa was accorded favourable terms for export restriction, the situation changed to such an extent that if the full export quota were taken up, there might even be a shortage on the local market. In other words, the producers might be interested in minimum rather than maximum quotas for the local market. From the point of view of James Finlay, the question of who administered the local market sales was no longer of significance.

Finally, in June 1938, approval was given to a tea-marketing scheme for East Africa, which came into operation in September. In effect, Brooke Bond became the East African Tea Growers' (EATGA) representatives and the main features of this controversial scheme were as follows.[53]

1 Producers were to pay transport costs of their tea from their factory to the distributor's packing factory.
2 The distributors (Brooke Bond) for its part undertook to supply all the necessary financial and sales organization and use their goodwill, trademarks and trade patents, although the packets would indicate that the tea was from the EATGA. In return for these services, the distributors were to receive a commission of 7½ per cent from the gross selling proceeds of the tea they handled.

At the beginning of 1938, there were eight producers within the East African Customs Union marketing branded tea. In addition, there were several brands in existence for very localized distribution, packed either by small growers or by bazaar firms that bought teas. These were all to be absorbed under the pool agreement in Kenya.[54] Ambangulu

---

53 MacWilliam, ibid., p. 89.
54 This arrangement meant that Brooke Bond controlled the marketing of all East African tea. Its monopoly over tea-marketing in Kenya lasted until 1977 when the KTDA took over its functions.

TABLE 18   *Total Tea Sales in 1937 in East Africa*

Divided between		Weight (lb)	%
Kenya Teas	Brooke Bond	1 250 000	56
	Buret	300 000	13
	African Highlands	250 000	11
	Jamji ⎱		
	Kapkorech ⎰	50 000	2
	SUBTOTAL	1 850 000	82
Uganda Teas	Buchanans	150 000	7
	Uganda Co.	75 000	3
	Miscellaneous	25 000	1
	SUBTOTAL	250 000	11
Tang. Teas	Ambangulu	125 000	5
	Miscellaneous	25 000	2
	SUBTOTAL	150 000	7
	TOTAL	2 250 000	100

Source: Brooke Bond memo, 1937.

Estate in Tanganyika joined the pool from the start and the Ugandan estates were to join later. The proportionate share in this tea trade is shown in Table 18.

The advent of the pool reduced the main brands to four, which covered 80 per cent of the tea trade in East Africa. This meant that

TABLE 19   *Kenya Tea Imports and Exports 1926–46 (alternate years)*

Year	Exports (£)	Exports (cwt)	Imports (£)	Imports (cwt)	Tea Duty (cents)
1926			61 127	6901	
1928	736	91	91 087	9969	45
1930	8 277	1 433	34 798	3788	40
1932	29 829	6 369	1 832	204	50
1934	113 489	22 362	1 639	170	50
1936	339 777	67 835	2 382	243	50
1938	508 050	85 440	3 186	338	50
1944	512 628	82 480	2 177	289	50
1946	534 240	79 920	37	1	100

Source: Colonial trade accounts.

TABLE 20   *Tea Acreage (East Africa) 1924–46 (alternate years)*

Year	Kenya	Uganda	Tanganyika
1924	382	118	
1926	3 156	188	
1928	5 593	297	
1930	10 052	360	
1932	12 034	721	
1934	12 662	1691	2739
1936	13 176	2629	4402
1938	13 681	2966	5265
1940	14 413	3524	5681
1942	15 313	4423	6302
1944	15 712	4528	6819
1946	16 239	4525	6808

Source: From 1928 these figures are from the Agriculture Dept, found in the Tea Controller's reports.

within sixteen years of establishing its trading organization in East Africa, Brooke Bond had managed to manoeuvre itself into a *dominant position, as far as both the growing and the marketing of tea were concerned*. Most of the profit that Brooke Bond was to make in subsequent years was derived from its position of control over the internal marketing of tea in Kenya.

TABLE 21   *Tea Production (in lb) in East Africa 1924–46 (alternate years)*

Year	Kenya	Uganda	Tanganyika	Total
1924	1 300			
1926	8 700			
1928	152 800			
1930	930 200			
1932	2 421 100	73 000	45 000	2 539 100
1934	4 024 700	123 700	45 000	4 193 400
1936	8 611 100	262 100	155 500	9 028 700
1938	10 840 500	490 400	522 000	11 852 900
1940	11 912 000	1 020 000	835 100	13 767 100
1942	16 250 000	1 928 600	1 416 900	19 595 500
1944	13 789 000	2 400 300	1 149 000	17 338 300
1946	12 277 000	2 648 800	1 480 900	16 406 700

Source: 1924–32 from the Agricultural Census 1933–46 from the records of the Tea Controller.

THE INTERNATIONAL TEA COMMITTEE AND THE INTERNATIONAL CORPORATION

It is now necessary to show how the *international* conditions of tea production determined the policy of the big tea companies such as James Finlay and Brooke Bond towards the tea industry in East Africa. We will concentrate on the methods used by local and foreign capital to pursue their respective goals.

Large companies are not merely concerned to 'carve an enclave' out of a particular production area, but are rather concerned to regulate and control conditions of production and marketing of that commodity worldwide. The James Finlay group, based in Scotland since the 1760s, built its empire on textile manufacture and trading and in the nineteenth century acquired large tea estates in India, Ceylon and Java.[55] By the 1920s this group was the largest single grower of tea in the world. Brooke Bond, on the other hand, was largely concerned with tea trading from the nineteenth century, which involved buying up tea in India and Ceylon and selling it at the London auction, as well as distributing bought teas under its famous brand name. Even after the company had invested in estates in India in the early 1900s, its main interest remained in the sphere of tea *marketing and distribution*.

The idea of restricting tea production and acreage was first mooted in 1920, as it was felt by the world's largest tea producers that if tea production was not regulated, the industry would face serious over-production in the years to come. It was after two abortive attempts at tea restriction in 1920 and 1930 that the first International Tea Agreement came into force in February 1933, when it was signed by the main growers in India, Ceylon and Indonesia. Unlike the earlier attempts at restriction, the International Tea Agreement (ITA) was binding on all tea-producers and backed by legislation of the respective governments. The combination of oversupply of tea worldwide and the depression had reduced prices well below the previous averages for producers in these countries. This gave cause for concern to the largest producers of tea who laid out the conditions of the Tea Restriction Scheme as follows:

1 tea exports should be regulated in order to restore the equilibrium between supply and demand;
2 governments of the producing areas should undertake to prohibit exports in excess of the agreed quotas;
3 the basis for regulation should be maximum exports reached by each country between the years 1929 and 1931;
4 no new planting should take place and seed exports to non-participating countries should be prohibited.[56]

---

55 *James Finlay & Company*, James Finlay & Co., Glasgow, 1963.
56 International Tea Committee reports, 1945, *KNA* 12/MAWR.

New entrants were to be prevented, for the restriction scheme was designed to *rescue the existing plantations in the old established tea-producing areas*. The purpose of the ITC's policy towards East Africa was to keep the industry as insignificant as possible. It was thought particularly important that the new tea-growing areas of the British Empire should join since the 'well-being of the whole industry' was at stake.

Initially, the Kenya government meekly referred the ITC scheme to the Kenya Tea Growers' Association (KTGA) for its opinion and since this body was dominated by the two companies with large interests in Ceylon and India, it would be expected to take a favourable attitude towards restriction. The dominance of large producers in the ITC was epitomized by the top personnel in the organization: the chairman of the ITC, which was set up to administer the scheme, was also the chairman of James Finlay, the holding company of African Highlands Produce in Kericho. It was hardly surprising that the two large companies which dominated the KTGA were to accept the terms of the scheme on behalf of the other growers, although some important modifications were suggested for its application to East Africa. There was to be no restriction on *exports* from East Africa, but Kenya growers would *cease all development*, providing that those growers who had just started development were allowed to complete economic units. The following formula was suggested: that planters who had 100 acres or more of tea and who had the means of disposing of their leaf to larger factories should be allowed to extend to a minimum economic area of 500 acres. Also that small estates and individual growers who sent their leaf to a central factory would be able to enlarge their areas to a maximum of 100 acres each. This would ensure that many small growers would not go out of business; but more important it was because the large companies at this stage were quite dependent on European growers' tea for throughput for their factories. Regulation based on standard exports was clearly impractical for East Africa for the immaturity of the tea left no proper basis for calculation.

The governors of Tanganyika and Uganda held different views to those of the KTGA. Indeed the administrations of all three territories faced a dilemma: acceptance of ITC regulations meant sacrificing the 'economic development' of the colony.

As has been pointed out, the local administration in Kenya usually took the side of the settlers in that they wished to develop industries in the country, thus taking an 'economic nationalist' position. Indeed, this position dominated the governors' conference held in October 1933 where it was resolved:

that the East African Governments feel bound to develop such East African industries as are possible within their territories but recognise that it is undesirable for increased production in East Africa to militate against the policy of tea export regulations adopted by Ceylon, India and the Dutch East Indies.[57]

The conditions of this first ITC agreement were finally accepted and the governments' attitude here can be seen as that of resignation. However, their opposition to the ITC regulations was to harden considerably, in direct response to political pressure from the settlers who represented the 'small' local tea-growers.

Whereas the Kenya government, taking its cue from the KTGA at this point, was prepared to limit its expansion between 1933 and 1939 to 1000 acres, the other two governments were not prepared to accept such a severe limitation. Meanwhile, in London, the ITC and large tea-producing interests were lobbying the secretary of state and in a memorandum urged speedy accession of East Africa:

> We are already seeing increasing quantities of tea coming into world markets from these dependencies, and do not see why the producers of East Africa should ride on our backs to take advantage of a situation which is created by a scheme such as this; in fact we are definitely of the opinion that only controlled production can save us from falling into a worse position than we have already been in, and we consider that we have a claim on British connections to assist us in this matter.[58]

After three weeks, the ITC accepted the KTGA amendment of freedom from export controls, but at the same time took the view that the actual expansion of planting desired by the East African growers was 'extravagant'. However, the acreage involved for East Africa was small and the area was merely fighting for the right to establish economic tea areas. The Kenya government, at this time responding to pressure from the large tea companies, managed to persuade Uganda and Tanganyika to accept the 'economic acreage' formula, thereby reducing their planned acreage.[59]

THE SECOND AGREEMENT 1938–43

It was decided in 1938 that the restriction scheme should be renewed for a further five years between 1938 and 1943. The agreement of the main participants was secured and the attention of the large producers then turned to East Africa, the formal approach being made through the African Tea Association in 1936. When the question of renewal was raised by the KTGA, the chairman of the African Highlands Produce Company (the James Finlay subsidiary) predictably took the

---

57 East African Governors' Conference (cable to Colonial Office, *KNA*, 10 October 1933); the settlers were a particularly powerful force in Kenya.

58 MacWilliam, op. cit., p. 90.

59 ITC report, op. cit.

line of the parent company and proposed unqualified acceptance of the scheme, the argument being that African tea-growers had benefited considerably from the higher tea prices realized as a direct result of the ITA scheme under which the regulating companies supposedly bore a 'heavy burden'. In other words, the large producers who dominated the ITC wanted to restrict exports from the new tea areas such as East Africa while encouraging the growers to sell a larger proportion of their tea on the *local* market. This was aimed at maintaining high prices on the international markets, a strategy which would serve their long-term global interests.

This ploy on the part of the dominant world tea-producers led to a revolt among the smaller tea-growers in Kenya, who had no interests outside East Africa, and who were therefore dependent on expanding their acreages and production. This group was tired of being coerced into accepting measures engineered by the large tea firms and they accordingly passed a resolution on the Second Tea Agreement at a KTGA meeting:

> this Association, having already agreed voluntarily to complete restriction as regards the opening up of new areas, conditionally on a like cessation of planting being observed throughout the African territories, is *not* prepared to undertake further participation in the new scheme in respect of import regulation.[60]

The smaller producers maintained that the young industry in East Africa had already made considerable sacrifices with regard to their own interests and 'those of the colony'. The Kenyan industry, they claimed, was only just beginning to pay its way and had borne considerable costs while developing the internal market. The resolution was passed overwhelmingly by KTGA members (who voted individually and not according to size). Despite such pressure, the ITC 'cartel' of large producers forced the KTGA to accept a further restriction of tea exports. The Ugandan and Tanganyikan administrations (representing producers outside the cartel) refused point-blank to accept the kind of export regulation imposed by the ITC on the KTGA.

The Kenyan administration began to heed to complaints of the small tea-growers, and in November 1937, the Acting Colonial Secretary (Kenya) sent the following memo to the governors' conference:

> There is the separate question of the development of the colony as a whole in the interests of its inhabitants, as distinct from the development of an industry by companies whose major activities lie *outside* the colony, and on whose interests a small extension of areas of planting in Kenya will have little or no effect . . . Several applications have been made recently by persons who desire to plant tea in

---

60 KTGA annual report, Kericho, November 1936.

suitable areas which have failed to respond to development under other crops (e.g. Nandi and Kaimosi districts) and the government desires in the interests of the colony to support these applications.[61]

Indeed, many small farmers during the 1930s had experienced a series of crop failures which left them with tea as the only alternative crop. After examining the claim from small European farmers, the Kenya government resolved to apply for 2220 acres for new entrants. It had no hope of support from the KTGA, where the interests of the large companies were paramount.

Kenya, along with Tanganyika and Uganda, now refused to sign the agreement for East Africa and the ITC had to consider granting some minor concessions by allowing the extension of *existing* tea areas to a total of 3000 acres for Uganda, Tanganyika, Kenya and Nyasaland. In a LEGCO debate in December 1937, the European tea farmers made their position clear: they would strongly oppose the renewal of the Tea Ordinance unless farmers in unsuccessful coffee areas were allowed to turn to tea-growing.[62]

The ITC, who were irritated by the delaying tactics of the East African governments and their constituents, finally agreed to grant an additional increment of 1300 acres for *new* planting in East Africa as a whole. The ITC also imposed a new advertising levy on East African tea in order to encourage local consumption, with a view to keeping tea away from international markets while prices remained low.

WARTIME CONDITIONS AND RENEWAL OF ITA

One might have assumed that the wartime situation, with the loss of several Far Eastern tea-producers, such as Indonesia, Burma and Japan, would have automatically led to the abandonment of tea restriction. On the contrary, the ITC resolved to recommend 'to the governments and producers concerned, that the existing agreement should be continued as it stands for the duration of hostilities'.[63] The ITC's concern over the loss of continental markets led them to only lower the export quota by 5 per cent.

The last ITC agreement had provoked considerable opposition from the smaller tea farmers within the KTGA and a resolution was passed rejecting participation in further restriction schemes.[64] The Director of Agriculture in Kenya sent a memo to the chief secretary asserting a defence of the East African tea industry:

61 Dept of Agriculture to the Hon. Chief Secretary, Nairobi, *KNA*, AGR, October 1939.

62 These details from: Memo from Dept of Agriculture to ITC, *KNA*, November 1943. Among the settlers of the tea-growers' lobby was Lord Francis Scott who had extensive interests in Kenya and Tanganyika.

63 Letter from ITC to Secretary of State for the Colonies 1 January 1942, *KNA*, AGR, 4/12.

64 Minutes of the KTGA, 13 July 1943.

the restriction scheme involves a disproportionate sacrifice on the part of the new and more productive areas such as East Africa, which would otherwise be in a position to exploit their comparative advantage . . . it would be a fallacy to ascribe the improvements in the tea market solely to restriction. The powers of the East African votes on the ITC appear to be limited.[65]

The position held by the local administration in Kenya was that the interests of Ceylon and India had fostered the tea agreements and renewals had been simply to maintain uneconomic estates at the expense of East African growers, whose yields by 1940 were two or three times higher than those on Indian estates. After considerable negotiation between the Kenyan administration, the Colonial Office and the ITC, the ITC consented that the tea agreement in Kenya should be extended for the duration of, and for six months after, the war, providing an allowance of 1000 acres per year was granted for new planting. The new acreage could be allocated to either new or existing planters, a provision which was a victory for the Kenyan administration.

The Kenya government further intervened to interpret the ITC regulations and set up a committee to decide on the distribution of the 3242 allotted acres. Out of this total they ruled that 39 per cent would go to new growers, 30 per cent to small growers and 31 per cent to large tea estates.[66] In January 1947, at a meeting of the territorial governments it was recommended that 'all acreage restrictions should be removed forthwith'.[67] In retaliation, the ITC banned all tea seed exports to East Africa, which did not concern tea-growers in Kenya unduly.

After the war, however, the ITC found itself under pressure on both metropolitan and local fronts. The ITC by 1947 had ceased to have the support of the Colonial Office, which was concerned that the ITA was contrary to the UN charter on commodities. The Committee therefore decided to retain some regulation of tea exports while removing restrictions on new planting.

THE EFFECTS OF THE INTERNATIONAL TEA AGREEMENTS ON KENYA

In 1947, questions were asked in the House of Commons about how the international regulation of the tea industry had affected Kenyan development. The Colonial Secretary replied that the tea industry in Kenya had not been adversely affected by the ITA since that area did

65 Memo from Director of Agriculture to Member for Agriculture, 18 October 1946, *KNA*, AGR, 4/12.

66 Memo to ITC from Dept of Agriculture, *KNA*, November 1943.

67 Conference of East African Governors, *KNA*, January 1947.

not meet either the export quotas or new acreage allowances.[68] It was indeed the case that under wartime conditions, although official policy had been to maximize production and quota figures, the Kenyan tea-growers had never fulfilled these quotas.[69] Nevertheless, from the time of the first agreement, the two large firms that dominated the KTGA deliberately failed to apply for the planting acreage to which Kenya was entitled. In the second restriction scheme, the first two seasons were lost to growers because of seed restrictions and wartime conditions had prevented many allotments from being effectively developed. Therefore, during the restriction years, only a limited form of development had taken place on Kenya's tea estates.

Even the large companies in Kenya had been prevented altogether from expanding their properties beyond the level of 1933. African Highlands Produce Company, for example, had 5032 acres of tea in 1934 and only 5492 acres by 1950.[70] From the point of view of the East African tea industry, therefore, the ITA experience had not been favourable. The ITC, for its part, constantly accused the East African territories of trying to 'exploit' the advantages of the scheme, without contributing to it or co-operating with the major producers.[71]

The foregoing discussion has shown the way in which a dominant world tea-producer (Brooke Bond) was able to establish its control over the conditions of tea production and distribution in Kenya before 1939. The International Tea Agreements (ITA) reflected the global dominance of the large tea-producers, notably James Finlay and Brooke Bond. Kenya's tea industry developed out of an interplay between domestic and foreign interests before 1950.

---

68 *Hansard*, vol. 393, 1947, in MacWilliam, op. cit., p. 26.

69 Wartime conditions rendered both finance and labour supplies a serious problem. Conscription of adult males in East Africa caused a labour shortage on the estates during the war.

70 Information from interview with the African Highlands Produce Company, Kericho, 1975.

71 MacWilliam, op. cit., p. 26.

CONCLUSION TO PART I

The preceding discussion has examined aspects of capitalist development in Kenya Colony before the Second World War. The establishment of colonial rule at the end of the nineteenth century required the military subjection of indigenous peoples and construction of basic infrastructure. After the funding of the Uganda Railway, the *metropolitan state* provided *minimal* financial support and expected that the colony itself would raise revenue by means of taxation and the export of crops. Due to the policy of self-sufficiency imposed by the metropolitan government and the conditions of economic depression in the late 1920s, the level of aid from Britain to Kenya was low.

The Kenyan administration during the interwar years was strongly influenced by the large estate farmers, who exercised a political monopoly over the means of representation and the producer boards. The settler class as a whole pushed for the extensive development of infrastructure and a high level of state subsidy for their farming enterprises. The *revenue* raised in the colony before 1939 was largely derived from taxes raised from the non-European groups. In the first decades of the twentieth century, settler agriculture was in a precarious position in terms of experiments with crops and shortages of labour. Once again the shortfalls in export revenue were made up by produce from African areas. The African population was gradually drawn into the monetary economy, although subsistence agriculture existed alongside the estate sector. The export of agricultural commodities from the colony up to the 1920s consistently increased in volume, although this was still less in value than the total product of African agricultural production.

In the early days of Kenya Colony, *finance capital* played its traditional role of facilitating the flow of primary products to the metropolis. Predictably, the bulk of the business of commercial banks in East Africa up to 1930 was commodity-financing. The strict criteria for granting loans tended to limit their use to the larger estate farmers. With the depression and collapse of commodity markets by 1930, the metropolitan state was forced to make provisions through the Land Bank to rescue the ailing sections of settler agriculture.

The *tariff structure* of Kenya Colony up to the Second World War reflected a balance between different sections of the settler class and

93

the indigenous population. A compromise was reached in the tariff committee of 1929 between the provision of cheap consumer goods for African and European consumers and the interests of settler agriculture. Reductions in imported foodstuffs were compensated for in 1929 by preferential transport rates for farming produce.

The examination of Kenya's *trading patterns* illustrates the degree of competition between firms of different nationalities for a share in the expanding East African markets for manufactured goods. It is evident that Britain's position as the dominant trading partner was being eroded by 1939. In particular, British manufactured goods such as cement were suffering competition from the newer industrial nations such as Japan and the United States. Britain's predominance in the world market could no longer be assured by free competition, and the system of imperial preference offered to the colonial territories in 1932 reflected this change.

The overview of *company formation* gives some indication of the nature and extent of business enterprises in the colonial economy before 1945. The first period, 1907–22, exhibits the limited scope of the first investments, which were mainly confined to the areas of land, property and agriculture. After 1922 the numbers and size of enterprises in Kenya increased substantially. Due to the racial barriers that surrounded production and distribution, European and foreign firms were largely predominant in the field of primary production, whereas Asian capital was confined to the sphere of trade. The level of investment in manufacturing before the war was limited to some basic primary processing.

Chapter 2 elaborates on the main characteristics of early foreign investment in Kenya. The main impetus behind the expansion of British firms into the colony was their drive to control the conditions of production in certain commodities such as coffee, tea, cotton and soda ash. *Merchant capital*, in the form of large British trading companies, acted as agents of British industrial capital by linking up East African markets for manufactured goods with metropolitan markets for raw materials. This form of commodity trading was carried out under competitive conditions which necessitated in some cases the move of firms into the production of commodities.[72] Most of the largest British firms in Kenya before the Second World War were involved in either primary processing or commodity trading. The only large-scale investment in minerals was the Magadi Soda Company which processed soda for export.

In general terms, the metropolitan government discouraged the development of manufacturing in East Africa, through fear that it would compete with home industries. Due to the greater autonomy of the colonial administration from metropolitan control, the national

---

72 Such as Baumann's investment in Ugandan coffee production.

processing industries in Kenya were protected to a greater extent than in Tanganyika or Uganda. However, British capital in Kenya in the interwar period was mainly confined to the production of raw materials for metropolitan markets. It was not until after 1945 that Britain's period of *laissez-faire* capitalism finally extinguished itself in the face of changing global conditions of accumulation.

PART II

CHAPTER 3

Kenya's Postwar Industrialization

Changes in the World Economy after the Second World War

The new era of capitalism which emerged after the end of the Second World War was marked by the hegemony of the United States in political, economic and military spheres. After 1945 there began a phase of *concentration and centralization* of capital on a world scale. By 1940 there had been a huge advance in United States industry which led to a fundamental upheaval in technology, organization of labour and relations of production after the war. This process involved the transformation of industrial organization and dramatic increases in labour productivity in all the capitalist metropoles. These changes completely altered the tendencies of international capital export. The traditional concentration of foreign investment in the field of plantations and raw-materials extraction changed in favour of a concentration of foreign investment in *manufacturing*. In metropolitan countries there was a shift from raw-materials processing to the development of oil-based synthetics. Capital exports in the postwar period, particularly after 1960, have been marked by the enhanced flow of capital *between* the advanced capitalist nations.[1]

However, the changed structure of the world economy in the postwar period was characterized by a huge *increase* in the absolute amount of capital exports from the major capitalist countries. For instance, in the period from 1946 to 1950, the net flow of private longer-term capital from the traditional capital-exporting countries (Britain, USA, France and Germany) averaged 1·8 billion dollars per annum. In the following decade it rose to 2·9 billion dollars per annum, reaching a peak of 3·6 billion dollars in 1958.[2] To these figures must be

---

1 These tendencies have been observed by both Marxist and non-Marxist writers on the world economy; for instance, E. Mandel, *Late Capitalism*, NLB, London, 1975, ch. 2; also J. H. Dunning, *Studies in International Investment*, Allen & Unwin, London, 1970, ch. 1.
2 Dunning, op. cit., p. 23.

99

added official donations and long-term loans. There were not only quantitative changes but qualitative differences between the capital exports of the prewar period and those of the postwar era. These are summarized by three main tendencies.

1   The significance of official government loans and grants as a proportion of total capital exports increased from the 1950s onwards. This is a reflection of the fact that the *state* in the advanced capitalist metropoles was to play an increasingly significant role in paving the way for private productive investment. This gave rise to a new form of both national and international finance capital, where both national and internationally based agencies combined state and private funds to support large-scale investment projects abroad. By the 1960s just under two-fifths of official long-term loan capital and one-tenth of private capital was channelled through bodies such as the International Bank and its affiliates (International Finance Corporation, International Development Association), the IMF, the Export/Import Bank, the EEC Development Fund and the EEC Investment Bank.[3] The main thrust of postwar international aid (from the USA) was to support disrupted European capitalism through the institutions of the Bretton Woods Agreement which had established the World Bank. The chief aim of the World Bank in the initial stages was to reconstruct the war-ravaged western capitalist countries. Such loans directed through international agencies plus government-to-government grants were almost always aimed at the development of infrastructure which is the essential prerequisite for investment. However, these types of large projects are usually not undertaken by individual capitals because they do not offer sufficient earning capacity in the short term. Therefore, official grants and loans in the postwar era have generally been used not only to finance projects which private capital is unwilling or unable to finance, but have also had an important long-term role as a catalyst to private investment by providing the necessary basic services and framework for capitalist expansion. This enhanced role of finance capital mediated through the state will be explored in some detail during the examination of the development of the CDC in Kenya.

2   Two connected features of the postwar period are the growing *multilateralism* of foreign investment and the *generalization* of the *capitalist mode of production* on a world scale. However, for most of the postwar period (up to the 1970s), America and Britain have supplied between 80 and 90 per cent of the world's international capital. Nevertheless, during this period, Britain's dominant position as capital exporter was gradually eroded by the United States.

3 ibid., p. 28.

This relative decline is reflected in the following figures: of the average total net exports of long-term private capital (1902 billion dollars) between 1951 and 1955, 67 per cent and 25 per cent were from the USA and Britain respectively, whereas between 1951 and 1964, of 2523 billion dollars, America constituted over 75 per cent and the UK only 15 per cent.

3   The final significant feature of this period is the predominance of the *multinational corporation* in larger units than before as the medium for conducting the flow of private capital overseas. Of the total figure of all private investment between 1951 and 1964, at least four-fifths took the form of capital for the establishment and operation of overseas enterprises and branch plants. It was in this era that the export of *capital* rather than commodities became the dominant tendency. This should be contrasted with the period of 'classical imperialism'. When Lenin wrote his famous treatise on imperialism in 1916, the vast proportion of international capital movements were not conducted through 'monopolies and cartels' (as Lenin implies) but rather took the form of portfolio investment,[4] while from the 1950s onwards, 75 per cent of this flow has been constituted by direct investment of multinational corporations. Before the Second World War, the fusion of capital into large centralized units had certainly started, although only on a limited scale. Bukharin correctly grasped that in the age of imperialism before the First World War the influence of cartels and international firms in the world economy was not as great as would appear at first sight.[5] The concentration and centralization of capital reached a new stage after 1945 with the takeover of smaller units of capital and the merger of firms within the same branch of production, a process that was further accelerated in the 1960s.

Thus, in the postwar era, the multinational corporation becomes the significant form of organization of large-scale capital. An additional stimulant to the creation of multinational corporations is the compulsion towards *vertical* integration, which is the main motive force behind the centralization of capital. Such vertical integration increasingly involves a combination of different production sites all over the globe, which correspond to the uneven development of raw-material sources, technological innovation and capital accumulation. The advancing level of accumulation in the capitalist metropoles through raised productivity of labour and increases in output put an expanding level of capital at the disposal of oligopolistic company formations.

4 V. I. Lenin, *Imperialism, the Highest Stage of Capitalism*, Progress Publishers, Moscow, 14th ed. He implies in this work in 1916 that the formation of cartels and large corporations had reached enormous proportions. It is suggested here that this stage of concentration of capital was not reached until after the Second World War.
5 N. Bukharin, *Imperialism and the World Economy*, Merlin Press, London, 1972.

These multinational enterprises become increasingly centralized and self-financing.

There has been an attempt above to outline the changes in the period of capitalism after the Second World War. It is now necessary to link these changes to the position of Britain in the world economy during this period and in turn to the effects of such changes on Britain's colonial territories. The dominance of US capital in the world economy, briefly sketched above, was to have long-term effects on Britain at the political as well as the economic level. The UK, from being a net creditor of 21·6 billion dollars before the war, emerged in 1945 owing about as much as it was owed, but within two years had become a net *debtor* to the tune of 2·6 billion dollars. This dramatic change in Britain's position in the world money market was mainly due to an increase in long-term obligations of 7·1 million dollars, owed to the USA and Canada. This was accompanied by an increase in Britain's short-term liabilities, almost entirely in sterling balances, of 14·1 million.[6] The countries of the British Commonwealth reduced their debts by about 12·5 billion dollars, mainly as a result of the accumulation of sterling balances arising from Britain's large wartime expenditures.

With British capital no longer being strong enough to compete with America on a global level, it was logical that *laissez-faire* capitalism should give way to a higher level of state intervention in the British economy. In response to such conditions there was a series of nationalizations in Britain's major industries between 1946 and 1950. The concept of a centrally planned economy emerged at a time when it was necessary for the continuance of the capitalist system for the state to act 'objectively' for capital as a whole, rather than remain confined to its traditional mediating role.[7]

The hegemony of American capital after the war also threatened Britain's global predominance at the *political* level. The new phase of expansion in the international capitalist system was facilitated by the generalization of commodity production and the free movement of capital across national boundaries. The existence of a large number of colonial territories controlled by Britain was clearly an impediment to the long-term expansion of the capitalist mode of production. In this respect, it is significant that the United States continuously pressed Britain to grant independence or self-government to its colonial territories.[8] After the Second World War, therefore, the state was to play a more active role in bolstering British investment in the colonial areas. Indeed, this was the basis of the emergence of a new British 'development policy' towards the colonial territories after 1945.

---

6 Dunning, op. cit., p. 21.

7 Much has been written on the changed role of the British state after 1945; see P. W. Bell, *The Sterling Area in the Post-War World*, OUP, London, 1956.

8 W. R. Louis, *Imperialism at Bay: The Role of the US in the Decolonisation of the British Empire, 1941–1945*, OUP, London, 1977.

Changes in Britain's Colonial Policy after 1945

What were the manifestations of such changes in the relation between capital and the state in Kenya Colony during the postwar period? The main emphasis of British policy towards the colonies before 1939 had been on the extraction of raw materials to supply British industries. In order to foster the needs of British industrial capital, in 1924 the *Empire Industries Association* was formed by prominent Conservative MPs and businessmen. This was an organization to campaign for imperial preference for raw materials entering Britain and the Association encouraged the Treasury to extend the system of railways in East and Central Africa.

Therefore, the 'Empire Development' propounded by Milner and Amery at the Colonial Office during the 1920s consisted of encouraging the development of colonial raw materials to service British industry.[9] Their chief instrument had been the *Empire Marketing Board*, founded in 1926 to advertise the marketing of empire produce in Britain. This board continued in business until the Ottawa Conference of 1932, which established a system of imperial preference for colonial raw materials to Britain. This organization continued to stress that 'everything in these distant colonies turns on the habits and needs of the great industrial countries, first and foremost, our own'.[10]

Even given the limitations of the role of the colonial state in the territories before 1939, there had always been in Kenya a dichotomy between the 'official' British policy towards the colony and that actually implemented by a local administration under pressure from settler 'clients'. Lord Lugard's philosophy of 'native paramountcy' (stressing the organic growth of native peoples) dominated official British policy towards the other territories in the 1920s.[11]

This 'live and let live' philosophy was, however, contrary to settler interests in Kenya, which involved the forcible curtailment of indigenous capitalism and coercion of the population in order to ensure supplies of labour for the settler estates.

The structure of the dependent British Empire rested on a series of negotiated constitutional arrangements which each colonial territory had made with the mother country. The powers of the Secretary of State for the Colonies were limited by the particular circumstances in which each territory had been acquired. It is important to note that before the Second World War, each territorial administration retained a high degree of initiative. An example of the way in which a colonial administration could be manipulated by local class interests was the consistent refusal of the settler-controlled LEGCO to sanction the income-tax proposals of the metropolitan administration. As the colo-

9 J. M. Lee, *Colonial Government and Good Government*, Clarendon Press, Oxford, 1967, p. 41.
10 D. Woodruff, *The Story of the British Colonial Empire*, 1939, p. 25.
11 M. Perham, 'Lugard', quoted in Lee, op. cit., p. 43.

nial regulations never prescribed a uniform pattern of administrative relationships with the territories, the Colonial Office had little control over development projects. In the case of Kenya Colony, the allocation of the colonial revenues which had been raised mainly from the African population, was decided through LEGCO – the Legislative Assembly, which was influenced by the dominant settlers.[12]

It has been shown in Chapter 1 that the first *Colonial Development Act* of 1929 was designed to provide funds which would service the interest on loans raised by the colonial governments which gave contracts to British firms. However, the economic depression in the western world in the late 1920s prevented most colonial governments, including Kenya, from raising sufficient loans. Indeed, it was the very conditions of economic depression which laid the basis for a change in British policy towards the empire. The curtailment of capital projects and the policy of retrenchment in the 1930s marked the beginning of planned directives from the metropolis.[13] More important was the competition faced by British firms in the world market, particularly from the newer industrial nations such as Japan. Colonial officers in several African territories before the Second World War complained that British firms were not competitive in producing 'appropriate' manufactured goods for colonial markets. The stage was thus set before the Second World War for a substantial change in the practice of central colonial policy in response to the altered needs of British industrial capital.

The actual practice of a central policy for colonial development and full-scale state intervention in the economy was gained by the experience of the Second World War. The prime object of Colonial Office measures towards the colonies during the war was to preserve the gold and foreign-exchange reserves of the UK. Colonial governments were instructed to restrict the import of consumer goods and instigate a system of import licences. By 1941, therefore, most of the colonies had been brought into some system of price control for their principal products and many of them were asked to join bulk purchasing agreements in order to maintain essential supplies for Britain during the war. The Secretary of State for the Colonies had sent a circular on economic policy which stressed the need to increase the flow of colonial supplies for war purposes and reduce to a minimum all colonial demands on the general resources of labour and materials.[14]

By the end of the Second World War, the formulation of a new colonial development policy became imperative as part of the measures of state intervention in the economy. The official version of the postwar 'new deal' for the colonies simply asserted a new version of

---

12 Lee, op. cit., p. 47

13 Powerful settlers were appointed to a series of government committees which determined the details of administration in the colony.

14 Lee, op. cit., p. 75.

'native paramountcy' where money and specialist personnel were to be provided for every colony to promote '*development and social welfare*'. There was certainly a greater degree of intervention in colonial economies than before the war and officials at the Colonial Office felt that socialist objections in Britain to the evils of monopoly capitalism in the colonial territories had been partly answered by the machinery set up for marketing colonial products during the war.

The immediate need of the British government after the war was to reduce the large dollar deficits, which amounted to around £311 million by 1948. The government was aware that one method of reducing these deficits and encouraging British firms was to channel government resources into colonial primary and industrial production. The *Commission on Colonial Primary Products* was to stress after 1947 that an increase in colonial production was to be seen not only as a measure to meet the immediate problems, but as a long-term contribution to European reconstruction plans. Furthermore, 'it will remain necessary to develop supplies outside the Western hemisphere and reduce European dependence on foodstuffs and raw materials from dollar areas, if the pattern of world trade is to be restored to equilibrium'.[15] The idea was to increase the exports of primary products from British colonies to America and dollar areas and to cut down the imports of manufactured goods from those areas. The latter aim was to be achieved by encouraging British firms to manufacture goods within the colonies themselves. Lord Trefgarne, the chairman of the CDC, articulated this policy:

> I mention these figures only to show the relative possibilities as between American imports of manufactured goods and of food and raw materials, and to show that sterling and the balance of world trade are likely to gain more from colonial products than from manufactured exports to America.[16]

Therefore, it is clear that increased agricultural production in Britain's African colonies would serve a dual purpose in that it would meet her own immediate food and raw-materials needs and assist the sterling balances. The longer-term aim of the metropolis after 1945 was to raise production in British industry, which had been adversely affected by the war effort. In any event, by 1939 in the colonial territories, British firms were facing increasingly tough competition from the newer industrial nations such as the United States and Japan, so that the logical move for British manufacturing firms after the war was to invest in colonial production behind tariff walls. The thrust of postwar development policy in Kenya served to support this process.

---

15 Annual report of the Colonial Development Corporation (CDC), 1948.

16 From a press reprint of a speech given by Lord Trefgarne on 22 June 1948 to an audience of Liverpool businessmen involved with colonial trade.

The chief instrument for implementing the new development policy in the postwar period was the *Colonial Development and Welfare Act* (CD&W) of 1940. This superseded the old CDA of 1929, which had provided only a small trickle of aid to the colonies before 1939. The CD&W Act made £120 million available to the colonial governments for a period of ten years and the further supplementary Acts of 1949 and 1950 increased the total amount to £140 million and extended the size of the central reserve, thus raising the amount which could be paid in any one year. About 40 per cent of the funds from this Act went towards education, health services, housing and water supplies.[17] The structural changes in the Colonial Office, implemented after 1945, did not change the financial relationship between Britain and her colonies. The programme of public expenditure inaugurated by the CD&W Act of 1940 was implemented through the existing administrative structures and each colonial administration remained responsible for balancing its own budget.

There was also a strong emphasis in postwar development policy, on raising the standards of skills and education. After the *Overseas Resources Development Act* of 1948, public corporations were intended to sponsor development in the colonies in various ways and it was expected that such bodies would train their own personnel. Development policy towards the colonies after 1945 involved laying the groundwork and providing the essential preconditions for the entry of private capital on a large scale.[18] It has already been noted that a feature of postwar capitalist development has been the enhanced role of national *and* international *finance capital* in stimulating the flow of private capital overseas.

After the war, the doctrine of the public corporation was sold to the colonies by the Colonial Office and each territorial government was at liberty to establish its own corporations, with the administrative structure strongly in favour of territorial bodies. The Labour government resisted pressure from the Labour 'left' to nationalize the large trading companies that operated in the colonies, but a compromise was reached whereby the newly established public corporations such as the *Colonial Development Corporation* (CDC) and the *Overseas Food Corporation* (OFC) would not interfere with the management of the trading companies but should buy a controlling interest in their share capital. The investment and loan funds put at the disposal of the CDC by the state were to be used to encourage the move of British capital into important areas of colonial economies not initially attractive to private capital. The *Overseas Resources Development Act* of 1948 was intended to act as the commercial counterpart to the CD&W Acts by

---

17 Lee, op. cit., p. 85.
18 As production units in the colonies became more sophisticated, the standard of labour efficiency would need to be improved.

providing for the creation of the two public corporations: the OFC and the CDC. The OFC was specifically designed to take over the management of the infamous groundnut scheme from the United Africa Corporation. The OFC had an initial capital of £50 million and the balance from the groundnut scheme was to be used for encouraging private capital into other food-growing projects in the colonial territories.[19] The OFC collapsed along with the groundnut scheme (which had absorbed most of its resources) in the early 1950s, and the corporation was formally dissolved in 1954.

This 'new deal' for colonial territories was concerned to provide these areas with extended infrastructure and services, with the hope that this would stimulate private investment in agriculture and industry. Economic services provided under the development plans were generally confined to such measures as the conservation of physical resources, provision of public utilities and research. The metropolitan state also set up national financial agencies such as the CDC and the OFC, which were intended to assist colonial enterprises where the initial capital expenditure was too heavy to attract commercial investors. The ultimate aim of the investment of such agencies was to hand over the projects to private capital.

The Postwar Kenyan Economy

There was a specific obstacle in the way of the expansion of capitalist relations of production and that was the *political* predominance of the settler minority. The new metropolitan policy to develop African cash crops cut across settler restrictions on indigenous capitalism. As international capital was closely tied up with the expansion of African cash-crop agriculture after 1945, settler political power was gradually undermined. The weakness of settler enterprises had been evident before 1939 and after the war enterprises were rapidly absorbed by foreign firms. By the late 1950s, settler hegemony in Kenya had reached its twilight and was to give way under nationalist pressure expressed through the Mau Mau.

CAPITAL FORMATION

The postwar years in Kenya Colony witnessed a rapid expansion of both agricultural and industrial production. This process was accompanied by a comparative *decline* in European agriculture as a proportion of total output. For instance, by 1954, for the first time in the history of the colony, the gross national product attributed to manufac-

---

19 A. Wood, *The Groundnut Affair*, Bodley Head, London, 1950, p. 85.

TABLE 22   Balance of Payments of Kenya 1929–46 and 1946–58 in £m

	1929	1930	1931	1932	1933	1934	1935	1936	1937	1938	1939	1946
Merchandise Trade												
Exports f.o.b	2·9	3·6	2·5	2·4	2·4	2·1	3·1	4·1	4·2	4·1	4·4	7·6
Imports c.i.f.	6·1	5·1	3·4	2·5	2·3	2·6	3·1	3·4	5·2	4·5	4·8	14·6
Invisibles												
Balance	−3·2	−1·5	−0·9	−0·1	0·1	0·5	—	0·7	−1·0	−0·4	−0·4	−7·0
Non-Factor Services Balances	1·6	1·6	1·4	1·3	1·4	0·5	1·8	1·8	2·0	2·0	1·8	2·5
Net Factor Payments	−0·9	−1·0	−1·1	−1·2	−1·2	−1·2	−1·3	−1·3	−1·3	−1·3	−1·3	−1·5
Net Current Transfers	−0·6	−0·6	−0·6	−0·6	−0·6	−0·6	−0·5	−0·6	−0·6	−0·6	−0·6	−0·1
Net Capital Imports												
Current Account Balance	−3·1	−1·5	−1·2	−0·5	−0·2	−0·8	—	0·7	−0·9	−0·3	−0·6	−6·1
Net Official Grants	—	—	—	0·1	—	—	—	—	0·1	0·1	—	0·4
Other Public	1·1	1·5	1·3	0·4	−0·3	−0·4	−0·6	−0·6	−0·8	−0·3	0·3	−0·5
Private	2·0	—	−0·1	0·1	0·5	1·2	0·6	—	1·6	0·6	0·3	6·2
Residual												

	1947	1948	1949	1950	1951	1952	1953	1954	1955	1956	1957	1958
Merchandise Trade												
Exports f.o.b.	10·5	12·4	13·7	20·8	27·8	30·0	24·7	25·9	31·6	36·3	35·4	40·1
Imports c.i.f.	21·0	29·4	36·8	31·5	53·1	58·6	52·3	61·8	73·7	69·0	71·1	61·8
Invisibles												
Balance	-10·5	-17·0	-23·1	-10·7	-25·3	-28·6	-27·6	-35·9	-42·1	-32·7	-35·7	-21·7
Non-Factor Services	0·9	1·8	3·7	2·9	4·7	5·0	4·5	8·9	9·7	7·8	4·0	4·7
Balances												
Net Factor Payments	-1·7	-2·3	-2·9	-3·8	-5·3	-4·9	-5·0	-5·0	-5·7	-6·9	-6·6	-7·0
Net Current Transfers	0·1	-0·1	-0·1	0·1	0·2	0·5	1·6	-1·5	-4·3	-4·5	-3·0	2·3
Net Capital Imports												
Current Account Balance	-11·4	-17·6	-22·4	-11·5	-25·7	-28·0	-26·5	-33·5	-42·4	-36·3	-41·3	-26·7
Net Official Grants	0·2	0·3	0·6	1·6	1·8	1·2	1·4	7·3	10·6	9·5	5·5	3·8
Other Public	-2·1	3·9	2·9	2·0	9·5	5·8	3·9	7·5	8·9	14·3	5·9	1·3
Private Residual	13·3	13·4	18·9	7·9	14·4	21·1	21·2	18·7	22·8	12·5	29·9	22·0

Source: Ord, op. cit.

turing industry was greater than that attributed to European agriculture.[20] Furthermore, there was a much greater reliance of the colonial economy on official grants and the inflow of new private capital also increased rapidly after 1945. Net official grants rose from £0·4 million in 1946 to £9·5 million in 1956 and private capital imports from £6·2 million to £21·2 million in 1953.

The largest proportion of capital formation *before* 1939 had been in European agriculture, which meant that by 1945 all the basic investments in land clearing, plantations and buildings had been made. Although at the time these investments were a heavy burden in terms of loan repayments, they did not need replacement by the 1950s and these fixed assets helped tô raise incomes in later years at no external financial cost. After the war, therefore, a larger proportion of private capital investment could be directed into secondary and tertiary industries which yielded larger and quicker returns. For instance, approximately half the private capital formation between 1946 and 1952 involved imports of plant and machinery and only 5 per cent involved construction work on European farms. There was a large absolute increase in capital formation attributed to 'other private sectors' (which includes industry) from £64·7 million to £123·8 million in the periods 1946–52 and 1953–8 respectively. The amount of capital formation attributed to European agriculture *declined*, not in absolute but in proportional terms, from 16·8% of the total in 1946–52 to 9·8 % in the 1953–8 period.[21]

By the 1950s, therefore, there had been a substantial increase in the level of capital accumulation in Kenya Colony. There was also a significant increase in the gross national product (GNP) in the immediate postwar years, which rose from £53 million in 1947 to £103 million in 1951.[22] The total African income, on the other hand (included in these figures), amounted to £26 million and £40 million in those years, leaving in the two years approximately £27 million and £63 million of other income out of which voluntary savings on any scale could be expected to come. The city treasurer of Nairobi made a rough estimate as to the amount of Kenya's voluntary savings in 1951 which he calculated to be around 10 per cent or somewhere between £3 million and £5 million. He further prepared a report on the amount of local money raised in Kenya between 1945 and 1952 which was estimated at £14 396 215.[23] Private capital formation was to reach its peak in 1956 when it amounted to £30·7 million or 21 per cent of the gross cash product.

---

20 *East African Royal Commission Report, 1953–5*, Govt Printer, Nairobi, 1955, p. 83.

21 H. W. Ord, 'The Kenya economy as a whole, 1929–1952; national income, investment and the balance of payments', mimeo., Edinburgh, 1976, p. 10.

22 East African Royal Commission report, 1955, p. 84.

23 ibid.

TABLE 23   *Kenya Gross Capital Formation 1946–58*

	1946–52		1953–8	
	(£m.)	(%)	(£m.)	(%)
Railways and Harbours	12·9	10·0	41·2	1·5
Other Public Sectors	30·1	23·4	60·2	24·1
Non-African Agriculture	21·1	16·4	24·6	9·8
Other Private Sectors	64·7	50·2	123·8	49·6
TOTAL	128·8	100·0	249·8	100·0

Source: Ord, op. cit.

FINANCE

It has been argued before that the role of finance capital channelled through the state or private agencies is to provide the necessary prerequisites for the interventions of private capital. Through official grants and loans to the colony in the postwar period, the state financed infrastructure which would encourage the inflow of new British capital. The level of direct aid increased in the colony after the war as did the flow of loan capital through commercial agencies. For instance, a large number of loans for the colonial territories were raised on the London market, assisted by Barclays Overseas Development Corporation. Between 1950 and 1952, these loans, destined for East African territories, averaged £17 million per annum.[24] These were mainly used by the local administration for infrastructure and services such as roads, railways, housing, education and health services. These grants and loans were supplemented by inflows of purely private finance capital from Britain and it is significant that of a total of £77·7 million borrowed by British African dependencies on the London market between 1945 and the end of 1952, some £48·6 million, or two-thirds, went into British East Africa.

In the postwar period, therefore, economic expansion must be attributed both to increasing *domestic accumulation* as well as an enhanced level of foreign capital inflow, serviced by finance capital. The basis for a large-scale capitalist expansion in the colony did not arise only out of the wartime conditions, but had been laid before 1939. During the 1930s, domestic expenditure had been squeezed to release domestic saving to service foreign-held debts and other statutory obligations. From 1933 to 1938 (inclusive) additions to official balances held abroad exceeded net inflows of grants or official loans. By 1935, more than 40 per cent of the GDP had been saved. Although the early postwar figures repeat for a time the large import gap of the 1920s,

---

24 These were later supplemented by loans from the IBRD, International Bank for Reconstruction and Development, details in the EARC report, op. cit., pp. 81–5.

with an even greater reliance on foreign saving, the burden of net factor payments abroad was reduced as a proportion of the GDP.[25] Even though macroeconomic statistics can only indicate general trends, it is evident that after the Second World War significant savings had been made in the national economy and the level of private capital formation was high.

AGRICULTURE

In the postwar period, economic expansion must be attributed to *increasing domestic accumulation* as well as an enhanced level of foreign-capital inflow. The basis for this accelerated growth of capitalism was laid before the war. Indeed, the move of private capital into industry after 1945 was made possible by the large savings accumulated from agricultural exports. During the war, the food products from East Africa were considered important and Kenya expanded its food production to cater for British demand for primary products. Wartime interference with shipping routes had also forced the colony into a further degree of import substitution for basic consumer items, while utilizing local raw materials (for example, oils, acids, bricks and chemicals). This demand stimulated both settler and African agriculture. Settler control of the marketing boards remained until the late 1950s, although metropolitan policy from 1950 onwards was to stimulate the development of African cash-crop farming. This latter aim was hindered by the racial segregation of Kenyan agricultural production and the dominance of white settlers.

Measures were taken by the administration which had the effect of enhancing commodity exchange, the most important being the granting of *individual land title* under the terms of the *Swynnerton Plan* of 1954. Under the auspices of this plan, the new marketing boards provided finance and expertise for pineapple, coffee, tea and pyrethrum growing in the African reserves. The combined effect of these measures was to stimulate the production of cash crops and further accelerate differentiation of the indigenous classes. Individual land titles, plus labour regulations, had the effect of creating a further divorce of labour from the means of production (land). The new pattern of ownership reinforced the existing class structure in the reserve areas, where the richer African farmers tended to predominate. The Swynnerton Plan assumed that about twenty years would be needed to complete the land consolidation process, but it was achieved by 1962. At this time, 300 000 farms had been consolidated and enclosed, which covered 2·4 million acres.[26]

---

25 Ord, op. cit., pp. 10–11.

26 Further details of colonial policy towards agriculture are to be found in M. D. MacWilliam, 'The managed economy: agricultural change, development and finance in Kenya', in D. A. Low and A. Smith (eds), *The History of East Africa*, Vol. III, Clarendon Press, Oxford, 1976, pp. 250–69.

Until security of title was available, neither the Land Bank nor the commercial banks would lend to African farmers. As the Land Bank's policies were not revised until just before independence, the state itself took on the task of providing finance capital for African agriculture. The plans for the development of agriculture in the reserves were speeded up in 1953, as it was hoped that these would help to remedy the problems surrounding the Mau Mau revolt. In 1953, the British government agreed to provide nearly £7 million (£5 million as a grant) to assist African agriculture. All these measures succeeded in enhancing the development of capitalist agriculture and the revenue earned by African producers from the newly established cash crops rose from virtually nothing to £4 million on the eve of independence.

The establishment of boards and committees for the regulation of the economy in Kenya from the wartime period onwards had two contradictory effects. It put a more extensive set of economic institutions in the hands of the dominant settlers and yet these bodies were funded and supervised by the metropolitan government. It is significant also that in mid-June 1945, the traditional channelling of business through the chief secretary was ended and the various government departments were grouped under members of the executive council. One of these was the Member of Agriculture and since this subject covered all communities, there could be *no separation* of agriculture into racial compartments as there had been before 1945. All of these changes ultimately undermined the position of the settler class, as they portended the 'opening up' of capital accumulation to all races. In the words of Wasserman, 'pressure on the settler farmer came both from the African peasant and the large plantation and commercial interests'.[27] It is significant that the most powerful sections of the settler class by the late 1950s had 'seen the writing on the wall' and were moving out of agriculture and into commercial concerns.

Therefore, it was in the interests of international capital to raise productivity in *all* sectors of agriculture, a process which was contradicted by the white political monopoly. It is no accident that the settlement schemes hurriedly drawn up in 1960 and 1961 also secured the financial backing of the World Bank and the CDC. The aim was also to bring about an intensification of high-grade agriculture in the Kenya highlands and thereby increase the production of commodities for the world market. For the first time, the metropolitan government openly accepted that African agricultural production was to supply commodities in preference to settler agriculture.

---

27 The process of settler decline is well documented in G. Wasserman, *Politics of Decolonisation, Kenya Europeans and the Land Issue, 1960–1965*, CUP, Cambridge, 1976, p. 24. For a further political history of the period, see G. Bennet, *Kenya, a Political History, the Colonial Period*, OUP, London, 1963.

TABLE 24   *Principal Items Exported from Kenya Colony in 1952*

	Value (£)	%
Coffee	7·1	28
Sisal	4·5	17
Wattle (extract)	1·7	7
Sodium Carbonate	1·2	5
Tea	1·3	5

Source: Colonial Office, Report on Kenya Colony, 1952.

EMPLOYMENT

Before 1939, the market for capitalist commodities in Kenya was restricted by the scale of production and the partial integration of the African population into the monetary economy. During the war years, however, with the presence of the armed forces and disturbance of shipping routes to Britain, there was an increased demand for agricultural products.

As commodity relations expanded, so did the number of Africans in wage employment. In 1942, there were only 179 085 registered labourers in Kenya Colony. By 1952, the total number of Africans in wage employment had risen to 438 702, 75 per cent of this number being composed of labourers and 25 per cent of clerical and domestic workers. Of the total number employed, 141 134 were engaged in the public sector, 196 000 in agriculture and 101 568 in commerce and industry.[28] By 1956, out of the total number employed, 43 per cent were in agriculture and forestry and 14 per cent in manufacturing, repairs and construction.To this extension in the wage-labour force must be added the increasing number of households drawn into the monetary economy through agricultural production.

In the field of *labour policy*, the government's aim was to create a stable workforce, in order to break the traditional pattern of male migrant workers moving from their rural homes to employment areas for limited periods. Following the *Carpenter Report* of 1954, the government, by means of minimum-wage legislation, began to try and secure an urban wage level which had no element of rural subsidy. Cowen's[29] analysis of 'Real wages in Central Kenya' concludes that the

28 Colonial Office reports on Kenya Colony for 1952 and 1956, HMSO, London. Unfortunately it is not possible to calculate exactly the numbers engaged in commodity production.

29 M. P. Cowen and J. Newman, 'Real wages in Central Kenya', mimeo., Nairobi, 1975, p. 1.

TABLE 25 *Estimates in Real Growth of Gross National Product Per Head 1929–58*

Date	Kenya Population (millions)	GNP Per Head at Current Market Prices		GNP Per Head at 1948 prices Monetary (£)	Monetary GNP Per Head at 1948 Prices (£ millions)	Price Indices	
		Subsistence(£)	Monetary(£)			Maize	Nyeri Farmer
1929	4·0	4·6	2·9	3·8	15·3	100	77
1933	4·2	1·5	1·6	2·7	11·3	33	63
1937	4·6	2·3	2·3	4·5	20·7	50	51
1939	4·8	2·3	2·0	3·5	16·7	50	57
1946	5·1	4·0	7·4	8·4	43·0	83	88
1948	5·4	4·6	10·2	10·2	55·3	100	100
1950	5·8	5·4	13·4	10·9	63·2	117	123
1952	6·5	11·5	14·8	9·3	60·5	250	169
1958	7·4	10·7	22·8	12·4	92·0	233	183

Source: Ord, op. cit., p. 12.

increase in production of estate agriculture and the active military presence served to stimulate the demand for all classes of wage labour. The shortages of labour during the war drove up money wages, but not fast enough to override the higher rate of price increases. Thus real wages remained constant and probably fell during and after the war, which was a strong factor behind the Mau Mau revolt.

This cost-of-living index gives a measure of price indices related to the consumption patterns of African farmers in Nyeri district and lower-paid labourers. From this it can be observed that in 1929, although African subsistence output contributed some 60 per cent of the GNP, this had declined to one-third in 1948.[30] What emerges from these estimates of wage labour and consumption is that the war years accelerated a rapid monetization of the economy which resulted in an all-round expansion in domestic production. This had been held up in the 1930s due to the world depression. It was against this background of expansion in production plus rising consumption levels, that capital moved not only into agriculture but also into industry after 1945.

Colonial Policy towards Industrialization

The arrangements for administering metropolitan aid to the colonies rested on initiatives from the territory concerned, but after the war-time experience of a *centrally planned economy* a strong precedent had been set for local administration. It is suggested here that the basis of settler predominance within the Kenyan state was being undermined in the postwar period by the expansion of both indigenous and foreign capital. Ironically, the Mau Mau revolt dealt the final death-blow to settler pre-eminence by enhancing metropolitan administrative control. The large increase in British aid to the colony in 1955, which amounted to £10·8 million, was part of the post-Mau Mau 'solution' for developing infrastructure and agricultural production in the African reserves. Table 22, 'Kenya's Balance of Payments', pages 108–9, illustrates these trends.

Investment in industry after 1945 was strongly encouraged by the metropolitan administration, in contrast with the prewar bias towards colonial primary processing. As early as 1949, the Ministry of Commerce and Industry in Kenya issued a press release emphasizing the 'new direction' of economic policy in the colony.

> Kenya is on the eve, as indeed is all of Africa, of large scale industrial development . . . this era began during the war, when abnormal conditions closed the usual sources of supply of many articles, and compelled East Africa to look more closely at its own industrial potential . . . there is no lack of capital. In 1948 alone,

---

30 Refer to Ord, op. cit., p. 12, table: 'Estimates in Real Growth of GNP Per Head, 1929–1958'.

£23 million was invested in new private and public companies and nine-tenths of this money went into industry . . . between 1945 and 1949, at least £54 million was invested in the equity of new companies in Kenya.[31]

The local administration tended to support metropolitan directives regarding the establishment of bodies to encourage both African agriculture and industry. In the 1950s the local administration played a more active role in promoting the interests of British capital in the Colony. Immediately after the war, Kenya was required to play its part in the defence of sterling, by reducing its non-sterling expenditure in 1952 to 85 per cent of the total figure for 1951.[32] Also, imports from Japan were to be reduced to certain 'minimum essentials' which did not include cotton textiles and there was a general restriction on the number of goods which could be imported from non-sterling areas. As a result of these measures, the value of trade with the non-sterling area fell by approximately £2 million.

The threat of competition to British capital in overseas markets caused many British industrial firms to move into *production* in those areas, under protected conditions. Indeed Lenin commented on this tendency with regard to European capitalism in the nineteenth century; 'International capital has not hesitated to settle within the tariff wall and establish itself on foreign soil.'[33] British industrial firms went into Kenya after 1945 to manufacture goods previously imported, a process that was strongly encouraged by the state.

POLICY

The *East African Royal Commission Report* (1953–5) embodied the main principles of Britain's new 'development' policy as it pertained to Kenya. The Commission outlined two measures by which the government should promote economic development, one which would remove existing disadvantages and the other which would offer special *inducements* to investors. In the first group was included provisions for infrastructure such as roads and water supplies. The inducements included subsidies, tax concessions and monopolistic privileges which were to be offered to overseas enterprises or immigrants as an incentive to settle in East Africa. They recommended that if these measures were insufficient to attract foreign investment, then the concessions should be increased. The Commission was of the opinion that East Africa was *not* in a good position to attract new capital from outside: 'there is the consideration that the economic importance *to* East Africa

31 Article, *EAS*, 21 June 1949.
32 Colonial Office report, 1952, p. 37
33 V. I. Lenin, *The Development of Capitalism in Russia*, Progress Publishers, Moscow, 4th edn, 1974, p. 493.

is greater than the economic importance of the area to external capital and enterprise due, among other things, to the size of the internal market'[34]

It was for these reasons that the colonial administration in Kenya was empowered to construct a special network of *inducements* to foreign capital, in order to stimulate industrial enterprises in the Colony.

TRAINING

One of the biggest perceived obstacles to the encouragement of productive investments in the colonies was the low standard of labour productivity. The labour force had to be shaped according to the needs of capital and the state was to assist in this process. Therefore, a considerable proportion of the aid administered to East Africa under the CD&W Acts of 1946 and 1950 was directed into training a skilled labour force to service industry as well as agriculture.

The position of the metropolitan government with regard to labour in the colonies was summarized by Sir G. Ord-Brown in a paper presented in 1945 in his capacity as labour adviser to the Secretary of State for the Colonies.

the dominant problem throughout East Africa is the deplorably low standard of efficiency of the worker, that is to say the exceptionally small output characteristic of the entire country, which has always been a conspicuous weakness in the East African economy.[35]

A subsequent statement by the Governor of Uganda in his foreword to the country's development plan indicated the nature of the official solution to this 'problem'.

Given better feeding and medical services, better conditions of employment and the stimulus of a full range of goods at attractive prices in the shops, it is surely not unduly sanguine to look for a marked improvement in the matter of idleness, indifference and irresponsibility which are such disturbing features of the present day African labourer and cultivator.[36]

The general solution to the problem of an unskilled labour force was for the state to play a more active part in education and training; the Member for Commerce and Industry in Kenya Colony at the same time put forward the official view of labour policy and concluded 'that we must direct the basis of education towards the technical and practical angle'. The Royal Commission supported this view.

---

34 EARC report, op. cit., p. 78.
35 Overseas Economic Surveys, British East Africa, HMSO, London 1948, p. 2.
36 ibid., ch. 10.

Here we submit that the difficulties which stand in the way of direct African participation in the field of industry are not primarily financial, but proceed from a lack of skill and experience . . . it is on the removal of this deficiency that a public policy, anxious to promote African participation in new development, should concentrate.[37]

Metropolitan directives to raise the standard of education in the colonial territories were carried out by the local administration in Kenya, particularly after 1955 when large amounts of direct aid were channelled into both education and services. Thus 43 per cent of the expenditure included in the development plans for all Britain's colonial territories was allocated to 'social development', which included education, housing and water supplies. Before the war, infrastructure in African areas had not been encouraged.

During the 1950s, trade and technical schools were established in addition to an increase in government-aided secondary schools. In 1956 there were a total of 389 718 government-aided primary schools and 2586 secondary schools in Kenya, and 54 146 intermediate schools. During this period four trade and technical schools were established at Kabete, Thika, Nyanza and Kwale. Towards the late 1950s, courses for adults were offered in accounting and bookkeeping. All these programmes were designed to shape a more highly skilled workforce which could service the expanding capitalist enterprises in the colonies.

TARIFFS

The use of import tariffs as a consistent form of protection for *local* industries was not formalized into a system until 1959. In 1946 the Development Committee noted:

We do not consider that tariff walls should be erected to bolster up uneconomic or inefficient local industries, and we do not think it right that the people of this country should be compelled by the Government's fiscal policy to purchase local manufactures when better imported articles are available under a normal import duty policy.[38]

Import protection before 1958 was granted to firms on an *ad hoc* basis and the introduction of a fully protective tariff system for local industry was largely in response to pressure from both local and foreign manufacturing firms. It was only after 1958 that a protective tariff system was included in the schedule, and this support for

---

37 ibid.
38 *Kenya Development Programme*, Govt Printer, Nairobi, 1946.

import-substituting industrialization was to be extended further in the 1960s.[39]

Despite these reservations, the tariff structure postwar represented a radical departure from that which had existed before the Second World War. The tariff structure had remained the same from 1930 (after the report of the Tariff Committee) until the war. During the war years a series of subcharges was introduced in the basic tariff with the object of maintaining revenue at as high a level as possible and discouraging the consumption of commodities which could not be regarded as essential. During the 1940s an automatic 10 per cent surcharge was imposed on manufactured items, a higher rate being imposed on some of these items produced locally. For instance, wood and unmanufactured timber carried a surcharge duty of 100 per cent; glassware, china and porcelain 100 per cent; motor spirit 66 per cent; sugar 100 per cent; tea 100 per cent; tobacco 175 per cent; dairy products (ghee, cheese, butter) 100 per cent; beer 25 per cent; soap 100 per cent; and wires 100 per cent. All of these items except motor spirit were produced locally.[40]

Wartime conditions had necessitated a certain degree of import protection even before it had become part of official policy. After the war, suspended duties were also imposed on certain manufactured goods and primary goods produced within East Africa, at the discretion of each territorial government. However, many potential investors before the 1958 scheme of protective tariffs were compelled to rely on duty remissions rather than direct protection. Even by 1955 it is clear that the attitude of the administration was shifting towards the provision of consistent protection for industrial projects. A government report, *Economic Assistance for Primary and Secondary Industries* (1955), emphasized the inadequacy of the existing duty drawback scheme:

> we consider that appropriate assistance to an industry should be granted to the industry as a whole . . . and this should be provided for by a special amendment to the customs tariff. It is reasonable that a local industry, to which protection is given, should enjoy protection up to a maximum of 20 per cent against a comparable finished product and 10 per cent against the imported equivalent semi-processed article. In a country where the setting up of new industry is still a venture carrying considerable risks, it is doubtful whether a fair return on capital employment is enough to induce owners of capital to face the risks.[41]

---

39 R. Eglin, 'The oligopolistic structure and competitive characteristics of direct foreign investment in Kenya's manufacturing sector', in R. Kaplinsky (ed.), *Readings on the Multinational Corporation in Kenya*, OUP, East Africa, 1978.

40 The Colonial Blue Books contain tariffs on all items, see 1938–46.

41 *Economic Assistance for Primary and Secondary Industries*, Govt Printer, Nairobi, 1955, p. 8.

It has been contended by Eglin[42] that the ultimate introduction of a comprehensive system of protective tariffs corresponds with the date of establishment of a foreign investment and most tariff protection was offered only after pressure had been exerted by the company concerned. For instance, in the case of cement, the British Standard Portland Cement Company consistently refused to install a cement plant until appropriate protective measures against imported cement were guaranteed by the administration. Indeed, from interviews with company directors I have confirmed the impression that foreign firms were impatiently waiting for a full protective tariff for import-substitution projects during the 1950s. The *ad hoc* system of protection utilized until 1958 was clearly inadequate for the long term.

It can be concluded, therefore, that after the Second World War the administration was gradually working towards a coherent policy of import protection in order to assist the development of an industrial sector. The institution of a comprehensive scheme of import duties in 1958 was the logical culmination of both the government's own policy and pressure from British industrial firms.

REGULATIONS AND ADMINISTRATIVE BODIES CONCERNED WITH INDUSTRIALIZATION

Various government bodies were created in Kenya from the war years onwards, in order to foster industrial development. The earliest of these was the *Industrial Management Board*, which was established in 1944 under the Defence Regulations for the purpose of supplying the armed forces with manufactured items such as crockery, sulphuric acid for batteries, pyrethrum and extract for cooking fat. The Board paid over its small profit to the Treasury in 1945 and then sold two-thirds of its holding to the CDC, with the Industrial Management Board retaining a one-third holding on behalf of its successor, *East African Industries Ltd.*[43] The type of enterprises which grew up under this umbrella of state support were engineering works, woodworkings, bricks, ceramics and tiles. The brick works were part of the East African Industrial Management Board and that portion of EAI was later sold to Refractories Ltd, while the soap-making business was hived off to Unilever Ltd in 1953.

The Industrial Management Board in turn had its activities taken over by the *Industrial Development Council* (IDC), a forerunner of the present ICDC. This body was established under Ordinance No. 63 of 1954 and was designed to 'facilitate the industrial and economic development of the colony by initiating, assisting or expanding industrial, commercial and other undertakings in the colony'.[44] The IDC was

---

42 Eglin, op. cit.
43 Memo on industrial development in Kenya, prepared for A. Hope-Jones, the Member for Commerce and Industry, by MCI, *KNA*, 16 May 1952.
44 ibid.

mainly a finance agency to support *new* industrial projects rather than those already under way. These new enterprises sponsored by the IDC were to take the form of partnerships with specialized industrial firms.

The recommendations of the report of the Development Committee summarized the government's policy towards industrial development. These included the following provisions: a system of industrial licensing, a government finance corporation to assist industrial development, a board of industrial research, extended electricity facilities, a trade advisory committee, a technical and commercial institute for industrial training and a factory inspectorate. All these provisions were incorporated in the general aim of the IDC which was to encourage and assist private enterprise to develop industries in the colony. These details of policy were made statutory during the 1950s and they laid the basis for state support of industrial development.

In addition to these measures, in 1946 the government appointed an economic and commercial adviser, who in 1948 became *Secretary for Commerce and Industry* (SCI). He was a member of the executive council and had his own executive powers. In 1948 a board of commerce and industry was appointed by a LEGCO resolution with the following terms of reference:

(1) to keep under constant review commercial and industrial aspects of customs and excise and to make recommendations to the SCI on any matters affecting industrial development;
(2) to advise the SCI on policy concerning the encouragement and development of industries and mining in the colony.

This board was a fully representative body including members nominated by the unofficial members' associations and the associations of chambers of commerce.

INDUSTRIAL LICENSING

From the outset, licensing for capital goods industries must be distinguished from licensing for primary products such as coffee, tea and pyrethrum, which was also introduced after the war. The overall direction of state policy towards industrialization in the postwar period was embodied in an *Industrial Licensing Ordinance* passed by the legislatures of Uganda, Kenya and Tanganyika in 1948. This came under the direction of the East African High Commission and the Ordinance vested executive powers in an *East African Industrial Council* in 1943. This Council was composed of one official and two non-official members from each of the three territories. This body was empowered to authorize the issue of licences for the manufacture of articles under the Industrial Licensing Ordinances (ILO), which were enacted in each of the three territories on identical terms.

The legislation of the ILO provided that: 'no person shall engage in

the scheduled industries without a licence granted by the council ... licences will be refused if the capital, skills, or raw materials
available to the applicant are deemed to be inadequate'.[45] The official
rationale for such a policy was to avoid what was called 'uneconomic
competition' between similar industries in the three territories. This
was interpreted by the Ordinance as meaning that a number of small
investments in industries being made immediately after the war were
undermining the prosperity of larger-scale investments.

The initial fervour by the administration in licensing industries soon
changed and whereas in 1942 there were thirty-four scheduled industries, by 1948 these had dropped to only six which included some
large-scale investments: leather and leather products, boots and shoes
(Bata), soap and vegetable oils (EAI), cement and acids.[46] This system
of licensing only a few large industries in each industrial branch
tended to support the *concentration of production* amongst several
large firms (often foreign). The decisions on which firms were to be
granted licences were taken on an *ad hoc* basis in response to requests
from individual firms. In 1958 the system of tariffs was rationalized
under a new schedule. By 1959 the industries scheduled under the East
African licensing legislation included: cotton-yarn piece goods and
blankets, woollen blankets, fabric from soft fibre, steel drums, glassware, metal window-frames and enamel holloware, Of a total of
twenty-four licences, only three were foreign.[47]

It is clear from an examination of these measures that by the late
1950s the government was working towards a coherent system of
protection for industry in the colony. The licensing system had the
effect of supporting the movement of capital into large, oligopolistic
units and a highly concentrated industrial structure emerged. Both
Asian and foreign firms were able to take advantage of government
protection in the development of their industrial enterprises.

The Industrial Structure in Kenya 1945–63

During the years following the war, capital flowed rapidly into the
manufacturing sector[48] and the bulk of this investment went into
import-substituting projects. In 1951 the value of the GNP attribut-
able to manufacturing industry amounted to £10 million or 12 per cent

---

45 ibid.

46 These did, however, include some of the largest industries in the colony at the time.

47 Reports of the East African Industrial Council, 1950s.

48 'Wartime conditions had diverted much world production from the manufacture of
consumer goods . . . the post-war political conditions and high taxation in some parts of
the world had caused capital to seek fresh outlets. Also balance of payments difficulties
had caused the Commonwealth to seek new sterling sources of raw materials and
manufactured goods.' (Paper presented to EAIC, January 1956, by MCI.)

of the total. By 1956 there were over one hundred manufacturing and industrial undertakings in the colony (employing over fifty persons), covering a wide range of items. Industrial growth accelerated the demand for wage labour and in 1951, of the total number of Africans engaged in wage labour, 10 per cent or 42 000 were employed in the manufacturing industry. The industrial wage bill was £20·8 million in 1957 and the net output rose from £27·4 million to £31·4 million between 1956 and 1957.[49]

The war period had generated a specific demand for consumer goods and the increasing number of Africans drawn into the monetary economy provided large potential markets for industrial products. Such markets were not confined to Kenya, for the East African Customs Union of 1924 had established a more or less 'free-trade zone' between the three territories. In the 1950s, there were consistent complaints from Asian businessmen in Tanganyika that the country's industrial development was being held up due to the influx of manufactured goods from Kenya. Tanganyika had a continual balance-of-payments deficit with Kenya and in 1955 trade statistics reveal that it imported four times more than its total exports to Uganda and Kenya.[50]

In Kenya the move of capital into industrial production was not exclusively controlled by foreign capital, and first we will consider the development of local Asian capital.

ASIAN CAPITAL

In the prewar period, Asian capital was largely confined to merchant concerns and some primary processing. The extension of Asian capital into manufacturing after 1945 must be placed in its historical context. The areas of accumulation for those of Asian origin in East Africa in the early part of colonial rule were restricted to trade and commerce by the regulations against non-whites holding land. Asian merchants were confined within urban boundaries, so that their only hope for expansion was into manufacturing or primary processing. The only agricultural holdings owned by Asians in Kenya were several sugar estates in the west of Kenya (Kavirondo), an area not settled by Europeans.

The question of access to land ostensibly remained open until the *Crown Land's Ordinance* (1915) which empowered the governor to veto land transactions between the races. Before that the Aga Khan had negotiated with officials to introduce Indian agriculturalists into East Africa.[51] This never reached fruition and the Indians were

49 ibid.

50 For an excellent account of the historic dependence of Tanganyika on Kenya for manufactured goods, see Martha Honey, 'Asian industrial activities in Tanzania', *Tanzania Notes and Records*, 1974.

51 R. C. Gregory, *India and East Africa*, Clarendon Press, Oxford, 1971, p. 435.

excluded from holding land in both the African reserves and the 'white highlands'. It was their juxtaposition between settler and indigenous capitalism before the Second World War which determined their role as traders and small-scale manufacturers in Kenya.

During the *Carter Land Commission* (1932–3,) Asian representatives along with the African members complained about the existing land regulations and requested an underdevelopment tax to force the cultivation or sale of European-owned land which was not being utilized. During the Commission, the Federation of Indian Chambers of Commerce in East Africa further complained that their trading operations were being restricted by the colonial government, in that trading centres could only be established within the reserves with the approval of the local native council and that the plots of land being allocated to them were too small and the terms of the leases limited to five years. The Indian contingent, on the basis of these objections, asked for the establishment of regular townships in the reserves which were gradually to emerge after this date.

Thus, by the 1930s, the Asian community was involved in a whole range of activities from building to shoe-making, but the main focus of their enterprise was on trading in commodities, acting as the link between the African producer and the (foreign) exporter of that commodity. In the period before the Second World War there were also quite a large number of Asians in clerical jobs for the colonial government; as carly as 1911, there were 1498 Indians in the employ of the government.[52]

Before 1945, very few Asian merchants had ventured into manufacturing, due to the constraints of capital and lack of credit facilities from European banks. There were, however, a few exceptions to this rule: the Premchand Brothers set up a factory to manufacture wattle extract and a cotton ginnery in the Thika municipality in the 1930s, having been prevented from establishing their factories in the 'white highlands'. Others were involved in small-scale grain-milling, sugar-refining, oil-refining and the manufacture of aluminium holloware. However, most Asians remained in the highly competitive sphere of retail trade. The colonial state also excluded them from exporting and importing directly until the 1940s through licensing regulations and they were compelled to buy and sell through the large foreign-owned merchant houses such as Smith Mackenzie. The competitiveness of such trade encouraged many of the larger Asian capitalists into manufacturing, even before the war. The pattern was for a merchant firm which had specialized in the import of one or two commodities such as cloth to move into the production of that commodity. The Thika Cloth Mills, for instance, were set up in the 1950s by the Nath Brothers, who were a prominent group of cloth traders.

---

52 ibid., pp. 435–6.

During the 1950s, the rise in consumer demand gave great impetus to industrialization and during this time restrictions on Asian enterprise were gradually lifted. Despite this change a few isolated incidents confirmed settler supremacy in the 1950s. For instance, when an Asian firm took over a match factory from Europeans in the late 1950s, the settler residents objected, and the firm was compelled to relocate its factory in Mombasa. During the same period another Asian industrial firm tried to extend the capacity of a subsidiary grain-milling operation, but they were refused permission to do so by the Ministry of Agriculture acting under pressure from the settler-dominated KFA.[53] These cases were indeed exceptional for this time when there was a generally more liberal official attitude towards the expansion of Asian-owned enterprises in the industrial sector.

ASIAN INDUSTRIAL DEVELOPMENT AFTER 1945

It is clear that the increased level of accumulation of merchant capital by 1945 and the expansion of markets for manufactured goods were to stimulate the move of the larger Asian merchant capitalists into industrial production. The problem of credit was to be overcome after the war and the new Banks of India and Baroda (set up in 1945) became most important in the financing of Asian industrial expansion.

The correlation between the institution of a protective tariff and the establishment of an industrial project, noted by Eglin, applied to both local Asian and foreign firms in the 1950s. Table 26 illustrates this point with regard to Asian enterprises. The structure of Asian industrial enterprises was similar to that of foreign firms during this period and there emerged a highly *concentrated* group of individual concerns. Like the foreign firms, Asian firms were also to expand through takeover of existing usually settler enterprises as well as by establishing new plants. After the war, a number of Asian firms had moved into manufacturing a wide range of products, including wood products, household goods, baking and confectionery, engineering and building materials. However, by the mid-1960s a higher degree of concentration in Kenyan industry had emerged and the largest proportion of Asian manufacturing was in the hands of a few large conglomerates.

The large-scale Asian industrial groups used takeovers in the 1950s and 1960s to consolidate their hold over particular branches of production, a tactic used by most capitalist enterprises at a certain stage of concentration. One of the most important industrial groups to emerge in the 1950s was that of the *Chandaria* family. By the 1970s this group owned fourteen industrial concerns in Kenya with investments ranging from wire to stationery manufacturing. Before the Second World War this family had been involved with importing and exporting com-

---

53 Information from an interview with a company director.

TABLE 26   *Protective Duties for Kenyan Industries*

Product	Company	Year Began Production	Duty Imposed	Year	Previous Duty
Pasta	House of Manji	1958	30%	1958	free
Matches	East African Match Company	1958	$\frac{8}{25}$ per gross box	1958	$\frac{3}{30}$ per gross box
Pressure Stoves	Kenya Aluminium Works	1958	22%	1958	free
Cotton Wool	African Cotton Industries	1961	25%	1963	free
Aluminium Sheets	Mabati Ltd	1961	25%	1961	free
Tomato Puree	Kabazi Canners	1958	30%	1960	free
Galvanized, Corrugated, Plain Metal Sheets	Kenya Aluminium Works	1963	25%	1964	12½%

Source: Kenya customs tariff schedules, in Eglin, op. cit., p. 14.

modities. In the 1950s they started moving into industry by taking over existing companies. The Kenya Aluminium Works, an aluminium holloware factory which had been owned by another Indian group since 1929, was taken over by the Chandaria family in 1954. This company was to act as a holding company for their further acquisitions and investments in industrial enterprises. A subsidiary of this firm, Kaluworks, established Kenya's first steel-rolling mills in 1963. This firm continued to monopolize production until foreign firms were to erect competing plants in the late 1960s. In a similar fashion, the group bought out the East African Match Factory in the late 1950s from its European owners. The Chandarias bought a 50 per cent share in this company in 1960 which they later increased to 75 per cent with the Khimasia family holding the remaining 25 per cent.

Using the Kenya Aluminium Works as their base, the Chandarias began to invest in new plant. In 1958 they set up a new factory to manufacture nails, East African Wire Industries Ltd, which, along with the purchase of Kaluworks, served to give the group a monopoly in this field of production.[54] The Chandaria 'empire' expanded further in the 1960s and its industrial concerns were served by a large, well-organized marketing network. By the 1970s, the firms were directed by one managing company, Comcraft Services, registered in Bermuda,

54 This information was derived from the files of these firms in the annual returns of the Registrar General.

which functioned as a managing agency, providing technical services for other local industries as well as its own.

The *Khimasia* family made similar moves after the war from trading into import-substituting industrial concerns. In the 1930s and 1940s they had traded in imported foodstuffs and cloth and in 1958 they established a factory to manufacture fruit squashes, mineral waters, jams and jellies, the products of which were marketed by the existing organization. Their direct move into production from trade was evident also when they established the Thika Cloth Mills (Nath Brothers) in 1959 to manufacture cotton and silk linings for the East African market. In 1967, the group consolidated its interests in food production by taking over Gibson & Company, a European-owned firm which controlled Kabazi Canners who manufactured a wide variety of canned fruits, vegetables and concentrates. This hold over one of the largest food-processing concerns in Kenya did not remain impervious to international capital. In 1970 Brooke Bond Liebig, in one of its attempts to diversify from tea production, bought a 30 per cent shareholding in Kabazi Canners, thereby controlling the marketing of its products in Kenya. Out of a total of all the companies owned by the Khimasias, six are industrial concerns and the rest are marketing and wholesaling agencies.[55]

Probably the largest Asian industrial complex in East Africa as a whole (during the 1960s) was that of the *Madvhani*. Unlike the Asian groups which had always been based in Kenya, this group used agricultural production and the processing of related products as the basis of its accumulation.[56] The empire of the Madvhanis in Uganda was based on sugar cultivation, processing, cotton ginneries and oil mills, all of which were established from 1939 onwards. From the profits generated by the sugar mills, the group diversified into steel-rolling mills, textile manufacture and glass production by the 1960s. The profits accruing from the highly competitive import trade were not likely to expand further, so that investment in production became the logical step. Exactly the same mechanism was in operation when they expanded into manufacturing in Kenya during the 1960s

From 1955 onwards, Madvhani-manufactured products had been sold in Kenya through their subsidiary firm, Muljibhai Madvhani Ltd, which had trading branches in Nairobi, Mombasa and Kisumu. The Madvhani group took the opportunity to extend their manufacturing units into Kenya during the 1960s in order to preserve their markets

---

55 Interview and annual returns, ibid.

56 The Ugandan Indians were not restricted in land ownership as the Kenyan Indians had been. The administration in Uganda was generally in favour of processing facilities being set up for the primary products of the country such as cotton ginneries and oil-refining plants. Despite the fact that the administration favoured metropolitan firms over Indian firms, large groups of Asian capital did move into primary processing even before the Second World War.

for industrial products. This expansion was carried out by means of taking over existing firms. An agreement was reached between the company and the Kenya government that the latter would grant first option to the Madvhani group for the purchase of industrial firms which had been declared bankrupt in Kenya.

Kenya Glassworks, for instance, was taken over by the Madvhanis in 1965 (from the Asians who set up the company in 1947) in order to expand their Kenyan market for glass products. In 1974 this company was estimated to control 70 per cent of the Kenyan market for glass bottles. The Kenya Rayon Mills were taken over by the Madvhanis in 1966 from the European owners who had declared the company bankrupt, and this firm corresponded with their Ugandan textile interests. Similarly, the Associated Sugar Company in Kenya was formed in 1965 to take over the assets of the former Kenya Sugar Company, which was in the hands of the receiver. This enterprise also fitted in with their large sugar-processing complex in Uganda. In 1966 the Madvhani group were able to buy a majority shareholding (60 per cent) in Kenya Towel Manufacturers, who were indebted to the Kenya Rayon Mills, and thus the group were able to further extend their interests in textile production in Kenya.[57]

Emco Steel Works, a steel-processing plant, was the only new investment which the group made in Kenya during the 1960s. The demand for steel in East Africa at the time was high and the Madvhanis were faced with the option of either expanding their steel-tube manufacturing plant in Uganda or establishing a new factory. There was clearly an advantage in setting up a plant in Kenya with import protection and by 1968 they had established a steel plant at Ruaraka, about 10 miles from Nairobi. This plant supplies the local market with steel bars, sheets and tubes, all of which are manufactured from local steel scrap. This firm, in 1974, supplied 70 per cent of the steel requirements of Kenya. The chief marketing company for the manufactured goods of the Madvhani group in Kenya is Kemulco Ltd, which is significant in that it represents a high-level alliance between the Asian industrialists and the indigenous bourgeoisie, thus providing an umbrella of political protection for the group's investments in Kenya.[58] Despite this rapid expansion in Kenya in the 1960s, the Madvhani group of companies (particularly after the Asian expulsion from Uganda in 1972) remained static and their chief aim in the 1970s was gradually to divest themselves of their Kenyan investments and transfer their capital out of the country. Indeed, the Chandaria group have already transferred their Kenyan firms to foreign-based holding

---

57 This information on the Madvhani group was obtained from an interview with the former company secretary of the firm in Uganda in June 1975 and from the annual returns of the Companies Registry.

58 The Kenyan partners were the chairman of Lonrho and his mother (from the annual company returns at the Registrar General's Dept).

companies in tax-haven areas such as the Channel Islands and Bermuda.

The investment of these large industrial groups in Kenya has been substantial and the value of the Madvhanis' fixed assets in Kenya and Uganda in 1972 was estimated at around £40 million (East African). I would estimate the asset value of the Chandaria empire in Kenya to be somewhere in the region of £15–20 million.[59]

Despite the potential recognized by writers such as Colin Leys of Asian industrialists becoming an 'industrial bourgeoisie' of a classic type, it is clear that the expansion of Asian capital in Kenya is strictly limited by *political* considerations. The reasons for the failure of this group to fulfil its potential as a domestic industrial class are to be located in the historical conjuncture of Asian capital in colonial Kenya. Asians in Kenya were never able to exercise political power, under either the colonial or post-colonial régimes, which would have sustained their accumulation. Their relative isolation gave rise to the emergence of family-business groupings which were reluctant to bring in outside capital and management. Many Asians, therefore, remained at the merchant level. These contradictions culminated in the gradual withdrawal of trading licences from non-citizen Asians from 1967 onwards in Kenya.

The more powerful sections of the Asian industrial class, however, have been able to deal with these problems by 'internationalizing' their operations and making political alliances at the local level. The largest industrial groups have been able to compensate for the threat posed by the 'economic nationalism' of the 1970s and have transferred their headquarters outside Kenya while remaining in the capacity of financiers and managing agents.

FOREIGN CAPITAL IN INDUSTRY

Although it is not possible to calculate exactly the amount of foreign and local investment in industry, it is clear that after 1945 there was a rapid inflow of foreign capital into both estates and industrial sectors. Ord has estimated that in 1958 more than one-third of privately owned assets in Kenya (outside African areas) was owned by non-residents.[60] This was largely made up of investments from multinational corporations. By the mid-1950s, foreign firms were manufacturing a wide variety of industrial products including shoes and leather, cement, paints, metal containers, vehicle parts, fruit, soft drinks, bicycle tyres and tobacco. Table 27 lists some of the major foreign investments in manufacturing from the 1940s onwards.

59 For further details on the Chandaria group, see R. Murray, 'The Chandarias: the development of a Kenyan multinational', in R. Kaplinksy (ed.), *Readings on the Multinational Corporation in Kenya*, OUP, East Africa, 1978.

60 Ord, op. cit., p. 9.

TABLE 27 *Major Foreign Investments 1945–63*

Company		Date Product	Owned by
Beverages and Food Products			
np	Schweppes (EA) Ltd	1954 soda drinks	Allsops & Schweppes (UK)
ext	Allsops East Africa	1954 beer	Allsops (UK)
np	Pepsi Cola	1953 soda drinks	Pepsi Cola (USA)
np	Fitzgerald Baynes	1953 soda drinks	Canada Dry (UK)
np	7-Up Bottling Co.	1954 soda drinks	7-Up Company (USA)
np	Kenya Canners	1950 canned fruits and vegetables	(a) Pickering & West (UK) (b) Delmonte (USA)
to	Associated Packers	1956 fruit squashes, puddings, juices, jellies	Mitchell Cotts (UK)
to	ABC Foods	1954 animal feeds	Baumann & Co. and Steel Bros (UK)
to	Lyons Maid	1959 ice cream	Lyons (UK)
np	Coca Cola Mid Africa	1956 soft soda drinks	Coca Cola (USA)
np	EA Tobacco	1954 Manuf. tobacco and cigarettes	British American Tobacco (BAT) (UK)
to	Kenya Orchards	1948 canned fruit and vegetables	Marshalls Ltd (UK)
ext	EA Breweries	1952 beer	Ind Coope (UK)
Non-Food Manufacturing			
np	Carbacid Manuf. Co.	1954 carbon dioxide	Carbacid (USA)
np	Robbialac Paints	1956 paints and varnishes	Robbialac (UK)
np	Leyland Paints EA	1954 paints and varnishes	Baumann & Co. and Leyland Paints (UK)
np	Cassmann Brown	1953 roofing felts	Cassmann (UK)
np	Sadolins Paints	1959 paints and varnishes	Sadolins
np	Jensen & Nicholson	1959 paints and varnishes	Jensen & Nicholson (Denmark)
np	East African Oxygen	1949 oxygen	British Oxygen (UK)
np	Bamburi Portland Cement	1953 cement	Amalgamated Roadstone Corp. (UK) Cementia Holdings AG
ext	EA Portland Cement	1956 cement	Assoc. Portland Cement
np	Avon Tyre Remoulding Co.	1958 bicycle inner tubes	Avon Tyres (UK)
ext	EA Bata Shoe Co.	1940 bicycle inner tubes 1958 leather and shoes	Bata Shoe Co. (Canada)

TABLE 27 *Cont.*

Company	Date	Product	Owned by
np E. African Stationery Manufacturers	1949	stationery	Dickinson Co. (UK)
np Metal Box EA	1948	metal containers	Metal Box (UK)
np Crown Cork Co. EA	1948	seals	Crown Seals (UK)
np Van Leer Containers EA	1952	steel drums, pails	Van Leer Containers (Holland)
np Shell Chemical	1952	industrial chemicals	Shell-BP (UK)
np Sterling Winthrop	1953	chemicals	Sterling Winthrop (USA)
np Finlay Industries Ltd	1952	brushes, wooden articles	James Finlay (Scotland, UK)
np E. African Oil Refinery	1959	refining of crude oil	Shell-BP (UK)
np Walpamur EA Ltd	1961	paints and varnishes	Walpamur (UK)

Key
ext extension of existing plant
to   takeover of existing firm
np   formation of new plant

This investment in industry took a concentrated form and each branch of production was dominated by one or several firms. In this sense the pattern can be characterized as oligopolistic rather than monopolistic. In only a few cases where a firm entered the market early, such as in the case of the British American Tobacco Company (BAT), was it able to establish a monopoly over production and distribution in all three East African countries. BAT had supplied the East African market with cigarettes and tobacco from its Ugandan factory since the 1930s. In Kenya it established a tobacco manufacturing plant in 1954 after obtaining an agreement with the government that it would be the sole purchaser of smallholder tobacco. Another example of a monopoly over internal sales at this time was the case of Brooke Bond. Other instances of firms with a dominant position in a single branch of production after independence were Firestone Tyres, British Oxygen, Lyons Maid and Gilbeys.[61]

The more usual form of foreign investment was the 'clustering' of two or more foreign firms in the same branch as an act of retaliation to defend particular slices of the market. Virtually all the new investments in industry after the war were made by firms which already had distribution agencies in the colony. Often, after the first firm invested

---

61 Eglin, op. cit., p. 7.

TABLE 28 *Tariff Protection to Foreign-Based Industrial Firms 1958–62*

Product	Company	Year Began Production	Duty Imposed	Year	Previous Duty
Industrial Ink	Coates Bros	1960	22%	1958	11%
Bicycle Inner Tubes	Bata Shoes	1958	90 cents per lb	1958	55 cents per lb
	Avon Tyre Remoulding Co.	1958	90 cents per lb	1958	55 cents per lb
Paints	Sadolins	1959	25%	1961	11%
	Leyland Paint Co.	1958	$33\frac{1}{3}$%	1963	11%
	East African Paints	1960	$33\frac{1}{3}$%		
	Walpamur	1961	$33\frac{1}{3}$%		
Vehicle Tyres	Michelin (Tanzania)	1962	S. $\frac{1}{25}$ per lb	1968	90 cents per lb
	G1 Tyre (Tanzania)	1969	S. $\frac{1}{50}$ per lb	1968	90 cents per lb
	Firestone	1969	S. $\frac{1}{50}$ per lb	1968	90 cents per lb

Source: Kenya customs tariff schedules, *Kenya Directory of Industries 1974*, in Eglin, op. cit., p. 6.

in a product, other importers would within a few years begin manufacturing under the same protective tariff as a means of defending their market share. For instance, the Leyland Paint Company of the UK established the first import-substituting enterprise in 1954 and they were followed within the next eight years first by Jensen & Nicholson and then by Sadolins and Walpamur in 1960. This type of 'overinvestment' has the long-term effect of creating a capacity largely in excess of the existing market. However, it is evident that these foreign investments were made with a view to capturing the whole East African market. During the late 1950s and early 1960s a series of subsidiary plants was set up by British industrial firms with investments in Kenya: these included Tanganyika Packers, the Metal Box Company (T), Dar Bottlers Company, BAT (T) Ltd, Business Machines (T) Ltd and Car and General Retreading Factory.[62] In the mid-1950s there was serious overproduction of cement from three factories, one in Uganda and two in Kenya. The British Associated Portland Cement Company was, by the mid-1960s, to unify the Kenyan plants under its parentage as well as establish a subsidiary in Tanzania and thereby capturing the whole East African cement market.

The duplication of industrial plants which began in the 1950s, reflects a type of competition between capitalist enterprises on an international level. In order to maintain their share of the market, large corporations are prepared to duplicate a product and withstand losses for several years. In some cases these firms reach agreements with each other to fix prices and determine market shares. For instance, in the case of paint in the 1950s, the four major producers formed a cartel and agreed to fix prices.

Another example where a conglomeration of foreign firms reached an agreement to divide up the market was in the case of oil. In 1958 an oil refinery was constructed to process imported crude and supply the entire oil demand of East Africa. Although BP–Shell constructed the refinery, the other oil companies Caltex, Esso and Shell took a share in the equity of the refinery. The companies collectively controlled prices and shares in the local market.[63] Metal Box and Van Leer Containers also divided up the market for metal containers from 1949 when they both established production plants in Kenya. Hence the pattern of import-substituting industrialization which began after 1945 in Kenya reflected a high degree of concentration among a few large firms.

This applies to both local and foreign enterprises in different branches of production. The cases of one firm establishing a monopoly

---

62 Honey, op. cit., p. 66.

63 Information from the file on the oil industry in the *EAS* Newspaper Cuttings Library, Nairobi.

For further details of postwar industrial investments, see N. Swainson, 'Foreign Corporations and Economic Growth in Kenya', PhD thesis, University of London, 1977, ch. 3, pt V.

over a branch were rare and it was more usual that two or more firms would dominate production. Due to the competitive conditions surrounding investment in manufacturing, by the 1960s foreign enterprises were often suffering from a marked overcapacity. This was to be only partly absorbed by the expanding markets for capitalist commodities during the 1960s.

The type of capitalist expansion which took place in Kenya after the Second World War was determined by a fusion of internal and external forces. On the one hand, substantial surpluses had been accumulated during the colonial period from agriculture, and most of the basic capital-intensive investment in infrastucture had been made. On the international level, capitalism was in the throes of a worldwide phase of expansion. The particular conjucture of postwar British capitalism was the threat of competition with the United States in the world market. Under these conditions the main motive force behind British investment in colonial industries was to defend their markets behind the tariff wall.[64] It is clear, for instance, that the institution of a protective tariff in the case of both local and foreign-owned industry was a major reason behind the decision to invest. It is no accident, therefore, that the metropolitan government after 1945 encouraged the extensive use of state support to promote investment in colonial territories such as Kenya.

This period is the watershed of capitalism in Kenya and it is characterized by the widespread subjection of labour to capital and the generalization of commodity relations.

---

64 It is not surprising that most of the foreign firms investing in Kenya between 1945 and 1963 were British.

CHAPTER 4

International Capital: Three Case Studies

The following three case studies illustrate different facets of Kenya's postwar corporate expansion. Each is concerned to illustrate the relationship between capital and the state in a new period of world capitalism marked by the *concentration* of capital.

East African Industries was an example of an import-substitution enterprise that was actually established by the government during the war. It was subsequently injected with capital and expertise by the CDC, a metropolitan-based finance agency and then hived off to Unilever in 1953. After the Second World War, the building boom in Kenya Colony stimulated a large demand for cement. Commercial firms were prepared to invest in large-scale cement production because markets had expanded and the state was prepared to provide protection and infrastructure for such an industry.

As most of Kenya's surplus was derived from agricultural production, it is not surprising that fruit-canning emerged after 1960 as one of the major industries. Once again, the colonial state in the 1950s played a central role in guaranteeing the viability of smallholder pineapple production. This industry required a very high level of state support, because of government investment in smallholder pineapple cultivation and the vulnerable state of world markets for the commodity. The study shows how the logic of large-scale capitalist production is followed through in the 1960s when the post-colonial state supported the establishment of Delmonte's virtual monopoly over conditions of pineapple production in Kenya.

By the 1960s each of these industries was dominated by one major world producer of the respective product and the studies illustrate the process by which Kenyan production comes to be linked with the world market. The focus in each is the mediating role of the state in this process.

The Colonial Development Corporation and East African Industries

The main arm of metropolitan policy in supporting development in the colonies was the *Colonial Development Corporation* (CDC). Where the size of markets and low productivity did not attract commercial investors, the metropolitan state provided two financial organizations to 'subsidize' areas of production for British industrial capital until these became profitable. In some cases, such as the groundnut scheme, the state finance organization, the *Overseas Food Corporation*, was actually formed to undertake an investment which had been instigated by industrial capital. The Unilever Company wanted to undertake a groundnut scheme in Tanganyika to supply their oil extraction plants in the West, but they did not wish to undertake the heavy capital investment necessary to establish large-scale growing areas in an undeveloped part of Africa. They managed to put pressure on the British government to finance the project directly with the United Africa Corporation as the managing agent. The government was favourable to these direct interventions to support industrial projects as there was a serious fats shortage in Britain at the time. The Overseas Food Corporation was set up by the *Overseas Resources Development Bill* of November 1947 with the main purpose of taking over the groundnut scheme from the managing agency of the UAC. This Bill created two bodies, the CDC with capital of £50 000 000 and the OFC with capital of £50 000 000. The groundnut scheme it was estimated would cost the government £25 000 000 and the balance was to be used to support other food-growing projects in the colonial territories.[1] Thus the initiative behind the fateful groundnut scheme came from industrial capital – in this case Unilever Ltd.[2]

The establishment of the CDC as a finance agency in 1947 was also an official response to the postwar need to increase production in Britain's colonial territories. It has been observed before that the 'official' rationale behind the establishment of the CDC was to increase productivity in order to reduce dollar deficits of the United Kingdom and its colonial territories.[3] This was clearly expressed in a speech given by Lord Trefgarne, the chairman of the CDC, to an audience of Liverpool businessmen in June 1948.

---

1 Wood, op. cit., pp. 26–31.

2 The groundnut scheme was unsuccessful in Tanganyika for a variety of reasons. One of the main problems arose from the use of lend-lease equipment obtained from American arms dumps after the war; most of the equipment was not suitable and few machines had spare parts. The sheer size of the project meant that the OFC board was not able to control the whole scheme. The capital costs of the operation became enormous and after several unsuccessful harvests the whole scheme was abandoned by 1954, having cost the British tax payers nearly £25 million.

3 CDC annual report for 1948.

expressed in approximate figures as the annual dollar deficit of the UK, you can take it as £500 million. As shown coldly in the accounts that represented the measure of the struggle of Britain and the outstretched generosity of the USA, both areas eager to redress the balance into which two wars have thrown their trade. This is the world background against which the productivity of the colonial territories must be viewed.[4]

Lord Trefgarne went on to emphasize that the immediate need of the United States was for raw materials rather than manufactured goods.

increasing the production of food in the area as a whole and if possible also the production of simple manufactured exports to America . . . many British Colonies have large dollar deficits . . . therefore it is sound policy to aim at greatly increased dollar exports of colonial products.[5]

In the words of the CDC report for 1948, this was to be done by

increasing the production of food in the area as a whole and if possible also the production of simple manufactured commodities. If this is achieved by developing new resources using labour which is, at present underemployed and capital equipment which is at present inadequate, a real increase in productivity will result.

The Corporation (like the OFC) had been created to implement these policies of the British government, but it was in structure designed to be less trammelled than either a central government department or a colonial administration. This form of corporation was to operate on semi-commercial criteria in order to promote investments in colonial production primarily in the area of agriculture and also industry. But the scope of the CDC was wide and covered 'any development project which is in the interests of the colony concerned and which has the prospect of being sufficiently remunerative to cover the cost incurred upon it'.[6] This last qualification distinguished the work of the two corporations, the CDC and OFC, from schemes undertaken under the Colonial Development and Welfare Act, for these two were to act *directly* in the role of finance capital to support productive capital. The conception behind the operations of the CDC was that projects should be judged by their commercial viability, although it was expected that some undertakings would make substantial yields which would counterbalance losses in other areas. The CDC accordingly invested directly in the share capital of enterprises, and provided loan capital for commercial undertakings and management

4 Lord Trefgarne's speech to Liverpool businessmen, 22 June 1948.
5 ibid.
6 CDC report.

contract facilities for some projects. Many colonial administrations encouraged private industrial capital by waiving import duties on development goods and supplies such as fuel for agricultural machinery and further pushed for the standardization of tax relief in each territory for projects relating to 'development'. The CDC considered that allowances for development expenses should be granted to potential investors and in particular cases the Corporation did succeed in reaching agreements with the colonial governments on matters concerning rents, royalties and the waiving of import duties on development goods.

By December 1949, there was a total of twenty-eight CDC undertakings in operation throughout the British colonies, with an aggregate capital of £14 187 000. Of these projects, one-third were in agriculture and the remainder in other activity divisions such as engineering, finance, factories and forestry. The actual form of the first twenty-eight CDC undertakings was mixed: seven subsidiary companies which were either wholly owned by the Corporation or in which they had a controlling interest; three investments where the CDC held a minority interest; three loans or debenture to commercial companies and one in which the Corporation acted as managing agent for the colonial administration.[7] This state financial agency, therefore, acted on a number of different levels in order to 'raise productivity' in the areas of both agriculture and secondary industry in the colonial territories. We will now turn to one particular CDC project in Kenya which was in fact the first industrial project the Corporation was to undertake. The case of East African Industries illustrates the role of international finance capital in laying the groundwork for the entry of industrial capital.

EAST AFRICAN INDUSTRIES

The Kenyan administration had, in 1942, sponsored the establishment of the *East African Industrial Management Board* to manufacture essential items, whose supply had been cut off during the war. These products included pottery, bricks, oils and miscellaneous chemicals. The plant was composed of various second-hand machines modified by engineering works in Kenya and the level of technology was rather low.

The government was pledged to dispose of its interests in the enterprise after the war and after 1945 some units of the plant were sold privately. However, there remained the main body of the factory comprising the pottery, the refractory plant, the hydrogenation plant, the sulphuric acid and the general chemicals plant. As this was the type of industrial activity the CDC was pledged to assist, the opportunity was not lost, and in 1949, *East African Industries* was formally consti-

---

7 ibid.

tuted and the CDC agreed to participate with the Kenyan administration in the operation. The Corporation subscribed £500 000 of the £750 000 shares of EAI, with the government holding the balance.[8] The agreement reached between EAI Ltd and the Corporation in December 1950 provided that the CDC should act as consultant and adviser to the company on management, financial control, factory administration and on all matters concerning the manufacture and sales of EAI products. For these management services the company was to pay the Corporation a fee calculated at a rate of 5 per cent of net profits in each financial year.[9]

From the outset there was a strong demand for EAI products due to the general shortage of manufactured goods during and after the war. However, the plant faced severe production difficulties due to under-capitalization and quite backward techniques of production. The most uneconomic unit of the factory was always the chemicals and acids plant which had to import virtually all of its components. The refractories and the pottery plant both relied largely on local materials, but the hydrogenation plant utilized cotton-seed oil from Uganda and copra oil from Tanganyika. Copra oil and cotton-seed oil were used in the preparation of Kimbo cooking fat, ghee and liquid oil from the earliest days of EAI's production and the regular supply, particularly of cotton-seed oil from Uganda, at a 'reasonable' price was a consistent problem.[10] In 1949, the company based their plans for an extension of the hydrogenation plant's capacity, on the availability of groundnuts from the Overseas Food Corporation project in Tanganyika, as well as cotton seed from Uganda. The former source of supply was never forthcoming in any quantity due to the failure of the groundnut-growing project by 1955, which meant that the EAI hydrogenation plant was largely reliant on Ugandan cotton seed oil.[11]

By 1950, the EAI plant was faced by severe production problems. This state of affairs was expressed by the general manager of EAI in 1949: 'the major effect of the commodity shortage is the necessity to carry larger stocks of imported material, thus tying up working capital. The loan capital obtained from the CDC may prove inadequate.'[12] This rising tide of production difficulties stemmed from both the

---

8 ibid.

9 Agreement between EAI and CDC, *KNA*, 7 December 1950. In addition to this fee, the Corporation was to act as the company's purchasing agent in Britain and for these services the CDC received further commission at the rate of 2½ per cent on the f.o.b. value of purchases after deducting all discounts and allowances, providing that the value of such items exceeded £10 000 on any one contract.

10 East African Industries, annual reports, (*KNA*) 1949–52. EAI later tried to encourage the establishment of a sunflower-seed cultivation scheme which would secure a local supply of oil for the hydrogenation plant, but the scheme was due to come into effect by the late 1970s.

11 The allocation of Ugandan cotton-seed oil to EAI in Kenya in 1952 was 3100 tons.

12 Papers prepared for an EAI board meeting in March 1952 (*KNA*, MCI).

TABLE 29   *EAI Sales (£)*

	November 1951	March 1952
Hydrogenation	51 346	16 342
Acid Plant	2 850	1 494

Source: Memo from the secretary of EAI to the directors and chairman, 21 April 1952.

difficulties in obtaining the imported inputs for the units that required them and also the limited amount of capital for expansion of fixed assets. A paper presented to an EAI board meeting in 1951 drew attention to some of the main difficulties faced by this new industry. First, a complaint was raised that an improvement in the quality of EAI products was desperately needed (as none of the products met international quality-control standards) and this would necessitate the immediate provision of additional equipment. Also the company's financial affairs were reported to be in chaos and no department in the EAI complex other than the hydrogenation plant had made sufficient profit in the previous two years to cover general overheads. Furthermore, with the exception of acid, these units were unable to supply the East African market, and all their products were substandard.

> without the assurance of protection against dumping there is no assured future for these industries in East Africa . . . we must either re-plan and re-equip all these projects with new plant and personnel, or else shut them down as quickly as possible.[13]

The EAI plant was plainly uncompetitive, and imported caustic soda was apparently available in East Africa for under £20 per ton, while EAI costs were around £42 per ton.

Nevertheless, the board considered that, given the previous capital inputs, it was not justified to abandon the plant altogether. The prognostications concerning the efficiency of EAI were reflected in their poor sales figures, shown in Table 29. The CDC, as EAI's managing agent, considered that bad organization was the root of the problems facing the plant. A CDC report on the fortunes of the project stressed: 'the problems confronting the company in realizing surplus stocks of material, stores and equipment cannot be over-estimated. Stocks of some materials represent several years' requirements.'[14]

The government was also thoroughly dissatisfied about the declining prospects of EAI and could hardly wait for a suitable opportunity to

---

13 EAI board report, op. cit.
14 Letter from the Secretary for Commerce and Industry (SCI) to the Member for Commerce and Industry, *KNA*, MCI, 1952.

offload the enterprise, but it is significant that most branches of government in the colony were against government involvement in a scheme that might compete with private enterprise. As a letter from the Secretary for Commerce and Industry to the Member for Commerce and Industry pointed out:

> You will recollect that there has always been an objection in commercial circles to the government competing with private enterprise, and that was one of the reasons why it decided to dispose of the interests of the old East African Industrial Management Board.[15]

During 1950, the Ministry of Commerce and Industry, EAI and the CDC held meetings to consider the future of the plant. The Kenya government was strongly in favour of disposing of its interest in EAI, as it did not wish to encourage fully state-owned enterprises. The MCI stressed that the EA Management Board plants, 'having been brought to a successful pilot stage of production should be expanded on a commercial basis'.[16] By 1951, therefore, the government had decided that it would provide no further assistance to the industry, as, in the words of SCI, 'EAI's approach to commercial competition seems to be somewhat pathetic'.[17]

THE ENTRY OF INTERNATIONAL CAPITAL

The CDC, therefore, was left with full responsibility for its 'pilot' scheme and the Corporation was required to find some method of salvaging this uneconomic plant. During 1952, the CDC had directed a policy of retrenchment and rationalization for EAI, but the Corporation itself did not have either the resources or the technical expertise to transform the plant and perpetuate its operations. It was at this point that the role of the CDC as a finance capital serving British industry was made explicit, and the Corporation decided to hive off the plant with all its capital equipment to a British firm. The CDC projects all encouraged the import of British capital goods at a time when these industries were suffering from inadequate capacity after the war. The EAI plant was to be no exception to this rule, for any extension or modification to the factory would involve not only the expertise of a particular firm but also the import of new machinery from British industrial suppliers.

The CDC invited the *Unilever Company* of the UK, with its long-established interests in the fats industry, to take over the ownership

---

15 Minute to the Member for Commerce and Industry (MCI) from Secretary for Commerce and Industry (SCI) *KNA*, MCI, 23 August 1950.

16 ibid.

17 Letter from SCI to MCI concerning government participation in EAI, *KNA*, MCI, 30 November 1950.

and management of the ailing EAI plant. The choice of a British firm to take over EAI was not mere coincidence. It will be recalled that the sister corporation set up in 1948 with the CDC was the Overseas Food Corporation (OFC), which had been primarily designed to administer the groundnut scheme in Tanganyika. The initiative for Unilever's participation in EAI in Kenya actually came from the CDC itself, but Unilever's interest in the Tanganyikan groundnut scheme no doubt strongly influenced the decision. By 1953 it was not yet clear whether the groundnut-cultivation scheme in the neighbouring territory would succeed. Indeed, the Unilever Company was clearly interested in investing in fats production in East Africa, as its original proposals for a groundnut scheme had been strongly influenced by its desire to diversify growing areas from West Africa.

Therefore, by the end of 1953, an agreement between the CDC and the Unilever Company had been concluded, with the international firm taking a 50 per cent equity interest, as well as taking the management responsibilities. Thus, by 1954 the whole ownership structure had been altered, leaving Unilever with 50 per cent, the CDC with 33½ per cent and the Kenya government with a 16 per cent interest through the Industrial Management Corporation. Despite their lowered equity interest in EAI, the CDC was still considerably committed to the project through the provision of loan capital, which in 1954 amounted to £35 000.

In 1954, the new management of EAI immediately modified the existing plant to conform with Unilever production methods. New machinery was installed to manufacture Unilever brands of margarine and cooking fats, which were aimed at low-income markets. Given that the oil refinery existed, the next stage was to assemble new plant in order to begin manufacturing soap and glycerine. As part of their process of 'rationalization', the new management during 1955 disposed of all those production units which were not directly connected with Unilever's interests. For instance, the insecticides and refractory businesses were sold in early 1956. EAI, under the control of Unilever, slowly recovered with the infusion of capital and expertise and the improvement was soon reflected in the firm's balance sheets. Whereas in 1950, the company made a post-tax loss of £1100, in the first year of Unilever management it made an after-tax profit of £35 000 and had a turnover of £328 000.

Meanwhile, the CDC continued to support the project through the provision of long-term loans. Under the agreement of 1953, the CDC had undertaken to lend £100 000, repayable on six months notice after ten years or thereafter. By the end of 1955, all this had been taken up and was used to finance current assets.[18] The soap project was financed by the capitalization of a bonus issue of shares, amounting to

---

18 Memo on borrowing powers of EAI, from EAI to MCI, *KNA*, MCI, May 1955.

£135 000, and further loans were granted by the CDC, the Industrial Development Bank and the Unilever parent company. In 1957, the soap plant began production of Unilever's brand products such as Sunlight, Lux toilet soap and Lifebuoy toilet soap, with the aim of covering the entire spectrum of Kenya's soap demands.

COMPETITION

When Unilever acquired its holding in EAI in 1953, the Kenya government offered the company an inducement that it would be able to buy its oil requirements at a price 'no less favourable than other users'.[19] This assurance indicated that the Kenya government would endeavour to protect the industry from the competition of Asian-owned oil mills in Uganda.[20] A memo to the Ministry of Commerce and Industry from EAI in 1949 suggested the purchase of new equipment in order to render the factory more competitive in relation to the other East African oil manufacturers:

> regarding the purchase of the new plant, our own plant is a four ton capacity and the other one has a ten ton capacity . . . we shall not be able to compete as regards costs on the local market, which is of a limited size, and unless we can sell entirely for exports we should shut down.[21]

In 1953, Unilever did install a new plant, although its production costs were still in excess of the Madvhani oil mills, due to the higher debt ratio of the Kenyan plant. Early in 1956, a question arose as to which of the two East African oil producers would secure a government contract to supply oils to the Kenyan prisons department. EAI pressured the Ministry of Commerce and Industry to support the Kenyan industry, and the latter pointed out, 'the terms must, of course, be competitive . . . but the wider implications of not patronizing our own industries would appear to merit the most serious consideration'.[22] It was ironic that according to the 'competitive' test of quality, the Madvhani firm won the tender.

A consistent state of competition existed between the Unilever plant in Kenya and the Madvhani plant in Uganda during the 1950s. In 1957, EAI's annual report stated that action was to be taken against Muljibhai Madvhani for an infringement of Unilever brand names (the Cow wrapper for instance was a copy of the Blue Band design). Clearly the Uganda firm was manufacturing products of similar quality for a

---

19 To K. Mackenzie, Treasury, from SCI (*KNA*, MCI). The retail price of EAI's soaps in the early 1950s was lower than that of imported products.

20 The largest oil mills in Uganda were those of the Madvhani group at Jinja.

21 Report on a visit made to Entebbe by officials of the Kenyan Ministry of Commerce and Industry to discuss the price of cotton seed oil for 1950, *KNA*, MCI.

22 Memo to the MCI from Asst MCI, 16 December 1957.

lower price. It was in order to compete for the lower-income market that EAI developed a brand of cheap-quality margarine in 1957. At this time the largest sales from EAI were of Kimbo and vegetable ghee (both cooking fats), for which cotton seed was used.

A further aspect of the competition between the Ugandan plant and EAI was the supply of *cotton seed*, which developed into a test case of Kenya's protectionist policy. The Ugandan firm had an advantage over EAI in that it could tender for cotton seed from the Uganda government at short notice, whereas the Kenyan firm was required to do so in advance. Despite pressure from the Kenyan administration, the Uganda government refused to allow EAI to have the same concessions as its local industry. The Ugandan company remained with an overall advantage over EAI until the early 1960s when that firm switched to imported palm oil instead of cotton seed as its basic raw material for the edible-oils plant.[23]

EAI by 1947 had diversified its production into a number of other areas such as toothpaste and fruit squashes in addition to soap and oils. The fats products still accounted for the largest proportion of the company's sales in Kenya, which were between 60 and 70 per cent in the mid-1970s. The remaining 30 to 40 per cent of its production was made up of soaps and detergents. EAI in 1976 controlled the largest share of the East African market for margarine, detergent and toilet soap, although in toothpaste it fell behind the American multinational, Colgate-Palmolive.[24]

Since the 1960s the CDC has gradually divested itself of its interest in East African Industries, which was not surprising as its chief aim in the 1950s was to foster infant industries and hand them over to private enterprise. As the post-colonial Kenyan government was anxious to maintain a share in large manufacturing industries, it bought the shares of the CDC. In 1977 the ICDC Investment Company increased its holding from 17½ per cent to 45 per cent, leaving Unilever with the remaining 55 per cent. There were rumours in 1977 that some Kenyan capitalists would take over EAI completely, and it is likely that this major consumer industry will be taken over in the future by either state or private investors.

The aim here has been to examine the role of one state financial agency, the CDC, in the context of its support for an important Kenyan industry. The CDC served from the postwar period to link up both agricultural and industrial production in the East African territories through a 'package deal' of management and loan finance. This case of direct investment in a pilot industrial project illustrated the role of state-finance capital: which was to help to build up enterprises that

---

23 This information was obtained from an interview with the chairman of EAI in June 1975. Palm oil is cheap and has a high fat content.
24 ibid.

TABLE 30   *Summary of EAI Balance Sheets 1950–73*

	Year of Formation	1950	1960	1965	1970	1973
Issued Capital	155 250	155 250	576 000	832 038	1 125 000	1 350 000
Net Assets	203 619	203 619	1 033 145	832 038	1 775 000	2 452 180
Net Profit	(1 100)	(1 100)	171 581	262 261	685 137	1 774 072
Profitability	(0·5)	(0·5)	1·6	3·1	3·8	7·2

Source: Annual reports of the Registrar General.

were not initially attractive to private enterprise. It is significant that the CDC were to hive off the EAI project to a prominent British fats manufacturer. State financial agencies such as the CDC were designed in the postwar era to provide the preconditions for the export of capital from the metropolis to the colonial territories.

Bamburi Portland Cement

This study will provide a more detailed example of the relationship between the local colonial state and foreign capital and how this effected the ultimate concentration within the industry. This study on the establishment of a cement industry in Kenya by foreign capital will focus primarily on the pressure exerted by the foreign company on the local Kenyan administration to grant concessions in order to cushion the 'infant industry' which would, in effect, serve to protect the potential cement industry from competition. The degree of success of these moves by the foreign company will be assessed in the light of the local state's extended capacity for infrastructure provision in the postwar period.

Cement is an example of a commodity where a measure of import substitution was necessary as far back as the 1930s, when the British product was experiencing severe competition with imported Japanese cement in East African markets. A partial processing of cement had begun in 1933 with the formation of the *East African Portland Cement Company* which set up a factory in Nairobi to grind cement from imported clinker. This company was formed as a partnership between the three main cement distributors in East Africa, Baumann, Smith Mackenzie and the African Mercantile Marine Company (20 per cent), with the two British cement suppliers, Tunnel Cement Holding (40 per cent) and Associated Portland Cement Company (another 40 per cent).[25] When the East African Portland Cement Company set up

25 Annual returns of the Registrar General.

the clinker mill in the 1930s and the British Standard Portland Cement Company in the 1950s established a full cement-processing plant at Bamburi, the chief aim had been to supply the local East African market, whereas by the 1970s local sales formed only half the Bamburi plant's cement production. We will trace the development of this industry which was primarily aimed at serving the local market and later expanded into an export industry.

Until the Second World War, in East Africa, the cement consumption of the area clearly did not justify the expenditure for a complete cement plant, despite the fact that the Kenya coast was ideally suited for such an enterprise with its abundant source of limestone.[26] In fact, the East African Portland Cement Company had clearly toyed with the idea of constructing a full cement-processing plant on the coast and just before the war this company had even purchased a stretch of land south of Mombasa island. The main obstacle, however, to any cement firm wanting to set up a large production plant in Kenya *before* the war was the consistent refusal of the government of the territory to protect the 'infant industry' against dumping of cement from abroad.

An *East African Standard* report in September 1951 on the cement industry in Kenya commented that:

> a considerable number of years ago other deposits on the coast, from which it was proposed to develop for cement manufacture were sterilised because the British government would not give the promoters of the scheme any protection against the dumping of Japanese cement.[27]

Clearly during the postwar era, large foreign-based industrial firms had a greater degree of success than before in extracting concessions from the local administration with regard to the protection of the colony's industries. The local administration was both able and willing to provide a more comprehensive range of infrastructure and protection for new industries. The success of the cement plant established at the coast in 1952 must be contrasted with the failure of the original cement-grinding company, East African Portland Cement Company, to obtain any reasonable concessions from the prewar administration.

The plant to manufacture cement which was set up at Bamburi between 1951 and 1952 was a partnership between two foreign-based firms, with the minority participation of a local capitalist, John Hughes. *Cementia Holdings AG* was an old-established firm of cement manufacturers which had lost many of its factories in Europe during the Second World War. In 1949, therefore, this firm wanted to establish production areas outside Europe and was considering three possible countries: Ireland, Australia and Kenya. The managing direc-

---

26 Limestone is the basic raw material for cement processing.
27 *EAS, KNA*, 6 September 1951.

tor of the Swiss firm estimated that production costs would be lower in Kenya than in the other areas.[28] Cementia then went into partnership with a British quarrying firm, the *Amalgamated Roadstone Corporation*, which also wanted to diversify its interests and production areas.

From the outset of the cement project, the postwar Kenyan administration gave strong encouragement to the company. Dr Mandl, the engineer who constructed the Bamburi cement plant, chose Kenya for several reasons: the unlimited supply of limestone from the coral coast, its proximity to the port and the good infrastructure facilities. The government were enthusiastic enough to provide the plant with further services. Beyond the obvious motive of encouraging secondary industries in the colony, the administration after 1945 had been under pressure from sections of the settler class concerning the high costs of cement.[29] The cement-grinding mill of the East African Portland Cement Company in Nairobi was insufficient to supply the rapidly expanding postwar demand for cement. Cement consumption had expanded from 25 000 tons in 1945 to 123 000 tons in 1950. Cement imports from Japan had been disrupted by the war, and supplies from British manufacturers were not enough to meet the booming demand. During 1951, in LEGCO there was a barrage of questions put to the Department of Trade and Supplies about the inadequate supply of cement in the colony and the high price of the imported commodity which, it was alleged, was adversely affecting the cost of living. A comment from the chairman of the Kenya Association of Building and Civil Engineering Contractors, in the *East African Standard*, presented another argument: 'Some of Kenya's leading firms of contractors may cease operation to save their dwindling capital if supplies of cement are not made available in the right places at the right time.'[30] Thus, in addition to a commitment towards encouraging industries in the colony after the war, the Kenyan administration had the further motive of wishing to placate various segments of the settler class, both the large contractors and the white petty bourgeoisie.

First, the company was granted generous terms for the lease of land on which to establish the plant.[31] Water and power were also extended to the plant from Mombasa by the administration. Royalties were to be on a sliding scale and affected the first 50 000 tons per annum that the company produced; after that time they were to be nominal. When the Bill was passed through LEGCO in 1951 (to authorize the manufac-

28 From the British Standard Portland Cement Company to Amalgamated Roadstone Corporation (UK), *KNA*, MCI, December 1951.

29 In October 1951, S. Cooke (Coast Representative in LECGO) put forward a motion questioning the government's handling of the 'cost of living' problem in the colony, *EAS*, 24 October 1951.

30 *EAS*, 16 July 1951.

31 From the Department of Lands to the Hon. Chief Secretary, Nairobi, *KNA*, MCI, April 1950.

ture of cement at Bamburi), the administration overrode the opposition from the Bamburi Residents' Association and adopted a law to
protect the company from being sued by the residents for 'noise or
other nuisance'. A report on the debate summarized the main issues:

> The government made available the area where the principal ingre-
> dients were known to exist, and gave encouragement to the project.
> There has been some opposition, not unnaturally from property
> owners in what is a beauty spot . . . from the Colony's point of view,
> the very substantial output will make an important contribution to
> the supplies of one of the basic commodities of all modern states,
> and reduce the dependence on imports in time of peace and in time
> of emergency.[32]

The most important concession to be extracted from the government by the company was the *anti-dumping legislation* which was
enacted as soon as the factory went into production and in October
1955 the legislation against dumping was passed. The administration
imposed a duty of 24s per 10 tons on imported cement, which, in
addition to the higher price of the imported equivalent after freight
charges, was sufficient to protect local cement.[33]

As part of the original agreement between the company and the
local administration, the government was to construct a branch railway
line connecting the plant (10 miles north of Mombasa) with the port-
head. This commitment was never honoured due to the diversion of
government funds to deal with the Mau Mau 'emergency' between
1952 and 1955. 'On the question of the bridge . . . in the next planning
period it is hoped to provide funds for this construction project. It will,
however, be appreciated that priorities must be dependent on the
position in regard to the Emergency and the funds available.'[34] The
funds for a railway were never forthcoming, and due to the heavy
expense involved in constructing a bridge and railway, the company
have relied on road transportation between the plant and harbour.

The Bamburi company further requested in 1955 that the government should give it assurances that no other cement industry would be
established in East Africa for the following ten years. This request was
put before the East African Industrial Council in 1955 (under the
Industrial Licensing Ordinances), but naturally enough the other two
territories rejected it, as they had no interest in a Kenyan monopoly of
the cement industry. Indeed, the Uganda Development Corporation,
in conjunction with a British cement firm, had reached an agreement in

---

32 'A cement industry in Kenya', *EAS*, 6 September 1951.
33 From Director of Trade and Supplies to British Standard Portland Cement, *KNA*,
MCI, January 1955.
34 From A. Hope-Jones (Minister for Commerce and Industry) to Dr F. Mandl
(managing director of Bamburi), *KNA*, MCI, 2 September 1955.

1952 to establish its own cement-processing plant at Tororo; this plant came into production in 1955.

The building of the Bamburi plant began in April 1952 and the works were in operation by early 1953. Originally, two kilns were installed with a capacity of 80 000 tons, but in 1955 a third kiln was added to increase output of cement to 120 000 tons per annum. These developments left Bamburi in 1956 in the position of supplying 60 per cent of Kenya's total cement consumption. The original aim of the company was to tap the rapidly expanding East African market for cement, as a letter from the British Standard Portland Cement Company at Bamburi to the Amalgamated Roadstone Corporation of the UK in 1951 makes clear: 'Export will only arise if production is not absorbed in East Africa and in such an unlikely event the obvious markets would be the nearest to hand.'[35] The Bamburi plant was by the 1970s primarily concerned with exporting cement, while the EAPC at Athi River supplied the internal market. The Bamburi plant's expansion into the export market after 1959 was due to various factors. There had been a rapid drop in cement consumption in East Africa at a time when the two other East African cement plants (EAPC at Athi River, and Tororo in Uganda) had increased their capacity. However, Bamburi from the 1960s was able to take advantage of the expanding Middle Eastern Market for cement and Kenya was the most convenient Indian Ocean source of supply.

Before the company at Bamburi was to commit itself to a major extension in 1955, a further list of requests for concessions was sent to the administration, which the BSPC felt to be justified given the 'additional capital to be invested and the risk involved'.[36] It repeated the demand for the government to give an undertaking that competition from other plants would be restricted.

It further asked for tax allowances for an initial period of two years after the extension was completed and these were granted for this period. In 1952, the company had requested the Ministry of Trade and Supplies in Kenya Colony to grant it sponsored shipment for the machinery that had to be transported from Germany and this had been granted.[37] In 1955, the same concession was granted to the company in the case of machinery required for the extension.

It is clear that the company at Bamburi hoped the government would protect its cement in East African markets as well as in Kenya, and in the same 'package' of requests it asked the Ministry of Commerce and Industry to guarantee 'that our product will find a continuing ready market in Tanganyika'.[38]

---

35 From BSPC to the Amalgamated Roadstone Corporation Ltd (UK), *KNA*, MCI, December 1951.

36 From BSPC to MCI, May 1955, op. cit.

37 The machinery for the BSPC plant at Bamburi was imported largely from Krupps Ltd in Germany.

38 From BSPC to MCI, May 1955.

The minister, A. Hope-Jones, outlined the government's position in his reply to Dr Mandl:

> as far as the government of Kenya is concerned, they would naturally be concerned to protect the investments in cement works made in the colony against unfair dumping of cement from abroad and that they would always be prepared to consider the position in the light of representations made by you and other cement works at present under construction in the colony.[39]

The Bamburi company, however, failed to halt the flow of Japanese cement into the Tanganyikan market, for it was in the interests of that administration to allow the influx of cheap sources of cement.

COMPETITION

By 1955, Bamburi had seen its request that no other cement works should be established for ten years by-passed as plans got under way for a cement plant at Athi River, after the discovery of limestone deposits. It has been observed before that this company had been looking for an opportunity to convert its cement-grinding plant into a full cement factory. Clearly, the administration was obliged to support this well-established local industry to the same extent as the BSPC company at Bamburi. In any event, the protective conditions surrounding cement production in Kenya had already been established by 1955, when the EAPC decided to construct a second cement plant in Kenya.

In 1957, therefore, work began on the cement plant at Athi River and the plant went into production in 1958, the construction having cost approximately £2 million. The capital expenditure, therefore, on the first 100 000 tons was double that of Bamburi and the factory was using the 'wet' manufacturing process which was more expensive in fuel.[40] Also, all the fuel for the plant had to be carried from the coast, a distance of some 250 miles. At this point there was no cross-shareholding between the two plants, at Athi River and Bamburi, as the EAPC had the majority of its shares owned by the Associated Portland Cement Company and the Tunnel Portland Cement Company (the Associated Portland Cement Company was estimated to be the second largest world cement producer in 1973, when it produced a total of 27·5 million tons of cement).

The demand for cement was buoyant for a period between 1955 and 1958, with a consumption in those years of 479 000 tons for East Africa and dropping to 412 000 tons (respectively). At the end of 1956, the plant at Bamburi announced that it would be extending its capacity by the beginning of 1958 to 160 000 tons per annum, having

39 From MCI to Mandl, 2 September 1955.
40 Memo from SCI to MCI, *KNA*, MCI, 10 October 1956.

taken into consideration competition from the Ugandan Tororo plant and the Athi River factory. The Athi River EAPC company was scheduled to produce 120 000 tons per annum by 1959 and the Tororo plant was to produce 160 000 tons by that year.[41] Therefore by 1959 the three East African cement plants were capable of supplying the internal demand for cement in the area. This position left the three plants in a serious state of competition from 1958 onwards, given that all the factories were operating at full capacity. The demand for cement dropped drastically from 1956. Dr Mandl, the managing director of BSPC at Bamburi, explained the conditions of overproduction to the Ministry of Commerce and Industry, 'until such time as the cement industries of East Africa receive wholehearted protection by the government of the three territories, they cannot do otherwise than reduce production.'[42]

The plant at Bamburi, however, had always had a competitive advantage over the other two plants at Tororo and Athi River, and despite complaints by the company that the government should ban all imports of cement, it is significant that the production level at Bamburi was never reduced in absolute terms in the 1950s despite the glut on the market. The advantage of Bamburi over the other plants clearly lay in their proximity to the port, which meant substantial savings on transportation of fuel from Mombasa to the plant and lower production costs.[43]

Furthermore, the railway taper rates rendered the Bamburi product cheaper, even given the distance of the up-country markets, as mile by mile the rates became lower. This situation left the Bamburi plant with a tactical advantage over the other two plants and it could, if it wished, force the others out of the market. Within Kenya, two different international firms faced each other in a state of direct competition, the Bamburi plant being owned by Amalgamated Roadstone of the UK with Cementia Holdings AG of Switzerland and the EAPC company being controlled by a dominant world cement-producer: the Associated Portland Cement Company with the Tunnel Portland Cement Company of the UK. Ultimately, the world producer of cement, the Associated PC Company, was to unite all the Kenyan sources of production under its ownership. But at this point the Bamburi plant was able to dictate the conditions of production. Accordingly in 1958, a formal *marketing arrangement* was concluded by the three East African producers, giving Bamburi the largest share of the local mar-

---

41 *EAS*, 27 December 1957.

42 *EAS*, 3 December 1958. In 1958 the exporting price of Israeli and Yugoslavian cement was below £4 f.o.b. per ton, which meant that even with the heavy tariff on imported cement, the product was cheaper than that manufactured in East Africa.

43 Capital expenditure on the Athi River plant was twice that of Bamburi for the first 100 000 tons.

ket with 37½ per cent, 33½ per cent to Tororo and 29 per cent to EAPC at Athi River.[44]

Bamburi was in effect able to dictate the terms of the area of the internal market to the other firms, given its position as the *largest* producer, well situated near to the Mombasa port. It was, however, only a matter of time before the two Kenyan plants were consolidated under the ownership of the Associated Portland Cement Company, the dominant world producer.

Given the glut on the local market, the Bamburi plant began to orient itself by 1959 towards the export market. In that year, for the first time, Bamburi *exported* more cement than it supplied to the local market, providing 130 000 tons and 95 000 tons respectively.[45] Therefore, the factory at Bamburi between 1959 and 1963 directed its output to the export market and production steadily rose.

CONSOLIDATION

It was obvious that cement production in Kenya could be organized more rationally if the Athi River and coastal plants were to be combined. At the end of 1963, the Amalgamated Roadstone Corporation of UK sold its shareholding in the Bamburi plant to Associated Portland Cement. The quarrying company sold its portion of the BSPC company at Bamburi because of the declining cement sales since 1958. Associated Portland Cement was then in control of 42 per cent of Bamburi's share capital and 40 per cent of the East African Portland Cement Company at Athi River. Both Kenyan sources of cement were brought under the dominance of a major world producer.

In 1964, the British company, the Associated Portland Cement Company, was able to consolidate its hold over the equity of EA Portland Cement by purchasing the Tunnel Cement Company's 39 per cent share in the Athi River plant. EAPC came under the management control of Bamburi, both plants being under the control of APC Company, the dominant world producer. There was a further move to tie up East African cement production by the formation of a subsidiary company of Bamburi in Tanzania in 1966, which was taken over by the Tanzanian government in 1969. The Tororo factory, formerly owned by the Uganda Development Corporation, ceased functioning in 1973 after Amin's dictatorship, and since that time the Ugandan cement market has been supplied entirely by Kenyan cement.[46]

---

44 Interview with the managing director, Bamburi Portland Cement, 1976.
45 ibid.
46 *EAS* Newspaper Cutting Library, file on *cement*. Since the early 1970s Kenyan cement has been supplied to Uganda through legal and illegal channels, often causing shortages in the Kenyan market. Apparently after 1971, Bamburi Portland Cement were asked to manage the Ugandan cement plant at Tororo, but they declined. It was obviously more profitable to serve the Ugandan market from the Kenyan plants.

In accordance with the independent Kenya government's policy of participating in the country's major industries, in 1971, the EAPC Company at Athi River (which supplied 80 per cent of internal cement requirements) offered 51 per cent of its shareholding to the Treasury. This left the Associated Portland Cement Company of the UK and Cementia Holdings with the remaining 49 per cent of EAPC's shareholding, as well as controlling 84 per cent of the Bamburi Portland Cement Company's equity. Since the cross-shareholding was established in 1964, the internal and external markets have been divided up between the two Kenyan plants, whereby in 1974 Bamburi supplied approximately 80 per cent of its production to the export market and Athi River about 90 per cent of its production to the internal market.[47] Thus, by the mid-1960s, the Associated Portland Cement Company managed to dominate the conditions of cement production in Kenya and Tanganyika.

The pressures of indigenous capitalism on the company did not only manifest themselves through the obtaining of equity shareholding in the firm through government corporations. Before 1971, the manufacturing companies had distributed their own cement, thus keeping their profit margins high and cutting out the role of 'middle-men' in the marketing of the product. However, the African trading class put pressure on the government in the early 1970s to allow the compulsory distribution of important commodities through appointed Kenyan agents of the Kenya National Trading Corporation (KNTC). Accordingly, in September 1971, an agreement was reached between the government and the company whereby the cement plants were to distribute cement only through the KNTC citizen agents, thus allowing the indigenous bourgeoisie a share in the profits of the cement trade.[48]

EXPANSION OF THE CEMENT PLANTS

The Bamburi coastal cement company had consistently expanded since 1953 until 1971 when production grew from 35 000 tons to 700 000 tons and these expansions were financed largely from capitalized profits. The most recent extension of the Bamburi plant was announced in October 1974; this, when it is completed, will raise Bamburi's cement production to 1 250 000 tons per annum. The extension will cost in total £8·5 million. The Commonwealth Development Corporation (once again in the role of finance capital supporting British industrial capital) was brought in to assist the company in this extension with a £1·8 million loan. Furthermore, the British government directly guaranteed another loan of £850 000 with a British merchant bank. Also, the firm involved in the construction of the new plant was a British company, Mowlem Ltd.

47 ibid.
48 *EAS*, 3 September 1971.

TABLE 31   *Cement Consumption and Production in Kenya and EA (000s tons)*

	1950	1952	1954	1956	1958	1960	1962	1964	1966	1968	1970	1972	1974
Cement Consumption													
1 Kenya	121	121	139	178	172	185	119	98	149	232	290	391	402
Total 2 E. Africa	278	289	334	400	411	394	309	340	454	605	800	n.a.	n.a.
Bamburi Exports			5	25	70	155	230	338	316	300	520	465	459
(BSPC Co.) Local Sales			70	101	97	98	52	46	76	131	180	278	249
Local Sales as a Proportion of Exports			140%	400%	140%	63%	23%	14%	24%	44%	35%	60%	54%
Total Production (Export)			75	126	167	253	282	384	392	431	700	743	708

Source: Interview with GI Manager of Bamburi Portland Cement Company, in Nairobi, 1975.

It is significant that the British government was to encourage the investment of British firms overseas. For this would require the input of capital goods from Britain at a time when the construction industry was experiencing a recession. Therefore, this British-based cement firm was to benefit from the intervention of a national financial agency at a later stage in its development.

This short analysis of the growth and consolidation of the cement industry in postwar Kenya has focused on the relationship between foreign firms and the colonial administration. The pressure exerted by these companies on the state has been considered in the light of the concessions granted to the cement industry in Kenya during the 1950s. Compared with the prewar period, the administration was prepared to provide extensive support through infrastructure and import protection for the 'infant' industry. Before the foreign firms would agree to begin construction, the administration agreed to enact anti-dumping legislation against imported cement. This of course gave the plant a competitive advantage over the imported product from the outset. After 1945, the Kenyan administration had larger funds at its disposal and was more willing to provide concessions to private capital in order to encourage import-substituting industry.

Kenya Canners and the Pineapple Industry in Kenya[49]

BACKGROUND

The setting up of a fruit and vegetable canning factory by both local and foreign capital in Kenya Colony after the Second World War was directly related to the dollar shortage which was affecting Britain immediately after 1945. British fruit-manufacturing firms wanted to expand into sterling areas to find alternative sources of raw materials. Their aim was to defend markets from the American 'giants' of the fruit-canning industry. American products had a strong hold over both British and continental fruit markets and in 1946, 25 per cent of US canned fruit products were sold to the United Kingdom.[50] In the words of the Governor of Kenya at the opening of the Kenya Canners fruit-processing plant:

> There is a unique opportunity because of the dollar shortages to capture a part of these markets with British colonial produce. In Canada, for instance, there is a large potential demand. Kenya Canners Ltd has been formed with the object of capturing these markets.[51]

Therefore, the Thika fruit-canning plant was set up specifically as an *export* industry to Europe and North America. In 1948, the managing

---

49 A longer study on the pineapple industry in Kenya was prepared by the author for the National Christian Council of Kenya (NCCK) in September 1976, as part of the project 'Who controls industry in Kenya?'.
50 *EAS*, 21 April 1950.
51 ibid.

director of Pickering & West, an English fruit firm, visited Kenya with the intention of setting up a fruit-processing plant. The governor directed him to a settler fruit farmer in Thika named Harries, and *Kenya Canners* was initiated as a partnership between the British firm and a group of settler farmers. The factory was built in the heart of the pineapple-growing district in Thika on a site adjacent to the newly established Metal Box factory, which supplied the tin cans.

From the outset of the pineapple-canning industry in Kenya, the state was to play a vital role in supporting both production and distribution. The *Swynnerton Plan of 1954* was designed to provide large-scale assistance to African smallholder crops and *pineapple* was made one of the designated crops along with tea and pyrethrum. The colonial state, therefore, was concerned to provide loans and technical assistance to smallholder growers, as part of its wider aim of fostering African agriculture.

As was usual in postwar industrial development, the foreign company, Pickering & West, did not commit its capital until certain basic conditions were agreed to by the local administration. The *state* undertook to provide all the essential services for the canning factory at Thika, such as water, roads and electricity. It also agreed to implement duties against canned imported goods to protect the local factory, even though its products would be aimed at the export market. The factory was formally opened in 1950 and was equipped to can other products such as beans and peas, as well as pineapples. However, the crops available for canning at this stage were totally inadequate in relation to the size of the plant. For several years after 1950, when the factory first started production, the cannery was dependent mainly on supplies from Harries's own plantations and some other European farmers, for the African smallholder pineapple scheme was as yet in its infancy.

The first expansion planned by the Kenya Canners factory in 1954 was accompanied by a host of demands to the local administration. The extensions were required by the planting programmes implemented under the African smallholder scheme which, it was calculated, would raise production from several thousand tons of fruit per annum to 10 000 tons by 1956. This rate of expansion the *East African Food Packers' Association* considered already posed processing and marketing problems and

> the canning industry does not feel justified in embarking upon the considerable capital commitments implicit in keeping with even this stage of development of pineapple growing under the present conditions. The full implication of the Swynnerton Plan must be appreciated because it must be realized that without the parallel development of the canning industry, further acreage of pineapples may become a liability rather than an asset.[52]

---

52 From the Hon. Secretary of the EA Food Packers' Association to the Secretary for Commerce and Industry, *KNA*, MCI, December 1954.

Thus, the Kenya Canners Company, the largest fruit-processing factory in Kenya, dominated the East African Food Packers' Association in its negotiations for assistance from the government. There were three areas in which the EAFPA felt that the government should directly assist the pineapple-canning industry: the high cost of sugar, high freight rates and competition from other Commonwealth countries for markets.

Kenya Canners, therefore, requested the government to play a more interventionist role in protecting the colony's 'infant industry'. The main request put forward in 1954 by the representatives of the canning firms, was that the government should *underwrite* the whole operation by guaranteeing an outlet for smallholder pineapples. This would act as an insurance policy for the industry in times of low prices on the fruit markets. Although pressure was exerted for this concession before the price of pineapples on the world market had plummeted, the minimum price legislation was delayed until 1958 when the *Canning Crops Board* was established.

In 1954, the EAFPA had demanded that the government should first guarantee a minimum price for five years of £16 per ton for graded pineapples to the producer and secondly reserve a sum (not exceeding £5 per ton) for tonnage of raw pineapple purchased for canning in any one year, to be paid to the processor should the industry be faced with a drop in world prices. 'Given these assurances, the processing industry will derive the degree of confidence necessary to put in hand the arrangements for increased plant, machinery and marketing facilities.'[53] The final demand was that the government should assist the industry's competitiveness on the world market by helping to obtain reduced freight rates, reduced duties on refined sugar and tariff protection against canned fruit imported into Kenya.

The government did agree in 1955 to pressure the metropolitan shipping lines to reduce their freight rates[54] for Kenyan produce, although price guarantees were not implemented until 1957.

The canning industry in Kenya was soon facing other production problems which instigated new demands for state support. Until 1955, all the three major pineapple-canning firms in Kenya, Kenya Orchards Ltd, Gibson & Company and Kenya Canners, used East African sugar from Miwani for their processing. During 1955, the sugar factories began to add sulphur to their sugar which had the effect of discolouring the cans. Therefore, at a time when the export market was at its best,

---

53 ibid.
54 In the above memo (December 1954), the secretary of the EAFPA submitted that the industry should be granted reduced shipping rates to UK markets, given their competitive position with regard to other world producers. The comparative shipping costs from Kenya and two other production areas were advanced.

Mombasa to UK	132s per measure
South Africa to UK	76s per measure
Australia to UK	132s per measure

the companies were forced to destroy part of their production. Kenya Canners had been pressing the government for some time to allow the canning factories to import white sugar, which was more suitable for canning than the local grades. The problem was that if the canning companies used imported constituents, they would lose the advantage of imperial preference when entering British markets. The local administration, therefore, agreed to an arrangement with the metropolitan government whereby the canning industry in Kenya would be able to use a certain quantity of imported sugar in its products without losing imperial preference. At the end of 1955 the Kenya government also allowed the canning firms a rebate on the duty paid on imported sugar.[55]

COMPETITION

By 1957 and 1958, Kenyan canned fruit was experiencing severe competition in international markets. This occurred at a time when pineapple production from the smallholder plots was mounting towards the capacity of the factory. By 1957, the total acreage under pineapple was 7000 acres, with approximately 25 per cent under European smallholders and 75 per cent under African cultivation.[56] Employment in the industry had increased from 804 persons in 1956 to 853 in 1957, of whom Kenya Canners employed about 80 per cent. The decline in pineapple exports due to world overproduction is illustrated by the fact that the quantity of Kenyan pineapples exported between 1956 and 1957 dropped from 6170 to 5150 tons (from £767 000 to £584 000 in value).[57]

For the first time since 1939, the UK market was saturated with tinned fruit, from Commonwealth and American sources. As 86 per cent of Kenya's pineapples were destined for UK markets, this was disastrous for the industry. For several weeks in 1957 Kenya Canners closed down its factory and refused to take any pineapples from the growers. The European growers managed to persuade the government to purchase the crop to avoid their ruin, but a longer-term solution to unstable markets was urgently needed. Kenya Canners took a tough line with the administration in Kenya: 'the financial position of the company is not fundamentally unsound and it is only doing normal business practice in ceasing to buy when it finds itself overstocked . . . the conclusion is that if the government wishes to increase the turnover of the company, it must supply more working capital'.[58]

The government had more than a passing concern with the fortunes

---

55 These details from Dept of Trade and Supplies to SCI, Nairobi, *KNA*, MCI, 21 March 1955. From 1955, the Kenya administration also imported in bulk the sugar required for the canning industry and then sold it to the factories at wholesale rates.
56 From Dept of Trade and Supplies to SCI, *KNA*, MCI, June 1955.
57 Survey of Industrial Production, 1957.
58 Memo from SCI to MCI, *KNA*, MCI, March 1957.

of the pineapple industry, as the African smallholder scheme was financed under the Swynnerton Plan. There was some debate as to whether the Industrial Development Corporation (IDC) should take a majority shareholding in the plant, a solution strongly pushed by the European farmers. The government had been considering direct intervention and in 1956 the Director of Agriculture had indicated that if Kenya Canners could not expand to meet African pineapple production, then the government would establish a cannery to handle African production. It was, however, significant that the government was against any form of settler control of the pineapple industry which would put African producers at a disadvantage. For instance, the proposal initiated by twenty-seven European pineapple farmers in Thika that there should be a takeover of Kenya Canners by a partnership composed of Europeans and the IDC was firmly rejected by the administration.[59]

The state resisted these takeover attempts of the European farmers, despite the fact that it was dissatisfied with the management of the British firm of Pickering & West. In 1958, the Kenya Canners plant was sold off to another East African based British firm, Afcot Ltd, a subsidiary of the Tanganyika Cotton Company. Afcot took 51 per cent of the shares, with the European farmers retaining 49 per cent.[60]

Instead of taking a direct interest in the Kenya Canners plant during 1957, the government decided to set up a *Canning Crops Board* to regulate the industry and salvage the smallholder pineapple scheme, in order to ensure an orderly expansion of the industry. It had powers to license acreages, fix prices and so on[61] and the main concession to the canning industry was a guarantee of minimum prices to the growers. The state had effectively agreed to underwrite the pineapple industry and subsidize its losses in times of slump in the world market.

CONSOLIDATION OF THE PINEAPPLE INDUSTRY AND ENTRY OF CALPAK

A recovery in the markets for canned fruits began in 1960. The wholesale prices of canned pineapples rose in Britain after a period of price-cutting amongst canners from 1957. During this time the prices paid to growers by the commonwealth canners fell from about £20 per ton to £5 per ton.[62] In order to take advantage of this recovery of export markets, the Kenya Canners plant needed capital to expand. Neither Afcot, which was essentially a trading firm, nor the group of settler farmers at Thika, had the means to effect such expansion.

---

59 Memo on 'Assistance to the pineapple canning industry', from the IDC to the Ministry of Commerce and Industry.
60 Annual reports of the company (Registrar General's returns).
61 *EAS*, 10 October 1957, report on Canning Crops Bill in LEGCO.
62 Report of the Tropical Products Institute Journal, in *EAS*, 11 May 1960.

In 1964, after a year's negotiation, the American-based firm the *California Packing Corporation* (Calpak) was granted the managing agency of Kenya Canners. In the words of the Tancot Newsletter in 1965, 'it is not our wish to sever our connection entirely, but the fact is that Calpak have the know-how, the marketing facilities and the financial resources to develop this industry properly, all of which we lacked'.[63] Calpak were one of the world's largest canned-fruit producers and they decided to invest in Kenya during the 1960s in order to control a competitor and develop alternative producing areas to the Philippines and Hawaii[64] where they had been traditionally located. Calpak's control over Kenya Canners was consolidated in 1968 when the conglomerate took 90 per cent of the firm's share capital leaving only 10 per cent in the hands of the original European firm, Air Harries & Company.

MONOPOLY CONDITIONS ESTABLISHED IN THE KENYAN PINEAPPLE INDUSTRY

Before examining the way in which Calpak shaped the conditions of pineapple production in Kenya according to its global requirements, it is useful briefly to summarize the features of this dominant world food corporation. In 1975, *Delmonte* (as Calpak became) had forty-seven canneries and dried-fruit plants world wide: twenty-nine in America itself, eight in Canada, three in Mexico, one in Venezuela, one in Britain, one in Italy, one in Greece, one in South Africa, one in the Philippines and one in Kenya. These canneries were supplied with fruit from a few selected areas of the world. In 1975, Delmonte had a total of seven huge plantations for bananas and pineapples (two in Hawaii, one in Costa Rica, one in Guatemala, one in Kenya and two in the Philippines). Their major pineapple-growing areas are the Philippines, Hawaii and, more recently, Kenya. Canned and dried fruits and other foods constituted around 70 per cent of the annual sales of the Delmonte Corporation, and in 1975 net sales amounted to 1279·3 million dollars, of which 891·5 million was made up of canned foods. The products of Delmonte are served by a worldwide network of distribution branches.[65]

DELMONTE IN KENYA

The first agreement between Calpak, the Kenyan Canners company and the Kenya government in 1965 involved the injection of K£5 million by the American firm in order to expand production. The first

---

63 Tancot Co. Newsletter, Nairobi, July 1965.
64 Calpak's motivation for diversifying from Hawaii during the mid- and late 1960s was prompted, among other reasons, by the power of the labour unions there.
65 Information from Delmonte annual reports.

phase of the expansion programme was to raise production from 20 000 tons per annum (which was the 1964–5 level) to 35 000 tons of canned pineapple by 1968. A new cannery was projected for the early 1970s which would raise production to 170 000 tons p.a.[66] This programme involved a radical restructuring of pineapple production in Kenya, covering numbers employed, productivity of labour and new machinery and cultivation techniques. In 1961, for instance, the Kenya Canners factory employed only 400 workers and this number increased to 650 between 1968 and 1970 (excluding the field staff which also expanded rapidly in size). By 1976, the total labour force of Kenya Canners in the factories and estates had risen to over 10 000 people.[67]

THE DESTRUCTION OF THE SMALLHOLDER SCHEME

Under the terms of the 1965 agreement, the government contracted to purchase the old Anglo-French Sisal Estate at Thika.[68] It so happened that this land was situated in a good pineapple-growing belt and it was agreed that the estate would be leased in sections to the company at a nominal annual rent. The general impression was that the company would develop its own estates at the same time as taking pineapples from the African smallholders.

After independence most of the European pineapple farmers in Thika district either sold out or switched over to coffee cultivation, due to the low prices offered by the factory for raw pineapples. The Swynnerton Plan of 1954 had aimed at reaching 30 000 acres under pineapple by the 1960s, although by 1965 there were probably no more than 10 000 acres of pineapple under smallholder cultivation. It was estimated in 1966 that African outgrowers earned £250 000 from the sale of fresh pineapple to the factory.[69]

Between 1965 and 1968, the government of Kenya encouraged further extensions of the smallholder pineapple scheme. Despite this, by mid-1967, Kenya Canners complained to the government that the company was operating at a loss because an insufficient throughput of pineapples. Indeed, the balance sheets for KC showed a net loss for the whole period of operation (until 1974).[70] In any event, the foreign corporation placed the onus for the failure to extend planting on the government. The essence of the problem was that however fast the government implemented extensions in the smallholder pineapple scheme, the method most suited to high turnover was the *estate* form.

---

66 *EAS*, 4 June 1965.
67 Delmonte information booklet, 1975, from KC in Thika.
68 This covered an area of approximately 12 000 acres.
69 *EAS*, 14 June 1967.
70 This can be explained by the practice of multinational corporations of transferring their profits out of the country in 'hidden' forms, such as depreciation, management and technical fees, rather than through declared profit.

From its first entry into Kenya in 1965 Calpak had expected the state to finance the smallholder growing side of the operation and therefore take the responsibility for its success or failure. In 1967, therefore, it was no surprise when the company requested the government to underwrite a loan to Kenya Canners of £250 000 from Barclays Bank, the loan being guaranteed by the Canning Crops Board. This loan was approved by Parliament in June 1967 and the Minister of Agriculture said that its main purpose was 'to arrest the decline of a very important enterprise which was processing many pineapples, most of which were grown by Africans, and help the company face the difficult conditions caused by increased competition'.[71] The loan to Kenya Canners was to be covered by a tax levied by the Canning Crops Board on pineapples delivered to the factory. Some opposition politicians soon launched into an attack on the government for supporting foreign enterprise in this way. Okelo-Ogongo (KPU, Kisumu Rural) said, 'it is wrong for the government to guarantee loans for private companies owned by foreigners . . . if possible the government should encourage the growers to form a co-operative and take over the factory.'[72]

In November 1967, the company managed to secure government co-operation to divert all large pineapples (suitable for canning) from the domestic market to the Thika factory, *until* their estates had reached maturity. The *Pineapple Development Authority* accordingly imposed a levy of 2s 75 cents per ton on all consignments of fresh pineapples destined for the local market. In 1968, KC found it impossible to meet its production target of 35 000 tons throughput of pineapples per annum, which had been projected in 1965.

In the same way as the colonial government in 1957 had placed the pineapple industry in a cocoon by guaranteeing minimum prices, so the post-colonial Kenya government agreed to restrict licences for pineapple-canning and growing. With these government guarantees, the KC was able to convert the system of pineapple production for export entirely from the smallholder to the *estate* form, which was more compatible with international production standards. Thus the pineapple-growing scheme, which had been initiated by the colonial government through the Swynnerton Plan, gave way to a more capital-intensive form of estate production under the direction of a dominant world fruit-processor. Kenya Canners, after 1968, began to phase out smallholder pineapples, and by 1972 the share of these pineapples as a percentage of the factory's throughput had dropped to around 25 per cent.

The immediate reason for the drawing up of a *new* management

---

71 *EAS*, 14 June 1967. Kenya Canners was apparently doing so badly at this time that it had to mortgage part of its assets to meet annual losses.

72 ibid.

agreement between the company and the Kenya government was that by 1968, Kenya Canners had failed to increase production to the planned 35 000 tons per year. Therefore, under the terms of the 1968 agreement the government agreed to purchase a further 20 000 acres of coffee estates and suitable land in Thika to rent to Kenya Canners section by section. The company immediately began to cultivate a further 5000 acres from this block in 1968 which began the large-scale switch of Kenyan pineapple production over to the *estate* form. This contract with the government gave the firm more or less exclusive growing rights for pineapple over the following ten years. Delmonte was to convert the land in Thika to intensively cultivated plantations using all the most modern scientific growing techniques.[73] Although it was never made explicit, it seemed likely that the government had acquiesced to Delmonte's demands that the smallholder scheme should be phased out.

From the late 1960s, therefore, it is clear that the company was intent on encouraging smallholder output only to the extent that it could be used to supply the factory until the newly planted estates reached maturity. It has been suggested to me that the reasons for this were that smallholder pineapples were not of a high enough quality for canning purposes. Delmonte could only control the product more carefully under closely monitored and scientific estate methods.[74] In July 1972, there were complaints in Parliament about the considerable difficulties being faced by smallholder pineapple-growers. In that month. A. K. Magugu called on Parliament to establish a select committee to investigate the plight of the pineapple farmers 'who are burdened with loans while their products were able to find no markets'.[75] The motion contended that the government had encouraged farmers in some parts of the country to grow pineapples as cash crops in 1966 and had advised them to mortgage their title deeds against loan advances. The MP for Juja, Mr Kahengeri, continued in the same way:

the government told the farmers that their pineapples would be bought by Kenya Canners, but subsequently the government bought some 25 000 acres of land and leased it to KC to grow pineapples, so that the small producers had nowhere to take their products. For five years now the government has failed and those

---

73 The technical advantages of large-scale pineapple production in terms of *output* are clear; FAO experiments in 1970 showed that pineapple cultivated (i.e. by smallholders) without use of nitrogen produced 12 tons of fruit per acre compared with 20 tons from a field using consistent applications of fertilizer and nitrogen. The smallholder scheme in Kenya was always underfinanced so technical standards and therefore the fruit produced were, by the 1960s, below international standards.

74 Interview with the company, August 1976, in Thika, Kenya. Of course, these methods made for a greatly increased productivity of labour.

75 *EAS*, 22 July 1972.

farmers are doomed. With this type of acreage going to Kenya Canners where will the small producer take his pineapples?[76]

The government attempted to explain this ambiguous situation when the Assistant Minister for Agriculture replied to the questions. He claimed that by September 1971, a sum of K£80 000 was outstanding on the loans and the situation was 'not healthy'.[77] Since the beginning of the smallholder scheme in the 1950s, a total of £10 million was outstanding in loans to farmers and the government considered that it would be a 'dangerous precedent' for these loans to be written off. In fact the government was obliged to absorb the losses of the smallholder operation, as it had tacitly accepted Kenya Canners' plans to convert pineapple cultivation entirely into the estate form. Therefore, having initially encouraged smallholder cultivation when the KC estates had reached maturity by the early 1970s, the firm was prepared to let smallholder production be eliminated.

The Kenya Canners company expanded rapidly in the late 1960s and 1970s, so that by 1975, the firm had approximately 80 000 acres[78] of land at various stages of development in the Thika district. The company had also invested heavily in new plant and machinery, and the total fixed assets of the firm rose from K£1 111 450 in 1971 to K£3 866 931 in 1974. These expansions were financed by a large proportion of *loan capital* which had been raised locally. In 1966, the Kenya government guaranteed a loan to the company of £125 000, with the parent firm Calpak giving another £75 000. Due to the construction of a new cannery by 1973 the debt level of KC had risen dramatically to £4·3 million, about 70 per cent of which was from the Development Finance Corporation of Kenya. Pressure from the Central Bank on foreign firms in 1974 required Kenya Canners to liquidate its debt in 1975 before it could remit its annual profit.[79]

The Delmonte corporation had succeeded in integrating Kenyan pineapple production into its worldwide system and through political alliances within Kenya had managed to win active government support for these moves. The agreements concluded between the Kenya government and Kenya Canners in 1965 and 1968 are in some ways unusual in the very favourable terms offered to the foreign firm. Apparently since that time this contract is used in the Treasury as an example of an agreement which goes against the 'national interest'.

Thus, from the outset, the pineapple industry in Kenya has enjoyed a high level of state support, which was carried over to the post-

---

76 ibid.
77 *EAS*, 29 July 1972.
78 This is only an approximate calculation derived from the Lands Registry in Nairobi.
79 Information of Kenya Canners' debt was obtained from the annual company returns in the Registrar General's Dept.

TABLE 32a   *Kenya Canners: Balance Sheet Summaries 1965–75 (K£s)*

Year	Fixed Assets	Current Assets	Liabilities	Net Assets	Profit and Loss
1965	165 236	228 008	218 743	174 501	(106 404)
1966	170 769	362 350	350 239	182 880	(227 582)
1970	451 315	696 318	1 031 049	116 584	(153 702)
1971	510 038	832 145	1 549 016	(206 833)	(54 179)
1973	1 111 450	1 117 978	1 821 389	408 039	(157 072)
1974	2 942 713	1 577 065	1 743 367	1 776 411	125 500
1975	3 866 931	3 784 114	3 915 739	3 735 306	194 606

TABLE 32b   *Trading Account: Sales (K£s)*

Year	Canned Food	Fresh Fruit	Coffee	Animal	Insurance and Freight
1974					
(gross)	2 097 114	57 821	217 655	4 695	242 597
(net)	2 017 960	15 902	10 903	906	—
1975					
(gross)	2 289 776	71 740	194 128	10 981	253 019
(net)	2 753 565	24 995	16 376	2 138	—

Source: Balance sheets of Kenya Canners Ltd, and Registrar General of Companies.

colonial period. This example illustrates the dependence of such export industries on world market conditions, for it was the pineapple factory's lack of competitiveness in the early 1960s that compelled the firm to sell out to the American fruit canning 'giant'. The major local shareholder of Kenya Canners before 1965 rationalized this trend after he had concluded the agreement with Calpak (Delmonte): 'I have reached the conclusion that if the Kenyan pineapple industry is to survive we will have to mechanize, the present trend is not towards the small crop . . . it is impossible to go on growing with the old methods'.[80] This perfectly expresses the rationale behind the absorption of small units of capital by larger ones as part of the worldwide process of capital *concentration*. Delmonte, in a period of ten years, succeeded in Kenya in establishing more or less monopoly conditions within the pineapple industry.

During the 1960s state loans had underwritten the industry as a whole and thereby encouraged the existence of dual forms of produc-

---

80 *Daily Nation*, 'Interview with Bob Harries', 11 November 1969.

tion. In the case of pineapples it is clear that the *estate* form was more suitable in technical terms, as a higher level of productivity was possible. It is significant that international capital can extract surplus value from labour in different ways. Brooke Bond, on the contrary, found that they could use smallholder tea production to their own advantage, by ensuring high production standards in the initial stages. The coexistence of the two forms of production, estate and smallholder, in the case of pineapples, did not fit into Delmonte's global scheme of production. Therefore, the smallholder scheme that was so heavily sponsored by the colonial government was gradually dismantled during the 1960s and replaced by large-scale plantations. To the international firm at that time it is clear that the *estate* form was able to raise productivity and ensure that the product would compete most favourably on the world market.[81]

---

81 Given the state of nationalist pressure on foreign firms by the mid-1970s, it seems unlikely that Delmonte's monopoly over the conditions of production and distribution of canned fruit will go unchecked.

CONCLUSION TO PART II

The focus in this section has been on the role of the state in postwar colonial capitalism. Britain's changed position in the world economy after 1945 gave rise to a more *interventionist* colonial policy. The metropolitan administration was active in providing grants for infrastructure and services, which were the essential prerequisites for investment of private capital.

During this period there was an expansion of commodity production in Kenya and an increase in labour productivity. The combination of a positive government policy and competitive conditions encouraged British firms to invest in industrial production behind the tariff wall. The local administration in Kenya after 1945 fostered new measures to protect and regulate the development of industries in the colony. These measures included tariff protection, duty refunds and industrial licensing. A highly concentrated structure of industry was to emerge, with each branch of production dominated by one or several firms. There were a few cases where one firm managed to establish near-monopoly conditions by entering the market before its competitors, as in the cases of cement and tobacco.

The movement of merchant capital into production after 1945 was evident among Asian as well as foreign enterprises. The state was prepared to support manufacturing investment from either local or foreign sources, in marked contrast to the prewar conditions. During the 1950s there was a degree of concentration of capital, in that both local (mainly Asian) and foreign firms expanded into larger units by the takeover of smaller firms.[82]

The enhanced role of state financial agencies in supporting the investments of British firms is illustrated in the first case study on the Colonial Development Corporation. This study on *East African Industries* shows the way in which the corporation supported an industrial project until it was ready to be hived off to private capital in the form of Unilever Ltd.

The study of the *cement* industry, on the other hand, shows the degree of support required from the state by foreign firms during the course of an industrial project. The concessions granted to the *Bam-*

---

82 These were usually European-owned.

buri Portland Cement Company by the Kenyan administration in the early 1950s were not part of a coherent tariff protection scheme but were rather in response to pressure from the company.

The case of *Kenya Canners* and the development of Kenya's pineapple industry shows the role of the state in stimulating African cash-crop agriculture for the world market. The state, through the Swynnerton Plan, directed large sums of loan capital into the development of a smallholder pineapple-growing scheme, while the processing plant was owned jointly by settlers and a British fruit-canning firm. The state was required continually to underwrite the pineapple industry in order to render its products competitive on the world market. Accordingly, a government parastatal was formed (the Canning Crops Board) to guarantee the growers a minimum price. The independent Kenya government was to subsidize this industry to an even greater extent than before. After 1965, the Kenyan government assisted an American multinational in consolidating a monopoly position over pineapple production. To this end, the government actively supported Delmonte's moves to phase out the smallholder growing scheme and develop large-scale estate cultivation of pineapples.

The postwar period was marked by a further extension of the capitalist mode of production in Kenya. Changes in Britain's position in the global economy gave rise to the development of an *interventionist* state. The power of the settler group was waning in the context of a greater degree of metropolitan control over the colony. As a result, Kenya became more closely integrated with the accumulation imperatives of metropolitan capital.

PART III

CHAPTER 5

Indigenous Capitalism in Kenya

The Colonial Period

This chapter will examine some of the dynamics behind the expansion of indigenous capitalism in Kenya from the colonial period. Unfortunately, not a great deal has been written on class formation in Kenya during the colonial period, which does hinder the analysis to a certain extent. However, some of the most extensive studies on the development of indigenous capitalism and the expansion of commodity relations in Kenya have been done by Mike Cowen, Scott MacWilliam and Apollo Njonjo for Central and Western Privinces respectively.[1]

These studies have illustrated the way in which an embryonic African bourgeoisie emerged from the 1920s onwards, based on new forms of commodity production founded on the direct employment of *wage labour*. Forms of primitive accumulation in the pre-colonial period were effected mainly by *hunting and raiding*, a process which was curtailed by the imposition of boundaries of white settlement in the colony from the early 1900s onwards. Political authority was granted by the colonial state to the leaders of particular tribal communities through chieftainships. By the 1920s, however, this traditional African leadership was being superseded by a 'new class' which had its basis in

---

1 The relevant works by these two are: M. P. Cowen, 'Capital and peasant households', mimeo., Dept of Economics, University of Nairobi, July 1976, and 'Wattle production in the Central Province, capital and household commodity production, 1903–1964', mimeo., Institute for Development Studies, University of Nairobi, July 1975; M. Cowen and K. Kinyanjui, 'Some problems of income distribution in Kenya', IDS Nairobi, Discussion Paper, March 1977; S. MacWilliam, 'Commerce, class and ethnicity: the case of Kenya's Luo Thrift and Trading Corporation, 1945–1972', paper presented to the Australasian Political Studies Association, Annual Conference, Sydney, August 1976, and 'Some notes on the development of commerce in Nyanza, 1900–1945', paper at African Studies Seminar, Murdoch University, Australia, June 1976. These essays will appear in *Capital and Class in Kenya*, (Longman, forthcoming). Other relevant works include: A. Njonjo, *The Africanization of the White Highlands: a study in agrarian class struggles in Kenya, 1950–1974*, (Princeton, PhD, December 1977); G. Kitching, 'The rise of an African petit-bourgeoisie in Kenya, 1905–1918', mimeo., 1975, *Journal of African History*, 1976.

the sphere of circulation. It had emerged from a group of skilled wage labourers of the early colonial period. Cowen shows how amongst this 'new class' the phenomenon of 'straddling' became important, i.e. individuals being involved at the same time in both permanent employment *and* private accumulation.[2] For instance, a teacher's position during the colonial period was an important means through which the individual capitalist could channel money capital into his own enterprises, either in trade or farming. This practice during the colonial period was extensive and has been described as the 'pervasive feature of the historical movement of indigenous capitalism'.[3]

This new class of local capitalists, therefore, had its basis in links between trade, commodity production in the reserves and salaried places within the state apparatus. This typified the spread of *capitalist relations of production* in colonial Kenya. There was, from the outset, a fundamental contradiction between this indigenous capitalist class and the class of European estate producers, which the colonial state usually resolved in favour of the latter.[4] From 1915 onwards African farming was confined within the reserves and through taxes and coercive measures the colonial state attempted to maximize the flow of African labour from the reserves to the estates.[5] This had the effect of *limiting* the expansion of indigenous capitalism within the reserves. Demand for particular commodities was, however, set by conditions on the world market for that commodity. New crops introduced in the reserves during the 1930s included tobacco, wattle, cashews and potatoes. African nationalist organizations and groups of farmers pushed for the removal of restrictions on the expansion of certain commodities such as coffee within the reserves. It was not until 1933 that the cultivation of coffee was permitted in African areas on an experimental basis and these areas were regarded as being far enough from European coffee-growing areas to avoid conflict. Nevertheless, coffee was not cultivated by Africans on a large scale until after the Second World War.[6]

The extension of commodity relations within the African reserves was subject to restriction by the colonial administration through licensing regulations and quality control. There was a twofold aim in these regulations: to reduce the demand for wage labour on African farms, and thereby enhance the supply of labour to European estates. The preservation of a strict racial preserve over production of commodities would finally serve to hold back the expansion of indigenous capitalism, which was potentially competitive with settler capital. Through these measures, before the Second World War, estate capital in Kenya

2 Cowen and Kinyanjui, op. cit., p. 15.
3 ibid.
4 For details refer to Chapter 1, pp. 21–31.
5 See van Zwanenberg, op. cit., chs 3 and 4 for further details.
6 For further details on African cash cropping before 1945, see Heyer, op. cit., p. 14.

was able to exercise almost total control over domestic marketing and processing of commodities, while curtailing the extent and location of African production. This control of agricultural production and marketing was the result of the articulation of estate capital through the colonial state.

Despite these restrictions, household commodity production in the African reserves expanded in response to demand from international firms for commodities such as cotton, tea, coffee, sisal, maize and groundnuts. Trading in these commodities within the reserve areas was carried on by both Asian and African merchants and the products were then bought and marketed internationally by the foreign merchant houses. For instance, the *value* of exports from African areas according to the statistics of the Agriculture Department rose from £175 000 in 1922 to £498 000 in 1938.[7] However, a *rapid* expansion in African commodity production was to take place *after* the war when the value of gross marketed output from small farms in all provinces rose from £1·04 million in 1945 to £4·6 million in 1955.

However, until all the restrictions imposed by the colonial state on African production were removed, there could not be a full-scale expansion of commodity relations. Until the *political* dominance of estate capital could be removed, indigenous capitalism would be unable to expand into production on any scale. The demands of African nationalists for representation within the colonial state from the 1920s onwards were partly a reflection of stifled indigenous capitalism. By 1945, however, no concessions had been made by the colonial state to the political demands of the African petty bourgeoisie. The Kenya African Union was compelled to unite the petty bourgeoisie and the 'masses' in a struggle to attain political independence. The unrelenting political opposition of indigenous capitalism to estate capital finally (after the Mau Mau revolt) stimulated political change in favour of that class. It is ironic that the Mau Mau movement, which involved violent attacks by dispossessed groups on both European and African capitalist farmers, was to be used to further the political ends of the indigenous capitalist class after independence. The leadership of the nationalist movement, representing the embryonic Kenyan bourgeoisie, was to gain a political settlement by the early 1960s which favoured indigenous capitalists at the expense of the broader masses who had fought during the Mau Mau revolt.[8]

The political and economic strength of the settler class during the postwar period was to decline rapidly. The weakness of settler capital

---

7 ibid., p. 24.

8 Although their conclusions were reformist, the ILO Mission Report to Kenya, *Employment, Incomes and Equality*, Geneva, 1972, documented the inequality and concentration of wealth in Kenya. Also Leys, op. cit., pp. 228–30, examines the way in which the Kenyan bourgeoisie (both Kikuyu and Kalenjin tribes) effectively carved up the most fertile areas of the Rift Valley while the problem of land shortage was shelved.

when faced with competition from foreign capital has been outlined earlier. After the Second World War, it has been shown that the colonial administration in Kenya fell more closely in line with the metropolitan colonial policy due to Britain's changed position in the world economy. The state apparatus in Kenya was restructured in favour of an expansion of African commodity production (tea, coffee, pyrethrum). These programmes were underwritten by British financial agencies such as the Colonial Development Corporation (CDC).

MERCHANT CAPITAL – THE GROWTH OF AFRICAN TRADE FROM THE 1940s

It is important to elaborate further on the nature of the African trading class before independence, as this forms the background to the larger-scale moves into production in the 1960s and 1970s.

It is clear that between merchant capitals there is a high degree of *competition*. Trade expanded in the African reserves from the 1920s onwards, and from the outset there was tough competition between the traders, both Asian and African. Small indigenous traders operating in the reserves acted as a link between foreign and Asian merchant firms and African commodity producers. Due to the proliferation in the numbers of traders in the reserves from the 1920s onwards, the colonial administration acted to control the numbers of traders in agricultural commodities through *licensing* ordinances. MacWilliam notes that colonial officials, with the Indian experience in mind, tried to prevent the development in Kenya of an indebted peasantry. This led to a multitude of rules preventing Africans from 'anything but minimal levels of borrowing, limited litigation to collect debts, attachment of property for the payment of debts, prior sale of crops to raise advance cash, selling of insurance policies to Africans and restrictions on collecting money by African associations'.[9] For instance, the *Credit to Natives Ordinance* of 1926 had imposed limits on the amount of credit which could be advanced by non-Africans to Africans, thus effectively blocking the expansion in size of African enterprises. The limit between 1926 and 1960, when the Act was finally repealed was 200s. However, after 1945, it became easier for the African petty bourgeoisie who wanted to form joint stock companies to obtain exemptions from the district commissioner of that area.

The demand by the African petty bourgeoisie for *state finance* to assist local enterprises had existed since the 1930s, although schemes for assisting African traders were not implemented until after the Second World War. After 1950, colonial funds were directed through the joint boards[10] of each province and schemes for *training* African

9 MacWilliam, 'Some notes on the development of commerce in Nyanza', op. cit., p. 16.

10 Joint Boards were instruments of local government concerned with 'native affairs' in the colony and they were composed of colonial bureaucrats and African representatives.

artisans and traders were set up in most locations. This coincided with a rapid expansion in the level of indigenous trade, stimulated by the wartime and postwar demand for agricultural commodities on the world market and the subsequent increase in commodity prices. A large number of demobilized African soldiers with small pensions expanded the ranks of the petty bourgeoisie, many of them struggling to carve a niche in the trade of the reserves.

So great was the postwar expansion in indigenous trade that the colonial administration sought to control the number of applications in certain areas for trading licences to establish shops and wholesale centres in the reserves. For instance, in Central Kavirondo, MacWilliam notes that, in 1946, out of 749 new trading licences issued, 632 were held by African traders. For the whole of Nyanza, data compiled by the provincial commissioner (PC) suggests that during the period between August 1945 and November 1946 one-fifth of approximately 3000 applications received for retail traders' licences were from demobilized soldiers. This was clearly a countrywide phenomenon. The colonial administration tried to control this process and in October 1946, a memo from the Acting Chief Secretary to all PCs tried to establish principles for allocating trade licences. The first principle was that there should not be more than one trader to 500 of the population – the second was that, wherever possible, licences should be issued to ex-servicemen who commanded 'reasonable resources'.[11]

It was this type of restriction on indigenous trade which provided the focus for the ideological attack of nationalist leaders on the colonial government. For instance, Oginda Odinga,[12] who set up the first nationalist political organization in Western Kenya, in his accounts of the establishment of his joint stock company in 1948, castigates the colonial authorities for placing obstacles in the way of indigenous traders.

> Far from encouraging African economic ventures, the government seemed set on producing obstacles. The British Labour government in power after the end of the war encouraged co-operative societies, but only ringed around with restrictions and control. When groups of Africans began individually to try and run co-operatives, the authorities worked to undermine their confidence and ability. We had hindrance on all sides and little assistance. We could not raise loans from banks because in African areas communal land ownership prevented individual land title which could be offered as security and banks would accept no other security . . . there was a network of trade regulations designed to 'protect' Africans but

---

11 These details are from MacWilliam, 'Commerce, class and ethnicity', op. cit., p. 5.

12 Oginga Odinga was one of the nationalist leaders of the 1940s and 1950s and he was vice-president of the Kenya Africa National Union (KANU) 1963–6, after which he left to form his own party, the Kenya People's Union (KPU). He was detained in 1969 after the banning of KPU and released in 1975; his attempts to re-enter Kenyan politics have been blocked by the government.

which merely served to militate against their economic initiatives and leave the monopoly of trade in the hands of Asians and whites.[13]

These attacks were largely polemical and represented the position of the indigenous capitalist class during the 1940s and 1950s. In fact, with regard to his own business enterprises Odinga had no difficulty in obtaining an exemption from the credit restrictions. The group of firms which were part of the Luo Thrift and Trading Corporation included the nationalist printing press, Ramogi Ltd. These business formations (albeit not very successful in financial terms) were important in advancing the political organization of the petty bourgeoisie in Western Kenya.

After the Second World War, when the realignment of forces within the colonial state favoured the expansion of commodity relations, the administration made a conscious effort to *encourage* African trade. The attempts to regulate the course of indigenous capitalism met with nationalist opposition; for instance, there was a strong hostility to the formation of co-operatives which were supervised by the state.[14] Trade advisers were appointed from 1945 onwards to assist indigenous merchants. In Nyanza for a time the PC opposed such an appointment through fear of antagonizing the Asian merchant community. This reflects the relative backwardness of indigenous capitalism in Nyanza compared with the Central Province, where in the 1930s local African traders were requesting the district commissioner to force Asian traders out of wholesale trade in certain commodities. In many of the reserve areas, however, Asian and African traders were locked in conflict. The colonial administrators after the war tended to interpret the marketing laws for commodities in favour of the African petty traders and to the disadvantage of Asian merchants. This prejudice related to a traditional colonial design to restrict the areas of operation of Asian merchant capital.

Therefore, the colonial government, before 1963, made provisions to both *encourage and regulate* the expansion of African merchant capital. After the war, one of the main aims of colonial business licensing regulation was to prevent excessive competition amongst indigenous traders. This position was summarized in an *East African Standard* article of 1959 on African trade:

> In general, any move to restrict trading is to be deplored but it seems that there is no alternative for an interim period of five to ten years than to restrict the number of retail outlets in the African areas,

---

13 Oginga Odinga, *Not Yet Uhuru*, an autobiography, Heinemann, London 1967, p. 89.

14 This point is made in MacWilliam, op. cit. (both papers), and the African resistance to the supervision of trade by the colonial government is made explicit in Odinga, op. cit., ch. 5.

allowing healthy, but not destructive competition. In addition to restricting the number of outlets in African areas, encouragement is needed for traders to specialize, perhaps by different rates of licences and fees. Loan funds to help African traders are limited, difficult to administer and provide only a drop in the ocean.[15]

The same article drew attention to district pressure groups (of African traders) who were pressing the government to erect barriers against 'foreign' traders (i.e. Asians) who were importing commodities into the reserves. The imbalance between Asian and African traders in terms of size and available capital was only to be remedied after the attainment of independence when indigenous capital was promoted by the state.

The colonial administration, therefore, attempted to foster a 'healthy' but not excessive spirit of competition. From the 1940s onwards it is clear that assistance programmes to African traders acted to bolster up the more established sections of the petty bourgeoisie. Thus the bulk of assistance to African traders in the 1950s was channelled not into new enterprises, but into firms and businesses that already existed. Accordingly, the Working Party on 'Assistance to African Traders, 1954–5' commented that the Kericho Joint Board:

> was of the opinion that it was desirable to make loans to existing traders as they were the most likely persons to have some knowledge of accounting and general commercial practice. As is known, the Kipsigis Traders' Co-operative has received a loan of £5000 from the Kericho Joint Board and it would seem that it is now functioning fairly efficiently . . . at present the banks give very little credit to Africans and Mr Blanford of the Standard Bank, Kericho, was of the opinion that they would do so only when African traders had proved their standing.[16]

Loans to African traders during the 1950s were administered by the joint boards of the local native councils and the colonial government provided advice to traders on accounting. The 1954–5 Working Party gave further criteria for the allocation of loans under the scheme:

> the four Joint Boards were of the opinion that while in theory it may be desirable to make loans for the encouragement of persons who are new to trading, in practice at this stage it is desirable to grant assistance only to those persons having some experience of trading and aptitude for commercial practice.[17]

---

15 *EAS* in *KNA* file MCI, on African trade.
16 ibid.
17 ibid.

Between 1958 and 1963 further loans were dispensed to African traders and small-scale manufacturers, although on quite a small scale. For instance, by the end of 1959, a scheme administered through the Industrial Development Corporation (IDC), but funded by the American ICA, provided grants to the local authorities for traders. In that year the scheme operated in twenty-six areas and loans totalling £121 000 had been made to 820 individual traders.[18] By 1962, the ICA scheme was extended to small-scale manufacturing as well and in 1962, £17 481 was committed to such projects (including sawmills, making of radios, motor mechanics and bakeries).[19] It is clear, therefore, that even before independence the larger traders were beginning to move into small-scale manufacturing.

During the 1950s the nationalists subjected the government to constant attack with regard to restrictions on African enterprise. In his speech during the budget debate in 1957, Tom Mboya, then the president of the Kenya Federation of Trade Unions, accused the government of discriminating against African traders in Dagoretti Village as they were required to erect premises in permanent building materials, whereas Asian traders were allowed to continue to trade in premises that had been constructed at a much lower standard. It is significant that during his speech Mboya hit not only at the government's enforcement of standards with regard to African traders but also at 'the difficulties placed in the way of Africans who wished to become *producers* as distinct from mere consumers'.[20]

AFRICAN TRADERS AND FOREIGN CAPITAL

Particular foreign firms were probably more instrumental in stimulating African trade than the colonial government's aid schemes to traders. Many had by the mid-1950s extended wholesale facilities to African traders in the reserves for distribution of their products. Among the first firms to Africanize the distribution of manufactured goods (retail) were Boustead & Clarke, the British East Africa Corporation, the Bata Shoe Company, Kettles, Roy & Tyson and the British American Tobacco. Certain foreign firms, notably BAT in the 1950s, were intent on encouraging the development of commodity relations in the reserve areas. BAT and other foreign firms were not in favour of government supported co-operatives in the 1950s[21] but they tended to encourage a more open system of distributorships of manufactured goods such as tobacco, cigarettes and shoes:

---

18 Answer from Minister of Commerce and Industry to a question on African traders' rights by T. Mboya in LEGGO, *EAS, KNA*, MCI, June 1960.

19 IDC memo, *KNA*, MCI, March 1962.

20 MCI file on African trade, *KNA*.

21 This is an area where the aims of both indigenous traders and foreign capital happen to coincide.

but the co-operative movement could be potentially dangerous in that it produces a limited range of consumer goods . . . it would be far better to allow complete freedom of distribution by them in competition against co-operative societies, and these concentrate on buying in bulk produce and selling agriculture implements.[22]

The BAT company had a strong interest from the 1950s in extending its *markets* in the reserves through the medium of African traders. It should be observed that 75 per cent of BAT-manufactured cigarettes in the 1950s were sold loose to the mass market. In 1955, this foreign firm exerted considerable pressure on the Working Party on Assistance to African Traders to provide conducive conditions for the development of markets in the reserves:

One of the ways in which we could give assistance to African traders is to get better roads into many of the areas at present not served. I am wondering whether we could possibly get anything out of the Swynnerton Plan fund for such matters . . . naturally there are outstanding Africans who are already capable of operating trade ventures on a sizeable scale, but their number is at present very limited, my view is that our major effort should for the time being be directed to the development of the ordinary retail African shopkeeper.[23]

BAT since 1958, when it was granted sole rights of purchase of African grown tobacco, has operated a virtual monopoly in Kenya over the manufacturing of tobacco and cigarettes. By 1967, more than 60 per cent of wholesalers for BAT products were African and more than 90 per cent of retail outlets were owned by Africans. In the early 1960s some of the African-owned wholesale businesses in tobacco and cigarettes had turnovers exceeding 500 000s per month.[24]

In general, therefore, foreign firms tried to encourage the emergence of an African trading class from the 1950s onwards (although wholesale distribution of the products of foreign firms was not fully Africanized until 1974). Firms such as East African Breweries, the EA Tobacco Company, Fitzgerald Baynes (later Schweppes), the Unga Flour Company and the Shell Oil Company, from the 1950s onwards operated *credit* schemes by which they would guarantee a sum of money in the bank for a trader operating on narrow cash-flow margins. This had the effect of encouraging the expansion of African retail trade. East African Breweries, for instance, which in the 1950s was owned and managed partly by Ind Coope of the UK and partly by local European settlers, had Africanized nearly all of its

22 The East African Tobacco Company (BAT) to the Working Party on African Traders, *KNA*, 1955.
  23 ibid.
24 *EAS*, 26 July 1963.

distribution in the up-country districts by 1960. This system tended to encourage the emergence of one or several powerful African traders in each district, and often those who managed to obtain a distributorship for a commodity such as beer or tobacco in the 1940s and 1950s would by the 1960s have accumulated enough money capital to move into production.[25]

It is clear, therefore, that between 1945 and independence in 1963 there was a substantial growth in the size of the African trading class. This move was encouraged by foreign capital, which in general wanted to expand the sphere of African commodity production and develop markets for its products. It has been shown that despite the fetters placed by the colonial state on indigenous capitalism in the early colonial period, this by no means halted the process of accumulation of *merchant* capital. This was, of course, the necessary prerequisite for conversion into productive capital during the late 1960s and 1970s. The victory of the nationalist movement which culminated in independence in 1963 represented a temporary alliance between the indigenous bourgeoisie struggling to throw off the fetters on its accumulation and the disaffected mass of the population who wanted an end to colonial rule. The contradictions inherent in this alliance were to manifest themselves in the politics of the 1960s.

In order to understand the configuration of Kenya's postindependence political economy it has been necessary to examine briefly the material basis of the African capitalist class during the later colonial period. The next part will show the way in which the indigenous capitalist class were able, after independence, to correct the imbalance in favour of the settler class by using the powers of the state to propel their own moves into production. Similar tactics of racial demarcation were utilized by the indigenous bourgeoisie after independence in order to break into areas of accumulation which during the colonial period had been exclusively dominated by settler and Asian capital.

The Post-Colonial State

It has been suggested that the bourgeois state in general, through its repressive and integrative functions, provides the preconditions for the process of production. The post-colonial state in Kenya has been dominated by the hegemonic fraction of indigenous capital and the apparatuses and functions of the state have been realigned since 1963 to foster the development of this class. The integrative functions of the

---

25 Some examples are P. Ngei, Jomo Kenyatta, James Muigai Kenyatta, Oginga Odinga and Njenga Karume, to name only a few.

post-colonial state in Kenya will be considered at both political and economic levels.

POLITICAL

The state institutions were inherited intact from the colonial régime, and these included a constitution, parliament and elected local government. The trappings of bourgeois democracy have been slowly eroded during the 1960s and 1970s as the ruling class gradually consolidated an immense amount of power in the hands of the *executive*.[26] Unlike in Tanzania, where this was effected by means of strengthening the party, in Kenya the ruling party, the *Kenya African National Union* (KANU), has been allowed to decline as an organization.

From 1963 onwards, the government was intent on asserting full administrative control over the country which was achieved through the civil service rather than the party. The size of the bureaucracy greatly increased in the post-colonial period and certain branches of government had their powers augmented. After 1963, the division of services that had accompanied regionalism was abandoned and all ministries resumed full control of their activities in the provinces. The entire provincial administration came under the control of the Office of the President, having been transferred from the Ministry of Home Affairs. The provincial administration in its turn was given a dominant role as agent of the executive, the provincial and district commissioners becoming chairmen of the security and intelligence commissions.[27] These had responsibility for all details of local administration including the licensing and control of public meetings. This network enabled the president and the executive to maintain a tight hold over district affairs.

Lamb[28] has pinpointed one of the most important aspects of the KANU leadership's strategy during the 1960s as being the transfer of control of critical local resources out of the hands of local politicians into the keeping of the bureaucracy. Since 1963, therefore, the local government has been increasingly deprived of its sources of patronage and it has become dominated by central government. The constitution has been gradually altered to confirm the concentration of power in the hands of the government.

The ruling group that surrounded President Kenyatta up to 1978 remained remarkably constant. The political role of this group has been to integrate different sections of the bourgeoisie through the state apparatus. A distinction must be made with regard to the bourgeoisie between those individuals dominant at political and economic levels.

---

26 For further details, see C. Gertzel, *The Politics of Independent Kenya, 1963–1968*, Heinemann, London, 1970.

27 ibid., p. 35.

28 Lamb, op. cit., p. 25.

Individuals at the top of the political structure provide for the maintenance and expansion of capitalist relations of production. On the other hand there are those businessmen who have organized politically to further their own economic interests.

The political splits within the bourgeoisie have been intense since independence, although the state has shown a remarkable cohesion. The most important threat to political stability in Kenya occurred after 1966 when a faction within KANU left the ruling party to form the Kenya People's Union (KPU). This group of politicians claimed that they were disillusioned with the way in which the Kenyatta government had betrayed the interests of the 'masses' after independence.

The programme of the KPU made a populist appeal to the exploited masses of workers and peasants drawing on very real contradictions of capitalism: landlessness, unemployment and corruption. This expression of opposition politics reflected the failure of the ruling group to integrate the petty bourgeoisie and the bourgeoisie proper. An example of this failure was the resort to tribal-based political appeals after 1969, a tactic which was not superseded by 'class-based' politics until the 1970s.[29] The government outlawed the KPU in 1969 and Kenya once again reverted to a one-party state. Nevertheless, the same type of dissidence continued within the ruling party, KANU, articulated by the 'radical' MP, J. M. Kariuki.[30] Between 1975 and 1977 a number of critical MPs were detained or imprisoned on criminal charges, and most of these were released in late 1978 after the death of President Kenyatta.

Thus it is clear from this brief summary of political events in postcolonial Kenya that there has never been a serious threat to the predominance of bourgeois state power in Kenya. The petty bourgeoisie have been placated at the economic level by the appropriation of non-citizen enterprise after 1967. Likewise, the discontent of workers and peasants has been partially appeased by such measures as the rise in the minimum wage in 1974 and the redistribution of former settler-owned lands respectively. The maintenance of political power in the hands of the ruling class is dependent on the continued effectiveness of this integration.

ECONOMIC

Another way in which the state provided the preconditions for capital accumulation after independence has been by harnessing the labour movement. The nationalist movement under the leadership of the

---

29 The assassination of Tom Mboya, a Luo minister in Kenyatta's government in 1969, was followed by tribal tensions between the Luo and Kikuyu.

30 Kariuki was killed in March 1975 in mysterious circumstances. For details of the Select Committee of Parliament appointed to probe his death, see the *Weekly Review*, 16 June 1975.

KAU from the 1940s had involved a broad alliance between all those indigenous classes oppressed by colonial capitalism, which included workers, peasants and capitalist farmers. This alliance was a temporary expedient to wrest political power from the British and when the indigenous bourgeoisie came to dominate the post-colonial state the labour movement was immediately curtailed. The new African government confined the labour movement by bringing the trade unions under the direct control of the government. After 1965, the *Confederation of Trades Unions* (COTU) replaced the *Kenya Federation of Labour* (KFL).[31] The Joint Disputes Committee became the Industrial Court in 1964, the purpose of which was to enforce a style of industrial relations which would regulate discussion within the existing free enterprise system, and provide the means of restraining wage demands. With the radical potential of the unions curbed, the government proceeded to tame the labour movement, a process which culminated in 1974 with a presidential *ban on strikes*. Since then industrial action has been muted and covert.

The following analysis of post-colonial capitalism concentrates on the secondary contradictions of capitalism in that it focuses on struggles between different sections of local and foreign capital.

INDIGENOUS CAPITALISM

In the first part of this chapter, the material base of the emergent Kenyan bourgeoisie has been considered. Despite restrictions placed on indigenous capitalism in the early colonial period by the settler-dominated administration, the significant trends in post-colonial Kenya have been a rapid expansion in the numbers of traders and bureaucrats. Secondly, during the 1970s, there has been a pronounced shift of indigenous capital from trade into production (both agricultural and industrial).

The primary sources of accumulation of capital in the post-colonial period have been real estate, farming, transportation and commerce. The rapid multiplication of indigenous enterprises in post-colonial Kenya has given rise to an intensive state of competition between merchant capitals. The logical outcome has been for capital to move from trade into production and the power of the state has been used to open up areas of accumulation such as large-scale farming. The first thrust of state support to indigenous capitalism involved the rapid transfer of land in the former 'white highlands' to Africans, through the settlement schemes.[32] The prime agricultural land of the Rift Valley fell into the hands of a small number of African capitalists, while the remaining area of European farming was subdivided

---

31 Further details in A. Clayton and D. C. Savage, *Government and Labour in Kenya, 1895–1963*, Cass, London, 1974, pp. 436–8.
32 These were funded by the British government.

amongst small peasant farmers and squatters.[33] The appropriation of land in the post-colonial period has been the single most important source of surplus value to African capitalists. Although the process of takeover ōf former European-owned farms began in the early 1960s, it was not completed until the mid-1970s. By 1975 several large foreign-owned estates still remained, producing certain commodities such as tea, although indigenous capital had begun to take over the most profitable agricultural sectors. For instance, Colin Leys has noted that between 1973 and 1975 about 90 per cent of the total acreage of foreign-owned coffee was sold to Africans (i.e. a total of about 25 000 ha.).[34] The forms of agrarian accumulation have been covered elsewhere, so the focus of this study will be on the expansion of enterprises in the commercial and industrial sectors.

Three main tendencies will be distinguished: the use of state powers to accumulate, expansion in numbers and size of firms (reflecting both competition and concentration) and, finally, the move of indigenous capital from the sphere of exchange into production.

The Use of State Powers to Support Accumulation

Colin Leys has emphasized the weakness and dependence of the petty bourgeoisie in Kenya.

> In practice, however, the shift from special assistance to protection can be seen in every field where the government tried to foster African capitalism – except those fields where it moved directly to the creation of monopoly without more ado. The effect of this was to create a new stratum of the African petty bourgeoisie, ensconced within the general system of protection and monopoly, in such a way as to serve and complement foreign capital, not to replace it.[35]

In his analysis of African capitalism in Kenya, Leys considered the use of political tactics to accumulate, such as monopoly and protection, to be a mark of 'dependency'. It is argued here, however, that these are standard procedures followed by any accumulating class and used throughout the history of capitalism. Nevertheless, it is clear that the post-colonial *state* plays an important role in providing indigenous capitalists with the advantages denied them during the colonial period. First, there will be a consideration of the way in which the Kenyan

33 For further details see Colin Leys, *Underdevelopment in Kenya*, Heinemann, London, 1975, ch. 3.

34 Colin Leys, 'Capital accumulation, class formation and dependency: the significance of the Kenyan case', Queen's University, Kingston, Canada, 1978, p. 22.

35 Leys (1975), op. cit., p. 149. Since his original study in 1975, Leys has changed his position on this issue; see Leys (1978), op. cit.

capitalist class have used the state to enhance their control over the commercial sector of the economy.

THE COMMERCIAL SECTOR

The indigenous capitalist class has since the 1960s used *legislative* means to gain a foothold in the commercial sector of the economy to the disadvantage of other racial groups. The preferential access to certain areas of the economy such as land and trade has been secured through the mechanism of *licensing*. (It will be recalled that the same tactics were used by the settlers during the colonial period.) The first legislation to this effect was the *Trades Licensing Act* of 1967, which excluded non-citizens from trading in rural and non-central urban areas and specified a list of goods which were to be restricted to citizen traders only. At that time these covered only a few basic wage goods such as maize, rice and sugar, but this list was extended in the 1970s. By 1975, therefore, the Kenya National Trading Corporation (KNTC) had granted distribution rights of a wide range of goods (both food and manufactured items) to citizen wholesalers. These included sugar, rice, maize, salt, soap, shampoo, sweets, matches, batteries, insecticides, hardware, cement, wire and tools.

The *KNTC* had been set up in 1965 with the intention of taking over the import-export trade but it came to be used more as the primary agency for the Africanization of *distribution* in Kenya. From 1967 onwards, the KNTC was used by the bourgeoisie in general as an instrument to accelerate their move into the wholesale and retail trade, formerly dominated by non-citizens of Asian origin. The agency system for produce and manufactured goods has been used by the dominant fraction of the indigenous bourgeoisie to procure also the most lucrative distributorships for goods manufactured by foreign firms, as well as primary agricultural products. The case of cement distribution illustrates this point; by 1974 the KNTC had forced the foreign cement manufacturers to distribute through agents chosen by the state corporation. In 1974, the five cement distributors for Nairobi included firms owned by prominent members of the Kenyan bourgeoisie; the chairman of Lonrho, an important MP and the brother of the KNTC chairman.[36]

There has indeed been considerable struggle between the larger businessmen and small-scale traders to obtain the most significant distributorships for goods. From the late 1960s there had been strong pressure from the small traders, represented through the Chamber of Commerce, to be allowed better access to the 'spoils' of wholesale trade through the KNTC. The battle between these two groups has been articulated since 1969 and reflects the balance of forces between

36 Nairobi Chamber of Commerce, minutes of the Africanization Committee, 1976.

foreign capital and a section of the Kenyan bourgeoisie. Those members of the Kenyan bourgeoisie with political and economic power have not pushed for compulsory measures to be imposed on foreign manufacturing firms. This is due to the incipient alliance between some Kenyans and foreign firms such as BAT, Cadbury Schweppes and Bata, who had operated sole agency systems for the retail distribution of their goods. This system proved to be an important source of profit to local traders back in the 1950s. However, by the 1960s, pressure was being exerted on *all* foreign firms to Africanize wholesale distribution of goods. Compulsory measures were most important for the bulk of the trading class: the petty bourgeoisie, who were generally *not* supported by the dominant fraction of the bourgeoisie who had their own alliances with foreign capital. It is not surprising that the pressure for compulsory measures emanated from the *Chamber of Commerce* which from 1969 onwards launched a campaign to encourage the government to impose legislation to ensure that the distribution (wholesale and retail) of all manufactured goods went through African citizens. The antagonism of the Chamber (representing the small traders) to that section of the bourgeoisie which had already benefited from monopoly retail distribution rights was expressed in a meeting of the Africanization Committee in 1974: 'the struggle waged by the Chamber for Africans to be given the distributive trade has only benefited a few privileged persons and who indeed have not been genuine businessmen nor are they members of the KNCC'.[37] The Chamber accordingly pushed for a larger *number* of traders to be given distribution rights from the KNTC. Once again the highly competitive nature of trading becomes apparent.

Due to the fact that some prominent Kenyan businessmen were already distributing goods manufactured by foreign firms, the Chamber was not able to successfully push for legislation until 1975. *The Kenya Association of Manufacturers* (KAM) was the mouthpiece of the alliance between sections of the Kenyan bourgeoisie and foreign capital, and it attempted to resist the moves to introduce legislation on distribution. The chairman of KAM (also the chairman of East African Industries, the Unilever subsidiary) implied that the Chamber's demands on the issue of distribution were unreasonable. The secretary of the KAM in a letter to the Minister of Commerce and Industry complained of:

> the continued harassment of industrialists by the Chairman of the KNCC. There is no doubt that the continued criticism of both foreign and local investors by Mr Macharia [KNCC Chairman], in his various addresses and public announcements is eroding many possibilities of expansion of the manufacturing side of the industrial economy.[38]

---

37 KNCC minutes, 9 August 1974.
38 Secretary of KAM to Kiano, Minister for Commerce and Industry, 9 July 1975.

The matter of compulsory distribution reached crisis point in 1975 and had to be personally arbitrated by the President, who in 1974 had made a statement to the Chamber that *all foreign firms* should appoint citizen distributors. However, this was not put into effect until 1975 after further pressure had been exerted by the Chamber on the Ministry of Commerce and Industry. An amendment to the Trades Licensing Act was then passed to the effect that all goods manufactured by foreign firms in Kenya should be distributed through KNTC-appointed citizen agents. The only firms to be exempted from these provisions were those producing semi-finished products for sale to other industries and those goods of a highly technical nature. This move cut out a substantial proportion of the wholesale trading profits to the foreign corporations and brought a wider range of commodities under the control of African merchant capital. This final concession by the government can be seen as an appeasement to the petty bourgeoisie.

CREDIT

Credit facilities for African enterprises have been extended considerably since independence. Exchange control was introduced through the Central Bank of Kenya in the mid-1960s. From then on all remittances of money abroad were subject to approval, and the conditions under which money is allowed to be remitted have been made considerably more stringent since the 1970s. In 1974, for instance, the Central Bank passed a directive restricting the amount of loans to be offered to non-resident individuals or companies (with over 50 per cent of shares held abroad). Non-resident firms were only allowed to borrow from local sources up to 20 per cent of the investment (including share and loan capital) whereas locally owned firms were able to borrow up to 60 per cent of their investment in the enterprise. All applications by foreign firms for local loans from 1974 onwards were subject to Central Bank approval: 'the intention of these instructions is to ensure that large companies who are able to secure finance from abroad use those facilities and leave local savings free for lending to small scale borrowers'.[39] It had been announced by the governor of the Central Bank, before these measures were implemented, that the Central Bank had granted more than £60 million in the form of loans to foreign-owned companies. Another move to conserve foreign exchange and make more funds available locally was the provision in 1974 that foreign firms were not allowed to remit profits or dividends to parent companies abroad until their local debts had been liquidated, a measure introduced to alleviate pressure on the balance of payments.

The government share in the foreign-owned banks in 1971 was also aimed at making a larger amount of money available to local enter-

---

39 *EAS*, 19 November 1974.

prises. In 1976, Kenya Commercial Bank had the remaining portion of its share capital (40 per cent) purchased from Grindlays by the government, thus bringing the bank entirely under local control. Certainly these provisions did make more money capital available to local businessmen. For instance, after the first nationalization move in 1971, the Kenya Commercial Bank recorded an increase of K£4·2 million or 225 per cent in lending to citizens between January and September of that year.[40]

Another notable feature of the post-independence period has been the large-scale extension of state credit institutions such as the Agricultural Finance Corporation (AFC) and the *Industrial and Commercial Development Corporation* (ICDC). The ICDC is the main source of state finance to the local commercial and industrial sector and the Corporation was the successor to the Industrial Development Corporation, which had been set up in 1954 by the colonial government. In 1975, the ICDC was funded 57 per cent from Kenya government funds, 18 per cent from commercial bank loans, 1 per cent from the Swedish government, 7 per cent from the West German government, 4 per cent from other foreign sources and 14 per cent from capital and revenue reserves.[41]

The central role of the ICDC in the post-independence period has been the financing of local trading and industrial enterprise but it also takes some equity shares in large foreign industrial projects. Between 1965 and 1971, the ICDC lent K£2·5 million as three-year loans to African citizens and between 1974 and 1975 total loan disbursements to 1087 citizen traders and industrialists amounted to K£2·7 million.[42] For the latter period (1974–5), from my own calculations, the average amount for each industrial loan was K£8723 and business loan K£2642.[43] About 80 per cent of the loans up to 1971 were advanced to indigenous traders in order to assist them in acquiring businesses from non-citizen Asians. After that time, however, most of the loans dispensed were used not for the purchase of businesses, but for the extension of existing enterprises. For instance, from a sample of 123 business loans disbursed between September 1974 and February 1975, approximately 95 per cent of the money advanced was used for the purchase of equipment and stock. Most of these enterprises were in the trading or service sectors.

The distribution of ICDC loans reinforced a pattern whereby credit was distributed to already-established enterprises and to those owning a number of other businesses. It is clear that the more powerful political elements within the bourgeoisie were always able to capture the largest proportion of state finance for expansion of their enter-

40 Leys, op. cit., 1975, p. 157.
41 ICDC annual reports, 1974 and 1975.
42 Leys, op. cit., p. 167.
43 Information from the ICDC files.

prises. Although security required for ICDC loans was not as large as that required to raise a commercial loan, a significant amount of assets in terms of land or property was demanded as security. This enabled the businessmen with the most significant amount of existing assets to acquire the largest amounts of loan capital from state banks. However, those involved in small trading have, to some extent, been appeased by the provision of business loans for the purchase of non-citizen enterprises. Nevertheless, there has been considerable competition to procure the most lucrative firms taken from non-citizens.

The small traders have consistently attacked the use of official positions within the state to advance business interests. This practice is indeed the hallmark of the present stage of indigenous capitalism, and it was officially sanctioned by the *Ndegwa Commission Report* of 1971, which permitted civil servants to maintain business interests while holding down government positions. Cowen has observed:

> the Africanisation and the expansion of State apparatuses, accompanied by the sweeping away of the restrictions which prohibited State employees or their wives from engaging in accumulation in private enterprise, accelerated the process of straddling between permanent State employment and accumulation in private enterprise.[44]

The extent of this practice was curtailed in the colonial period by the existence of a code of regulations which prohibited public servants from engaging in private enterprise.

It was the use of positions within the state to further business interests that prompted the Chamber of Commerce in 1975 to pass a motion deploring 'the existing situation whereby nearly all the country's senior civil servants have become deeply entrenched in private business activities'.[45] The Chamber blamed the Ndegwa Commission for sanctioning such practices and demanded that the government review the report. Continuing in the same vein they urged the government also to liberalize the security requirements with respect to loans offered to African businessmen. This correctly insinuated that the bulk of loans to African traders and industrialists were being used by the *larger*-scale capitalists who were already well established in trade and/or manufacturing. Thus, the small trading class were clamouring for better access to state support in order that they also could join the ranks of the bourgeoisie.

PROCUREMENT OF BUSINESSES FROM NON-CITIZENS

The taking over of non-citizen businesses is a *political tactic* to create preconditions for the further expansion of indigenous capitalism. *All*

---

44 Cowen and Kinyanjui, op. cit., p. 11.
45 *EAS*, 25 April 1975.

sections of the bourgeoisie have been concerned to appropriate businesses from non-citizens, but the actual apportionment of the 'spoils' has, of course, been the subject of tough political battles. Once again, the main ideological thrust of the Africanization moves has come from the petty bourgeoisie. It has been shown before how this group relied on legislating further control over commerce which tended to be dominated in the pre-independence period by Asian and foreign capital.

From the early 1970s, a tough Africanization programme was established for the commercial sector. The overall aim of the government towards the commercial sector, in response to the pressures outlined above, was expressed in a report of an *ad hoc* committee on Africanization in 1972:

> the Africanisation of Commerce and Industry is the surest way by which Africans can hope to control the economy of this country. They must, therefore, be assisted by the government to overcome the obstacles which have been placed in their way. Our examination of the problems facing new African businessmen has revealed serious loopholes which have been exploited by the immigrant communities to their best advantage. Unless these are tightened it is unlikely that many African businesses will progress beyond the retail trade level . . . in the employment sector, for instance, non-African businessmen have employed many tricks to keep Africans away from business ventures. The Government has tried through the assistance of the KNTC, ICDC and the Joint Boards to assist Africans to come into business, but non-African businessmen have made it difficult for Africans to rent business premises by refusing to let them or by inflated rents.[46]

The Trades Licensing Act which had been in force since 1967 established the guidelines of the Africanization policy as it affected the commercial sector, by excluding non-citizens from trade in certain areas. By the early 1970s, many non-citizens were still present in the small-scale commercial sector. The next stage in the move against these traders was to use the provincial trade officers of the Ministry of Commerce and Industry to introduce more stringent procedures for the renewal of trade licences. Between 1972 and 1975, in all the central trading areas in Kenya's largest towns, Mombasa, Nairobi, Kisumu and Eldoret, a large number of non-citizen businesses were served with notices to quit their premises by the provincial trade officers. This forced non-citizen owners to sell their shops to citizens. In many cases there were not immediately enough African traders with sufficient capital to purchase the businesses, so they would sometimes be taken over by a citizen Asian or a partnership composed of the

---

46 Ministry of Commerce and Industry, report of an *ad hoc* committee, 1972.

original owner and an African Kenyan. However, the provincial trade officers, who held files on every business in their areas, gradually imposed more stringent conditions on the disposal of business licences of the former non-citizen premises.

For instance, in 1975, the Ministry of Commerce and Industry issued 463 notices to quit to non-citizen businesses in Nairobi, including several large supermarket chains. The minister warned that 'the Government will view seriously any window dressing in businesses by the former owners or bids to obtain licences by illegal methods'.[47] Africans who took over these businesses were given five months to complete negotiations and raise funds for the business. In 1975, sixty-nine of these businesses issued with notice to quit were actually owned by *citizen* Asians. This was a direct move on the part of particular African businessmen to gain hold of some Asian-owned enterprises, among which were the major Nairobi food wholesalers and importers. One of the largest supermarket chains in Nairobi, which was involved in wholesale trading and import of food and consumer items, was given notice to quit along with the other sixty-nine citizen Asian enterprises. Negotiations immediately got under way between the Asian owners and a group of prominent Kenyan Africans. After nine months, an agreement was reached between them, and the company was re-formed as 'Uchumi' Ltd in 1976, the new firm being jointly owned by the KNTC, ICDC Investment Company and Kenya Wine Agencies Ltd and managed by the Italian Standa Group.[48] Kenya Wine Agencies is a front for a powerful group of Kenyan capitalists.

It can be seen, therefore, that measures taken to Africanize the commercial sector after 1967, using state coercion to enforce the takeover of businesses owned by non-citizens *and* citizens of Asian origin, have served to advance the African bourgeois class as a whole. By using political tactics against these minority business groups, the bourgeoisie have laid down the preconditions for a future expansion of indigenous capitalism. It can be seen that the dominant fraction of the bourgeoisie in economic terms have managed to make the most use of these coercive measures to Africanize the commercial sector, although some of the most powerful and racist rhetoric has emanated from the petty bourgeoisie.

Company Growth: Number and Size of Firms – Concentration

The second feature of capitalism in Kenya in the post-colonial period which applies to both local and foreign-owned enterprises is that of

---

47 *EAS*, 22 March 1975.
48 *Daily Nation*, 4 February 1976.

concentration. In this part there will follow an examination of the nature of business enterprise in Kenya and the relative position of African firms within each economic sector will be compared with that of Asian and European firms. In the following analysis, it has been convenient to employ the same racial categories for companies that are employed by the Registrar General's Department. The use of such racial categories reflects the prevailing ideology of Africanization within the Kenyan bureaucratic structure. Thus, the racial classification of firms which was begun during the colonial period was continued after independence but with a different bias.[49]

Joint stock companies were formed for the first time in Kenya in the early 1900s, but the first *African* companies were not formed until after the Second World War. It has been shown in Chapter 3 that after the war the advance of commodity relations and availability of ready money stimulated the formation of businesses by petty traders, demobilized soldiers and salaried officials. The actual formation of joint stock companies by Africans during the colonial period had been restricted, particularly by the limitations placed on borrowing between Africans and non-Africans, under the Credit to Natives Ordinance of 1906 and 1926. Although it became easier to obtain exemptions after 1945, this Ordinance was not repealed until after 1960.[50]

In 1946, twenty-four private African joint stock companies were formed for the first time, the majority of these firms trading in primary commodities. Some of the earliest of these firms were the Ukamba Fuel and Charcoal Supply Company, the African Growers and Produce Company, the Luo Thrift and Trading Company and the Kenya Fuel and Bark Company. These firms were all formed between 1946 and 1948 by members of the African petty bourgeoisie who were mainly traders, farmers or teachers.[51] It is significant that the last two companies, the Luo Thrift and Trading Corporation and the Kenya Fuel and Bark Company, were started in Western and Central Kenya by Oginga Odinga and Johnstone Muigai respectively, who were active leaders of the nationalist movement. The state of emergency declared in 1953 at the height of the Mau Mau movement served to virtually seal off the Central Province from the rest of Kenya and, as most of the new joint stock companies were formed by the Kikuyu, it is not surprising that the expansion of African enterprises in the mid-1950s was drastically curtailed. It can be observed from Table 33 that between 1953 and 1954 the number of registered African firms dropped to zero and only picked up again after 1958.

---

49 Despite the obvious ideological use by the Companies Registry of such racial categories, it is unfortunate to conduct this analysis along these lines, as it is not an indication of *class*. Even given these limitations, the empirical observations are useful.

50 For details of this legislation, see O. K. Mutungi, 'Business organisations and the Africanisation of commerce and industry in Kenya', PhD thesis, Yale University, 1974.

51 This information on early African companies was obtained from the annual returns, Registrar General's Dept.

TABLE 33   *Number of Private Companies Forming in Kenya between 1946 and 1973*

Year	European (%)	Asian (%)	African (%)	Mixed (%)	Total No.
1946	44	40	15	1	162
1947	44	43	11	1	205
1948	60	30	6	3	239
1949	61	33	3	3	233
1950	66	28	1	5	221
1951	62	33	2	3	248
1952	65	30	2	4	244
1953	69	29	2	—	189
1954	64	33	—	3	243
1955	70	28	—	6	351
1956	63	54	1	3	324
1957	67	29	1	3	341
1958	57	37	1	5	231
1959	50	43	2	5	270
1960	50	42	4	4	300
1961	39	49	7	5	271
1962	38	50	8	4	233
1963	45	42	5	8	360
1964	35	34	19	11	427
1965	28	34	25	12	427
1966	30	36	19	15	458
1967	26	35	23	16	516
1968	20	30	33	16	561
1969	14	38	28	20	806
1970	13	37	30	20	866
1971	15	39	33	13	984
1972	17	30	37	16	825
1973	15	24	46	15	885

Source: Annual returns of the Registrar General, summary of yearly statistics.

Table 33 also illustrates the rapid growth in the number of Asian-owned enterprises after the Second World War; by 1961 the number of Asian firms registered for the first time exceeded the 'European' group with 134 and 105 companies respectively. African firms gradually increased as a proportion of *new* private firms being formed in Kenya, and in 1972, 310 African firms exceeded for the first time the 248 formed by the Asian community. By 1973, African firms constituted nearly 50 per cent of all private firms forming in that year and if the mixed group is included (which after 1969 included over 80 per cent African partners), then it can be concluded that from 1973 onwards companies owned by Kenyans formed the largest proportion, about 60 per cent of all new companies forming in Kenya.[52]

The European group of companies consist of approximately 50 per cent of firms owned directly from abroad, but the decline in the numbers of these firms forming in Kenya does not indicate a fall-off in foreign investment, but rather reflects *concentration* amongst existing firms. Foreign firms have tended to consolidate by the 1970s by means of expanding their existing enterprises and taking over smaller firms. Table 33 simply shows in numerical terms an absolute increase in the number of new firms being formed by indigenous Kenyans. Another indicator of the expansion of African capitalism through enterprises has been the almost complete takeover of business partnerships by African traders. African partnerships in 1954 constitute only 11 per cent of the total number on the register (12 487), whereas ten years later, in 1964, African firms had risen to 54 per cent of the total, and by 1973, they constituted over 80 per cent of the total 55 589 business partnerships in Kenya. Business partnerships cover the small trading and service sectors, as they cannot have more than two partners and are not protected by limited liability.

The formation of enterprises provides individual capitalists with a means whereby they can further their own accumulation. The movement of capital into corporate forms, although it does not alone signify increased levels of accumulation, can be said to create the preconditions for further capitalist expansion.

CAPITAL FORMATION AND SIZE OF ENTERPRISES

The basis of this analysis is a sample of private companies listed in the Registrar General's Department for the years 1965, 1969 and 1973, which covered a total of 485 firms. Table 34 shows the number of firms within each community for 1965 and 1973, with the size dispersion for each of the populations. There are, however, a different number of companies within each population of firms, which consist of 121 African firms, 198 Asian firms, 99 European and 67 mixed. It was also possible to examine the relative share of each of the major populations in three different size groups.

Of the 99 European firms in the sample, 40 per cent are foreign-owned, and the rest are those owned by Kenya residents. The following conclusions are drawn from the analysis.

European firms   In 1965 these predominated in the small size group (75 per cent) and next in the large size group (18 per cent). By 1973, the participation of all firms in each of the size groups is more evenly spread between the three size groups with the largest proportion being in the largest size group (42 per cent).

---

52 ibid.

TABLE 34   *Sample of Private Firms Registering in Kenya in 1965 and 1973*

1965	Size GP 1–499	(K£s) (%)	500–10 000	(%)	10 000	(%)	Total With Issued Capital
African	(33)	94	(2)	6	(0)		(35)
Asian	(45)	56	(12)	15	(24)	29	(81)
European	(42)	75	(4)	7	(10)	18	(56)
Mixed	(17)	81	(2)	9·5	(2)	9·5	(21)
TOTAL	137		20		36		193
1973							
African	(34)	28	(70)	58	(17)	14	(121)
Asian	(25)	12	(97)	49	(76)	38	(198)
European	(23)	23	(34)	34	(42)	42	(99)
Mixed	(10)	15	(31)	46	(26)	39	(67)
TOTAL	92		232		161		485

Source: ⅓ list sample conducted in 1974 total number of companies: 485.
Notes: The total number of firms in 1965 is smaller due to the fact that the base year was 1965 which means that some of these firms had not yet registered issued capital. Mixed means a combination of ownership between the communities, therefore it is rather a dubious category.

Of the 99 European firms, 50 per cent were owned directly from *abroad*.

This table has not been weighted so some of the increase in size can be attributed to inflation rather than increase in company size.

Asian firms In 1965 these were found mainly (55 per cent) in the small size group whereas by 1973 50 per cent of the Asian firms were found in the middle size range, with 38 per cent in the larger size group. Therefore, the significant movement of Asian firms between 1965 and 1973 was from the small to the middle and large groups. Once again an indication of capital concentration. In 1973, the largest size group (£10 000+ paid-up capital) was dominated by Asian and European firms with 38 and 42 per cent respectively.

African firms These show a similar pattern of expansion in size between 1965 and 1973, with the largest proportion of firms moving from the small to the middle size group. By 1973, the largest number of firms were located in the middle size group (58 per cent) with 28 per cent in the smallest group and only 14 per cent in the largest group. The lower participation in the largest group of African firms compared with those from the other two communities can be explained by the comparatively retarded progress of African company formation due to the circumscribing of African capitalism under the colonial régime. Given

TABLE 35   *Activity Sectors of 485 Private Companies*

Sectors	Asian (%)	African (%)	European (%)	Total
Agricultural Production ⎱ Dealing in Agricultural Products ⎰	6	46	10	77
Mining and Quarrying	2	1	4	8
Food and Beverage Manuf.	3	1	1	8
Clothes and Textile Manuf.	7	2	2	18
Chemicals, Plastics and Wood	3	—	4	9
Metal, Iron and Steel Manuf.	3	—	2	8
General Engineering	10	1	11	31
Transport (Land, Air and Water)	—	2	7	11
Investment and Finance	3	2	16	25
Real Estate and Property	7	7	8	30
Building and Construction	2	1	8	14
Import/Export, Managing Agents	10	7	11	39
Travel and Tour Operators ⎱ Hotel and Catering ⎰	4	5	8	20
Wholesale Merchants	10	14	—	37
Retail and Services	26	10	5	68
Educational Printing	5	2	4	18
Miscellaneous	—	—	—	1
TOTAL %	100	100	100	
TOTAL NO.	198	123	101	422

Source: 1974 sample of private companies.
Note: The 'mixed' category has been excluded due to its indefinite ownership.

this reservation with regard to African firms, it is possible to observe that there has been a rapid increase in the numbers of firms (particularly in the Asian and African groups) between 1965 and 1973; these firms have in general also increased in size. African firms can be expected to expand more rapidly in the future, given the present level of state support to indigenous capitalism.

TYPES OF ENTERPRISE

Having examined the relative size of firms in different communities, it is important to ascertain the sectors in which the firms of each community are concentrated. Accordingly, a breakdown into sectoral activities is shown from a sample of 485 private firms (Table 35). This analysis shows that *European/foreign* group of firms predominate in three main sectors: investment and finance (16 per cent), general engineering (11 per cent) and import/export/managing agents (11 per cent). (In this sample many large foreign firms have been excluded.)

The largest proportion of *Asian* firms in this sample remained in the wholesale/retail sectors (36 per cent), the next in order of significance being manufacturing and engineering combined (25 per cent). With the expansion of African capital into the commercial sector, supported by the state, it seems likely that Asian firms in this sector will be gradually forced out. This might give rise to further moves into manufacturing. *African* firms during the present phase of primary accumulation of capital, not surprisingly, have predominated in the areas of agricultural production (45 per cent), wholesale and retail trade (24 per cent), real estate and property (7 per cent) and import/export (6·5 per cent). As this sample was conducted on a 1973 sample of firms, it has tended to overlook the move of African firms into manufacturing which began on a larger scale after 1975. After independence, the wholesale expansion of African capitalism has been in *agricultural* production.

INDEBTEDNESS OF FIRMS

In order to determine the sources of money capital available to capitalist enterprises in Kenya, an examination has been conducted on the relative indebtedness of companies from the sample of 485 companies. The analysis shows that the proportion of African sample companies with debts is higher than the other populations and also that these firms have a higher proportion of debt capital to paid-up capital than the other groups. However, the proportion of Asian firms (domestic capital) with mortgages is not appreciably lower than the African firms, 19 and 28 per cent respectively. The percentage of loan to issued capital is substantially higher for African firms, with an average of 25 per cent compared to 3·4 per cent for Asian firms. In this phase of indigenous capital accumulation, it is not surprising to find such a high level of indebtedness of firms. Indeed, in a period of high inflation it is not unreasonable to invest in enterprises initially using a high proportion of loan capital. The probable reason for the low level of debt of the European/foreign group of firms in this sample is that unless foreign firms undertake large expansions, they are able to be self-financing due to their generally larger size and links with a parent company.

The differences in the *sources* of this finance are equally important. The small number of mortgages taken out by the European/foreign group were owed entirely to branches of foreign banks such as the Standard Bank and the National & Grindlays. Asian firms were also dependent on branches of Indian banking capital such as the Bank of Baroda. There has, indeed, been a strong connection between Asian industry in Kenya and Indian sources of credit, most of the Indian banks having been established in Kenya after 1945.

TABLE 36   *Relative Indebtedness of 485 Private Firms in 1973*

Group	Total in Each Community	Total with Mortgages (%)	Total with Mortgages (no.)
Asian	198	18·7	37
European	99	5	5
African	121	28	34
Mixed	67	23	15

Source: 1973 Sample of Private Firms, Registrar General of Companies.

African firms, on the other hand, present a different pattern of reliance on *state* finance rather than on commercial banks. Out of a total of fifty-three mortgages taken out by this group, thirty-eight were with some form of government credit agency such as the Agricultural Finance Corporation, the Land Bank of Kenya or the ICDC. It is the case, however, that since the 1973 sample, a larger number of African enterprises are using commercial banks as their main source of credit, as their existing security increases.[53] But the role of the *state* in bridging the gap in credit at this early stage of capitalist expansion is important.

Links between Local and Foreign Capital

INTERLOCKING DIRECTORSHIPS

So far, the autonomous development of African firms since independence has been observed. A second pronounced trend of indigenous capitalism at the present stage has been the moves by the state to Africanize positions within the foreign corporations *and* to localize the ownership of foreign corporations.

Indigenous capitalism, however, does not operate independently of international capital and there is a high degree of *interlinkage* between foreign and domestic capital in Kenya as in many other parts of the world. Since independence in Kenya, the expansion of foreign capital has been restricted by the state from entering some areas such as land and commerce. There has also been the participation of both state and private Kenyan capital in foreign-owned enterprises, particularly after 1973.

This examination of ownership and directorships, although it does not explain the movement of capital, does indicate certain trends. The aim of my 1974 directorship study has been to compare the types of ownership and management linkages in enterprises amongst the

53 An interview with the Commercial Bank of Africa in 1977 bears out this contention.

TABLE 37   *Kenya's Top Fifty Directors (by number of directorships)*

(a)   Nationality

	African/Citizen	European/Citizen	British
1967	5	4	41 = 50
1974	18*	18	13 = 49
	(including two citizen Asians)		

(b)   Professions

	Civil Servants and Politicians	Professions	Foreign Companies*	
1967	7	6 accountants	CDC	2
		2 advocates	Lonrho	3
			M. Dalgety	1
			James Finlay	1
1974	13	2 accountants	CDC	2
		7 advocates	Lonrho	4
		1 medical doctor	James Finlay	2
			M. Dalgety	2
			United Transport Co.	1

Sources: 1, 1974–5 Sample of private and public companies in the Registrar General's Dept, selected by myself.
2, National Christian Council of Kenya, directorships study in *Who Controls Industry in Kenya?* (1968).

*From the full fifty directors, the remainder were full-time owners or managers of local firms.

'top fifty' directors in Kenya (in terms of numbers of firms), with a similar study conducted by the National Christian Council of Kenya in 1968. This 1974 study indicates the changing patterns of management within large corporations and the expanding number of firms actually owned by the African directors. Despite the limitations of conducting such an analysis, due to the fast-changing positions within companies, some important patterns can be observed. The 1974–6 study, conducted by myself, is not directly comparable with the NCCK directorship study of 1968, as the latter made no attempt to examine the ownership of companies but was based on the number of directorships. It can be assumed, however, that in the 1968 'top fifty' list, most of the directors held positions exclusively in foreign firms; only very few owned shares in the companies in which they were directors. In addition to this, the overall number of African directors was small. Table 37 illustrates the patterns of citizenship and professions amongst the directors for 1968 and 1974.

202   INDIGENOUS CAPITALISM IN KENYA

Table 37 shows the largest proportion of directors in 1974 to be Kenyan citizens; whereas in 1968, 82 per cent of the directors were British citizens. By 1974, the situation had changed and of the top fifty directors, thirty-six were Kenya citizens. From the latter group, half were African citizens and the others of non-indigenous origin (usually European residents). The remaining thirteen British directors were virtually all managers of foreign firms on contract.

By the 1970s, most longstanding European and Asian residents in Kenya had been compelled to become citizens if they wanted to continue either as salaried personnel or as businessmen. Since 1967, the Immigration Department, taking directives from the Kenyanization Bureau, strictly enforced a system of employment contracts to limit non-citizen access to managerial positions in both the public and private sectors. For instance, Jack Block, owner of a large hotel chain in Kenya and fourth on the 1974 directors list, changed his citizenship from British to Kenyan between 1967 and 1974. His family had been residents in Kenya since 1918. The European and Kenyan Asian citizens must be considered as part of the Kenyan bourgeoisie in the sense that the change in nationality is merely a confirmation of their class position.

The participation of Asian directors in the 'top fifty' study for 1974 seems to be diminished, the main reason being that the largest industrial groups such as the Chandarias and the Madvhanis have expanded through concentration, not the formation of new enterprises. The most notable members of the large Asian industrial groups in the 1974 study were P. K. Jani, a Kenyan citizen, and M. P. Chandaria, a British citizen.

The directorships attributed to foreign firms remained largely the same between 1968 and 1974, the most significant firms in terms of number of subsidiaries being Lonrho, James Finlay and Mackenzie Dalgety (the latter was taken over by indigenous capitalists in 1975). However, the marked difference between 1968 and 1974 is that the majority of the managers of foreign firms were African Kenya citizens. For instance, the chairmen of both Lonrho and Mackenzie Dalgety by 1974 were Kenyans. These appointments represented a strategic alliance between the foreign firm and prominent members of the indigenous bourgeoisie.

The two chairmen of foreign companies are examples of the 'younger generation' of businessmen who have had long periods of higher education abroad and at a young age were appointed to the boards of these major foreign firms in the early 1970s. They are typical of a pattern of indigenous managers using the foreign firm to acquire their *own* capital for investment. Furthermore, this group of Kenyan managers of foreign firms have often tried to buy into the same firm after a short period as managing director or chairman. For instance, Mackenzie Dalgety was formerly one of the largest foreign-owned firms in Kenya with investments in import/export trade, agriculture and manufacturing, and had a share capital in 1974 of over £2 700 000. In 1975, this firm had the largest portion of its equity (60 per cent) purchased by a local firm, Mawamu Holdings, which was jointly owned by the chairman of Mackenzie Dalgety and the chairman of Lonrho East Africa. This is probably the largest foreign firm to be taken over by local capitalists/managers, but the tendency is unmistakable. For instance, in 1976 the managing director of a major foreign paint company bought a controlling interest in the same foreign subsidiary.

By 1974, there had been a high degree of Africanization of management within foreign firms, and just as there is an interlinkage between positions within the bureaucracy and private enterprise, so there is an overlap of permanent managerial positions and development of private holdings. This practice is not discouraged by foreign corporations as they can potentially gain a more secure alliance if their manager is a businessman in his own right. This process, however, has led to conflicts, and some firms would not wish to encourage the local manager to take over that subsidiary.

It should not be assumed from the above, however, that the only large-scale capitalists are those who developed through alliances with foreign capital. The 'autonomous' process of accumulation of merchant capital has been noted from the 1940s onwards. Not only has there been an increase in the proportion of Kenyan citizens holding directorships in 1974, but the significance of the directorship study lies in the extent to which those individuals have developed their *own firms*. This applies to all Kenyan citizens, whether African or European. In the political alliances of the 1950s and early 1960s, Asians tended to be excluded from the pact between the European 'progressive' capitalists and nationalists. (This expresses their failure to develop a political base in Kenya up to the present.)

In 1968, only one of the five Kenyan directors, Charles Rubia (an assistant minister and an MP), owned shares in one of the firms in which he also held a directorship, whereas by 1974,[54] only two out of seventeen Africans did *not* list any shareholding in companies, one being a full-time civil servant and the other an executive of the CDC. The notion of African capitalists as an impotent collection of managers and 'agents' for foreign capital is not exhibited in this directorship study of 1974. For instance, two of the top ten directors, the fifth and

---

54 It should be borne in mind that my own ranking of the 'top fifty' directors is bound to be dated very quickly as by 1977 there are likely to be many more indigenous Kenyans in top company positions who have their own companies. My list also does not include many senior politicians and government ministers. Given these reservations, the 'top fifty' ranking must be considered as an estimate only in 1975. R. Kaplinsky has conducted an examination of Kenya's top directors as part of a revised edition of *Who Controls Industry in Kenya?* (National Christian Council of Kenya, forthcoming).

the ninth, *owned* the largest number of their firms, thirty-three and twenty respectively. Only two Kenyan directors in the 'top fifty' list for 1974 formed their own companies *after* having attained senior management positions in a foreign corporation.

The top fifty Kenyan directors are themselves strongly interlinked through *ownership* of enterprises, which reflects a common class background irrespective of race. A table not included here illustrates a set of interlinkages between members of the indigenous bourgeoisie. It shows nine common shareholders in seventeen companies, all of which are locally owned. A former minister is linked through two companies with a large group of firms owned by a Nairobi doctor. These firms are in the areas of drugs manufacture and distribution, transportation and tourism. In 1976 a prominent Kenyan industrialist (thirty-first on the top fifty list) was in partnership in three companies (two in manufacturing and one in contracting) with another government minister. There is another set of interconnections in four firms, three investment companies and one flower-exporting concern.

It is necessary in this context to distinguish between those individuals who occupy places in the political order and those who are primarily businessmen.

It is clear from the 'top fifty' list for 1974–5 that a larger number of the Kenyan directors have developed their *own* enterprises at the same time as holding down professional or executive occupations. In general, the network of ownership and management outlined above shows a *strong overlap* between class places within the bourgeoisie between bureaucratic and political positions and the professions. It is a mistake, therefore, in the Kenyan context to distinguish a separate bureaucratic class. Also, at this stage of accumulation there is *not* a high degree of separation between the owning and managing classes, who are often interlinked. Nor at this stage in Kenya is there a distinct separation between agrarian and industrial capitalists.

CASE STUDIES ON KENYAN DIRECTORS

In order to illustrate more closely the patterns of capitalist expansion in post-colonial Kenya, two directors have been chosen (fourth and fifth on the 'top fifty' list). Block and Karume are both Kenyans, and the racial difference is subordinate to their class location. Their careers reflect a prevalent trend: the expansion of merchant capital into industry. Although the directorship study does not in any way measure accumulation, it is *indicative* of certain patterns of capitalist development.

(a) *Njenga Karume*
Karume is one of the foremost members of the industrial bourgeoisie during the 1970s. He had little formal education and first entered

business in the early 1950s when he began transporting timber from Elburgon to Nairobi. The proceeds from this concern were used to open a bar in Kiambu. He was detained for one year during the 'dragnet' of Kikuyus in the Central Province during the state of emergency, which temporarily halted his progress, along with many other African businessmen at the time.[55] His break away from the highly competitive orbit of small traders came in the late 1950s when he managed to expand his beer distribution business after having obtained the agency from East African Breweries for one-third of the distribution rights of their products in Kiambu district. By the early 1960s, he was the sole distributor of EAB products for that district which involved a high monthly turnover. From beer distribution, Karume extended his operations to transporting, having built up a fleet of vehicles by the early 1960s. Like many other larger African traders, by 1963, he was well entrenched in trade and services. After independence, a further expansion in the scale of his business operations took place.

After 1968, Karume began to move out of the ranks of the large-scale traders into production and between 1968 and 1972 he made new investments in saw-milling, tea-processing and the manufacturing of shoes, drugs and bricks. In all of these manufacturing enterprises, Karume owned a part or the controlling interest in the equity, the only exception being his interests with other Kenyans in a K£3 million pharmaceutical factory established in 1974 by a Yugoslavian company and the ICDC, each of the three partners holding one-third of the equity. The shoe factory was established by Karume and some ex-Bata employees. This local shoe-manufacturing firm had 70 per cent of its share capital held by Karume, with the remaining 30 per cent being owned by the five ex-Bata directors and a Nairobi lawyer.[56]

By the time of the 1974 directorship study, Karume was a director of thirty-six firms. In thirty-three companies, he held a direct interest in the equity.[57] In 1976, his only three foreign firms (directorships) included Guinness East Africa, the United Transport Company and the Agip Hotel. This presumably has some connection with his beer distribution and transporting businesses. It would appear that Karume only joins the boards of foreign companies if these enterprises are compatible with his existing interests. This is another example of the *interdependence* of domestic and foreign capital.

Karume's powerful position in the emerging industrial bourgeoisie in Kenya is confirmed by his strong political base. In 1973, he became chairman of the newly formed Gema (Gikuyu, Embu and Meru

---

55 These details are from 'The man behind Gema', *Weekly Review*, 19 May 1975.

56 For details of the conflict between the Bata Shoe Company see the case study in Chapter 7, pp. 264–73.

57 Calculated from annual returns of the Registrar General.

Association), which was ostensibly an ethnic association, but in fact has come to represent large-scale Kenyan capital. This organization did not only confine itself to financing election campaigns and political rallies, but it has become at the economic level one of the main supports of the move of indigenous capital into production. It was in order to finance such moves that in 1973 the Gema Holdings Corporation was set up as a public company to act as an investment agency and bank for indigenous capital.[58] A group of Kenyan businessmen, including Karume, had through Gema in 1976 raised over K£1 million for industrial projects, out of a K£2·5 million share issue.

From 1975 onwards this corporation directly took control of several large industrial enterprises, in that year acquiring one of the largest brick and tile manufacturing plants in Kenya, formerly owned by an American multinational. Other investments in industry are under way (either through direct participation or through the provision of loan finance) and it seems likely that the Gema group of capitalists will command the move of indigenous capital into industry. This corporation has acted to link up capital raised in the agricultural and merchant sectors with industry, and it is the clearest instance of the large-scale *concentration* of indigenous capital.

(b) *Jack Block*

Block was one of the top Kenyan directors in 1974 with thirty-six places on the boards of foreign firms, thirty-three of which he owned partially or wholly. The pattern of expansion of his enterprises from trade into production is typical of his class position and in this sense he is directly comparable to Karume. A brief outline of the history of the Block family 'empire' in Kenya before independence shows a similar pattern of expansion.

The father of the present chairman of the Block holding company in Kenya, J. Block, arrived as an immigrant from South Africa in the 1900s and, having no resources of his own, was assisted by Lord Delamere with some credit, which enabled him to purchase a small farm in Kiambu. From that time onwards he built up a cattle-trading business and from there moved into the wholesale and retail trade as a general merchant. In 1947, he had accumulated a substantial amount of merchant capital and in that year the family bought the first of their chain of hotels, the New Stanley Hotel in Nairobi. This marked the start of one of the largest *local* catering and hotel networks in Kenya, which by the 1970s included hotels, game lodges and air safaris. Block's location in the Kenyan bourgeoisie was established even before independence; in 1964 he was deputy president of the Kenya

---

58 For discussions of the Gema organization, see *Weekly Review*, 19 May 1975, and 2 February 1979.

National Farmers' Union and president of the Rotary Club.[59] Although the Block family were allied with the settler bourgeoisie before independence, their interest in large-scale business enterprises confirmed their subsequent political alliance with the African bourgeoisie.

By 1963, the interest of the Block family had largely shifted out of agriculture and into trade and services.

By the late 1960s, the family 'empire' took on the familiar form: a consolidation of holdings while moving into new spheres of agricultural and industrial production. From that time into the 1970s, apart from their existing holdings in tea estate and hotels, they had expanded into sisal production, air safaris, meat- and food-processing, brick-manufacturing and mining. In most of the projects, Block has incorporated other Kenyan partners, although the hotel chain remains wholly owned by the Block Investment Trust. One of the most important firms owned by Block outside the hotel was one concerned with importing and distributing machinery and equipment, and he also had a wide range of investments in finance, real estate, import/export, marketing agencies, and so on. The interlocking ownership of the firm highlights a set of alliances between the Block family and other top Kenyan politicians and businessmen (both European and African).

Therefore, as in the case of Karume, the process of accumulation of merchant capital took place initially independently of contacts with foreign capital. Of his thirty-six directorships in 1974–5, Block was on the board of two large foreign firms: Lyons Ice Cream and 20th Century Fox.[60] The latter American-based film distributor appointed Block chairman of their Kenyan subsidiary in 1968, and the group includes interests in the entertainment and catering trade: New Theatres, 20th Century Investments, Drive-in Cinemas, and so on. The connection with this American-based cinema distributor seems not unrelated to Block's interests in the catering and hotel business.

Therefore, Block and Karume are but two examples of early industrialists who have emerged from the merchant capitalist class of the 1940s and 1950s. The example of these two individuals represents a similar pattern: the move of merchant capital into production and then the formation of links with foreign capital. In neither case were their business empires formed as a spillover from foreign capital. It is clear that links with foreign firms become obvious to them in terms of their existing enterprises.

By examining the 'top directors' in general and through the case studies, two tendencies emerge: one is the expansion of existing hold-

---

59 All these details are from a file on the Block family in the *EAS* Newspaper Cuttings Library, Nairobi.

60 Information from the annual returns of these companies (Registrar General's Dept), and accurate as far as possible between 1974 and 1976.

ings and the other is the practice of individual capitalists using foreign firms or other professional positions to support their own enterprises. The directorship study has illustrated the interlocking character of capitalist development, and the links between local and foreign firms which have been outlined in the framework of capitalist interdependence. It is considered misleading, therefore, to assume *a priori* that an indigenous capitalist class can develop only as an appendage of foreign capital.[61]

Move of Indigenous Capital into Production – Restriction of Foreign Capital

The expansion of capitalism in the postwar period in general is related to the world economy and this corresponded with an expanded level of domestic accumulation of capital. By the time the nationalists gained political control of the state in 1963, indigenous capital was poised for a move into production (first agricultural, then industrial). During the early 1970s, when the samples for this research were conducted, the evidence to support the move of indigenous capital into industry was not available and the most notable feature of domestic company formation was the concentration in the areas of agriculture and trade. However, the process of movement from trade into industry has been indicated by the case studies, and further examples to illustrate this trend will be brought out in the section on finance capital in Chapter 6.

However, even before the buying into foreign-owned industrial enterprises suggested above, the state played a major role in 'localizing' some of the country's major industries under foreign control. This includes complete government control of the power industry and Kenya Commercial Bank, the East African Oil Refinery (51 per cent) and the East African Portland Cement Company (51 per cent).[62] This does not in all cases mean full local control over management, but obviously the taking of the majority shareholding institutes the machinery for a further extension of such control. By 1976, the list of government participation (either through investment of ICDC or the Treasury directly) included most of the *major* industrial sectors.

Parallel to the expansion of state capital into foreign-owned sectors, there has been a movement of private domestic capital into production. This has taken the form of either the establishment of new enterprises (usually with financial support from the state) *or* the buying into existing foreign-owned enterprises. For instance, in the 1970s domestic capital has encroached on several areas of production previ-

---

61 Which is suggested by the dependency approach.
62 Appendix 6 at the end of Chapter 6 shows government participation in private industry in Kenya.

ously dominated by foreign capital, such as the tea industry, shoe and tanning industry, and soap, bricks and ceramics production. It has been shown how the local managers of two large foreign firms (a trading conglomerate and a paint firm) bought controlling interests in these enterprises between 1974 and 1975. Also an American brick-making concern was taken over by the Gema Corporation in 1975.

There are also a number of local enterprises which have set up in direct competition with powerful multinational corporations in the same branch of production. Two notable examples of this trend are the Tiger Shoe Company and the Chui Soap factory. Individual capitalists often break into a particular branch of production dominated by a multinational corporation, with assistance from the state.

By 1976, state financial institutions *and* commercial banks were extending large amounts of credit to local industrialists, as well as to foreign firms. The Kenya Commercial Bank and the Industrial Development Bank had just begun special loan schemes for African industrialists by 1977, and quite a number of new industrial projects were owned entirely by African capitalists. These enterprises employ quite a large number of people and cover a range of activities: iron and steel manufacture, pharmaceuticals, oil and air filters, leather shoes, soap, radios and food-manufacturing.

Therefore, as indigenous capital advances into industrial production in Kenya, the state will play a central role in assisting such development, in terms of finance and protection. Parallel with the advance of indigenous capitalism in Kenya, in the 1970s a number of state mechanisms have developed to *regulate* and control foreign corporations. Despite the fact that the mechanisms for controlling foreign investment in Kenya are not as extensive as in countries such as Nigeria and India, where indigenous capitalism is more advanced, the foundations have been laid. The most important government bodies established to this effect in the 1970s were the *Capital Issues Committee* and the *New Projects Committee*.

The *Capital Issues Committee* of the Treasury was set up in 1971 to vet all issues of capital stock with a view to cutting down on capital outflow from Kenya. This is probably the single most important instrument of nationalist control over foreign capital in Kenya by the mid-1970s. The aim of the CIC since its inception has been to encourage foreign firms such as the Bata Shoe Company and Brooke Bond Liebig to issue a proportion of their share capital on the Nairobi Stock Exchange, in order to promote a higher level of local ownership of large corporations. This tactic was not successful in the sense that, at the present stage of indigenous capitalism, the purchasing of shares by individuals is not an established pattern. What has emerged is a pattern whereby the CIC pressures a foreign firm to issue a proportion of its share capital on the Nairobi Stock Exchange, upon which 20 per cent or more will be purchased directly by the Treasury.

The CIC has a record of imposing relatively tough conditions on some foreign corporations. Langdon[63] has noted that it readily rejects applications for overdrafts. In addition, the CIC has tried to control transfers of stock between citizen- and non-citizen-owned firms. For instance, the committee between 1973 and 1975 managed to block several attempts by Lonrho to take over local firms. However, several other takeover attempts were successful due to political intervention from some top politicians. Langdon[64] concludes that although the CIC does constrain multinational corporations in some respects, overall it does not represent an important control on these firms. The committee in my view is an important control instrument, and it must be borne in mind that the systematic operation of such nationalist measures depends also on the coherence of the bourgeoisie in question. Here it has been suggested that at this early stage of indigenous capitalism there is a high degree of conflict between different fractions of the bourgeoisie, particularly between industrial and merchant capital.

The New Projects Committee

This was set up in 1973 by the Ministry of Commerce and Industry with the aim of regulating the flow of foreign capital into industry. It is a ministerial committee which includes representatives from the Ministry of Finance and Planning, the ICDC, the Development Finance Corporation of Kenya and civil servants from the relevant ministries.[65] The committee critically evaluates proposed industrial projects against a list of criteria in the 'national interest' such as employment created, use of local raw materials, introduction of new skills and foreign exchange savings. These are set against the type of protection (duty remissions and so on) demanded by the multinational concerned. Most of the bargaining from the side of the firms is centred on the issue of the type and extent of import protection. The terms of participation of local businessmen are also considered in drawing up the conditions under which the investment is made. Government policy has tended to favour alternative industrial locations to Nairobi or Mombasa. It was only after 1976 that a higher proportion of industries began to be constructed outside the existing urban centres.[66]

This committee is also susceptible to political intervention which obviously skews its effective functioning; this is further compounded by its incapacity to evaluate effectively some of the highly technical projects. There have been several cases where the New Projects

63 S. Langdon, 'Multinational corporations in the political economy', in R. Kaplinsky (ed.), *Readings on the Multinational Corporation in Kenya*, OUP, East Africa, 1978, p. 179.
64 ibid., p. 180.
65 ILO Mission Report, op. cit., p. 439.
66 For instance, the textile mill at Nanyuki and a vehicle assembly plant at Thika.

Committee has actually turned down a project, but powerful local interests involved have exerted pressure to reverse the decision. However, once indigenous capital moves on a larger scale into industrial production, it is likely that such control mechanisms on foreign capital will be developed more effectively.

In this chapter, there has been an examination of the origins of the African merchant class of the 1940s and 1950s which by the late 1960s and 1970s was poised for a move into industrial production. The African capitalist class up until the 1970s was predicated on agricultural production and their involvement in industry was limited. From the mid-1970s, however, there has been a marked tendency for domestic capital to move into industrial concerns where the rate of profit is higher than in trade, with greater possibilities for establishing a dominant position over the market. These moves are being strongly supported by the Kenyan state, mainly through the credit institutions. Individual capitalists are able to use special access to state mechanisms to support their enterprises against more established foreign concerns.

The increase in the number and size of African-owned companies from 1965 onwards has been noted in this chapter. Although the formation of enterprises does not in itself measure accumulation, it provides individual capitalists with a *means* through which they can accumulate. The directorship study also illustrates the expansion in the numbers of enterprises owned and controlled by local capitalists. A dual process of expansion of businesses both autonomously and connected with foreign capital has been outlined, and the two are not mutually exclusive. The case studies on Karume and Block have illustrated that the precise mode of capitalist expansion cannot always be attributed to links with foreign capital.

It is clear, however, that the *state* will play a central role in supporting the move of indigenous capital into production in the future.

CHAPTER 6

Foreign Capital in the Post-Colonial Economy 1963–76

Forms of Foreign Investment in the Post-Colonial Period

During the so-called 'classical' phase of imperialism (before 1939), the bulk of foreign investment in Kenya went into primary production and plantations. Changing conditions in the world economy after the Second World War stimulated the entry into Kenya of British manufacturing firms which began to invest directly in production. This intensified penetration of foreign capital into the area corresponded with the generalization of commodity relations.[1] Therefore, in Kenya, as in many other African countries after 1945, import substitution industry was developed by both local and foreign capital.

In Kenya, the enhanced dominance of international capital in the colonial state after 1945 tended to counteract settler political supremacy and support the ultimate transition to political independence of a nationalist government under the hegemony of an African bourgeoisie. The post-colonial period witnessed a further phase of *expansion* of foreign capital in Kenya, characterized by the export of productive[2] capital from advanced capitalist countries. These trends can be explained by a shift in emphasis in the world economy, which began after 1945, towards the export of *capital* goods (machines, vehicles and equipment). Import-substituting industrialization in the new countries has directly stimulated the western capital goods industry.[3]

The medium through which capital is exported in this advanced stage of imperialism has been the *multinational corporation*. These

---

1 These changes in the world economy have been discussed more fully in Chapter 3.

2 For further details of these trends in the world economy see W. Schoeller, *International Competition between National Average Conditions of Labour*, Economics Research Bureau, Dar es Salaam, 1976.

3 The lack of Department I (capital goods) sectors and the predominance of primary processing for export of consumer goods production has been a notable feature of Third World industrialization.

conglomerates have grown greatly in size and complexity and reflect the increasing level of capital concentration on a world scale. During the post-colonial period in Africa, after the mid-1950s, this concentration of capital into fewer units has become increasingly *international* in character. The worldwide strategy of multinational firms has been to dominate existing and potential markets of the developing regions.

Despite the fact that the world economy is at present dominated by a relatively small number of corporations in particular areas of production, the laws of capitalist *competition* have not been eradicated. The struggle to gain a foothold in national markets reflects inter-imperialist rivalry on a global scale. The concentration of enterprises into ever-larger units is carried out mainly through merger and takeover of smaller units. This process is evident in Kenya from the mid-1960s onwards. The dominance of multinational corporations in the world economy has led to a further division of labour[4] based on product specialization. This is due to the fact that the MNCs can take the utmost advantage of price differentials in purchase of raw materials and labour power. The global range of their operations enables them also to adjust to nationalist pressure in a particular area.

The changes in the world economy after 1945 certainly prompted British firms into manufacturing in addition to the more traditional plantation sectors. The first phase of investment in import-substitution industry in Kenya began during and after the Second World War, and was to develop further during the post-colonial period. After 1963, the bulk of foreign capital flowed into the *manufacturing* sector, which corresponded with the move of indigenous capital into agriculture. After the land settlement schemes (between 1962 and 1964) the independent Kenya government prevented foreign firms from purchasing land, which was considered the preserve of indigenous capitalists.

Despite the concentration of foreign capital in import-substituting industry, by the 1970s there were indications that some multinationals were investing in primary processing for export (such as cashew nuts, dried vegetables, tinned fruit, and so on).[5] The Latin American experience suggests a limited potential for import substitution in the long run. This is particularly where Department I (machinery and capital goods) and Department II (consumer goods) sectors are poorly integrated, with a heavy reliance on the import of machinery from the imperialist countries.

---

4 For a descriptive account of the present division of labour under the multinational corporation, see C. Tugendhat, *The Multinationals*, Pelican Books, Harmondsworth, 1973, pp. 139–41.

5 The 1979–84 *Development Plan* (Kenya) expresses the government's shift in policy away from import substitutions into primary goods and food-processing. For further details on the current growth of 'agri-business', see J. Collins and F. Lappe, *Food First: Beyond the Myth of Scarcity*, Houghton Mifflin, New York, 1977.

In- Kenya from 1945 onwards, foreign capital was concentrated through a process of merger and takeover, and the large British trading firms (such as Mitchell Cotts and Mackenzie Dalgety) began to invest directly in manufacturing. This was not an isolated phenomenon, but was part of a worldwide transformation of merchant into industrial capital.[6]

The expansion of foreign firms after 1963 was marked by the consolidation of existing enterprises and by the entry of new firms from both British and non-British sources. For instance, several British firms invested in post-independence Kenya by means of taking over existing firms. Lonrho is a prime example of this process, and between 1966 and 1973 the multinational corporation acquired approximately fifty subsidiaries in Kenya. The British American Tobacco Company (BAT) consolidated its monopoly hold over cigarette manufacturing and distribution by purchasing the Rothman's subsidiary in 1966. Brooke Bond, the dominant estate firm in Kenya, in 1971 bought out the last significant European-owned tea estate in Kericho district, and also bought an interest in a local fruit and vegetable canning company in 1970.[7]

By the 1970s, however, the patterns of foreign investment began to change in Kenya, as the joint venture or partnership form became predominant. This involved a link-up between international finance agencies, foreign industrial firms, and local state or private capital. The joint venture form has been described by Mandel as 'becoming one of the most important features of the late capitalist or neo-colonialist phase of imperialism'.[8] In Latin America and India[9] this form of partnership investment has been common since the 1940s and 1950s (with some variations between different countries), but in Kenya it did not become dominant until the 1970s which corresponded with the growth of indigenous capitalism. Indeed the partnership form of foreign investment has become the hallmark of postwar capitalism, and in some respects it has emerged in response to pressures exerted by the bourgeoisies of newly independent countries.

The contemporary forms of foreign investment in industry represent a complex unity of financial and industrial capital. Foreign control of the industrial sector through direct ownership has been superseded by management and technology 'packages', as the relations between MNCs and host countries take on more subtle forms. It is hoped that the case of Kenya will demonstrate some of these tendencies.

---

6 For a demonstration of this process, see G. Kay, *Development and Underdevelopment, a Marxist Analysis*, Macmillan, London, 1975.

7 For further details of takeovers refer to company files, *EAS* Newspaper Cuttings Library, Nairobi.

8 E. Mandel, *Late Capitalism* NLB, London, 1976, p. 347.

9 See K. K. Subrahamniam, *Import of Capital and Technology*, New Delhi Press, 1972, p. 44.

Sources of Foreign Capital and Branches of Production

Before considering the recent move of foreign capital into manufacturing after independence, it is important to outline the *sources* of such capital inflow. After 1963, the number of foreign investors in Kenya increased, as many firms that had traded with Kenya during the colonial period from the USA, Germany and Japan hastened to set up production units within the country. During the mid-1960s Kenya pursued an 'open door' policy with regard to foreign investment, and once a firm had obtained a 'Certificate of Approved Enterprise' under the Foreign Investment Protection Act there were few constraints. These relatively liberal conditions encouraged an initial spate of investments in Kenya from abroad. Appendix 1 lists the major foreign firms which invested in Kenya after 1963, by country of origin.[10]

Unfortunately it is only possible to estimate the level of foreign investment in Kenya from different countries; see Table 38. Investment from the United States has probably risen faster than any other country since 1972 due to the strategic importance of Kenya as a pro-western ally on the Indian Ocean.[11] Most of the major British multinationals entered Kenya during the colonial period, the most significant exception being Lonrho. The major influx of large foreign firms *after* 1963 has been derived from non-British sources, while the existing British firms have expanded by takeover of existing enterprises. It is fair to estimate from the available figures that *Britain* was still the largest single investor in Kenya during the mid- and late 1970s.

The only available breakdown of equity investment by sources tends

TABLE 38   *Estimated Book Value of Foreign Investment in Kenya in 1972*

Country	K£m.	% of Total
UK	87	67
USA	26	20
Germany	6	5
France	5	4
Japan	1	2
Total	130	100

Source: S. Langdon, 'The political economy of foreign investment', mimeo., 1976.

10 For a discussion of the chief foreign firms operating in Kenya by sector, see S. Langdon, op. cit.

11 In 1976 Kenya took out a security assistance agreement with the United States.

to confirm the above assumptions for 1968. From the East African Investment Survey, the equity of foreign firms was divided as follows between sterling and non-sterling areas:

Foreign Equity in Kenya

Sterling K£'000	%	Non-Sterling	%	Total foreign K£'000	%
35 186	71	14 446	29	49 632	100

Therefore, investment from the *sterling area* predominated in 1968, with the greatest proportion coming from Britain and only a small percentage from Canada and Australia.

In this section the intention is to show the main *areas of foreign investment* in Kenya since 1963, by illustrating two tendencies: the general move of foreign capital away from estates and into the manufacturing sector, and the increased level of local ownership of the main economic branches. The enhanced level of local ownership of the economy from 1970 onwards can be largely attributed to *state* participation. The issue of control through joint ventures will be considered in the section on management contracts.

First, it is useful to obtain some estimate of the *absolute* size of foreign capital inflow into Kenya. Unfortunately, the most recent statistics available in 1975 were for 1972 (derived from the Annual Investment Survey of the East African Statistical Department).[12] This survey calculates the accumulated value of foreign investment in Kenya from a coverage of about 1000 firms with balance-of-payments transactions. Table 39, accordingly, calculates the value of foreign investment in Kenya for 1965, 1968 and 1972. There has been an absolute *increase* in the amount of private foreign investment in Kenya since 1965, with equity remaining the most predominant form of capital inflow and loans next in importance. Although loans remained at 38 per cent of the total between 1965 and 1972 (with a 10 per cent drop in 1968), it is likely that this proportion will rise over time.

Appendix 2 shows foreign and local *equity* distributed by sector for the years 1965, 1968 and 1972, and broken down into local and foreign. Most of the firms in the balance-of-payments survey will be foreign, although the sample does include also some locally owned firms. The equity table illustrates a gradual *localization* of the equity of Kenya-based companies. In 1965, 1968 and 1972 the proportions of local to foreign equity were respectively, 37:63, 36:64, and 44:54. Thus, by 1972, just under half the total equity of the 1000 sample firms was owned by *citizens* (either state or private shareholders). This change can be attributed to the increasing moves by the Kenyan state

---

12 These figures were provisional and are therefore subject to change.

TABLE 39   *Foreign Investment Total for Kenya 1965, 1968 and 1972*

	K£000s	%
1965		
Total Foreign Equity	47 049	57
Long-Term Loans	31 566	38
Accounts with H. Office	3 841	5
TOTAL	82 456	100
1968		
Equity	49 632	56
Long-Term Loans	25 105	28
Accounts with H. Office	13 645	15
TOTAL	88 382	100
1972		
Equity	55 912	58
Long-Term Loans	36 662	38
Accounts with H. Office	4 581	4
TOTAL	97 155	100

Source: EASD Investment Survey.

to purchase shares in large foreign companies in some of the major sectors of the economy.

Regarding the distribution of foreign equity between sectors, the EASD statistics also show a declining proportion of foreign equity in the agricultural sector,[13] with an increasing amount going into the manufacturing sector. The drop in foreign equity in the 'miscellaneous manufacturing sector' (Appendix 2) reflects the participation of *state* capital in the major industrial sectors after 1970, notably oil-refining, power and lighting, meat-processing and cement. For instance, the building construction and electricity sector, in which foreign equity was reduced from 58 to 19 per cent between 1968 and 1972, can be explained by the fact that the government took over 100 per cent of the share capital and management of East African Power and Lighting from a British multinational in 1971. However, by 1972, one of the significant industrial sectors in which the Kenyan government had not taken a share was the chemical concern which manufactured chemicals

13 Economic Survey statistics up to 1976 show that the manufacturing sector is assuming a greater importance in the economy as a whole, while agriculture is not expanding at the same rate.

and soda ash, owned by the British conglomerate ICI.

In this sample of mainly foreign-based firms, most wholesale and retail enterprises will have been omitted as they do not have balance-of-payments transactions. The wholesale/retail contributions in this survey cover exclusively the operations of the major oil firms in Kenya such as Shell-BP, Caltex and Mobil. At that time these firms still retailed their oil directly. However, in the 'mining and quarrying' sector, foreign equity ownership moved from 88 per cent foreign in 1968 to 67 per cent local in 1972, due to the fact that the government took a controlling interest in the East African Oil Refineries at Mombasa.

LOANS

Appendix 4 shows the amount of loans advanced to Kenya-based companies for 1965, 1968 and 1972, as part of the EAC investment survey. There has been an *absolute increase* in the size of total loan capital (accumulated) between 1965 and 1972, when it rose from K£31·5 million to K£38·4 million. The changing proportion of loan capital in different sectors is significant. In 1965, the largest proportion of finance was extended to the wholesale and retail sector (40 per cent), and mining and quarrying (22 per cent). In 1968, the two largest sectors with loan finance were mining and quarrying (29 per cent) and building construction (18 per cent). Of the total amount of loan capital going to Kenya-based companies in 1972, 37 per cent of the total was directed towards miscellaneous manufacturing, which supports the contention that foreign investment is increasingly directed towards manufacturing sectors and takes the form of loan finance.

However loan capital did not become pronounced in foreign investment until the mid-1970s, a period that escapes the cover of the EASD investment survey of 1972.

THE MANUFACTURING SECTOR

Before examining in more detail the participation of foreign capital in the different industrial sectors, it is necessary to place manufacturing in the context of the *Kenyan economy* as a whole. In 1974, manufacturing constituted 20 per cent of capital formation in Kenya's monetary sector, although this was to drop to 16 per cent in 1975 during a worldwide recession. The numbers engaged in manufacturing industry rose steadily during the 1960s from 13 per cent in 1965 to 17 per cent in 1975 (of the total numbers engaged in the private sector). As Kenya is primarily an agrarian economy, it is not surprising that agriculture remains the largest single source of wage employment, even though the proportion of those employed in this sector did fall from 53 to 41 per cent between 1965 and 1975. The failure of capitalist production to absorb the population at a sufficient rate has given rise to a consistent expansion in the numbers of self-employed or 'informal sector' occupations. Those self-employed and unpaid family workers rose from 54 000 in 1973 to 57 500 in 1976. The most rapid increase has been of the so-called 'informal establishments' in the urban areas, whose numbers rose from 41 400 in 1973 to 94 000 in 1976.[14] Although coverage of the self-employed sector cannot be entirely accurate due to the difficulties of collecting the data, it is fair to assume that the numbers of such occupations will increase in future.

Another example of the central position of the state with regard to accumulation and employment is the large numbers engaged in the public sector. It is clear that the functions of the state have been greatly expanded in the post-colonial period and it is not surprising that by 1975 the public sector employed 42 per cent of the total engaged in wage labour.[15]

SURVEYS OF INDUSTRIAL PRODUCTION

The most detailed analysis of the manufacturing sector in Kenya can be found in the Industrial Census[16] conducted by the Statistics Division of the Treasury from 1965 onwards, on all manufacturing firms employing more than five workers. The most comprehensive of these studies were carried out between 1967 and 1972. These illustrate that the *gross product* in the manufacturing and repairs sector as a whole rose from K£41·8 million in 1967 to K£60·8 million in 1972, while the numbers engaged in this sector rose from 54 971 persons to 76 336 over approximately the same period. Appendix 3 shows the proportion of GDP in each industrial sector accounted for by citizen- and non-citizen-owned firms, the distinction between these two being made on the basis of equity ownership above 50 per cent. Table 40a summarizes the size of GDP produced by local and foreign firms within the three broad sectors of the Industrial Census.

Table 40a shows that up to 1972 foreign firms dominated all three of the basic industrial sectors in Kenya, although the proportion of 'local' GDP increased in all three sectors between 1967 and 1972. There has been a slow 'localization' of GDP which is more evident in some sectors than others. The most significant proportional changes in the share of the GDP between local and foreign-owned firms are as shown in Table 40b.

Foreign firms remained controlling the largest share of GDP in textiles, paper products and transport equipment. However, it is likely that by the mid-1970s foreign control would have diminished, given

---

14 All these statistics are from the Economic Surveys between 1965 and 1976, Govt Printer, Nairobi.

15 Employment in the public sector has risen more rapidly than in the private sector as a whole and in 1971 there would be some manufacturing included in the public sector.

16 The 1972 Industrial Census was not completed by 1977.

TABLE 40a   *GDP – Industrial Census 1967 and 1972*

	1967			1972		
	Local (%)	Foreign (%)	K£000s	Local (%)	Foreign (%)	K£000s
Mining and quarrying	7	93	1 820·5	19	81	1 951·1
Building and Construction	13	87	4 524·5	25	75	11 007·5
Manuf. and Repairs	29	71	31 191·00	37	63	60 847·3

Source: Industrial Census for 1967 and 1972, Treasury.

TABLE 40b   *Contribution of Locally Owned Firms to Sectors of GDP*

	1967	1972
Wood Products	28	75
Footwear and Clothing and Made-up Textiles	14	47
Misc. Manufacturing	29	56
Chemicals and Petrol Products	5	43
Non-Metallic Minerals	2	33
Printing and Publishing	21	33
Transport Equipment	12	20

the increasing level of state intervention in industry. The 'localization' of the petrol and chemicals sector can be accounted for by the government investment in East African Oil Refineries in 1971.

The largest sectors in terms of *size* of GDP in 1972 were chemicals and petrol products (17 per cent), food (15 per cent) and tobacco and beverages (14 per cent). The food sector was largely locally owned if tea is excluded (Brooke Bond Liebig) while tobacco was then dominated by the East African Tobacco Company (BAT). It was predictable that in 1971 the largest sectors (in terms of GDP) also registered the highest amount of profit, with *basic industrial chemicals and petroleum* at K£2·4 million, *beer, malt and tobacco* at K£4·1 million and *cement* at K£1·7 million.[17]

The biggest sectors in terms of GDP and profit were not necessarily the largest *employers* of labour in the industrial sector. According to the Industrial Census of 1971, the highest numbers employed were in rolling stock, textiles and sawn timber. This confirms the fact that the

---

17 Industrial Census, Statistics Division of the Treasury, 1967–71.

major industrial branches in Kenya are *capital intensive* and use a relatively small amount of labour compared with the output. Foreign firms have tended to concentrate in the more capital-intensive sectors such as the petrol and chemicals, cement, tobacco and paint industries. The ILO Mission Report to Kenya[18] found that where both foreign and local firms were found in the same branch of production the local firms tended to be more capital intensive than the foreign ones. It is clear that the type of technology employed does not relate to the ownership of the firm but rather the prevailing conditions in that branch of production on a world level.[19] The ILO study of 1972 also discovered that foreign firms have much *lower labour costs* per unit of output than local firms, even though they employed the same type of technology. This confirms the fact that international corporations, through better supervision and organization of labour are able to extract a higher rate of surplus value from production. Therefore, foreign investment since the 1960s has concentrated in the capital-intensive manufacturing sectors.

PROFIT

Obviously the goal of any capitalist enterprise is to extract as high a rate of profit as possible from its operations, and in this respect there can be no distinction between the ownership of enterprises. However, multinational corporations with their headquarters abroad will attempt to repatriate the largest amount of profit realized from their operations in 'host' countries. Due to their global structure and organization, these corporations have attempted to maximize levels of repatriated profit beyond declared profit by utilizing various accounting techniques on a world scale. For instance, subsidiaries of MNCs *transfer the prices* of their products in order to conceal their actual profits in any one area. The common technique of foreign firms is to under-invoice exports and over-invoice imported components, in order to cut down their declared profit levels. The ILO in Kenya found evidence of overpricing of imported intermediary goods from the parent company to the extent of 20 or 30 per cent more than these goods would fetch on the open market.[20]

This pattern of *hidden profit* amongst multinationals operating in developing countries is not isolated to Kenya, and cases cited in relation to Latin America illustrate a similar trend. For example, in Columbia, subsidiaries of multinational pharmaceutical firms have

---

18 ILO Mission Report to Kenya, 'Employment, Incomes and Equality', Geneva, 1972, pp. 446–52.
19 A function of capitalist competition.
20 For further details, see ILO, op. cit., p. 454.

been recorded as paying 155 per cent more than the normal export price of goods imported from the parent company.[21] The rate at which over-invoicing is possible depends on the branch of production concerned; pharmaceuticals would seem to be a case where a high rate of over-invoicing is possible. Likewise, exports are heavily *underpriced*, and a study of such practices in Mexico, Brazil, and Argentina show that some 75 per cent of the subsidiaries examined had underpriced their export products by 50 per cent relative to prices received by local firms for similar products.[22] In relation to the situation in Kenya, the ILO estimated in 1971 that over-invoicing of intermediate goods probably more than *doubled* the real outflow of surplus from the manufacturing sector as compared with the declared profits and dividends.[23]

However, since the early 1970s there has been government pressure (mainly through the Capital Issues Committee) on firms to reinvest a higher proportion of their profits in Kenya. Since 1974, firms with a high repatriation rate have had their local borrowing rights restricted by the Central Bank. This disincentive on repatriation would seem to have stimulated reinvestment in Kenya.[24] Another form of 'hidden profit' is through the payment of management and technical fees to parent companies from the local subsidiary. The government has attempted to cut down on the level of these payments by placing a 14 per cent withholding tax on such remissions since 1974.[25] It is, however, impossible to measure *exactly* the level of profit outflow from Kenya, declared or undeclared. Further nationalist restrictions in Kenya on foreign investment will tend to cut down the level of capital outflow, but the techniques utilized by the MNCs are just as likely to become more sophisticated. For instance, the new partnership form of foreign investment gives the framework for a much tighter control over the actions of foreign firms, but on the other hand with the use of technical and management agreements the foreign firm has scope to maximize profits through service payments if it remains unchecked.

Although the repatriation of profit is a significant issue, especially with regard to nationalist controls, it is clear that this in not the only source of 'drain' from the Kenyan economy.

---

21 For further details of this practice, see R. Muller, 'The multinational corporation and underdevelopment in the Third World', in C. K. Wilber (ed.), *The Political Economy of Underdevelopment*, New York, 1974.

22 ibid.

23 ILO, op. cit., p. 455. In 1973 a Swiss firm was appointed by the government of Kenya to check on over-invoicing by foreign firms. It is not clear what impact this measure had in terms of curtailing the practice.

24 The diversification projects undertaken by Brooke Bond Liebig in the 1970s have been partly attributed (interviews) to the pressure exerted on the company regarding the repatriation of its profit from Kenya.

25 S. Langdon, 'Multinational corporations in the political economy', op. cit., p. 161, discusses the aspects of the taxation system which affect multinational corporations.

New Forms of Foreign Investment in the 1970s

FINANCE CAPITAL AND MANAGEMENT CONTRACTS

In this section, the new forms of capital investment through partnership will be examined. Virtually all large industrial projects undertaken since 1972 have taken the form of partnerships between local capital (either private or state), a foreign managing agency and a technology supplier, with loan capital being provided by an international financial agency. The case of Kenya is not isolated, and this movement reflects an advanced phase of *internationalization* of capital on a world scale. This new phase has involved to a great extent the fusion of banking and productive capitals at both national and international levels.[26]

The large financial agencies such as the German Development Agency, the International Finance Corporation (World Bank), the Industrial Development Bank and the Commonwealth Development Corporation include both national and international development bodies, and these have been the main source of finance for industry from the 1970s onwards. These agencies constitute a complex link between money and productive capital on a *world* scale, and they provide financial and management services while a foreign industrial firm usually provides technical inputs plus management for a particular project.

FINANCE CAPITAL

Since independence in Kenya, there has been a great increase in the number of branches of international and national financial agencies. Earlier, the role of the CDC was considered in its historical context as facilitating the investment of British industrial firms in the colony. After independence, with the extension of investment sources to other capitalist countries, several different financial agencies entered Kenya. The main function of these agencies has been to support infrastructural development (roads, water, irrigation), agricultural projects, and more recently to invest directly in industrial production. From 1974 onwards, in Kenya, there has been a clear move by international agencies to provide loan and equity funds for the expansion of large-scale agro-industrial complexes aimed at the *export* market. For instance, in 1975, Pan-African Vegetable Products started operations to manufacture dehydrated vegetables (bought from outgrowers) for the export market. This project, with a capital cost of K Sh. 30 million,

---

26 V. I. Lenin, *Imperialism, the Highest Stage of Capitalism*, Progress Publishers, Moscow, 1968, 1st end, 1920, observed this tendency.

was a partnership between several different finance agencies: the IDB, the ICDC, Barclays Overseas Development Corporation and Sifida Investment Company (Geneva), with the technical management being provided by Bruckner Werke (KG), a West German multinational.[27] The products of this project were to be marketed by both Sifida and Bruckner Werke, which illustrates the way in which banking and productive capital operate in close collaboration.

The role of the *national* finance capitals should perhaps be distinguished from the *international* agencies such as the branches of the World Bank. National financial agencies such as the CDC and the German Development Agency are concerned to fund productive investments which involve the importation of machinery, equipment and expertise from one of their own national industrial firms.

The international agencies and the World Bank in particular seem prepared to encourage agricultural and industrial production undertaken by local or foreign capital, or a mixture of both. For instance, the IDB in Kenya has since 1975 extended special credit facilities to African-owned industrial projects. The World Bank also plays a major role in stimulating peasant production of primary commodities for the world market, such as tea and cotton. In order to illustrate in more detail the new forms of finance capital in the present phase of capital export, there will follow an examination of the role and structure of some different credit institutions in Kenya. The role of three state credit institutions in Kenya will be examined, all of which were set up after 1963.

INDUSTRIAL DEVELOPMENT BANK

The IDB was established in 1973, which was about the beginning of a new era of investment in Kenya. This bank is owned directly by the Kenya government, with an authorized share capital of K Sh. 40 million, shared between the government (49 per cent) and the ICDC (26 per cent), with 12 per cent each held by the National Bank of Kenya and the Kenya Assurance Company. The main line of credit is from an international source, the *World Bank*, which by the end of 1975 had provided the IDB with K Sh. 28·9 million under two lines of credit. The World Bank also provides the IDB with management advice and project evaluation services.[28]

It is interesting that the IDB, in addition to World Bank credit, also received lines of credit from Morgan Grenfell & Company (in association with the Export Guarantee Department of the UK), and from the German Development Corporation. This German and British finance capital links up with the World Bank to fund industrial projects in Kenya.

---

27 Information from the annual reports and accounts of the IDB for 1975 (Kenya Govt).
28 ibid.

The IDB's borrowing capacity is limited to three times the amount of its unimpaired subscribed capital. The aim of the IDB finance is to promote industrial projects by four different means:

(1) provision of medium- and long-term loans,
(2) direct equity investment,
(3) provision of guarantees for loans from other sources,
(4) underwriting security issues, shares, etc.

The IDB was specifically designed to support investments in *new* productive enterprises rather than re-financing existing enterprises. The IDB is aimed at supporting *large*-scale enterprises as the ICDC confines its sponsorship to projects costing up to K£50 000. Therefore, the IDB will provide funds for projects in excess of that amount. The bank usually only provides up to 50 per cent of the total capital cost of any new project, although consideration is sometimes given to the financial requirements of expansion programmes of existing enterprises. In most projects, the IDB takes a proportion of equity capital and provides additional loan finance for the enterprise. In 1975, the bank made fifteen investments and loan commitments totalling K£3·9 million.

The bank supports the projects of both local and foreign enterprises, and these are largely for import-substitution industry rather than for export. In 1975, the bank invested (through equity and loan finance) in a total of twenty-four industrial undertakings, five of which were wholly owned by African capitalists. The five locally owned enterprises were involved in the manufacture of bricks, vehicle spare parts and water pipes, tyre retreading, toilet paper rolls and cassettes – all for the local market. In 1976, the IDB started a special loan scheme for African industrialists. Out of a total of twenty-four IDB-supported projects in 1975, four were oriented towards the export market: one for both local and export (fertilizers), with the rest being mainly import *substitution* enterprises. Of this total, the only investment in an extension was a p.v.c. pipe unit at the Metal Box factory in Thika.

The following four sectors from the Annual Report (1975) were those into which IDB channelled the bulk of its funds in 1975:

Fibre, textile and garment manufacture	20·6%
Chemicals and pharmaceuticals	15·2%
Food and animal feeds	14·3%
Hotels and tourism	12·9%

During the 1970s the Kenya government has requested World Bank funds for a wide variety of projects in both import-substituting industry and large-scale agriculture.

DEVELOPMENT FINANCE CORPORATION OF KENYA (DFCK)

This is another Kenya-based financial institution first established in 1963. It is owned jointly by the ICDC, the CDC, the German

Development Corporation and the Netherlands Finance Company. These DFCK shareholders have provided K£3 million by way of income notes and subscribed approximately K£2 million under separate loan agreements. Unlike the IDB, the DFCK's financing facilities are primarily directed towards the establishment *and* the expansion of manufacturing industries. Investment in the tourist industry, forestry and fisheries is also undertaken, provided that the projects can be shown to operate on a commercial basis. Therefore, during the 1960s, the main thrust of the DFCK's finance was towards the support of *existing* industrial and agricultural enterprises; by the mid-1970s investment in new projects was also considerable.

In 1975, the DFCK had committed loan and equity finance to a total of fifty-one different enterprises, eighteen of which were locally owned. In 1975, of the seven new projects in which the DFCK invested, three were owned by African industrialists.[29] The three largest sectors in which the DFCK invested the largest proportion of its loan capital in 1975 were textile and allied industries (22 per cent), hotels (16 per cent) and civil engineering and allied industries (11 per cent).

During 1975, the DFCK had committed K£890 000 to five new projects, which made a total investment through equity and loans of K£6 970 000.[30] In 1975, the corporation opened up a new line of credit with Manufacturers Hanover Export Finance Ltd (London), and in that year negotiations started with the European Investment Bank for further lines of credit. The Kenya government in the case of such loans from the EIB must act as guarantor. This again illustrates the role of the state in facilitating investment in productive enterprises.

EAST AFRICAN DEVELOPMENT BANK (EADB)

The EADB was set up in 1963 ostensibly to support industrial projects in all of the three East African territories. Even before the formal break-up of the community in 1977, about 80 per cent of the loan facilities were being utilized for Kenyan projects.[31] During 1975, for instance, the bank made investments totalling K£3 625 000 in seven projects, one in Tanzania, one in Uganda and five in Kenya. The three East African countries together subscribed 93 per cent of the share capital, while the commercial banks (Barclays International, Grindlays, Standard, Post-Och Kredit Banken) held the remaining 7 per

---

29 From DFCK annual reports and accounts for 1975. These African-owned industrial firms are engaged in printing, shoe-manufacturing and soap-making.

30 ibid.

31 The imbalance between the industrial development of the three East African states had its roots in the colonial period although it was to become more pronounced after independence in the early 1960s. From the 1940s onwards foreign-owned industrial firms had set up projects in Kenya with the aim of supplying the markets of Tanzania and Uganda.

cent. Lines of credit are offered to the EADB by the Swedish Development Agency (SIDA). In 1976, for instance, the IBRD extended a second line of credit to the EADB, amounting to US $15 million. The amount of loan capital dispensed per project by the EADB between 1974 and 1975 rose from K£245 000 to K£518 000, and by 1975 the bank had a cumulative loan disbursement of K£11 980 000. This in itself reflects the growing size of Kenya's industrial sector.[32] The EADB invests in extensions of existing enterprises as well as in new projects, and in terms of size of investment the following three sectors are the most significant: textiles, salt and iron and steel. Most of the projects are import-substitution rather than export-oriented industries.

The role of the British finance agency, the CDC, has been examined in some detail in Chapters 3 and 4. In the post-independence period, the corporation extended its support for the smallholder tea industry and other agricultural projects, as well as supporting housing schemes in the urban areas. The CDC has not concentrated exclusively on funding industrial projects, as the agencies above have done; most of its projects are directed towards agriculture and service industries. Another international agency operating in Kenya since the early 1970s is the International Finance Corporation (a subsidiary of the World Bank) whose function is to link up foreign and domestic capital. The IFC began to invest in industrial projects in Kenya from 1974 onwards.[33] It is clear that these large national and international financial agencies play a prominent role in supporting productive investments in the economy.

THE COMMERCIAL BANKS

It has been illustrated earlier that the commercial banks entered East Africa in the wake of British colonialism, and then acted in the role of 'conventional' finance capital by providing book-keeping services for productive capital. The largest banks established during the colonial period were Barclays, National & Grindlays and the Standard Bank. As these British Banks were the first to enter East Africa from the late nineteenth century, it is not surprising that after independence they still handled the largest amount of banking business in Kenya. By 1975, these three banks, along with the two state-owned banks, the National Bank of Kenya and Kenya Commercial Bank (formerly National & Grindlays), together handled 70 to 80 per cent of the credit

32 EADB annual reports and accounts for 1970–5.

33 World Bank aid to the Kenya government will not be considered here as we are mainly concerned with the 'private' sector. But it is important to note that the largest proportion of World Bank aid to Kenya has been directed towards *infrastructure* (roads and water). A smaller proportion has gone directly into agricultural production such as the tea smallholder scheme.

facitlities offered to private enterprise in Kenya.[34] Other smaller private banks which established branches in East Africa after 1951 include the Nederlandsche Handel-Maatschappij (1951), the Bank of India (1953), the Bank of Baroda (1953), Habib Bank (Overseas) (1956), Ottoman Bank (1958), Commercial Bank of Africa (1962) and the Uganda Commercial Bank (1965).[35] This expansion in banks of non-British origin in East Africa marks the intensified penetration of international finance capital into the area after the Second World War.

All these banks operated independently until 1971 when the government took a 40 per cent share in National & Grindlays and formed the Kenya Commercial Bank. The KCB took over seventy-eight of the eighty-one branches owned by Grindlays Bank in Kenya, although the other three branches remained part of Grindlays Bank International (K). In 1976, the government took over the remaining minority interest of Grindlays in the KCB (40 per cent), thus making it a wholly government-owned bank. Grindlays remained with one branch to manage foreign business.[36]

At the same time (in 1971) the Kenya government proposed that Standard Bank DCO and Barclays should amalgamate and the government take 50 per cent of the new bank. For some reason these plans never materialized and the management and ownership of these two banks remained in foreign hands. One of the pronounced aims of the government investment in Grindlays and the formation of Kenya Commercial Bank was to enhance the amount of money capital available to Africans. In 1972, after one year of government ownership, the KCB announced that lending to Kenya citizens rose from K£2 million to K£6·3 million. Furthermore, the government, through the Central Bank, has sought to direct banking policy more closely.

Unlike the national and international financial agencies discussed earlier, the *function* of the commercial banks is to provide mainly short-term loans for trade, agriculture and industry. In some cases, banks participate in the equity of large industrial projects in Kenya, but this is unusual. However, it is important to bear in mind that there is quite a high degree of interlinkage between the large commercial banks and the so-called 'development' finance agencies. For instance, Barclays Bank (UK) has a subsidiary, the Barclays Overseas Development Corporation, which supports industrial and agricultural

---

34 This estimate was made by the general manager of the Commercial Bank of Africa, interview, Nairobi, April 1977.

35 W. T. Newlyn, *Money in an African Context*, OUP, Nairobi, 1967, p. 54. The Uganda Commercial Bank was the first entirely indigenous bank in Africa. Commercial Bank of Africa is another bank to become 'Africanized' in terms of participation; for instance in the 1960s, co-operative societies in Tanzania owned shares in the bank. In the 1970s a substantial amount of the CBA shares in Nairobi are held by indigenous capitalists.

36 See *EAS*, 10 November 1970, for information on the history of Grindlays Bank.

projects in developing countries through equity participation and loan capital.

However, the most important traditional function of the commercial banks in East Africa is the financing of trade in *agricultural commodities* such as *coffee and tea*.[37] Since the early colonial period, primary commodities such as tea, coffee and sisal have dominated the export bills of all three East African countries. When commercial banks finance commodities, they advance credit to a customer after having taken title to a commodity against firm sales, by means of a letter of credit from an overseas buyer. The government, since 1976, has been putting pressure on the commercial banks in Kenya to extend at least 25 per cent of their credit resources to agricultural projects (which does not include commodity trading). It has apparently been difficult for the commercial banks to meet this target, and the Central Bank did not have appropriate enforcement mechanisms.

The smaller banks in Kenya have increased the size of their operations since the 1960s, although Kenya Commercial, Standard and Barclays still controlled around 80 per cent of banking business in 1977. For instance, the Commercial Bank of Africa (part of the SFOM group), a subsidiary of the Bank of America, expanded rapidly in size between 1974 and 1976 when its borrowing resources rose from 9 million dollars to 70 million dollars.[38]

The commercial banks operate in the sphere of circulation and provide all the complex arrangements for productive capital from the start to the finish of the process of capital accumulation. The linkages between banks on a world scale have become increasingly complex and dominated by fewer giants, who expand and concentrate by means of take-overs of smaller units. There is a high degree of interlocking ownership, for instance, between American and British banks. Barclays Bank is the largest British bank and the world's fourth largest and it has expanded by merger and takeover. Despite the fact that American banks at present own portions of British banks, in 1973, Barclays acquired the First Westchester National Bank of New Rochelle for 52 million dollars. This was one of Barclays' successful bids to take over American banks in that year.[39] This is merely one example of the global interlinkage between finance capitals. British-owned commercial banks have tended to dominate Kenya's commercial banking due to the historical connections between East Africa and the British metropolis.

It has been shown that there is also a close interlinkage between western merchant banks and new 'state' development agencies, whose combination represents an important new form of finance capital. It is

---

37 In the 1975 Economic Survey, coffee and tea comprised K£35·2 million (21 per cent) and K£22·9 million (14 per cent) respectively of Kenya's total exports by value.
38 Interview with CBA, April 1977, op. cit.
39 *EAS*, 30 October 1973.

clear that *finance capital*, through state agencies and private merchant banks, plays a central role in supporting the move of both foreign and domestic capital into *production*. Therefore, the role of various national and international agencies and development banks is of utmost importance when examining Kenya's links with the world economy.

MANAGEMENT CONTRACTS

It has been stressed that the prevalent form of foreign investment in the 1970s is through *joint ventures* between local and foreign capital and international financial institutions. The conditions under which such projects are established are laid down by the management contracts and technical agreements taken out usually between the government and the foreign firm.[40] The partial ownership and regulation of projects by the government theoretically gives the 'host' country a chance to control the conditions under which foreign firms transfer the whole technological 'package' to an overseas project. Much has been written with regard to technology agreements in Latin America, suggesting ways in which governments can improve their bargaining techniques with multinational firms. The management contract usually involves a complex package of technical, managerial and financial components all of which must be evaluated by the host government. Vaitsos[41] has suggested that the issue of technology purchase and foreign investment should be placed within a strict bargaining framework, which can be adjusted according to the different characteristics of each industry. In Kenya, management contracts are negotiated by the Treasury and representatives of the relevant ministries. The project evaluation by the New Projects Committee of the Treasury has been shown before to be relatively inconsistent and susceptible to political pressure. There is a recurrent problem of ensuring adequate evaluation facilities within the government bodies to deal with complex technological issues.

The Treasury has the power to bargain with the foreign firm to gain conditions from the project that are more advantageous to the 'national' economy. Each management contract takes a similar form and the variations between them depend on the technical characteristics of the project and the type of political interventions to which it is subject. In general the terms of management contracts cover common factors such as financial arrangements, government concessions, level of protection and fees to be paid to the parent company for technical

---

40 The technical agreement is normally drawn up separately from the management contract and is usually confidential.

41 C. Vaitsos, 'The process of commercialisation of technology in the Andean pact', in H. Radice (ed.), *International Firms and Modern Imperialism*, op. cit. His aim is to encourage host governments to 'improve' their bargaining techniques with foreign technology suppliers.

and management services. It is obvious that the foreign firms will push for the highest fees possible and for quite a high level of management control (particularly at senior levels). It is on these points that the government bodies will usually attempt to push for more favourable terms. The following discussion summarizes six management contracts taken out between the Kenya government and foreign firms between 1965 and 1975. There will be a separate consideration of the terms.

FINANCIAL TERMS

In general, the financial conditions laid down in the management contracts will conform to the prevailing government regulations. In some of the cases in our list, the amount of loan capital required for the project is explicitly stated. For instance, a chemical firm required K£609 000 in 1970 when the contract was drawn up and security for the loan was to be provided by the subsidiary company. In some other cases the management contract will specify the *source* of the loan capital, as well as limitations on borrowing rights of certain projects. The six examples used here exhibit marked differences in the terms of concessions. For instance a canning firm during the 1960s made an agreement with the government which permitted that firm to borrow locally up to 50 per cent of the total investment in the project (including both fixed and current assets). On the other hand, another industrial firm in 1973 had its local borrowing restricted to 40 per cent of the share capital. In part this might reflect the changing Central Bank regulations, which by 1974 had restricted the amount of local borrowing for all foreign firms to 20 per cent of the share capital, while local firms were permitted to borrow between 40 and 60 per cent of their total investment.[42]

The differences between the last two firms also suggest that a superior political alliance might have overridden state regulation. The canning firm was able to take out a large number of mortgages with local banks which amounted approximately to between K£2 and K£3 million between 1968 and 1975. Between 1975 and 1976 the company liquidated this debt, largely due to tougher Central Bank regulations concerning the transfer of dividends and fees by firms with large amounts of local debt.[43]

Some of the contracts established the method of procuring loans from the parent of the subsidiary firm in Kenya. In the case of a paper mill, for instance, loans took the form of retention of fees owed by the subsidiary to the parent company. In some cases the rate of interest repayment on the loans to the parent would be fixed at a certain percentage.

---

42 For a discussion of Central Bank regulations, refer to Chapter 5.
43 This firm also had a mortgage with its parent company.

GOVERNMENT CONCESSIONS

Each contract makes specific demands on the government to provide protective measures for the new project and these usually depend on the nature of that enterprise. It has become standard practice in the case of import-substitution projects for the firm to request adequate tariff protection against imported products from abroad, and also tax rebates on intermediate goods. The discussion of Kenya's postwar industrialization in Chapter 3 outlined the degree of government concessions granted to 'infant' projects. Due to the limited markets in countries such as Kenya, an extensive degree of protection is required from the government by the potential investor. One firm in our list which manufactures a range of maize starch and glucose products set out a four-page list of items which it was to manufacture, and requested the government to impose import duties of between 30 and 50 per cent.

Most foreign firms investing in a particular sector of production will try to ensure that the same type of protection is not extended further to another firm making the same product. The East African Industrial Licensing Ordinances from the 1950s onwards did attempt to avoid duplication of plants in the East African region. This was not, however, effective, due to the diverging national interests of the three East African countries.[44] The most blatant examples in recent years of duplication of projects within Kenya occurred in the vehicle assembly sector. In 1974 agreements were reached between the government and three different foreign firms to establish vehicle-assembly plants to supply the local market. These included Leyland (Kenya) Ltd, General Motors and Associated Vehicles Assemblers (owned by Lonrho, MacKenzie Dalgety and local partners). In 1978 it was announced that a fourth plant would be constructed to assemble Fiat vehicles. The first three vehicle-assembly firms reached agreements with the government concurrently whereby they would each receive import protection and duty remissions for the assembly of their respective range of vehicles. The viability of these four plants in a market as limited as that of Kenya has been questioned by both foreign advisers and the New Projects Committee, which has not affected the outcome. Nevertheless the government has tried to ensure through the contracts that all these assembly plants make efforts to use a higher proportion of locally manufactured components.

Out of this sample of contracts, the most favourable concessions were granted to the canning company which was assisted in the procuring of suitable land for expansion.[45] In this case the foreign firm was able to secure a virtual monopoly over that branch of industry in

---

44 The possibility of fully extending export markets to Uganda and Tanzania was cut short after the border closure between Kenya and Tanzania in 1977.
45 Foreign firms cannot purchase land directly in Kenya.

Kenya. From this sample it would seen that by the 1970s the government was becoming more strict about the conditions placed on foreign partners in industrial ventures. The provisions covering utilization of raw materials, training of local personnel and utilization of local credit were becoming increasingly specific.[46]

MANAGEMENT FEES

One of the ways in which foreign firms extract profit from their operations in countries such as Kenya is through the imposition of management and technical fees on the subsidiary companies. Once again the rate and type of fees are always subject to bargaining between the host country and the foreign firm. Technology fees tend to be standard within the same firm, although the form by which the fees operate varies between different firms. For instance, the management fees to be paid by the Kenyan subsidiary to the parent paper-manufacturing firm amounted to 2 per cent of yearly net sales in excess of K£2 million and 3 per cent of yearly sales in excess of K£3 million. The technical fee for the first phase of construction is usually distinguished in a management contract. In the case of the paper mill, the parent was to be granted equity shares in lieu of technical fees incurred in the construction of the plant.

The method of payment also differs from contract to contract but it is usually specified from the outset. For instance an American chemical firm requested payment of 2½ per cent from net profits, and wanted this to be paid to the parent company in US dollars. The canning firm on the other hand wanted the option for payment in foreign currency. It seems to be general practice that the proportion of fees charged on sales escalates with absolute size of sales and profit. In the early 1970s, the Kenya government introduced a withholding tax on management and technical fees paid to parent companies as a means of discouraging large remittances abroad. It is difficult to ascertain whether this has been effective in cutting down the level of remittance from this source.

TRAINING AND PERSONNEL

Management contracts between host government and foreign firms are likely to specify the numbers of expatriate technical and managerial staff required to implement each stage of the project, with a view to phasing out most non-citizen posts. In the 1970s the Kenyanization Bureau of the Ministry of Labour became increasingly strict in demanding precise schedules from foreign firms for the replacement of expatriates by Kenyans and the provision of training schemes for local

---

46 It is not possible to ascertain exactly the degree to which various concessions were the result of bargaining between the government and foreign companies.

staff.[47] During the preparation of management contracts, therefore, the Bureau is consulted on the question of training and personnel.

When a new factory is constructed, foreign managers are permitted to employ a number of expatriate technical staff for an interim period until Kenyans have been trained to take over the positions. The paper mill contract for example, initially earmarked 190 expatriate positions which were mainly technical, while twenty-six Kenyans began training with the parent company overseas. Most management contracts establish a deadline for the withdrawal of all or most of the expatriate staff. Nevertheless, the posts of general manager and often production manager are often reserved for representatives of the foreign company. In another of the sample contracts the firm agreed to Africanize all management positions within the company (except for the general manager) within seven years of the start of operations. In the case of one of the vehicle-assembly firms, the government encouraged the establishment of a local training school for factory staff.

In considering some management contracts it has been possible to generally define the areas of interlinkage and control over technology, finance and labour which host governments and foreign firms exercise over productive enterprises in Kenya.[48]

Conclusions

In this chapter the main features of foreign investment in post-colonial Kenya have been outlined. The form of such investment has been subject to change since independence in the early 1960s, which is a reflection of both the advance of indigenous capitalism and the internationalization of capital on a a global level. The Kenyan state during the 1970s exerted an increasing amount of pressure on foreign firms to localize their operations in terms of ownership and management. The growth of Kenya's manufacturing sector in the late 1960s and 1970s has been marked by the extension of government ownership in all the major sectors. It is not surprising, therefore, that the partnership form of investment between foreign firms, financial agencies and the state and/or private capital has become predominant. Foreign capital in the post-colonial period has flowed mainly into the manufacturing sector, and interests in the traditional plantation areas have been subject to pressure from indigenous capitalists.

---

47 For discussion on the workings of the Kenyanization Bureau in Kenya, see N. Swainson, 'The Bata Shoe Company and the transfer of technology in Kenya', a paper prepared for the African Association of Political Science project on training in MNCs, Dar es Salaam, November 1976.

48 Here we have not discussed the use of patents and technology packages in any great detail. This is due to the secrecy which surrounds such deals.

Furthermore, the Kenya government, after 1970, has attempted to supervise more closely the conditions under which foreign firms operate in the country. Both Chapters 5 and 6 have illustrated the development of control mechanisms on foreign capital in the post-independence period, and it is likely that these will be extended further in the future as the Kenyan bourgeoisie consolidate their power. Nevertheless, at the present stage it is evident that the government bodies concerned with supervising foreign investment operate imperfectly. This state of affairs has been attributed to two main factors: first the highly technical character of industrial projects which cannot be effectively evaluated under the existing system. Furthermore, persistent intervention at the political level in the case of particular projects, presents an obstacle to the consistent application of nationalist controls on foreign capital. It is suggested here that these controls will only function effectively when the state reaches a higher level of autonomy in support of the Kenyan bourgeoisie.

The discussion of management contracts in the last part of this chapter illustrates the formalized relationship between foreign capital and the host government at a point in time. This process has involved the formation of strategic alliances between foreign firms and sections of the Kenyan bourgeoisie. It is clear from the whole discussion that, despite the limitations, Kenya has actually constructed the *machinery* through which to control foreign capital in the interests of indigenous accumulation. This has been carried out in the context of the advance of indigenous capital into production and an increasingly high level of government ownership in the industrial sector.

APPENDIX 1   *Major Foreign Firms in Kenya after 1963, by Country of Origin*

Firm	Business	Parent Company
1 UNITED KINGDOM		
(a) *Investors before 1963*		
East African Oil Refineries	Oil refining and distribution	Shell–BP
East African Industries	Manuf. of oils, fats, soap, toothpaste, fruit squash	Unilever
Gailey & Roberts	Import, servicing and assembly of agricultural equipment	United Africa Co.
Metal Box (Kenya)	Metal containers	Metal Box
Baumann Co.	Primary processing, manuf. of paint and animal feeds, machinery import	Steel Brothers
Brooke Bond Liebig (Kenya)	Processing of tea, coffee, cinchona, tara, fruit and veg. canning	Brooke Bond Liebig
East African Portland Cement	Cement manuf.	Associated Portland Cement (UK) and Cementia Holdings AG
Bamburi Portland Cement		
East African Road Services	Transporting	British Electric Traction (BET)
United Touring Co.	Tourism and transport	BET
Mitchell Cotts (EA)	Trading, primary processing	Mitchell Cotts
EA Tobacco Co.	Tobacco and cigarette manuf.	BAT
Twiga Chemical Industries	Chemicals manuf.	Imperial Chemical Industries (ICI)
Magadi Soda Co.		

Finlay Industries	Manuf. of brushes and household goods	James Finlay (Scotland)
African Highlands Produce Co.	Tea growing and manuf.	James Finlay (Scotland)
Cadbury Schweppes (EA)	Chocolate and soft drinks manuf.	Cadbury Schweppes
(b) *Investors after 1963* Lonrho East Africa & subsidiaries	Primary processing, textiles and vehicle manuf., property, printing, estates	Lonrho
Mowlem Construction Co.	Road construction	Mowlem
Marshalls (EA)	Machinery import and servicing	Marshalls
2 USA Coca Cola EA	Manuf. soft drinks	Coca Cola
Firestone Tyres	Manuf. of tyres and rubber products	Firestone
Union Carbide	Manuf. batteries	Union Carbide
Fluorspar Co. (Kenya)	Fluorspar mining	Continental Ore (with Bamburi P. Cement)
Kenya Canners	Canning of fruit and veg.	Delmonte
Singer Industries	Sewing-machine assembly	Singer
Esso EA	Oil distribution	Esso
3 JAPAN Kenya Toray Mills	Manuf. synthetic textiles	Mitsui
Ataka	Engineering	Ataka
African Radio Manufs	Assembly of radios	Sanyo

Firm	Business	Parent Company
4 GERMANY		
Hoechst Drug Co.	Manuf. pharmaceuticals	Hoechst
Panafrican Vegetable Products	Veg. processing	Bruckner Werke and others
Siemens EA	Engineering	Siemens
Kuhne & Nagel	Transport and managing agents	Kuhne & Nagel
Hobby Hotels (EA)	Tourism	n.a.
5 INDIA		
Raymond Woollen Mills	Manuf. of textiles and wool	Raymond Textiles
Panafrican Paper Mills	Manuf. of paper	Oriental Paper Mills
6 AGA KHAN		
Diamond Trust (Holding Company)	Property, finance, hotels	Aga Khan Foundation (Geneva)
7 HOLLAND		
Twentsche Overseas Trading Company	Import and export	Twentsche Trading Co,
8 DENMARK		
DCK	Flowers and fruit for export	n.a.

(This list was drawn up in 1976 and is therefore subject to rapid change; there will have been some omissions.)

APPENDIX 2(a)   *Equity Capital Held by Kenya Companies, 1965 and 1972 (K£000s)*

Industry group	Kenya		Other EA countries		Foreign countries		Total	
	1965	1972	1965	1972	1965	1972	1965	1972
Services Incidental to Agriculture	1	12			99	88	485	8 585
Agriculture	27	26	5	1	68	73	14 053	11 929
Mining and Quarrying	4	67			96	33	852	300
Food Manufacturing	82	85	1		17	15	3 113	5 885
Beverage Industries	79	92	2		19	8	9 816	7 895
Chemical Industries	16	12			84	88	4 525	5 996
Transport Equipment and Repairs	70	76	1	3	29	21	3 023	3 831
Misc. Manufacturing Inds	11	36	1	6	88	57	10 290	19 025
Building Construction (inc. light and water)	25	83	2	1	73	16	10 072	10 993
Wholesale and Retail Trade*	14	10	2		84	90	11 828	11 582
Building Societies and Other Financial Institutions	51	47	5	4	44	49	3 202	10 119
Real Estate	43	15	1		56	85	1 082	1 255
Road Transport	32	40	1		67	60	685	1 483
Other Transport Services	91	81	1		8	19	590	723
Misc. Personal Services	82	59		1	18	40	1 253	4 599
TOTAL (K£000s)	26 155		1665		47 049		74 869	104 170
% of total	35		2		63		100	

Source: EAC Statistics Division – *Investment Survey.*
*This category is largely made up of oil retailing.

APPENDIX 2(b)   *Equity Capital of Companies in Kenya, 1968*

Industry Group	Kenya (%)	Other EA (%)	UK and other Sterling (%)	Non-sterling Areas (%)	Total K£000s
Services Incidental to Agriculture					585
Agriculture	23	5	59	13	16 341
Mining and Quarrying Oil Prospectg	11		85	3	901
Food Manufacture	82	8	15	3	5 453
Beverage Industries	58	5	36		1 000
Chemical Industries	7	3	86	6	3 898
Transport Equipmt Manuf. and Repair	73	2	18	6	4 213
Misc. Manufacturing	21	2	40	37	12 017
Bldg Constr. incl. Light and Water	39	1	57	1	10 747
Wholesale and Retail Trade	18		22	60	8 665
Bldg. Societies and other Financ. Inst.					1 139
Real Estate					1 026
Road Transport	45	1	41	12	8 868
Other Transport (incl. Communication)	23	2	62	13	1 989
Misc. Personal Services	38		15	47	789
TOTAL	26 324	1675	35 186	14 446	77 631

Source: East African Investment Survey, provisional.

APPENDIX 3   *Percentage of Gross Product by Nationality of Shareholding/Ownership (K£000s)*

	Citizens		Non-Citizens	
	1967 (%)	1972 (%)	1967 (%)	1972 (%)
Mining and Quarrying				
Metal Mining		81	100	19
Crude Petroleum and Natural Gas			100	
Stone Quarrying, Clay and Sandpits	40	34	60	66
Other Mining and Quarrying		3	100	97
TOTAL K£000s	131·4	376·9	1689·1	1575·6
	7	19	93	81
Manufacturing and Repairs				
Food (plus Tea in 1972)	62	60	38	40
Beverages and Tobacco	59	52	41	48
Textiles	10	15	90	85
Footwear, Clothing and Made-up Textiles	14	47	86	53
Wood Products (excl. Furniture)	28	75	72	25
Furniture and Fixtures	26	45	74	55
Paper and Paper Products		6	100	94
Printing and Publishing	21	33	79	67

	Citizens		Non-Citizens	
	1967 (%)	1972 (%)	1967 (%)	1972 (%)
Leather and Fur Products	9	15	91	85
Rubber Manufactures	13	35	87	65
Chemicals and Petrol Prods	5	43	95	57
Non-Metallic Mineral Prods	2	33	98	67
Metal Products	24	24	76	76
Non-Electrical Machinery	24	36	76	64
Electrical Machinery	63	61	37	39
Transport Equipment	12	20	88	80
Misc. Manufacturing	29	56	71	44
TOTAL (%)	29	37	71	63
TOTAL K£000s	8929.5	22 320	22 261.6	38 626.7
Building and Construction				
Electrical, Structural				
Steel Back, Erectors				
Plumbers	8	21	92	79
Other Building and Construction	14	25	86	75
TOTAL (%)	13	24	87	75
TOTAL K£000s	581.6	2661.5	3942.9	8346

Source: Census of Industrial Production for 1967 and 1972, Central Bureau of Statistics, Treasury. The response rate for this survey was around 80 per cent for 1972.

APPENDIX 4(a)   *Long-Term Loans Outstanding from East Africa and Rest of the World, in 1968 (K£000s)*

Industry Group	1965 (%)	1968 (%)
Services Incidental to Agric. and Agric.	11	10
Mining and Quarrying (incl. Refinery)	20	29
Food Manufacturing		3
Beverage Industries		
Chemical Industries	7	3
Transport Equipment, Manufacturing and Repairs		5
Misc. Manufacturing Industries	8	7
Building Construction (incl. Electric and Water Supply)		17
Wholesale and Retail Trade	44	9
Building Societies and Other Financial Institutions Real Estate	9	1
Road Transport and Other Transport		12
Misc. Personal Services (Hotels, Cinemas)		4
TOTAL PERCENTAGE	100	100
TOTAL	31 566	25 105

Source: EAC Statistics Division, Investment Survey, provisional.

APPENDIX 4(b)   *Amounts Outstanding in Long-Term Loans in Kenya, 1972 (K£000s)*

	Kenya (%)	Other EA Countries (%)	Total Non-Residents (%)	Grand Total (K£000s)	% by Sector
Agriculture	44	48	56	3 330	9
Food Manufacturing	48		51	4 301	11
Beverage Industries	86		13	3 041	8
Chemical Industries	20	13	80	892	2
Transport Equipment, Manuf. and Repairs	39		61	1 877	5
Misc. Manufacturing Inds (incl. Oil-Refining)	54	316	45	14 040	37
Wholesale/Retail Trade	37	546	96	5 608	15
Building Societies and Other Financial Institutions plus					
Real Estate	41		59	3 001	8
Road Transport and Other	4	6	96	253	1
Misc. Personal Services	39		61	2 073	5
TOTAL				38 416	

(Estimates prepared for East African Community Investment Survey, therefore no totals given.)

APPENDIX 5   *Industrial Census: Numbers Engaged, 1968, 1969, 1970 and 1971*

Industry	1968	1969	1970	1971
Mining and Quarrying				
Metal Mining and Petroleum Prospecting	596	486	355	324
Stone Quarrying and Non-Metallic Mineral Mining	1 560	1 744	1 880	2 065
TOTAL	2 156	2 230	2 235	2 389
Manufacturing				
Meat and Dairy Products	3 259	3 294	3 662	4 177
Canned Fruit and Vegetables	1 799	2 051	1 661	1 777
Grain Mill Products	1 705	1 761	2 080	2 285
Bakery Products	701	703	699	960
Sugar and Confectionary	2 285	2 523	2 772	2 894
Miscellaneous Foods	931	937	1 021	1 107
Beer, Malt and Tobacco	2 763	2 806	2 703	2 888
Soft Drinks	439	514	633	809
Textiles	6 442	6 479	6 627	7 621
Footwear and Clothing	2 347	2 781	4 096	4 339
Sawn Timber	3 925	4 451	4 990	5 383
Furniture and Fixtures	725	870	905	1 243
Paper and Paper Products	1 178	1 262	1 427	1 535
Printing and Publishing	1 732	1 834	2 075	2 290
Leather and Leather Prods	486	797	990	1 052
Basic Industrial Chemicals and Petroleum	732	718	818	824
Paints, Soap and Oil	853	929	1 090	1 261
Pyrethrum Extract	216	205	101	366
Miscellaneous Chemicals	787	1 028	112	1 199
Clay and Glass Products	557	596	740	929
Cement	980	1 064	1 100	1 181
Other Non-Metallic Products	442	474	563	829
Metal Products	2 752	3 038	4 087	4 673
Non-Electrical Machinery	408	555	565	409
Electrical Machinery	2 292	3 193	3 645	4 145
Shipbuilding and Repairs	1 246	1 127	1 243	1 390
Railway Rolling Stock	7 215	7 417	10 756	10 725
Motor Vehicle Bodies	623	639	999	1 257
Motor Vehicle Repairs	3 557	3 514	3 874	4 251
Aircraft Repairs	951	991	1 053	1 228
Misc. Manufacturing	643	847	1 190	1 312
TOTAL	54 971	59 398	69 277	76 336

Industry	1968	1969	1970	1971
Building and Construction				
Electrical Contractors,				
Plumbers and Borehole				
Drilling	1 446	1 885	1 806	1 827
Building Construction	7 062	7 842	8 049	10 510
Civil Engineering,				
Painting and Minor Repairs	1 486	1 489	3 834	4 508
TOTAL	9 994	11 261	13 689	16 845

Source: Central Bureau of Statistics, Ministry of Finance and Planning.

APPENDIX 6   *Government Ownership in the Private Sector, 1976*

(a) Companies Wholly Owned by Government or Statutory Board(s)

Company Name	Government Body
African Diatomite Industries	ICDC
Uchumi House	ICDC
Kenya National Trading Corp.	ICDC
Kenya National Properties	ICDC
Kenya Industrial Estate	ICDC
Kenya Cashew Nuts	ICDC and Maize and Produce Board
Boma's of Kenya	KTDC
Homa Bay Lodge	KTDC
Kenya National Travel Bureau	KTDC
KTDC Hotel Management Co.	KTDC
Mt Elgon Lodge	KTDC
Sunset Hotel	KTDC
Development House	AFC and ADC
Industrial Development Bank	Treasury ICDC KNA and NBK
Lands	ADC
Kenya National Assurance Co.	Treasury
Kencom House	Treasury
Kenya Power Co.	Treasury
Kenya Pipeline Co.	Treasury
Kenya Commercial Bank	Treasury
Kenya Airways	Treasury
National Bank of Kenya	Treasury
Tana River Development Co.	Min. of Power and Communications
Chinga Tea Factory Co.	KTDA
Chebut Tea Factory	KTDA

Company Name	Government Body
Githongo Tea Factory Co.	KTDA
Githambo Tea Factory Co.	KTDA
Ikumbi Tea Farmers Co.	KTDA
Imenti Tea Farmers	KTDA
Kangaita Tea Factory	KTDA
Kambaa Tea Factory	KTDA
Kenyanyaini Tea Factory	KTDA
Kap Koros Tea Factory	KTDA
Kiamakama Tea Factory Co.	KTDA
Kebirigo Tea Factory Co.	KTDA
Letein Tea Factory Co.	KTDA
Mataara Tea Factory Co.	KTDA
Nyakoba Tea Factory	KTDA
Nyasiongo Tea Factory	KTDA
Ragati Tea Factory	KTDA
Tehat Tea Factory Co.	KTDA
Thumaita Tea Factory Co.	KTDA

(b) *Companies where Government or Boards Have a Controlling Interest*

Company Name	Government Body
DFCK	Government
EA Sugar Industries	DFCK
EA Power and Lighting	Min. of Power and Communications
Chemilil Sugar Co.	DFCK
EA Oil Refineries	Treasury
EA Portland Cement	Treasury
Kenren Fertilizer Co.	Treasury
Leyland Kenya	Treasury
South Nyanza Sugar Co.	Treasury
EA Fine Spinners	ICDC
Fluorspar Co. of Kenya	ICDC
Minet ICDC	ICDC
Kenya Wine Agencies	ICDC
Kenatco	ICDC
Kenya Engineering	ICDC
Kenya Mining Industries	ICDC
Mea Garments	ICDC
First Permanent (EA)	DFCK
Housing Finance of Kenya	Min. of Housing
Kenya Building Society	HFCK
Mumias Sugar Co.	Treasury
Meru Mulika Lodge	KTDC
Marsabit Lodge	KTDC
Tea Hotel	KTDC
Zimmerman's	KTDC
Seed Driers	ADC
Nzoi Sugar Co.	ADC

(c) *Companies in which Government or Boards Have a Minority Interest*

Company Name	Government Body
Associated Battery Manufacturers	ICDC
African Radio Manufacturers	ICDC
African Retail Traders	ICDC
Block Hotels	ICDC
Brackenhurst Hotel (1944)	ICDC
Brollo Kenya	ICDC
Bamburi Portland Cement	ICDC
BAT Kenya	ICDC
Brooke Bond Liebig (Kenya)	Treasury/ICDC
CPC Industrial Products	ICDC
Ceramic Industries	ICDC
Claude Neon Lights (EA)	ICDC
EA Industries	ICDC
Eslon Plastics of Kenya	ICDC
ESA	ICDC
EA Fine Clothing	ICDC
EA Fisheries	ICDC
EA Packaging Industries	ICDC
EA Breweries	ICDC
Firestone (EA)	ICDC
Infusion Kenya	ICDC
ICDC Investment Co.	ICDC
J. W. Kearsley (Kenya)	ICDC
Kenya Fishnet Industries	ICDC
Kenya Bowling Centres	ICDC
Kenya Industrial Plastics	ICDC
Kenya Canners	ICDC
Kenya Toray Mills	ICDC
Kiambaa Industries	ICDC
Kenya Peanuts	ICDC
Kenya Industries	ICDC
Lake Baringo Fisheries	ICDC
Lamu Fisheries	ICDC
Nairobi Airport Services	ICDC
Nakuru Chrome T. Co.	ICDC
Nakulines	ICDC
Pan African Vegetable Products	ICDC
Pan African Paper Mills	ICDC
Polysynthetic (EA)	ICDC
Pulp and Paper Co.	ICDC
Raymond Woollen Mills	ICDC
Sokoro Fibre Boards	ICDC
Salt Manufacturers	ICDC
South Coast Hotel	ICDC
Seracoating	ICDC
Sewing Thread	ICDC
Tanneries of Kenya	ICDC

Company Name	Government Body
Tiger Shoe Co.	ICDC
Union Cambridge (Kenya)	ICDC
Umoha Enterprises	ICDC
Wananchi Saw Mills	ICDC
Welded Steel Pipes	ICDC
Air Kenya	KTDC
African Tours and Hotels	KTDC
Embu Hotels	KTDC
International Hotels	KTDC
Kenya Safari Lodge	KTDC
Lake Naivasha Hotel	KTDC
Mountain Lodge	KTDC
Panafric Hotel	KTDC
Robinson Hotel (MSA)	KTDC
Safari Lodge Properties	KTDC
Tourism Promotion Services	KTDC
The Ark	KTDC
Tourism Enterprises	KTDC
Associated Vehicles Assembly	Treasury
Bata Shoe Company	Treasury
CMC Holdings Co.	Treasury
Grindlays Bank (Kenya)	Treasury
Elgon Tea Factory Co.	ADC
Eliato Kenya	ADC
Kenya Livestock and Estate	ADC
Kenya Co-operative Creameries	ADC
BAT Developments (Kenya)	ADC
KFA	ADC

These figures are based on estimates for 1976 and are therefore subject to constant change.

Abbreviations

KTDA	Kenya Tea Development Authority
KTDC	Kenya Tourist Development Corporation
ICDC	Industrial and Commercial Development Corporation
ADC	Agricultural Development Corporation
AFC	Agricultural Finance Corporation
HFCK	Housing Finance Company of Kenya
NBK	National Bank of Kenya
KNAC	Kenya National Assurance Company

CHAPTER 7

Case Studies of Three Multinational Firms in Kenya

The intention of these case studies is to explore the levels of collaboration and competition between local and foreign capital in post-colonial Kenya. For this purpose three firms have been selected, Brooke Bond and Bata, dominating one branch of production and Lonrho, a contemporary form of conglomerate with a wide variety of interests. In these cases, the mediation of the state in the relation between foreign corporations and certain sections of the Kenyan bourgeoisie is of particular concern.

Brooke Bond Liebig and the Tea Industry in Kenya

The background to Brooke Bond's intervention in East Africa during the 1920s has been outlined earlier. Before the Second World War, this international tea firm, which specialized in tea marketing rather than production, had managed to establish a monopoly over tea distribution in East Africa. Tea production was restricted between 1934 and 1947 during the period of the International Tea Agreements as a result of a global strategy on the part of the major tea-producers.[1] Once tea prices had risen after the Second World War, the expansion of tea acreage was once more permitted and even encouraged by the dominant tea-growing firms in Kenya.

This analysis aims to show the way in which Brooke Bond and other large foreign tea-growing firms continued to dominate the conditions of tea-production in Kenya after 1945.

EXPANSION OF BROOKE BOND AND THE KENYAN TEA INDUSTRY AFTER 1945

After the Second World War there was a rapid expansion in the Kenyan tea industry, and about five new tea firms with Indian interests decided to buy estates in Kenya. In addition to this, the two major tea producers, Brooke Bond and James Finlay, undertook large-scale

---

1 See Chapter 2 for the early history of the Kenyan tea industry.

expansion programmes to increase tea output in their Kenyan subsidiaries. The major thrust behind this expansion of the international
tea companies after 1945 was the export market, where prices had
risen dramatically from pre-war levels.

Therefore East Africa and Kenya in particular were in a favourable
position to develop their respective tea industries in the years following the Second World War. Production costs of tea (both land and
labour) were lower in East Africa than in India and Ceylon and this
factor, plus lower company taxation, encouraged the entry of new tea
firms and the expansion of existing firms. The Brooke Bond Company,
as one of the largest tea-growers and the monopoly tea distributor in
Kenya, will be the focus of the following discussion.

BROOKE BOND —INNOVATIONS AND IMPROVEMENT IN TECHNIQUES

Brooke Bond in the 1950s embarked on an expansion programme
which involved both new planting (by taking over existing estates) and
improvement in plucking and manufacturing techniques. The bulk of
Brooke Bond's new tea-planting took place between 1947 and 1960,
and by 1958 the company had 2909 hectares of mature tea area.[2] Table
41 shows that yearly tea production rose from 4·15 million kilogrammes to 7·09m kg of made tea between 1958 and 1968. Brooke
Bond built four new factories in the 1950s and three in the 1960s,
making a total of eight green-leaf factories, plus one instant-tea factory
by 1976.[3]

The greatest innovation in tea-planting methods came after 1960
when the bulk of Brooke Bond's new planting had already taken place.
Improved tea strains were made possible with the advent of vegetative
propagation (VP), which is a method of growing selected cuttings from
existing bushes or clones. This enabled the selection of high-yielding
varieties from different types of tea bushes and the smallholder tea-
planting programme of the 1960s was able to take greatest advantage
of the new process. This method of tea-growing improved the standards of tea in the long term for both smallholders and estates. The use
of herbicides after 1959 also improved yields of all tea plants.[4]

However, the substantial improvement in the standards of Kenyan
tea from after the Second World War can be attributed to improved
plucking techniques which involved the better organization of labour.
The major aim of all large MNCs is to *improve the productivity* of
labour in the long term and the case of tea is no exception. From the

2 Information from the Brooke Bond Liebig Company in Kenya.
3 Annual reports and accounts of Brooke Bond Liebig Kenya Ltd, 1975, and old
records of the Brooke Bond Company at Kericho.
4 Details from an interview with a senior group manager (Brooke Bond) at Kericho in
1974.

TABLE 41   *Brooke Bond Kenya Ltd, Statistics on Tea Production 1958–75*

Year Ending 30 June	Total Production (kg of made tea)	Yield/Hectare (kg of made tea)	Hectares	Cost of Production (cents per kg of made tea)
1958	4 146 402	1425	2909	458
1959	4 650 0`3	1559	2982	368
1960	4 756 971	1536	3097	386
1961	4 275 155	1324	3238	443
1962	5 434 284	1556	3492	383
1963	6 113 306	1655	3707	366
1964	6 815 518	1728	3942	350
1965	5 797 388	1394	4156	403
1966	6 637 267	1566	4238	388
1967	5 312 838	1210	4391	496
1968	7 095 101	1588	4466	427
1969	7 904 577	1753	4508	407
1970	9 051 905	1987	4565	353
1971	7 659 420	1679	4562	419
1972	12 038 035	2213	5440	377
1973	12 919 434	2365	5462	374
1974	10 446 283	1912	5465	460
1975	11 414 074	2089	5465	497

Source: Brooke Bond Liebig Kenya Ltd.

Notes: 1 Buret Tea Company purchased in 1971.
           2 Made tea to green leaf – multiply made tea by 4·5.
           3 Labour cost approximately 35 per cent of cost of production

1950s onwards, labour was ordered to pluck the tea leaf more finely: pluck only the top three or four leaves and the bud. Previously, plucking had been quite random and the quality of leaf not closely controlled. These improvements in plucking methods had the effect of raising the overall standard of the manufactured tea.[5]

The major changes in Brooke Bond's *manufacturing* techniques came also around 1960 when the firm began a change over from the orthodox method of production to the CTC method (crushing, tearing and cutting). The traditional method of tea manufacture, the orthodox method, first employed in India and then East Africa, involves the withered tea leaf being revolved inside large rollers. This was a labour-intensive method for the tea had to be fed into the rollers by hand. The CTC method, however, involves a cutting and tearing mechanism which chops the tea up much more finely in a shorter period of time. The finished tea from the CTC method has become increasingly popular on the world market due to its quicker infusion time and stronger taste. The main advantage to the company of this method is in the labour saved and the shorter production time.

Another innovation in the manufacturing process was 'trough withering', a process that was modified in the late 1960s so that a deep bed of green leaf could be dried by a warm air flow introduced from the steam power of the factory. This change conserved production time. The final innovation in factory techniques of tea production came in the mid-1960s with the GWA system of fermenting the tea leaf, which gives a more careful control over the process. All these improvements were made *inside* the existing factories.

Innovations and research and development are not usually carried out at the parent company level, but at the research institutes in producing areas. Brooke Bond Kenya, for instance, sponsors the Tea Research Institute at Kericho. The main function of such research in the subsidiary companies is not to create new products, but to perfect existing processing techniques and raise the productivity of labour through improvement in the means of production. Instant tea, the only entirely new product introduced in Kenya, was developed by the parent company. The instant-tea factory, which was opened in 1973 in Kenya, cost £1 million to construct and had a capacity to process 7 000 kilogrammes of powder per week and 5 million kilogrammes per annum. This project uses highly sophisticated equipment developed by the parent company and originally employed only seventy-six skilled labourers.[6]

The improvements in manufacturing techniques from 1960 onwards have had the effect of raising the yield per hectare of made tea in the

---

5 Kenya teas did not catch up in quality with those from Ceylon and India until the late 1960s when these improvements had begun to be effective.
6 *Sunday Post*, 9 June 1974.

Brooke Bond subsidiary. The firm's yield per hectare in Kenya has increased by 50 per cent between 1958 and 1975, from 1425 to 2089 kilogrammes of made tea. It is significant that the costs of production have not fallen drastically since 1958, despite the investment in improved processing techniques.

Increased labour costs in the 1970s (which constitute approximately 35 per cent of the total production bill) have accounted for the rise in overall production costs. The amount of labour employed in the tea factories has been held constant, but the estates staff have expanded with the improvement in tea-plucking standards. Increased oil and transport costs have also raised production costs. By 1976, Brooke Bond employed a total of 12 315 people, 121 in management, 189 supervisory staff (not unionizable), and 1090 unionized staff, making a total of 10 915 unionizable staff.[7]   The bulk of the latter group are employed on the estates.

Since the 1950s, the company has been able to concentrate capital, improve techniques of production and raise output levels. In 1963, BBL's tea production constituted 34 per cent of Kenya's total production, whereas by 1973 this proportion had fallen to 23 per cent, which can be explained by the increase in smallholder production.[8] In the 1960s and 1970s, Brooke Bond has expanded its output rapidly without extending its tea area, mainly through improved manufacturing and growing techniques.

DIVERSIFICATION AND TAKEOVER

Since 1969, Brooke Bond has diversified its production away from tea and coffee in order to lessen its dependence on primary products. The price of tea on the world market is relatively 'inelastic': it never rises or falls dramatically. Most of the diversifications undertaken by Brooke Bond in the 1970s have been in the food and beverage sectors.[9] BBL was only able to maintain its monopoly marketing position for the internal market (established in 1938) until 1977, when the Kenya Tea Development Authority (KTDA), through an umbrella company, Kenya Tea Packers Ltd, took over all the tea-marketing functions in Kenya.[10]

Brooke Bond's new phase of expansion (1969–1975) took place as part of a merger in 1968, at the parent-company level, of Brooke Bond and Liebigs Meat Company (UK) to form Brooke Bond Liebig Ltd. This merger linked up Brooke Bond's beverage interests with one of

---

7 Information from the Kenyanization Bureau of the Ministry of Labour, Nairobi.

8 See Tea Board of Kenya statistics, and those of BBL (Kenya).

9 Making an obvious connection with their international food and beverage marketing concerns.

10 For further details of this takeover, see 'Tea in Kenya', Weekly Review, 8 September 1978.

Britain's largest meat and extract processors, who had been operating in East Africa since the 1930s.

By 1969, the government had taken over the Liebig production plant at Athi River, but the marketing of the canned meat products remained in the hands of the Brooke Bond Liebig Company until 1974 when it was taken over by the Kenya Meat Commission. Brooke Bond had consolidated its interests in the food and beverage sectors, when in 1967 it took a 30 per cent interest in Kabazi Canners, a fruit and vegetable canning plant owned by Asian industrialists. Therefore, by 1970, the Brooke Bond Liebig subsidiary in Kenya distributed a variety of canned foods, tea and coffee on the local market. The company distributed these products up to 1974 through 250 African retail agents,[11] but after that time it was compelled to distribute its products through citizen wholesale agents, cutting down the foreign firm's profit margin in the distribution of the product.

The firm undertook other diversifications in the late 1960s in Kenya. In 1968 it took over an existing fishing fly-tying factory in Kericho. In 1969, it bought a K£30 000 interest in a local financial institution, East African Acceptances Ltd. However, the largest proportion of Brooke Bond Liebig's profit in the 1970s was still derived from tea and coffee (both growing and marketing). After the Second World War, in Kericho district, the Brooke Bond Company had consolidated its tea-growing area by taking over small settler tea estates which were in financial difficulties. This was the usual method when large units of capital absorbed the weaker ones.[12] Brooke Bond in 1971 acquired its last tea estate from European farmers – the Buret Tea Company – for K£850 000, thereby adding 2100 acres of mature tea area to its estates. Brooke Bond raised a loan with Grindlays International in order to assist with the purchase of this firm. This takeover raised Brooke Bond's area of mature tea in Kenya from 4562 hectares in 1971 to 5440 hectares in 1972, and *made tea* production rose from 7 659 420 kilogrammes in 1971 to 12 038 035 kilogrammes in 1972.

By 1972, Brooke Bond had consolidated its tea-growing area in Kericho, where it owned a total of 14 956 hectares of agricultural land. The remaining land area was devoted to blue gum estates, which provide fuel for the tea factories, dairy farming, and new crops such as tara and cinchona. In 1972, the company's overall interests in Kenya were divided into the following sections; 75 per cent in estates (mainly tea and coffee), 15 per cent in marketing, canning, packing and distribution and 10 per cent in trading, warehousing, fishing flies, travel and hotel interests.[13] In the 1972 Annual Report, the managing direc-

11 Annual reports and accounts of BBL.
12 Concentration of capital involves the absorption of weaker units of capital. The instability and fragility of settler capitalism has been outlined in Chapters 1, 2 and 4.
13 BBL (Kenya), reports and accounts for 1973.

tor expressed the company's intention to 'move away from further expansion in the agricultural sector – tea, coffee, etc., and consolidate in the trading and marketing divisions'.

However, since 1968, the company, as part of a global diversification move, has expanded the estates division to include some *industrial* crops, notably *tara* and *cinchona*. These crops were developed by Brooke Bond at Kericho and it was the first time they had been cultivated on a plantation basis. In 1975, the estates division had 347 hectares of tara. The latter is the powder from the pods of spinosa trees and it is a rich source of two chemicals, tannic and gallic acids. World consumption of tara is estimated to be in the region of 6 000 tons per year. Although by 1974 only 5 tons of Kenyan-grown tara were shipped to Scotland for the tanning industry, it was estimated that by 1979 tara production would reach 900 tons per annum.[14]

Cinchona trees are stripped and *quinine* salt is extracted from the bark, which is then used in the drugs industry and mineral water preparation. In 1975 the company had 650 hectares of cinchona, with plans to develop another 100 in the following two years. In the first year of sales of quinine bark to Europe in 1974, the company made (gross) sales of K£250 000.[15] The cinchona estates are potentially a most profitable diversion for Brooke Bond Liebig.

The two examples of crop diversification mentioned above indicate a shift in the company's interests at a global level away from the traditional areas of tea and coffee into specialized industrial crops.

BROOKE BOND 'GOES PUBLIC' IN KENYA

Brooke Bond Liebig, by 1972, was the third largest foreign company in Kenya (by asset value) and had been registered in Kenya for fifty years.[16] In 1971, the Treasury in Kenya began to pressure the firm to issue shares to the public on the Nairobi Stock Exchange, as previously the firm had been a private company with 99 per cent of its share capital owned by the parent firm in London. After lengthy negotiations with the government, BBL agreed to reconstitute itself in Kenya as a public company and offer a proportion of its shares to the public. After some negotiation over the pricing of the shares, BBL issued about 11 per cent of its local share capital in Kenya as shares amounting to K£750 000.[17] The main aim of the government had been to encourage the participation of local capital in one of the major foreign

---

14 This information is from the *Sunday Post*, 9 June 1974, and the BBL (Kenya) reports and accounts for 1975. The gallic acids obtained from tara are used in the manufacture of paper and dyes.

15 Interview with financial director, BBL (Kenya) in 1974, Nairobi.

16 Nairobi stockbroker's report in 1971.

17 Annual returns (Registrar General) for the BBL (Kenya) Co., 1972.

firms in the country, but only a small number of private investors bought 2 per cent of the share capital. The government itself, as part of its policy of localizing the equity of large foreign firms, took 11 per cent leaving 87 per cent of BBL Kenya's equity in the hands of the British parent company. This move appeased nationalist pressure on the company and also enabled the firm to raise money on the local stock exchange.

Brooke Bond's recent investment in industrial crops which are grown intensively on existing land is one way in which large foreign corporations can adjust to nationalist pressure in the host countries.

SMALLHOLDER TEA AND NATIONALIST PRESSURE ON BROOKE BOND

This section will assess the relationship between foreign estate companies, notably Brooke Bond, and the smallholder tea scheme in Kenya. This follows the fortunes of smallholder tea production into the 1970s and identifies the indigenous class interests operating within the tea parastatal, the Kenya Tea Development Authority.

Estate tea production after 1945 expanded rapidly, a process which was dominated by Brooke Bond and the James Finlay Company. From the 1950s onwards there was a parallel development of smallholder tea cultivation. This scheme was instigated by the colonial government under the Swynnerton Plan to develop cash crops in African areas and it was later funded by two other agencies, the CDC and the World Bank. The first smallholder experimental plots were started in Kericho as early as 1949 and small peasant farmers were given between one-third and one acre of land on which to cultivate tea. The materials were then advanced by the government, which the growers had to repay through a cess on the green leaf payment. From 1950 onwards the smallholder scheme spread into the Central Province. After a while, the estate tea firms, notably Brooke Bond, George Williamson and African Highlands Produce (James Finlay) worked in collaboration with the government to ensure quality control over smallholder tea. Many Brooke Bond personnel were seconded to the scheme in order to instruct African farmers on the growing of tea. The board co-ordinating the tea scheme was the *Special Crops Development Authority* (SCDA) which later became the Kenya Tea Development Authority (KTDA). The SCDA was composed of government staff and experts from the commercial tea companies, African representatives from the growing areas and estate company representatives. In 1950, the first smallholder tea factory was constructed in the Central Province, at Ragati, by an engineer seconded from Brooke Bond. It was initially designed to process 1 million pounds of tea per annum. Until other smallholder factories had been constructed, the growers sold their leaf to the estate company factories of Brooke Bond, George

Williamson and James Finlay. Once a smallholder factory was constructed in a growing area, the tea-growers were required to pay a cess on the sale of green leaf to the factory.[18]

It is clear that from the outset the dominant tea-estate firms, such as Brooke Bond and James Finlay, played an important role in shaping the conditions under which the smallholder tea scheme developed. Brooke Bond, for instance, acted as advisers on tea-growing and also assisted in the linking up of British machinery suppliers and the smallholder tea factories. Before Africans were trained to operate the factories, the major tea companies in Kenya, Brooke Bond, James Finlay and George Williamson, provided management and technical assistance to the smallholder factories. This enabled them to directly influence the smallholder tea scheme from the growing to the processing of tea. In the early 1950s, Brooke Bond had been reluctant to assist the scheme, fearing that the development of smallholder tea might affect its own dominant position. Soon, Brooke Bond realized that it could fashion the smallholder tea scheme to its own advantage. The condition of Brooke Bond's participation in the smallholder development was that the government remove the threat of illegal, sundried tea to its low-cost market. The government responded and in 1964 the colonial regulations against sundried tea were confirmed in an Ordinance which banned its sale in Kenya.[19]

The three major tea companies were able to work the smallholder tea scheme to their own advantage by controlling *plucking* standards from the first stage of smallholder development. The tea firms insisted that the smallholder leaf be of a higher standard than the estates – that only two leaves and a bud should be plucked – and this was to be enforced through a team of leaf officers employed by the SCDA and later the KTDA. This meant that Brooke Bond was able to purchase the higher quality smallholder tea and blend it with its own lower-quality tea. The unit costs of production for smallholder factories were obviously higher, a price which was borne not by Brooke Bond but by the government parastatal (KTDA).

Table 42 shows the rapid expansion of smallholder tea production between 1963 and 1973. In 1963 estates constituted the largest proportion of planted tea area in Kenya (80 per cent) and by 1973 the smallholder tea area had expanded from 3527 to 32 000 hectares, during those ten years, thus making up over 60 per cent of Kenya's tea area. A further large extension programme was projected for 1974–8 that involved the construction of twenty-two new factories, bringing the total number of KTDA factories to fifty in 1978. The KTDA was to run these factories independently of the estate firms, although the factories for 1979 would operate under an initial management contract

---

18 The cess was to cover the costs of factory construction and planting materials.
19 For further details, see 'tea' file in KNA.

TABLE 42   Tea Area and Tea Production in Kenya 1963–78

Date	Planted tea (ha) Estates	smallholders	Total	Area Planted over 5 Years Old (ha)	Total Production (kg of made tea)	Total Exports (kg)	Local Consumption
1963	17 921	3 527	21 448	13 510	18 082 363	15 082 363	2 728 727
1964	18 591	4 471	23 062	14 659	20 242 630	16 422 313	3 820 217
1965	19 327 (66%)	5 429 (34%)	24 756	15 937	19 823 174	16 823 174	3 766 235
1966	20 102	7 238	27 340	17 756	25 418 658	23 283 084	2 135 574
1967	20 809	9 269	30 708	19 893	22 811 614	18 115 977	4 695 637
1968	21 329	12 233	33 562	21 488	29 762 490	27 839 247	1 924 243
1969	21 840	14 685	36 525	23 062	36 060 527	32 951 903	3 108 564
1970	22 289 (55%)	17 985 (45%)	40 274	24 756	41 077 594	33 851 055	5 659 381
1971	22 838	20 528	43 366	27 340	36 289 854	30 072 656	5 691 416
1972	23 268	26 495	49 763	30 708	53 322 469	47 483 857	5 838 612
1973	23 635	31 161	54 796	33 562	56 578 100	50 528 200	6 049 900
1974	24 355	34 380	58 735	36 525	53 439 668	49 696 800	7 057 987
1975	24 336 (40%)	37 206 (60%)	61 542	40 274	56 729 780	52 499 500	7 400 000
1976 (prov)	24 534	41 412	65 951	43 366	61 984 457	59 154 500	8 000 000
1977 (est)	25 250	42 500	67 750	49 763	67 500 000	60 000 000	7 500 000
1978 (est)	25 500	45 500	71 000	54 796	75 000 000	67 250 000	7 750 000

Source: Tea Board of Kenya, annual statistics.

Estimates include KTDA's planting plan to be completed in 1978.

Average yield estimated at 1500 kg of made tea per hectare per annum

In 1977 exports exceeded the estimates due to high international prices – approximately 63 000 000 kg (est. on first six months' sales).

of six months with the foreign tea firms. This extension programme was funded by the World Bank, the CDC and the West German Development Agency. In 1974 there were 79 000 registered African tea-growers, and after the expansion scheme in 1978, there were an estimated 100 000 smallholders in Kenya.[20] This can be compared with Brooke Bond's operation which in 1975 employed 14 754 unskilled labourers.[21]

At this point it is important to outline the basis of exploitation of smallholder tea-producers by international capital. Clearly, the smallholder scheme would not have been encouraged by Brooke Bond if that firm was not able to extract surplus from production. There have been several attempts to conceptualize the relationship between the peasant household and international capital. Cowen[22] has noted that 'where households are subject to quantity and quality controls over production, where labour is subject to supervision by capital and the producer price is tantamount to a wage, the household approximates a wage worker.' Another writer[23] has explained how in some situations it is more beneficial for capital to dominate agriculture by controlling the conditions of reproduction of the small farmer rather than expropriating him. This is because capital is saved certain costs which it would have to bear if it were to organize production directly.[24] The fact that the smallholder farmer invariably grows some of his own consumption requirements means that capital is able to purchase commodities from the farmer at a price that is below the value of his labour power.

Indeed the low price paid to the tea-growers in the early 1970s gave rise to considerable discontent. In 1975, the growers were paid in the form of first and second payments from the factory. After deductions, the farmer at that time received only 57 cents per kilo of green leaf plus a yearly bonus which depended on the efficiency of the respective factories. These two forms of payment brought the total payment to the grower in that year to between 60 and 80 cents per kilo of green leaf. By 1976, in response to such conditions, some tea-growers were turning from tea to more lucrative pursuits such as dairy cattle. A letter to the *Daily Nation* from a Meru tea-grower expressed this dilemma:

Unless the government steps in and forces the KTDA to pay substantially more (no less that 2/- per kilo without deductions) to the

---

20 Annual reports of the KTDA.

21 The balance between the 10 915 unionizable staff and this figure can be explained by the use of temporary labour during heavy plucking seasons.

22 M. Cowen, 'Capital and peasant households', mimeo., Nairobi, 1976. For further discussion of the issue, see J. Banaji, 'Modes of production in a materialist conception of history', *Capital and Class*, no. 3, 1977.

23 Henry Bernstein, 'Underdevelopment and the law of value: a critique of Kay', RAPE, no. 6, August 1976.

24 Overheads for the smallholder tea farmer are low.

farmers, I for one and probably more will follow the good example set by the Meru farmers. My 3 acre tea crop is certainly out during the coming dry season and I will go in for potatoes, vegetables and cattle which pay more in comparison.[25]

With the hike in international tea and coffee prices in 1977, the price paid by the KTDA to the tea-growers in Kenya was raised to 2s per kilo. However, the price of this commodity is closely tied to the international tea market, even though the fluctuations in tea are never so great as in the case of coffee.

Through its control of tea marketing, Brooke Bond has been able to take advantage of smallholder teas. Before 1977, when the KTDA took over Brooke Bond's marketing arrangements, the smallholder factories, along with the other commercial tea plants in Kenya, sold 10 per cent of their monthly production to the Brooke Bond packers at Kericho. This was then blended and packed by the foreign firm and sold on the local market under its own label. The rest of the smallholder tea, along with the estate production, is sold either at the Mombasa (about 15 per cent) or the London auction where Brooke Bond will once again buy up a sizeable proportion.

The tea trade from East Africa handled by Brooke Bond is substantial. The overall amount of production in Kenya in 1973, for instance, was 60 million kilogrammes of made tea. Of this total Brooke Bond contributed 23 per cent, and about 51 million kilogrammes (85 per cent) of the total exported from Kenya went overseas, the balance of 15 per cent being sold on the local market under the Brooke Bond label.[26] Of the total exported, Brooke Bond handled approximately 21 million kilogrammes (41 per cent) through its exporting company in Mombasa. The balance from the exports either from smallholder or commercial tea factories would be exported directly on contract or sold at the London auction.

NATIONALIST PRESSURE ON BROOKE BOND

The dominant position of Brooke Bond in Kenya's tea industry has not been taken lightly by either the smallholders or members of the Kenyan bourgeoisie. The state of exploitation of the Kenyan tea-growers by international capital has been the focus for attack by opposition groups. During a parliamentary debate in 1974 on the K£5 million CDC loan for smallholder tea extension, there were strong attacks on the monopoly marketing company (BBL) and also on certain individuals within the smallholder parastatal (KTDA) who were alleged to be making extensive use of their government positions to support their

---

25 *Daily Nation*, 20 September 1977.
26 These statistics are from BBL's annual reports and accounts for 1973 and 1974 and the Tea Board of Kenya

own business interests. Mr J. Seroney (a former MP detained in 1976) called for the activities of the KTDA to be decentralized in order that growers should control the operations of the industry to a greater extent. Another MP asked for the operations of the KTDA to be made more accountable to the growers by being made a public company: 'this would stop its current exploitation by certain people and ensure that there was not unnecessary borrowing'.

Martin Shikuku (an ex-assistant minister, detained in 1976), a vociferous spokesman of the petty bourgeois 'opposition' faction, during the same debate, accused the KTDA of being in league with the 'foreign exploiters'. He maintained this partnership was 'sucking the blood and sweat of the Kenya tea growers', and he wondered why 'Britain, a country where no tea grows, should be able to control the tea industry of this country'.[27] These attacks were not only aimed at the foreign firm that controlled tea-marketing in Kenya, but also pointed to a group of Kenyan farmers with positions inside the KTDA who it was felt were using the organization to further their own interests.

In this context it is relevant to distinguish between those individuals with executive positions who channel their money income into private holdings, and those officials who *directly* use their positions to support accumulation. The case raised here conforms to the latter example.

Since 1972 Brooke Bond has been prevented by the government from buying further agricultural land in Kenya. Brooke Bond had hoped that by issuing some of its share capital on the Nairobi Stock Exchange, it would appease nationalist pressure on the company. By 1975, the Treasury had increased its share in the capital of Brooke Bond Liebig Kenya to approximately 20 per cent, a move which was engineered by the Capital Issues Committee. Indeed it was this nationalist control body that was to check Brooke Bond's expansion in other respects.

Although BBL's interests in Kenya are mainly in tea production and marketing, coffee became an important subsidiary crop from the 1960s. In 1973, for instance, Brooke Bond exported 8 million kilogrammes of coffee from Kenya, and had 1500 ha under coffee in the Kiambu district.[28] The clash with local capital came in 1972 when Brooke Bond made an unsuccessful attempt to take over a profitable local coffee estate which had formerly been owned by European farmers. The shareholders of the coffee company accepted Brooke Bond's offer, but the takeover was subsequently rejected by the Capital Issues Committee.[29]

Only a short period elapsed before another bid for the coffee company was made by a Kiambu farming company owned by some prominent Kenyans connected with the KTDA and the Gema organization.

27 *EAS*, 24 April 1974
28 BBL (Kenya)'s annual report and accounts for 1974.
29 Information from J. Donovan, stockbroker's report, in 1972

It was evident that a section of the bourgeoisie had used the powers of the state to support their own accumulation in this case at the expense of a foreign firm. Since 1972, therefore, Brooke Bond has not attempted to extend its land area, which would directly conflict with the interests of farmers. This kind of nationalist pressure has led the company to extend into new production areas.

The same group of indigenous capitalists who have been concerned to prevent Brooke Bond from expanding their land area have invested in the private cultivation of tea, outside the smallholder system. In both Kiambu and Kericho districts during the 1970s, several local farmers have developed their own tea estates, selling their leaf either to an estate factory or to the KTDA. To take an example of this trend: in the Limuru and Kiambu districts, north of Nairobi, the total area of planted tea was 5705 ha. Of this total, 2889·5 ha were owned by the KTDA smallholders and 2815·6 ha by private tea-growers (including companies and individuals). Of this area, the following portions were owned by private growers:

639·9 ha Brooke Bond
267   ha Karirana Estate (Inchcape/Mawamu Holdings)
907   ha
Total Companies: 907 ha
Private Individuals: 1909 ha[30]

The latter group of 'private individuals' consist of Kenyan farmers who have purchased land in the district since independence.[31] This group was predominantly composed of members of the Kenyan bourgeoisie, including a top Gema official, some senior employees of the KTDA and several cabinet ministers. Four of these capitalist farmers with large tea estates in Kiambu in 1968 invested directly in their own tea factory in order to process the tea grown on their respective estates. This factory operates independently of the KTDA and of the foreign tea companies, and exports tea directly abroad on contract.

Two of the principal shareholders of the firm had been involved in the tea parastatal. Their positions had undoubtedly helped them to develop their own tea schemes. This 'assistance' is likely to have taken two forms: first, these people have obtained skill and contacts in the tea industry through the KTDA; second, some materials and/or finance may filter through from the parastatal to the private enterprises.

The conditions of production in the Kenya tea industry have been examined here in the context of the historical dominance of one foreign tea company: Brooke Bond Liebig Ltd. The discussion has demonstrated a *concentration* of production in the tea industry through improved techniques and increased labour productivity. This

30 Tea Board of Kenya licence holders, 1974–5 (estimates).
31 This area was formerly a settler preserve.

process culminated in Brooke Bond's *consolidation* by the takeover of existing tea estates in Kenya. Brooke Bond established its monopoly over internal tea-marketing in East Africa as early as 1938. The culmination of nationalist pressure against this monopoly came in 1977, and happened to coincide with a dramatic increase in tea prices on the world market. In early 1977, in response to these high international prices, the KTDA for several months withdrew from the 'pool' tea-buying arrangement and sold its tea directly abroad. At the end of 1977, the KTDA went further and *took over* the 'pool' organization from Brooke Bond Liebig (Kenya), thus depriving the multinational of an important source of profit. Although this action served to impose a local control over internal tea-marketing, it does not free Kenya from the caprice of the international market, as 80 per cent of the country's tea was exported in 1977.

On the production side by the 1970s, the smallholder tea area in Kenya was larger than that of the foreign-owned estates, and by 1980 the estates should constitute less than 30 per cent of the total. From 1971, it has been shown that Brooke Bond was prevented from expanding its land area, as this was regarded as the sole preserve of the indigenous bourgeoisie.

This study has shown the way in which a major export industry has been brought further under local control with the support of the state.

The Bata Shoe Company in Kenya

Shoe production is essentially an import-substituting industry and the intention here is to show the way in which one foreign firm in Kenya came to dominate the conditions of production in this branch. The relationship of the multinational firm to indigenous production in that area is subject to scrutiny.

The Bata Shoe Company was one of the first investments of a non-British company in Kenya Colony before the second World War. Bata was originally set up in Czechoslovakia during the 1914–18 War and by the 1920s the firm was expanding into other countries, including Europe, Africa and America. By 1935, the Bata Shoe Company had several factories and distribution points in Africa and it decided in that year to set up a marketing branch in Mombasa to serve the East African region. The Bata subsidiary soon realized that there was an increasing demand for low-cost rubber and canvas footwear, so the firm began manufacturing rubber shoes in 1939.

Wartime conditions in Kenya caused the Bata Shoe Company to move up-country, to an area 20 miles north of Nairobi where the conditions were suitable for the construction of both a leather factory and a tannery.[32] Wartime conditions also affected the global organiza-

---

32 J. Okwissa, 'Industrial location, the case of the Bata Shoe Company', BA thesis, Dept of Geography, University of Nairobi, 1976.

tion and after the German invasion of Czechoslovakia in 1939, the headquarters of the firm was shifted to Canada, where it has remained ever since.

BATA ESTABLISHES MONOPOLY CONDITIONS IN THE SHOE AND TANNING INDUSTRIES

During the 1950s, the business of the Bata Shoe Company included the manufacture of tanned leather, leather and rubber shoes as well as the export of raw hides to Europe. After 1955, modern machinery was installed at Limuru for shoe-making, and revolving bats replaced pits in the tannery. Like most import-substitution industries, the Bata plant, along with the other two tanning firms in Kenya, under-utilized their capacity in the initial stages.[33] From the 1950s, Bulleys Tannery (owned by Tom Booth Ltd of Ireland) and Bata operated the largest tanneries in Kenya, with the former concentrating on the export market, while Bata used most of its hides for shoe production.

This excess capacity and high unit costs of production encouraged these firms to press for government support in the form of duties against imported Indian leather. The government responded by imposing a duty on imported leather which ranged from 21 to 29 per cent, depending on the type of leather, and this was increased to 30 per cent in 1960.[34] Due to the overproduction of leather in Kenya during the 1950s, the Bata Shoe Company lobbied the colonial administration to encourage the development of artisan shoe-making. The idea was that this small-scale shoe-making sector would absorb the excess capacity of the Bata tanning plant. It is evident that in this case an international firm found that a local production sector complemented its own interests.[35]

Between 1955 and 1965, 10 to 15 per cent of Bata's tanned leathers were sold to artisan shoe-makers.[36] By the 1970s, however, the numbers of artisans had dwindled due to their inability to compete with machine-made shoes and because of their high unit costs of production. Although the BSC encouraged government assistance to African shoe-making, it was opposed to any support being given to African tanneries. Indeed, given the limited markets for leather, it was logical that it would discourage any further leather production in Kenya. Predictably, the administration followed the company's advice and

---

33 See M. P. Cowen, 'Wattle production in the central province, capital and household commodity production, 1903–1964', mimeo., Institute for Development Studies, Nairobi, 1975, for further details.

34 See N. Swainson, 'Multinational corporations in Kenya: two case studies, pineapple canning and shoe production', for the NCCK, Nairobi, 1976.

35 S. Langdon, in a case study on the Bata Shoe Company in Kenya, in 'Multinational corporations in the political economy of Kenya',PhD thesis, Sussex, 1976, implies that international firms inevitably stifle local enterprise.

36 Information from the Bata Shoe Company at Limuru.

dampened proposals for the development of African tanning in the rural areas.

Until the early 1960s most of Kenya's hide exports were in raw form and by 1966 the BSC processed one-quarter of all tanned hides in Kenya. In 1960, Bata exported its first consignment of 'wet blue' (partially tanned hides) and after this date the export of raw hides was phased out.

SHOE PRODUCTION – EXPORTS AND LOCAL SALES

Bata's shoe production from the outset was aimed at serving the mass market in East Africa. It is not surprising that the sales of Bata's shoes in Kenya increased very rapidly from the 1950s onwards as the monetary economy expanded and shoes entered the consumption basket of African wage workers. Due to their lower price, *textile* and *rubber* shoes have formed the largest proportion of Bata's total output. Although most of Bata's shoes are sold on the local market, the firm has always managed to export a small number to neighbouring African countries. From the 1950s, the export level of shoes fluctuated between 6 and 14 per cent of Bata's total production, until 1966 when it jumped to 30 per cent. During the 1970s exports accounted for around 30 per cent. In the past Tanzania and Uganda have taken the largest proportion of Bata's shoes from Kenya, for instance, in 1970 these two countries imported 1·7 million pairs of shoes valued at K£899 874; by 1974 this number had dropped to 446 025 pairs.[37] The border closure in 1977 terminated Bata's exports to Tanzania, although a proportion continued to be exported to Uganda. Bata's primary aim in setting up a plant in Kenya was to capture the internal market for shoes. The early entry of the firm into the region with limited markets illustrates the way in which capital seeks to expand the market for its products over time.[38] Despite the emergence of competitors to the firm's hegemony in Kenyan shoe production, the internal market still offered ample potential for expansion.

THE BATA PRODUCTION PROCESS

During the 1950s, the Bata complex at Limuru contained a rubber plant, a leather workshop, a tannery and a bicycle tyre plant. In 1955, 500 operatives employed in the leather plant turned out approximately 1000 pairs of leather uppers per day, while the rubber plant made 1500 pairs per day and employed 200 workers. The production of rubber and plastic shoes requires sophisticated machinery and the amount of profit made on synthetic footwear is higher than that from

37 Annual trade accounts for Kenya.
38 Bata conducted large-scale advertising campaigns in the 1950s to persuade Africans of the advantages of wearing shoes.

TABLE 43　Bata Sales in Pairs of Shoes

	Retail (%)	Wholesale (%)	Export (%)	Total (pairs)	No. of Employees
1951	43	57	0	871 224	
1952	37	63	0	1 031 763	
1953	32	57	11	1 128 336	
1954	26	65	8	1 571 879	525
1955	27	70	3	2 104 618	577
1956	30	64	6	1 988 374	686
1957	26	68	6	2 398 054	709
1958	27	65	8	2 229 400	646
1959	30	64	5	2 112 203	728
1960	35	55	10	2 086 583	767
1961	33	52	14	2 646 934	904
1962	10	75	14	2 278 348	964
1963	12	81	7	2 994 610	970
1964	37	57	5	3 481 076	992
1965	25	70	5	5 625 082	1000
1966	20	50	30	5 831 632	981
1967	20	37	43	4 730 219	944
1968	21	47	31	5 643 377	1059
1969	23	46	31	5 967 423	1092
1970	24	53	23	6 471 077	1183
1971	22	51	26	7 482 472	1349
1972	24	60	16	7 520 013	1459
1973	27	65	8	7 279 988	1367
1974	17	77	6	7 835 703	1305
1975	23	68	8	7 639 451	1301
1976	—	—	—	—	1500

Source: Bata Shoe Company, Limuru.

leather footwear. Bata has tended to concentrate on manufacturing low-cost synthetic shoes and in 1975, out of 8 million shoes manufactured, 2 million were made from leather and 6 million from textile, rubber, or plastic.[39] The synthetic shoes require a high level of imported inputs, which are in most cases obtained directly from Bata subsidiaries abroad. The Bata organization is vertically integrated and the firm controls the global sources of inputs into shoe manufacturing. For instance, since the 1950s the BSC in Kenya has obtained rubber from its own plantations in West Africa. The leather shoe plant at Limuru, on the other hand, utilizes mainly local hides. In order to illustrate the relative labour intensity of leather shoe-making: in 1970 from 7·5 million pairs of shoes manufactured by Bata, 5·5 million were from rubber and textile compared with only 2 million leather shoes, with the two plants employing 650 and 400 workers respectively.[40]

Bata has invested in several other production areas connected with its basic plants. For instance, in 1957 the company opened a rubber plant, which was closed in 1972 due to competition from the Avon Tyre Company. In 1974 a more successful side-line was introduced when a leather-board section was opened to manufacture a leather-type product of compressed shavings from the tannery. Bata uses about 30 per cent of this production for the manufacture of suitcases, bags and shoe-soles, while the remainder is sold to local artisans. The capacity of the leather factory was expanded by 23 per cent in 1974.

Like any other multinational firm, Bata has sought over time to advance its manufacturing techniques and raise labour productivity. The emergence of particular techniques of production is usually in conformity with the company's global organization. From an interview with Bata, Langdon has noted that during the 1960s a new technique was introduced for making boots whereby two workers could make 500 boots while the older, less mechanized technique employed thirty-five workers to make 800 boots.[41] The main reasons offered by the company for such changes were that the new technique saved labour, turned out a product of good appearance and also used a machine that was sent from another Bata subsidiary. From the other case studies, it is clear that capital is constantly seeking to improve the means of production, which invariably involves reducing the numbers of workers. The constant improvement in production techniques has been accompanied by a rising rate of profit for the firm in Kenya. Langdon has noted that Bata's sales expanded by 66 per cent between 1967 and 1972 and in 1974 the company made a trading profit (before tax) of K£1 042 961 with a net asset value of K£972 068.[42]

---

39 Bata Shoe Company, Limuru.
40 ibid
41 Langdon, Bata study, op. cit.
42 ibid.

LABOUR AND TRAINING IN BATA

The increased productivity of labour in the Bata company has been ensured through training programmes carried out at the factory level. This advancing productivity of the Bata labour force is illustrated by the fact that in 1954 the company employed a total of 525 workers when the total numbers of pairs of shoes turned out by the factory was 1·6 million; by 1974 Bata employed double the number of workers and 1305 employees produced nearly five times more – 7·8 million.[43] The sophistication of the machinery employed after the mid-1960s necessitated a specialized and skilled labour force.

It was to this end that Bata established a technical training school at Limuru as early as 1955 for basic training in all aspects of shoemaking. This was phased out in 1967 and replaced by on-the-job training, in the context of higher general education standards in Kenya. After a basic training, management trainees would be sent into different sections of the factory and later on to more specialized courses overseas in such subjects as leather work, design and engineering.[44]

The declared policy of the Kenya government since the late 1960s has been to put pressure on foreign firms to *Africanize* their management structures and provide comprehensive training schemes to that effect. The *Kenyanization Bureau* set up in 1967 consistently pressured Bata behind the scenes to Africanize its management more rapidly. The figures show that the overall number of Kenyan managers in the firm has risen fast since 1968, when there were sixty expatriates; for by 1976, out of a total management staff of 200, only twenty non-citizens remained. The Kenyanization Bureau during the 1960s did arbitrate several conflicts between African managers and the BSC and also offered the company assistance in recruiting Kenyan personnel. Nevertheless, the company has been insistent on retaining foreign personnel at the head of most production departments. The Kenyanization Bureau has insisted on exact timetables for the phasing out of expatriates and by 1979 the aim was to leave only five expatriates in top managerial positions (such as managing director, production manager, etc.).

Bata, therefore, encourages management training *inside* different Bata companies. Operatives are trained by supervisory staff on the job, and they are selected after a short written test. In 1975, operative wages ranged from 463s basic to 1300s per month, at a time when the minimum wage in Kenya was only 300s. The workers needed to fight for recognition of their union, the Kenya Shoe and Leather Workers'

---

43 Statistics from the BSC at Limuru.

44 Details on the training school are to be found in *Bata Magazine*, no. 5, May 1961, *EAS* file on the BSC. Trainees after 1967 were required to have Higher School Certificate or government trade tests.

Union, in 1961. This union has generally supported the Africanization of management positions within the company.[45]

BATA AND INDIGENOUS ENTERPRISE

Distribution

Since 1970, local entrepreneurs have entered the shoe and leather business at the levels of both production and distribution. From the mid-1960s, Bata established a comprehensive 'business advice service' designed to assist all its wholesale dealers in book-keeping, display, salesmanship, and so on. Before 1974, the thirty-six retail outlets for Bata shoes were owned by the company, which also provided loans to traders for the purchase of stock and displays.[46] Since the regulation in 1974 that foreign firms should distribute their goods through local shops, all Bata outlets have been taken over by Kenya citizens.

Indeed, the Africanization of Bata's distribution system has provided an important source of accumulation to many African traders. The margin of profit for these traders is high. For instance, a dealer in 01 Kalou in 1968 had a monthly turnover of 13 000 pairs of shoes, and this was in a remote district of the country.[47] Although the firm still maintained a close hold over the way in which its products were distributed, after 1974, 77 per cent of Bata's shoe production passed through the hands of citizen wholesalers.

Production

The predominant feature of indigenous capitalism in the post-independence period in Kenya has been the move from trade into production; shoe-manufacturing is a good illustration of this trend.

In 1972, five senior African managers at Bata left the firm and established their own shoe-making plant with finance from a prominent Kenyan industrialist, Njenga Karume. Karume and a Nairobi lawyer held 60 per cent of the shares, with the five executive directors holding the remaining 40 per cent. The technical problems of establishing the factory were solved by the fact that the five ex-Bata employees had all come from different departments within that organization, covering most of the important areas of shoe-making; the design, rubber factory, tannery, leather factory and accounts.[48]

At the time of their resignation, the five managers had been with

---

45 For instance, refer to a letter from the Kenya Shoe and Leather Workers' Union to the director of the Kenyanization Bureau, 1969.

46 Information from the BSC, Limuru.

47 *EAS* file on the BSC.

48 The general manager of the local shoe firm had formerly been the assistant manager of the leather factory at Bata.

Bata for periods of between six and sixteen years and most had been trained abroad in their respective skills. The general manager of the Tiger Shoe Company made the following comment on his position in the Bata management hierarchy: 'we were given responsibility without authority, which becomes frustrating'.[49] Two of the managers who 'defected' from Bata's management team were in line for departmental manager positions, and would possibly have been in line for the post of production manager in the Kenyan company.

The local firm made it clear that the problems surrounding the setting up of an enterprise in direct competition with a large multinational related not to skills but to finance. In addition to the managers, several Bata operatives left to work with the local firm, although they soon returned to the multinational, which was able to pay higher wages.[50]

Due to the difficulties facing the infant company in raising funds for machinery, it was forced to make most shoes by hand. The leather for such shoes was obtained from local tanneries. The knowledge which the managers had obtained through their previous experience with Bata was important in ensuring the initial success of the enterprise. During the following two years, the firm was able to raise commercial bank loans to purchase shoe-making machinery.

However, Tiger did experience some difficulties in obtaining supplies of certain components (adhesives, eyelets, etc.) in the first year of its operation. This has been attributed to the hostility of the dominant multinational, which tried to prevent Tiger from obtaining imported supplies of eyelets. The conflict had to be mediated at the highest government level before Bata would agree to grant the local company a supply of eyelets from its own licence.[51] Despite these initial problems, Bata adjusted to the new competitor. In an interview I conducted with Bata in 1976, it was claimed that the success of the local firm could be attributed to the excellent Bata training! As Bata itself had some political alliances, it is clear that in the early years of its operation the local shoe company relied on its own political connections (the main shareholder being the national Gema chairman) to ensure its survival.

In fact, in the short term, the Tiger Shoe Company presented little immediate threat to Bata's dominant share of the Kenyan shoe trade. Even after its 1975–6 expansion, the capacity of the local factory was 1000 shoes per day or 260 000 per year, which can be compared with Bata's production figure for 1975 of 7·6 million. It is, therefore,

---

49 From an interview with the general manager of the Tiger Shoe Company, Nairobi, 3 August 1976.

50 For instance, in 1975 the average monthly wage for workers at Bata and Tiger was 580s and 350s per month respectively.

51 This is noted by Langdon, op. cit., and confirmed by another source.

unlikely that Tiger will seriously threaten Bata's predominant hold over the Kenyan shoe market in the immediate future. Nevertheless, the local firm has expanded fast from small beginnings, and once the enterprise demonstrated a modest success, it was opened up to state financial support. Between 1975 and 1976, Tiger sold K£25 000-worth of shoes and employed fifty operatives.[52] In 1975, the firm announced a major expansion in its factory's capacity that was to cost K£275 000, K£125 000 of which was to be provided by the DFCK, with the ICDC taking an equity interest of K£25 000.[53] The remaining K£75 000 was put up by the existing directors of the company.

Until 1976, Tiger did not compete directly with the BSC, as it concentrated on manufacturing high-quality leather shoes for the high-income market. Bata's interests lie largely in the low-income market for synthetic-based shoes. However, the Tiger extensions in 1976 include an injection moulding machine that makes possible the production of p.v.c., rubber and plastic footwear.

After 1976, Tiger pressed the government to place a ban on imported shoes in order that it could secure the high-cost market for leather shoes.[54] Although the rates have been raised, it is unlikely that a complete ban will be imposed, given the relative strength of merchant capital at this stage.

Clearly Tiger's main competitive disadvantage was the fact that it had to purchase leather from other tanneries, whereas Bata could utilize its own supply. The most logical step for the local firm in these circumstances was to acquire its own tannery. In 1975, it was significant that Tiger's major shareholder, Karume, joined the board of directors of Bulley's Tannery, Kenya's second largest tanning concern. By the next year, Karume and other Kenyan businessman had bought a controlling interest in this firm, thereby enabling them to integrate leather production into their shoe-making enterprise.

A further 'spill-over' of skills from the BSC into indigenous enterprise occurred in 1976, when a new tanning company was set up at Sagana, the construction being supervised by the former assistant manager of Bata's tannery. The pattern of the local shoe company was being repeated: individuals with technical training from the multinational corporation leaving in order to establish their own concerns. Indeed, the high price of leather on the world market during the late 1970s plus expanding internal demand will encourage the growth of further tanneries and local shoe-manufacturers. This could have a snowball effect and ultimately challenge Bata's hold over the internal market.

---

52 Interview with the general manager, op. cit.
53 DFCK annual report for 1975.
54 The cheapest leather shoes in 1976 retailed for between K.Sh.60s and 70s.

CAN BATA MAINTAIN ITS MONOPOLY?

The multinational produced 8 million pairs of shoes in the year 1976; 3·9 million square feet of upper leather and 106·4 kilogrammes of bottom leather, and between 10 and 20 per cent of this leather was exported.[55]

Like any other large international firm in Kenya, Bata has built up certain high-level alliances in order to protect its position. An indication of such methods was the issue by the BSC of 'goodwill' shares to prominent Kenyans in 1975. Forty-two lots of shares worth K£2000 each were issued to members of the government (including ministers and chairmen of parastatals), and private businessmen.[56] There is, however, no reason to assume that these alliances will remain static.

This study has traced the way in which a foreign firm developed a particular branch of production over a period of thirty-seven years in Kenya. The rapid increase in Bata's rate of production took place in the context of an expanding monetary economy from the 1950s. For the post-independence period, Bata more or less managed to maintain a monopoly over the conditions of production and distribution of shoes in Kenya.

Despite these conditions, it has been shown that domestic capital can operate in the same sphere of production if it has the necessary finance and political backing. It is clear that a local shoe firm that wishes to compete with Bata will have to employ the same capital-intensive methods of production. The 'spill-over' of skills from the multinational into other competing enterprises is a trend not confined to the shoe-making sector alone. As the process of indigenous investment in the shoe-making sector proceeds, it is likely that Bata's monopoly will slowly be undermined.

Lonrho in Kenya

The final case study concerns one of the largest and most powerful British conglomerates in Africa. Unlike the other two cases, Lonrho was not confined to one branch of production or distribution and it entered Kenya after independence. The firm enjoyed a phenomenal growth rate between 1967 and 1977, in Kenya and elsewhere in Africa, and it has developed a wide range of interests in production, distribution and finance. Lonrho (the London and Rhodesia Company) was first incorporated in 1909 to acquire mining rights and shares in mining companies in Southern Africa. Over a period of fifty

---

55 Information from the BSC. It is likely that Bata will export a higher proportion of semi-tanned leathers in wet-blue form when the international price is high.
56 Return for the Bata Shoe Company, 1975 (Registrar General of Companies).

years, up to 1960, Lonrho expanded these interests and made further investments in property, ranching and agriculture in both Rhodesia and South Africa. In August 1961, Lonrho acquired mining and motor trading companies from R. W. Rowland, who became the joint managing director of the company with A. Ball.[57]

From that point onwards, Lonrho expanded very rapidly, mainly through the takeover of existing companies rather than internally generated investment in new plant. Like many other western conglomerates during the 1960s, the company passed through a period of expansion, diversification and concentration. To give some indication of the rapid pace of growth in the 1960s: in 1962 the company's pre-tax profits were £0·2 million, and a decade later in 1972 they had reached £16·3 million and by 1974 had jumped to £46·5 million. The firm's turnover between 1972 and 1974 rose from £184 million to £349·2 million, and between 1963 and 1967 the group's net assets increased from £3·5 million to £15 million.[58]

Lonrho acquired existing firms using various different means. Sometimes the companies were purchased by the issue of shares and loan stock in Lonrho itself; at other times Lonrho would buy out a firm (such as Cominière) and pay in European currency at well below the value of the assets of that firm in Africa. The Slater-Walker deal in 1969 involved the issue of 1 200 000 fully paid Lonrho shares to the owners of that firm. The way in which Lonrho financed its takeovers of large groups of companies in Africa gave rise to much speculation in the City of London by 1971. From the 1960s onwards, Africa remained Lonrho's main sphere of investment, although the firm also expanded its interests in Europe and the Middle East. Indeed, the bulk of Lonrho's turnover at a global level was derived from its investments in East and Central Africa as the following breakdown of the firm's turnover in 1974 shows:

	£ million
East and Central Africa	157·02
Europe and Others	64·38
South Africa	25·99
West Africa	101·81
TOTAL	349·2[59]

From 1971 onwards, the firm began to work towards a large-scale link-up between Arab resources and capital with the areas of sub-Saharan Africa in which Lonrho traditionally operated. Rowland was reported as saying in 1973: 'The combination of Western technology,

---

57 From J. Sebag and Co. (auditors), report on Lonrho, 1972.
58 Lonrho, annual report and accounts, 1974. In 1974, Lonrho had 90 000 employees, only 3000 of whom worked in the UK.
59 Report, op. cit.

African resources and Arab money will be an unbeatable combination – that is where Lonrho's future lies'.[60] In 1972, in order to further these aims, Lonrho set up Lonrho Arab International to co-ordinate invest- ments in the Middle East. Lonrho also became a partner in the newly formed Arab International Bank.[61] Lonrho, in its contacts with both the Middle East and Africa, adopted a strategy sympathetic to nation- alism, and its role became increasingly that of broker and financier rather than a direct owner of projects. In the context of rising national- ism in both Arab and African countries, this policy showed a high level of political awareness which is common to many advanced interna- tional firms. Rowland, in expressing support for Arab claims to control their own oil industry, made the following comment;

> I am totally in sympathy with this type of revolutionary capitalism, if you have that you will not get nationalised. It is much better that they should use their money this way than on buying Russian arms and there is no greater opportunity than in Independent black Africa. Clearly the future of a company like this depends on being able to take part in this development.[62]

The way in which Lonrho has cultivated political alliances in black Africa illustrates the strategy of multinational firms in an advanced state of imperialism. It has already been shown that most multinational firms in Kenya, during the 1970s, have preferred the role of managers and financial agents to that of direct owners. Lonrho as an interna- tional firm is not unique, although its style in forging political alliances has been unusually flamboyant. It was this mode of operation that led the British Prime Minister, Mr Heath, to label the firm's activities after the boardrooms crisis of 1973 as 'the unacceptable face of capital- ism'. This merely indicates that the actual style of Lonrho 'let down' the reputation of the bourgeoisie as a whole, which is why the firm was so heavily castigated by 'established' business interests in the City of London. The only exceptional feature of Lonrho during the 1960s was the fact that this large multinational had a few institutional investors and, in an age of advanced capitalism when ownership is usually divorced from management, up until 1975 Rowland himself was both the managing director and the major shareholder of the company.[63] After that time, Kuwaiti investors bought 50 per cent of Lonrho's shares, although the management of the firm is still personally directed by Rowland.

It was the unorthodox character of Lonrho's management that led to

---

60 Article in *African Development*, June 1975. The link-up with Arab capital has been extended further after 1976 when the Kuwaitis bought a large block of Lonrho's share capital.

61 S. Cronje, *Lonrho*, Penguin Books, Harmondsworth, 1976, p. 191.

62 *AD* article, op. cit.

63 Cronje, op. cit., p. 241.

the famous Lonrho boardroom crisis of 1973, in which a group of 'conservative' directors tried to remove Rowland, claiming that he was mismanaging the firm and that his method of takeovers was causing liquidity problems within the company. The type of alliances which Rowland had built up with the African bourgeoisie came to the fore at this time. Rowland called on the support of three African managing directors of Lonrho subsidiaries, Udi Gecaga (Kenya), Tom Mtine (Zambia) and Gil Olympio (Ivory Coast), to give evidence in his favour. This defence was successful and the shareholders voted for Rowland's continued management of the Lonrho company, implicitly endorsing his large-scale moves into black Africa.

Despite the gloomy prognostications on the future of the Lonrho company in 1973, by the end of 1974, in generally depressed market conditions, Lonrho emerged as one of the 'top ten' companies in Britian, having a capitalization of over £10 million. Lonrho's success lay in its ability to procure finance and achieve high rates of return in investments over a short period of time.[64]

LONRHO IN KENYA

Lonrho's interests in Kenya, by the 1970s, were substantial. Although it is not possible to ascertain the exact size of Lonrho's operations in 1974 it was reckoned to be the *largest* international firm operating in Kenya (in terms of asset value).[65] It is the intention here to examine in more detail the nature of the links between this foreign firm and sections of the indigenous bourgeoisie in Kenya. First, it is necessary to outline in chronological order Lonrho's largest investments in Kenya since the mid-1960s.

Lonrho moved into East Africa between 1966 and 1967, which was part of the firm's strategy of extending its interests northwards from Southern Africa. In Kenya, as in many other African countries at the time, the tactics of Lonrho's expansion were the same: the takeover of existing enterprises. These purchases were not effected at random, but were rather part of the firm's continental strategy. Many of the East African takeovers were effected in Britain at the parent company level. In 1967, Lonrho made its first important acquisition in Kenya and Uganda, of *Consolidated Holdings*, a large printing and transporting firm with several subsidiaries, which also controlled the *East African Standard* newspaper. Lonrho acquired the company by buying out the shares held in Britain. This group controlled the largest printing and stationery manufacturing concerns in Kenya.

The next area in which Lonrho invested was in estates and primary production. In July 1967, Lonrho took a 50 per cent interest in the

---

64 Lonrho in Kenya, for instance, insists on a project having a rate of return in the first five years of at least 20 per cent.

65 This calculation was from a reputable firm of Nairobi auditors in 1974.

Tancot Company (Tanganyika Cotton Company), an estate company which had been operating in Tanzania and Kenya since the 1920s, growing sisal, tea, cotton and coffee. By the mid-1960s, this firm had expanded into brick-manufacturing and specialized vehicle assembly. The remainder of the share capital was not purchased by Lonrho until 1972, when the shares were bought in sterling. This firm represented Lonrho's typical pattern of takeover: the assets of the firm were undervalued. There was a useful connection between the first two Lonrho 'empires' in that Tancot also manufactured Roneo Vickers office equipment under licence, which was then marketed by Stationery and Office supplies of the Motor Mart Group.[66]

In December of the same year, the Lonrho group took over the *Express Transport* group which operated vehicles and warehouses in all three East African countries. This was a profitable company, and was responsible for the warehousing and dispatching of Kenya's entire coffee crop and part of Uganda's as well. This company was owned by groups of nominees in sterling countries (Jersey and England) and Lonrho simply bought out the controlling equity in sterling. The fourth group to be taken by the Lonrho company in East Africa was the *Motor Mart and Exchange Company* which was involved in vehicle importing and distribution. This organization handled the distribution in East Africa of General Motors vehicles and it had a number of subsidiary companies including Industrial Machinery Ltd. This takeover was part of a large deal worth £3·9 million by which all the financial interests of Slater-Walker Securities in East and Central Africa were absorbed by the Lonrho company.[67] Among the other Slater-Walker interests in East Africa acquired by Lonrho as part of this deal was the large wattle-extract concern, the East African Tanning and Extract Company, which virtually controlled the conditions of wattle production in Kenya. Slater's had acquired this firm from Forestal Land and Timber early in the same year, 1969.

Therefore, by the late 1960s Lonrho had bought into four large groups of enterprises which operated in all three East African countries. All of these enterprises included in the Lonrho deals had been operating in East Africa for twenty or thirty years. By the mid-1960s most of these groups were overextended and in need of drastic rationalization and infusion of capital, which Lonrho was to take advantage of when it came to the conditions of purchase. Once again, the logic of capitalist concentration is evident: of larger units of capital absorbing smaller ones. In 1967, *Lonrho East Africa* had been formed in Kenya to co-ordinate the Lonrho group interests in the whole of East Africa. The first phase of investment in East Africa, therefore,

---

66 This information is from two sources: the Registrar General of Companies, and the file on Lonrho in the *EAS* Newspaper Cuttings Library in Nairobi.

67 The book value of Slater-Walker assets taken over by Lonrho in East Africa is estimated at £6 million, *Daily Telegraphy*, 24 April 1969.

took the form of *taking over* existing concerns. After 1970, however, further investments in Kenya have been made from the reserves of the holding companies.[68] These four groups of companies formed the basis of Lonrho's organization in East Africa. The following are the basic management divisions within Lonrho East Africa:

(1) motor – Motor Mart and Exchange (vehicle distribution and assembly);
(2) manufacturing – Consolidated Holdings (printing newspapers and transporting);
(3) general services – Express Transport Company (travel property acquisition and transport services);
(4) estates – Tancot (coffee, tea, cotton, wattle and sisal estates and assembly of agricultural machinery and implements);
(5) management – East African Investment Trust (overall management organization which co-ordinates operations and research).

These basic management divisions relate to the central organization of Lonrho at the parent company level.

Subsequent Lonrho investments in East Africa have taken place on a piecemeal basis with the aim of *consolidation* of its existing holdings. For instance, in 1971 Lonrho acquired *Westlands Motors* from some local European businessmen, which added the important Toyota franchise to Lonrho's vehicle trading group. In 1973, the East African Tanning and Extract Company took over the Kenyan Tanning and Extract Company, an Asian firm which had been the competitor to EAT & E Co. since the 1930s, thus completing a monopoly over wattle-growing and extract-manufacture in Kenya.[69]

After this period of consolidation, which can be said to have ended around 1974, a new phase of *expansion* began in Kenya. Lonrho began to change its tactics and invested in *new plant* in Kenya for the first time. These changes were part of an overall strategy of the parent company in Africa and reflected on Lonrho's part a response to nationalist pressure.

By this time, Lonrho had invested in most of the major economic sectors in Kenya, but was likely to be blocked from further takeovers. These Lonrho investments in *new* plant between 1974 and 1975 have included a textile factory at Nanyuki and a vehicle-assembly plant near Mombasa. The decision to move into production directly was no doubt related to Lonrho's global strategy, and in the case of the vehicle-assembly plant it is clear that competition from other vehicle importers prompted import-substitution manufacturing under protected conditions. The vehicle-assembly plant in 1975 cost K£1·4 million to construct and was designed to assemble Ford,[70] Mazda, Datsun, Mer-

68 Interview with U. Gecaga, chairman of Lonrho East Africa in Nairobi, 1974.
69 Annual returns of the Registrar General for those companies.
70 IDB annual report for 1975.

cedes, Peugeot and Toyota commercial vehicles. The conditions under which the management contract was drawn up for this enterprise involved a high level of political mediation.

Like many other large foreign corporations, Lonrho has changed its style of operations in the 1970s and has entered into partnerships with the Kenya government and financial agencies in the formation of new projects. These partnerships are undertaken for reasons of political protection as well as financial convenience, and we have seen that they constitute the most common form of foreign investment in the developing economies. For instance, the Nanyuki Textile Mill,[71] which went into production in late 1976, is a joint project between Lonrho managing agents, David Whitehead & Sons and the German Development Bank. This project cost a total of K£6 million and has an annual capacity to spin, weave and finish 10 million linear metres of cloth for local consumption.

After 1974, Lonrho was closely involved with local private capital in extensive urban redevelopment schemes in Nairobi. There has been some overlap in the interests of the Kenyan managers of Lonrho and the foreign company itself in these schemes. This is one example where the local managers of foreign firms use the firms as sources of money capital for their own investments. Lonrho has undertaken several business ventures in co-ordination with the large pool of Kenyan industrial capital raised by the Gema organization. This is all part of Lonrho's alliance with powerful sections of the Kenyan ruling class.

The size and influence of Lonrho in the Kenyan economy, however, have not passed unobserved. Indeed, in many African countries the firm, with its high-level political alliances, has been particularly susceptible to nationalist attack. What has been singled out by these groups has been the way in which some sections of the Kenyan bourgeoisie, in collaboration with the foreign company, have managed to further their own interests by using their positions within the firm. It is important, therefore, to examine the political context of Lonrho's investment in Kenya since the mid-1960s. When Lonrho began to take over Kenyan companies in mid-1967, the Kenya People's Union (KPU), the opposition party, strongly attacked Lonrho in a resolution condemning the change in management and ownership of the *East African Standard* newspaper group to a company with 'South African connections'.[72]

The issue was brushed aside until 1969 when the opposition party once again took up the question of Lonrho's adverse effect on the Kenyan economy and they pinpointed the alliances which the firm was making with prominent Kenyans. Mr Lumembe (MP) criticized 'those Africans who are appointed company directors, some of whom have

---

71 The Nanyuki Textile Mill went into liquidation in 1977, allegedly as a result of competition from illegal imports.
72 *EAS* 12 June 1967, Lonrho file, op. cit.

ten, twelve and even thirty directorships'. The leader of the KPU opposition party, Oginga Odinga, said in the same debate that he had asked the Minister of Commerce and Industry to let him know 'what he is doing about some of our people who are being used by foreigners in certain businesses'.[73] These complaints against Lonrho almost always emanated from a section of the petty bourgeoisie struggling to become part of the bourgeoisie itself, and therefore being opposed to the benefits which a section of the ruling group were obtaining from their alliances with foreign capital. Lonrho was always singled out for attack due to the publicity which surrounded the company and the open nature of its political alliances in Kenya and elsewhere.

These attacks on Lonrho in the 1960s were not accompanied by any formal nationalist control over Lonrho, as the firm's major acquisitions took place when the country still had a very liberal policy towards foreign investment. However, the Capital Issues Committee of the Treasury after 1972 attempted to restrict Lonrho's moves to take over more local firms. In some cases these restrictions were successful and in others not. Due to increasing nationalist pressure with regard to Africanization of top management of foreign firms since 1968, Lonrho responded by Africanizing the most strategic positions within its East African hierarchy. The alliance between Lonrho and the ruling section of the Kenyan bourgeoisie was formally cemented in 1973 when Udi Gecaga (the son-in-law of the President) was appointed to the London board of Lonrho and promoted from managing director of the local firm to chairman.[74] Also, a prominent member of the Luo community was appointed personnel manager for the group in late 1972.

It was the extensive publicity given to the leadership struggle within the Lonrho parent company in 1973 which led to renewed public attacks on the company within Kenya. During the 'boardroom crisis', Udi Gecaga, along with other Lonrho managing directors from Africa, supported the unorthodox Mr Rowland in his efforts to retain control of the Lonrho company. The British Prime Minister, Mr Heath, was not the only one to consider that the Lonrho company had broken the rules of the capitalist game. The boardroom crisis served as another reminder within Kenya of the powerful influence of the Lonrho company within the economy. In May 1973, J. M. Kariuki, the vociferous Assistant Minister for Tourism and Wildlife,[75] took up the line of the banned opposition party and accused the Lonrho company of ' buying out all the firms in Kenya' and he urged the government to investigate the activities of the Lonrho group of companies. Kariuki proposed a radical solution, that the government should act immediately in order

---

73 *Daily Nation*, 1 October 1969. Some of the most virulent attacks on Lonrho have been channelled through the *Daily Nation*, as the *Standard* is owned by the firm. The *DN* is owned by the Aga Khan group.

74 *EAS*, 25 May 1973. Gecaga was managing director of Lonrho EA from 1971.

75 J. M. Kariuki was assassinated in 1975.

to 'see the firm's balance sheets to ensure that the monies earned in Kenya did not go outside the country and if need be nationalize all the companies that had been bought by Lonrho'.[76]

Kariuki was a more sophisticated member of the opposition group and he went further than his KPU predecessors in providing evidence against Lonrho. He produced documents before the Parliament to show that Lonrho had borrowed locally a sum of approximately K£13 million in order to buy out several Kenyan firms, in addition to which he listed most of the Lonrho takeovers since 1967. I have roughly estimated that Lonrho's declared debt in Kenya in 1975 was approximately K£8 614 000.

Kariuki further attacked the policy of the Lonrho company in Kenya and charged that the *East African Standard* group of companies employed racial discrimination in differentiating between the salaries of African and European employees. Mr Kariuki further claimed that Lonrho

> has even removed some Africans in top positions because they did not happen to toe the line, and replaced them with those Africans who support the policy of certain individuals. The Minister of Finance must check on how the companies bought by Lonrho were transferred.[77]

Kariuki repeated these allegations against Lonrho on British television.

This opening attack gave rise to a stormy debate in the Kenyan Parliament which lasted several weeks and drew out the divisions within the bourgeoisie. The Kenyan High Commissioner in London was immediately anxious to reassure British investors in Kenya of the 'stable' climate of the Kenyan economy.

> The Kenyan Government has not found it necessary to pronounce itself on the Lonrho affair despite the fact that the Lonrho group has considerable interests in Kenya. In spite of this non-committal attitude, Kenya's name has been dragged into the Lonrho affair by the mass media insinuating a particular stand. This has inevitably created a certain amount of anxiety in financial and commercial circles on broader issues concerning Kenya's investment policy . . . it reamins the cardinal principle of the Kenya government's policy to attract foreign capital and expertise in developing the country.[78]

Kariuki further developed his conspiracy theory in the Kenya Parliament when he claimed that the Lonrho organization was 'an associa-

---

76 *EAS*, 10 May 1973, 'Kariuki raises Lonrho affairs in the Assembly'.
77 ibid. He was presumably referring here to members of President Kenyatta's family.
78 *EAS*, 31 May 1973.

tion created to penetrate African politics by using businesses to gain power'.[79] This is, of course, in reverse order, for any foreign capitalist enterprise operating in a particular social formation will attempt to build up alliances to protect its interests. The Lonrho chairman was provoked into replying that those making such attacks on Lonrho should repeat the allegations outside Parliament. Another MP asked the Minister for Commerce and Industry to institute a commission of inquiry to investigate the activities of Lonrho and other large foreign firms operating in Kenya. At this point the mother of Lonrho's chairman, J. Gecaga (a nominated MP), came to the defence of her son's 'comprador' position in the Lonrho company by saying that at least he was an African in charge of a large foreign company, whereas many other foreign companies did not have local people in top positions. She went on to attack Kariuki personally, accusing him of being envious of her son's well-paid position within Lonrho.[80]

The government, in reply to these criticisms, was confident enough to respond and produce an almost complete list of Lonrho-owned firms in Kenya; and the Minister of Commerce and Industry simply gave assurances that 'the government will not allow itself to be pocketed by Lonrho or any other foreign firm operating in Kenya'.[81] The appropriate verbal concessions had been made to the petty bourgeois opposition, and the issue subsided.

The next opportunity for the 'opposition' elements in Parliament to use the Lonrho company as a platform to attack the government presented itself less than a year after the London boardroom crisis, in February 1974 with the UN consultancy deal. Early in 1974, various OAU countries, at the instigation of Amin of Uganda, attacked an oil consultancy agreement that had been reached between the secretary general of the OAU and the Lonrho company. This was on the grounds that there had not been adequate consultation with OAU members before such an agreement had been reached with an 'imperialist' company which had extensive interests in Southern Africa. In fact, there is strong evidence to suggest that many of the foreign ministers were aware beforehand of the details of the oil deal, but did not condemn it until the heavy publicity given to the issue made it expedient to do so. The Kenyan petty bourgeoisie did not lose this opportunity to attack their own ruling group, particularly as the lead had been taken by their populist Ugandan neighbour. The Kenyan Vice-President and an MP (now detained) expressed opposition to the Lonrho oil deal. The former commented:

> signing an agreement of this nature would be against the leadership of the OAU and Kenya was not a party to it . . . it would be further contrary to the UN sanctions against Rhodesia if we independent

---

79 ibid.
80 ibid.
81 *EAS*, 18 May 1973.

African nations who have made a big noise against Rhodesia would now accept Lonrho, a firm deeply rooted in Rhodesia and South Africa, to be oil agent between us and the Arabs.[82]

Once again the chairman of Lonrho in East Africa issued a denial of such accusations, saying that the company's motives had been misinterpreted and that Lonrho was at that time looking north and trying to cut its ties with the white-dominated south. The oil consultancy deal had been part of Lonrho's overall strategy to link up its African and Arab interests but, as in some other cases, the gamble of the company did not seem to pay off. The company a few months later withdrew quietly from the oil consultancy deal in order to avoid further adverse publicity in the African countries in which it operated.

We have concentrated in the above sections on the opposition to the alliance between Lonrho and the dominant fraction of the Kenyan ruling class. It was contended earlier that some sections of the indigenous bourgeoisie in Kenya have used alliances with foreign firms to further their own business interests. All the top Kenyan managers of Lonrho, particularly the chairman himself, have during their time as executives been able to engage in private accumulation. From the 1974 study of directorships in Kenyan companies, Gecaga comes third with a total of thirty-eight directorships. Of these firms, seven were owned by himself and all of them were acquired by him *since* 1974. Of these firms three were investment companies (mainly in property), two were distributors of manufactured goods, one was a transporting company and the last was an importing agency. Gecaga also had a small share in a large wattle-extract company purchased by the Lonrho company in 1974.[83] In addition to investments in land, property and trade, Gecaga has, during the 1970s, moved into large-scale farming, and has also acquired land and urban property. One of his most significant investments was in Mawamu Holdings Ltd, a local firm formed in 1975 with Ngengi Muigai (chairman of Mackenzie Dalgety), to take a controlling interest in a large foreign firm, Mackenzie Dalgety.[84]

The expansion of the Lonrho conglomerate in Kenya illustrates the meteoric rise of a firm through the tactics of takeover and political alliances. During the 1960s Lonrho took advantage of Kenya's liberal investment laws, and bought into some major areas of the economy. The spectacular progress of Lonrho's development in Kenya has instigated some tough political battles between different sections of the bourgeoisie. Economic nationalists who would like to see a greater proportion of the economy under domestic control have been angered by the nature and extent of Lonrho's interests in Kenya. It is likely that with the political realignment since the death of Kenyatta in 1978,

82 *Sunday Nation*, 17 February 1974.
83 From annual returns to the Registrar General of Companies.
84 ibid.

Lonrho's privileged political position may be subject to some change. Nevertheless, the study has suggested that managers of international firms such as Lonrho are not only political intermediaries between local and foreign capital, but are also active businessmen in their own right.

Conclusion to Case Studies

In the first two case studies (on tea and shoes), the main emphasis has been on dominant international firms expanding to control the conditions of production in their respective branches. The studies have attempted to link these developments to the global strategies of the two firms, Brooke Bond Liebig and the Bata Shoe Company. Both these firms were set up during the colonial period in Kenya, and the level of state support given to the industries is considered. These firms form an interesting contrast in that tea is primarily an *export* commodity, while shoe production involves largely import-substitution to serve the local market. In the later parts of both the Bata and Brooke Bond studies, there has been an attempt to evaluate the position of the dominant foreign firm with regard to recent nationalist pressure and the emergence of indigenous production in those branches. The movement of indigenous capital into both tea and shoe (and leather) production in Kenya by the 1970s has presented a challenge to multinational dominance in those sectors. For instance, in 1977 the government tea parastatal (KTDA) took over the internal tea-marketing functions which Brooke Bond had monopolized since 1938.

The final Lonrho study reveals a different pattern of corporate expansion from the previous two, in that the firm established itself in Kenya through buying existing enterprises. The firm began its initial expansion through takeover in the mid-1960s and by the next decade had accumulated over fifty subsidiary companies. In the 1970s, the firm altered its tactics and began to invest money raised from its existing operations directly in production. The firm by the mid-1970s had extensive interests in the Kenyan economy in the areas of trading, primary production, real estate and manufacturing. This meteoric rise to pre-eminence in Kenya has been achieved in the context of a set of alliances between the multinational and prominent members of the ruling class. It is suggested that the indigenous managers of some foreign corporations are able to use their positions to support their private accumulation.

These studies and the whole discussion in Part III conclude by confirming the interdependence between domestic and foreign capital during the present phase of imperialism. It is clear that these economic factors do not operate in isolation, and the state is crucial in mediating the relationship between foreign capital and the indigenous bourgeoisie.

Conclusion

This book has sought to detail some of the features of capitalism in Kenya from the colonial to the post-colonial period. The first two parts examined the development of corporate accumulation in the context of the settler economy. The aim has been to show the mode of corporate expansion after outlining the relationship between capital and the state in three different historical periods. The book does not attempt to analyse class formation, although it has been necessary to identify the dominant class forces in each of the three historical sections.

It is clear from the discussion in Parts I and II that colonial capitalism in Kenya took different forms from that experienced by the other two East African territories (under protectorate and mandate rule respectively). Uganda and Tanganyika were more closely integrated into the orbit of metropolitan accumulation than was Kenya. The political autonomy of the settler group ensured that the area developed its productive forces to a greater extent as a basis for the *internal* accumulation of capital. The outright suppression of industries in Tanganyika and Uganda by the Colonial Office in the 1930s, because of the threat to British markets, had no parallel in Kenya.[1] The state in Kenya between the wars played an extensive role in supplying labour for the estates and raising revenue to develop infrastructure. The administration up to 1939 was highly protective of the settler economy and there was some political and financial independence of the colony from the metropolis.

The three case studies in Part I show the mode of expansion and operation of international firms in both production and distribution. Foreign investment in Kenya during this period was mainly limited to estate agriculture and mineral exploitation, for instance, tea and soda ash. The case of the tea industry indicates a contradiction between the imperatives of metropolitan and local accumulation, whereas the other cases of company expansion exhibit the intensive state of competition between merchant capitals which drove the latter into production.

By the 1930s Britain's era of *laissez-faire* capitalism was beginning to wane, which was to have a decisive impact on postwar patterns of capitalist accumulation in Kenya Colony. After 1945 international capital underwent a new phase of outward expansion under the hegemony of the United States. Given the declining position of Britain in the world economy, the state was compelled to play a more interventionist role. The 'new deal' for colonial territories after 1945 served to

---

1 In the 1930s a blanket factory and Ugandan sisal plant were destroyed by the government.

integrate Kenya more thoroughly into the global capitalist system. For instance, the British financial agencies began to take on a pivotal function with regard to colonial development. Through the Colonial Development Corporation and other agencies, the metropolitan state for the first time in Kenya directed a large amount of aid into infra-structure and African cash-crop agriculture. At the same time, British manufacturing firms moved into Kenya and began to manufacture goods behind the tariff wall, which was the logical outcome of world market competition and the concentration of capital. These changes initiated the break of settler dominance over agricultural production in Kenya, and led to the transfer of political power to the nationalists in the early 1960s. The colonial state in Kenya became incapable of reconciling class antagonisms and by the late 1950s it was evident to the metropolitan government that the interests of the capitalist system in Kenya could best be maintained by the transfer of political power to an indigenous class.

The discussion of *post-colonial* Kenya departs most obviously from the current explanations of 'economic dependency' of Third World countries. At the time of independence in Kenya it was clear that the African merchant class were poised for a move into large-scale capital-ist production. Once the political constraints of colonial rule were removed, the indigenous bourgeoisie were able to move rapidly into agriculture and commerce and by the 1970s into manufacturing as well.

However, the argument in Part III does not support the thesis of 'independent' industrialization put forward by Bill Warren.[2] He has claimed that the increased institutional control over domestic economies has enabled Third World countries to attain a degree of independent industrialization based on the home market. Warren has attempted to prove too much from dubious UN statistics on industrial growth rates[3] and this type of argument cannot take into consideration the degree of integration between the rural and urban sectors, nor productivity in the agricultural sector. He does not provide much evidence to support his contention that the enhanced power of peripheral capitalist states has led to an overall weakening of imperial-ism. Warren's bold attack on the 'dependency' orthodoxy can only be commended in so far as it drew attention to a serious flaw in current left debates, which fail to distinguish between development within the framework of capitalism and socialist revolution. They deny any pro-gress of the former because of the absence of the latter, which only results in a utopian conception of socialism. Nevertheless, Warren's general position on 'independent capitalism' fails to periodize capital

2 B. Warren, 'Imperialism and capitalist industrialization', *NLR*, no. 81, 1973.
3 ibid. For a critique of Warren's thesis, refer to J. Petras *et al.*, 'Imperialism and the contradictions of development', *NLR*, no. 85, 1974.

in the same way as the dependency theorists. The particular characteristics of capitalist development in different eras of capital are
assumed to be unproblematic by both Warren and Frank.

This study has shown that the forms of foreign investment in Kenya
have changed between the 1960s and 1970s from direct ownership
over the means of production to indirect control over use values
(technology, etc.). The particular forms of industrialization in Kenya
by the 1970s reflect a certain stage in the development of the productive forces. For instance, by the 1970s industrial processes in Kenya
involved mainly assembly-line operations, although the advance in
manufacturing has encouraged some degree of integration between
capital and consumer goods industries. This is where generalizations
about the nature of peripheral development must be placed in their
historical specificity. Kenya, for instance, has built up a technical
capacity in its import-substitution industries despite the lack of essential fuels such as coal or oil. Such industrial development has been
assisted since the colonial period by Kenya's dominant position in East
African markets, for most foreign projects since 1945 were designed as
centres of production and distribution for the entire region.[4]

It is maintained in this book that at the present stage of imperialism
there is a high degree of *interdependence* between all capitalist countries – be they advanced or developing. What are the specific problems
associated with capitalism at the peripheries? Technological dependence[5] has been identified as the main link in the chain between the
newer capitalist countries and the metropoles. In post-colonial Kenya,
for instance, local capitalists have extended their sphere of accumulation into manufacturing which has brought them into *collaboration and
competition* with foreign capital. Although our empirical studies of
industrial and corporate development in Kenya have illustrated a
general pattern of *localization* of capital, it is not possible to claim that
this trend will continue *ad infinitum*. Nationalist measures are normally used to support domestic capital *at a certain stage* of early
capitalist accumulation. The conditions of world capitalism are not
static and a vigorous phase of import substitution at this point in time
does not mean that Kenya might not at a later date become relegated
to the camp of countries which produce semi-finished raw materials for
the world market.[6] A new international division of labour would seem
to be under way in the 1970s where different areas produce specialized
primary or industrial goods for the world market. For instance, in

---

4 The process of Kenyan domination began in 1924 with the East African Customs
Union which allowed agricultural products to pass into Tanganyika duty free.

5 A sophisticated analyst of technological factors is F. H. Cardoso; see, for instance,
his 'Dependency and development in Latin America', *NLR*, no. 74, 1972.

6 Indeed the Kenyan Development Plan for 1979–84 has outlined a shift in industrial
policy from import-substitution projects to food and raw-materials processing.

several Latin American countries (Chile and Brazil, for example), the import-substitution phase would seem to have lost its impetus and given way to primary processing for export. Similarly the 'runaway industries' of South-East Asia which produce textiles, clothing and electrical components for western markets hardly conform to Warren's independent industrialization model. A great deal of work remains to be done on the conditions of global accumulation which have given rise to such trends.

There is little doubt that since the early 1900s there has been a significant degree of capitalist development in Kenya. By the 1970s we have outlined the emergence of an indigenous bourgeoisie which has its basis in the large-scale employment of wage labour in both agriculture and industry. However, this process has been fraught with contradictions such as the failure to absorb the labour force fast enough, giving rise to pressure on land, unemployment, and so on. At the political level, the Kenyan ruling class have been required to integrate competing capitalist interests and keep down popular movements. There have been only a few serious threats to the hegemony of Kenya's ruling class,[7] and there has been a remarkable maintenance of state power in the face of bitter factional disputes. Colin Leys concluded in 1975[8] that the alliance between the auxiliary bourgeoisie and foreign capital was an unstable one, particularly in the context of increasing pressure from the popular masses.

By 1978 these predictions had not been borne out. Even after the death of President Kenyatta in August 1978, the ruling class proceeded to realign at the political level with remarkable cohesion.[9] Whether the change of leadership within the ruling group, led by Arap Moi as President, will succeed in maintaining the fragile alliance between the petty bourgeoisie and the bourgeoisie proper remains an open question. Indeed by October 1978 the new President began to strike at the former power structure by attacking corruption, removing certain government officials and putting ceilings on land transfers. These changing alignments within the power structure might herald a long-term shift in the present pattern of accumulation.

The general conclusion of this study is to reject the notion of an antonomous capitalist path that is free from contradictions. Ann Philips has correctly censured underdevelopment theory for obscuring the essence of the problem by asking the question 'Can capitalism

---

7 The most serious threats to the stability of the ruling group since 1963 occurred in 1969 with the death of Mboya and the banning of KPU, and to a lesser extent in 1975 with the assassination of Kariuki.

8 Colin Leys, *Underdevelopment in Kenya, the Political Economy of Neo-Colonialism*, Heinemann, London, 1975.

9 For reports on the political transition refer to the *Kenya Weekly Review* for late August and September 1978 and the London *Times*.

promote development or does it necessarily produce underdevelopment?'[10] All that such underdevelopment theorists are really saying is that ideal development *cannot* occur under capitalism, which is hardly a novel revelation. The traditional Marxist writers on the world economy (Lenin, Rosa Luxemburg and Bukharin) may have differed in their interpretation of the location and motives for the export of capital in the early twentieth century, but they were agreed that the process of transformation to capitalism was marked by the *uneven* development of productive forces. Lenin made this clear in his exposition on the development of capitalism in Russia:

> the progressive role of capitalism may be summed up in two brief propositions: increase in the productive force of social labour and the socialization of that labour. But both of these facts manifest themselves in extremely diverse processes in different branches of the national economy . . . an equally thorough transformation must, by the very nature of capitalism, take place in the midst of much that is uneven and disproportionate: periods of prosperity alternate with periods of crisis, the development of one industry leads to the decline of another, there is progress in one aspect of agriculture . . . the growth of trade and industry outstrips the growth of agriculture.[11]

Indeed the festering and unresolved 'national questions'[12] in the advanced capitalist countries are clearly a product of the failure of the bourgeois states to integrate their own 'peripheries'. Marxists should return to the laws of accumulation which govern uneven development, rather than asserting the structural dependence of peripheries on the centres.

With regard to Kenya, this book has merely outlined aspects of corporate accumulation, but the crucial questions for the future should concern the nature of *class forces* which have emerged out of capitalist development in the region. Future work should focus on such areas as the type of integration of pre-capitalist and capitalist modes of production, the growth of the working-class, and so on.

Two parallel and contradictory tendencies have been exhibited in post-colonial Kenya: the development of a domestic bourgeoisie and a rapid internationalization of the global economy. In comparison with large multinational firms in Kenya, indigenous capital is small and insignificant. Nevertheless, at the *present stage* of accumulation in

10 Ann Philips, 'The concept of development', in *RAPE*, no. 8, 1977, p. 20.

11 V. I. Lenin, *The Development of Capitalism in Russia*, Progress Press, Moscow, 1974, p. 603.

12 Many dependency theorists assume that the national question has been solved in the advanced countries – Quebec and Scottish nationalism illustrate the falsity of this proposition.

Kenya it is still the case that value formation is *nationally* based and the state is able to support the interests of the internal bourgeoisie. During the independence period, within the limits set by Kenya's position in the global economy, the indigenous bourgeoisie have extended their control over the means of production. In the last instance it matters little to the Kenyan worker or peasant whether his exploiters are based in Nairobi or London, for the ultimate contradiction is between labour and capital, whatever its nationality. However, the locus of the class struggle must necessarily be *within* the social formation.

Sources

Archives, Libraries and Government Bodies

Foreign Office Library, London
Macmillan Library, Nairobi
East African Community Library, Nairobi
The Nation Newspaper Cuttings Library, Nairobi
Companies Registry (Department of the Registrar General), Nairobi
Lands Registry (Ministry of Lands and Settlement), Nairobi
Old records of private firms
Kenya National Archives (KNA)

Colonial Sources

Colonial Office publications (reports, surveys, etc.)
Department of Overseas Trade reports
Colonial Blue Books (annual until 1962)
Annual trade accounts for Uganda and Kenya
East African Royal Commission report, 1953–5
Reports of the East African Industrial Council, 1950s
Colonial Office reports on the Colony and Protectorate of Kenya, 1952 and 1956
Overseas Economic Survey on British East Africa, 1948
Ministerial memos in the Ministry of Commerce and Industry files, *KNA*
LEGCO debates for the colonial period, Macmillan Library
R. J. M. Swynnerton, *A Plan to Intensify the Development of African Agriculture in Kenya*, Nairobi, 1955
Colonial (later Commonwealth) Development Corporation (CDC), annual reports and accounts, 1948–76

Official Sources after Independence

Kenya Tea Development Authority (KTDA), annual reports and accounts, 1964–76
Industrial and Commercial Development Corporation (ICDC), annual reports and accounts
Development Finance Corporation of Kenya (DFCK), annual reports and accounts
Industrial Development Bank, annual reports and accounts
East African Development Bank, annual reports and accounts
East African Community, *Treaty for East African Co-operation*, rev. edn, 1972
East African Authority, *Economic and Statistical Review*
Kenya Statistical Abstracts, 1966–, Statistics Division of the Treasury
Kenya Development Plans, 1964–79, Ministry of Finance and Economic Planning

Kenya Economic Surveys, 1963–78, Ministry of Finance and Economic Planning
Investment Surveys of the East African Community, Statistics Division of the Treasury
Industrial Census, Statistics Division of the Treasury
Agricultural Finance Corporation annual reports

Private Sources

Commercial Bank of Africa, annual reports and accounts
Nairobi stockbrokers' reports
Economist Intelligence Unit reports on Kenya
Barclays Overseas Economic Surveys on Kenya
Kenya Association of Manufacturers' annual reports
Chamber of Commerce (Nairobi), reports of committees

Kenyan Newspapers

East African Standard
Sunday Nation
Daily Nation
Sunday Post (discontinued after 1975)
Kenya Weekly News (discontinued after 1962)
Weekly Review (a political weekly, 1975–)

Journals

Journal of Modern African Studies, Gaborone
Review of African Political Economy, London
Africa Contemporary Record, London
Africa Development, London
Journal of East African Research and Development, Nairobi
East African Economic Review, Nairobi
New Left Review, London
Monthly Review, New York
Canadian Journal of African Studies, Ottawa
Africa Review, Dar es Salaam
Capital and Class, Oxford
Economy and Society, London
Journal of Contemporary Asia, London

Unpublished Theses

M. P. Cowen, 'Wattle in Kenya, capital and household production', Cambridge University, 1978, PhD
Martha Honey, 'Asians in Tanzania', University of Dar es Salaam, forthcoming, PhD

S. Langdon, 'Multinational corporations in the political economy of Kenya', University of Sussex, 1976, PhD

M. D. MacWilliam, 'The East African Tea Industry, 1920–1956', Oxford University, 1958, MA

Scott MacWilliam, 'Ethnicity and Class in Kenya', University of Toronto, forthcoming, PhD

Apollo Njonjo, 'The Africanization of the white highlands: a study in agrarian class struggles in Kenya, 1950–74', Princeton University, PhD, December 1977

J. Okwissa, 'Industrial location; the case of the Bata Shoe Company', Dept of Geography, University of Nairobi, 1976, BA

M. G. Redley, 'The politics of predicament: the white community in Kenya, 1918–1932', Cambridge University, 1976, PhD

Bibliography and Suggested Reading

East Africa

A. Amsden, *International Firms and Labour in Kenya: 1945–70*, Cass, London, 1971

C. E. Barker, M. Bhagavan, P. V. M. Collande and D. Wield, 'Industrial production and transfer of technology in Tanzania; the political economy of Tanzanian enterprises', mimeo., Dar es Salaam, 1975; Zed Press, forthcoming

G. Bennet, *Kenya, a Political History, the Colonial Period*, OUP, London, 1963

Sir M. Blundell, *So Rough a Wind: The Kenya Memoirs of Sir Michael Blundell*, Weidenfeld & Nicolson, London, 1964

E. A. Brett, *Colonialism and Underdevelopment in East Africa, the Politics of Economic Change, 1919–1939*, Heinemann, London and Nairobi, 1973

A. Clayton and D. C. Savage, *Government and Labour in Kenya, 1895–1963*, Cass, London, 1974.

M. P. Cowen, 'Concentration of sales and assets: dairy cattle and tea in Magutu, 1964–1971', IDS, Nairobi, working paper no. 146, 1974

M. P. Cowen, 'Wattle production in the Central Province, capital and household commodity production, 1903–1964', mimeo., Institute for Development Studies, University of Nairobi, 1975

M. P. Cowen, 'Capital and peasant households', mimeo., Dept of Economics, University of Nairobi, 1976, to be published in Scott MacWilliam and M. P. Cowen (eds), *Essays on Capital and Class in Kenya*, Longman, London.

M. P. Cowen and K. Kinyanjui, *Some Problems of Capital and Class in Kenya*, Discussion Paper, IDS, Nairobi, 1977

M. P. Cowen and J. R. Newman, 'Real wages in Central Kenya, 1924–1974', mimeo., Nairobi, 1975

M. Dilley, *British Policy in Kenya Colony*, 2nd edn, Cass, London, 1966

H. Fearn, *An African Economy*, OUP, London, 1961

M. von Freyhold, 'On colonial modes of production', Dept of History seminar paper, University of Dar es Salaam, 1977

M. von Freyhold, 'The post-colonial state and its Tanzanian version', *RAPE*, no. 8, April 1977

F. Furedi, 'The social composition of Mau Mau in the Highlands', *Journal of Peasant Studies*, no. 1, 1974

C. Gertzel, *The Politics of Independent Kenya*, Heinemann, London, 1970

R. C. Gregory, *India and East Africa*, Clarendon Press, Oxford, 1971

W. Lord Hailey, *An African Survey*, rev. edn, OUP, London, 1956

B. Herman, 'Some basic data for analysing the political economy of foreign investment in Kenya', mimeo., Nairobi, 1972

J. Heyer, 'A survey of agricultural development in the small farm areas of Kenya since the 1920s', IDS, Nairobi, working paper no. 194, 1974

E. Huxley, *White Man's Country: Lord Delamere and the Making of Kenya*, 2 vols, Macmillan, London, 1935

E. Huxley, *Settlers of Kenya*, Greenwood, Connecticut, 1975 edn

International Labour Organization (ILO), Mission Report to Kenya, *Employment, Incomes and Equality*, Geneva, 1972

R. Kaplinsky (ed.), *Readings on the Multinational Corporation in Kenya*, OUP, East Africa, 1978

J. Kenyatta, *Suffering Without Bitterness*, EAPH, Nairobi, 1968

J. Kenyatta, *The Challenge of Uhuru: The Progress of Kenya, Selected Speeches*, EAPH, 1971

Gavin Kitching, 'The rise of an African petit-bourgeoisie in Kenya', *Journal of African History*, 1976

Gavin Kitching, 'Modes of production and Kenyan dependency', *RAPE*, no. 8, 1977

G. Lamb, *Peasant Politics, Conflict and Development in Muranga*, Julian Friedmann, Sussex, 1974

S. Langdon and M. Godfrey, 'Partners in underdevelopment; the transnationalization thesis in a Kenyan context', *Journal of Commonwealth Politics*, March 1976

S. Langdon and M. Godfrey, 'The state and capitalism in Kenya', *RAPE*, no. 8, 1977

J. M. Lee, *Colonial Development and Good Government*, Clarendon Press, Oxford, 1967

Colin Leys, *Underdevelopment in Kenya, the Political Economy of Neo-Colonialism*, Heinemann, London, 1975

Colin Leys, 'The post-colonial state', *RAPE*, no. 5, 1976

Colin Leys, 'Capital accumulation, class formation and dependency; the significance of the Kenya case', mimeo., Queen's University at Kingston, Canada, 1978

Norman Leys, *Kenya*, Hogarth Press, London, 1924

J. Lonsdale, 'The growth and transformation of the colonial state in Kenya, 1929–1952', history seminar paper, Cambridge University, 1977

J. Lonsdale and B. Berman, 'Accumulation and control: the making of the colonial state in Kenya, 1888–1929', ASA Annual Conference, September 1978

H. MacWilliam, 'The East African Royal Commission', in D. A. Low and A. Smith (eds), *A History of East Africa*, Clarendon Press, Oxford, 1976

Scott MacWilliam, 'Commerce, class and ethnicity; the case of Kenya's Luo Thrift and Trading Corporation, 1945–1972', mimeo., Australia, 1976

Scott MacWilliam, 'Some notes on the development of commerce in Nyanza', mimeo., Australia, 1976

Both of the above papers appear in Scott MacWilliam and M. P. Cowen (eds), *Essays on Capital and Class in Kenya*, Longman, London, forthcoming

Mahmood Mamdani, *Politics and Class Formation in Uganda*, Heinemann, London, 1976

P. Marris and T. Somerset, *African Businessmen*, EAPH, Nairobi, 1971

Tom Mboya, *The Challenge of Nationhood, Speeches and Writings*, Praeger, New York, 1970

Tom Mboya, 'It is African and it is socialism', sessional paper no. 10, Nairobi, 1969

Robin Murray, 'The Chandarias; the development of a Kenyan multinational', in R. Kaplinsky (ed.), *Readings on the Multinational Corporation in Kenya*, OUP, East Africa, 1978

G. Mutiso, *Kenya: Policies, Policy and Society*, EALB, Nairobi, 1975

W. T. Newlyn, *Money in an African Context*, OUP, East Africa, 1967

National Christian Council of Kenya Working Party, *Who Controls Industry in Kenya?*, EAPH, 1968

J. R. Newman, *The Ukamba Members' Association*, TransAfrica Publishing House, Nairobi, 1975

G. Oates, 'The Colonial Office, Kenya and development, 1929–1945', conference paper for the Cambridge History Conference, 1975

O. Odinga, *Not Yet Uhuru, an Autobiography*, Heinemann, London, 1967

H. W. Ord, 'The Kenya economy as a whole, 1929–1952; national income, investment and balance of payments', mimeo., Edinburgh, 1976

M. Perham, *Lugard; the Years of Authority, 1895–1952*, Collins, London, 1960

C. Rosberg and J. Nottingham, *The Myth of Mau Mau*, Praeger, New York, 1966

W. MacGregor Ross, *Kenya From Within*, Allen & Unwin, London, 1927; repr. Cass, London, 1968

John Saul, 'The unsteady state: Uganda, Obote and General Amin', *RAPE*, no. 5, April 1976

Issa Shivji, *The Class Struggles in Tanzania*, Tanzania Publishing House, Dar es Salaam, 1976

M. P. K. Sorrenson, *The Origins of European Settlement in Kenya*, EAPH, Nairobi, 1968

Nicola Swainson, 'Company formation in Kenya, with particular reference to the role of foreign capital', IDS, Nairobi, working paper no. 267, 1976, in revised form for R. Kaplinsky (ed.), *Readings on the Multinational Corporation in Kenya*, OUP, East Africa, 1978

Nicola Swainson, 'The role of the state in Kenya's postwar industrialization', IDS, Nairobi, working paper no. 275, 1976

Nicola Swainson, 'Case studies of the leather-shoe and pineapple canning industries in Kenya', mimeo., Nairobi, 1976, for the NCCK rev. edn of *Who Controls Industry in Kenya?*

Nicola Swainson, 'A case study of the transfer of skills – the Bata Shoe Company in Kenya', mimeo., Dar es Salaam, November 1976, prepared for the African Association of Political Science project on 'Multinational Corporations in Africa'

Nicola Swainson, 'The rise of a Kenyan bourgeoisie', *RAPE*, no. 8, 1977

Nicola Swainson, 'The role of the state in Kenya's postwar economic expansion', paper presented at the Canadian Association of African Studies Conference, Ottawa, May 1978

Nicola Swainson, 'State and economy in post-colonial Kenya', *Canadian Journal of African Studies*, Winter 1978

R. L. Tignor, *The Colonial Transformation of Kenya*, Princeton University Press, New Jersey, 1976

G. Wasserman, *The Politics of Decolonialisation: Kenya Europeans and the Land Issue, 1960–1965*, CUP, Cambridge, 1976

R. D. Wolff, *Britain and Kenya, 1870–1930; the Economics of Colonialism*, TransAfrica Publishing House, Nairobi, 1974

A. Wood, *The Groundnut Affair*, Bodley Head, London, 1950

C. C. Wrigley, 'Kenya; the patterns of economic life', in E. T. Harlow and E. M. Chilver (eds), *The History of East Africa*, Vol. 2, Clarendon Press, Oxford, 1965

R. van Zwanenberg, *Colonial Capitalism and Labour in Kenya, 1919–1939*, EALB, Nairobi, 1975

R. van Zwanenberg and Anne King, *An Economic History of Kenya and Uganda*, EAPH, Nairobi, 1975

General

Samir Amin, *Accumulation of a World Scale; a Critique of the Theory of Underdevelopment*, 2 vols, MRP New York, 1974

Samir Amin, *Neocolonialism in West Africa*, Penguin, Harmondsworth, 1973

Samir Amin, *Unequal Development; an Essay on the Social Formations of Peripheral Capitalism*, Harvester, Hassocks, Sussex, 1976

G. Arrighi and J. Saul, *The Political Economy of Africa*, MRP, NY, 1969

S. Avineri (ed.), *Karl Marx on Colonialism and Modernisation*, Doubleday, New York, 1969

J. Banaji, 'Modes of production in a materialist conception of history', *Capital and Class*, no. 3, 1977

P. Baran, *The Political Economy of Growth*, MRP, New York, 1957

M. Barratt Brown, *The Economics of Imperialism*, Penguin, Harmondsworth, 1974

Henry Bernstein (ed.), *Underdevelopment and Development*, Penguin, Harmondsworth, 1973; 2nd edn, 1976

H. Bernstein, 'Underdevelopment and the law of value; a critique of Kay', *RAPE*, no. 6, August 1976

Henry Bernstein, 'Sociology of underdevelopment verus sociology of development?' in David Lehmann (ed.), *Development Theory: Four Critical Essays*, Frank Cass, London, 1979

M. Z. Brooke and H. L. Remmers, *The Strategy of Multinational Enterprises*, Longman, London, 1970

N. Bukharin, *Imperialism and World Economy*, Merlin Press, London, 1972

F. H. Cardoso, 'Dependency and development in Latin America', *NLR*, no. 74, 1972

A. Foster Carter, 'Neo-Marxist approaches to development and underdevelopment', in E. de Kadt and G. Williams (eds), *Sociology and Development*, Tavistock, London, 1974

M. Dobb, *Capitalism Yesterday and Today*, Unwin Bros, London, 1958

J. Dunning (ed.), *International Investment*, Penguin, Harmondsworth, 1972

J. Dunning (ed.), *The Multinational Enterprise*, Allen & Unwin, London, 1972

A. Emmanuel, *Unequal Exchange*, NLB, London, 1971

A. Emmanuel, 'White settler colonialism and the myth of investment imperialism', *NLR*, no. 73, 1972

A. Gunder Frank, *Capitalism and Underdevelopment in Latin America*, MRP, New York, 1969

A. Gunder Frank, 'The development of underdevelopment', in *Latin America: Underdevelopment or Revolution*, MRP, New York, 1969

P. C. W. Gutkind and I. Wallerstein (eds), *The Political Economy of Contemporary Africa*, Sage, London, 1976

P. Hirst, 'Economic classes and politics', in Alan Hunt (ed.), *Class and Class Structure*, Lawrence & Wishart, London, 1977

A. G. Hopkins, 'On importing Gunder Frank into Africa', *African Economic History Review*, vol. 2, no. 1, 1975

G. Kay, *Development and Underdevelopment; a Marxist Analysis*, Macmillan, London, 1975

M. Kidron, *Foreign Investment in India*, OUP, London, 1965

F. M. Lappe and J. Collins, *Food First: Beyond the Myth of Scarcity*, Houghton Mifflin, New York, 1977

E. Laclau, 'Feudalism and capitalism in Latin America', *NLR*, no. 67, 1971

E. Laclau, 'The specificity of the political – the Poulantzas-Miliband debate', *Economy and Society*, vol. IV, 1975

V. I. Lenin, *Critical Remarks on the National Question*, Progress Publishers, Moscow, 1951 and 1976

V. I. Lenin, *Imperialism, the Highest Stage of Capitalism*, Progress Publishers, Moscow, 14th edn, 1968

V. I. Lenin, *The Development of Capitalism in Russia*, Progress Publishers, Moscow, 1974

Colin Leys, 'Underdevelopment and dependency: critical notes', *Journal of Contemporary Asia*, January 1977

Rosa Luxemburg, *The Accumulation of Capital*, Routledge & Kegan Paul, London, 1963 and 1971

H. Magdoff, *The Age of Imperialism*, MRP, New York, 1969

E. Mandel, *Marxist Economic Theory*, Merlin Press, London, 1972

E. Mandel, *Late Capitalism*, NLB, London, 1976

Karl Marx, *Surveys from Exiles* and *Revolutions of 1848*, ed. D. Fernbach, NLB, London, 1973

Karl Marx, *Capital*, Vols 1–3, Progress Publishers, Moscow, 6th edn, 1976

Karl Marx and F. Engels, *On Colonialism*, Progress Publishers, Moscow, 6th edn, 1976

P. McMichael, 'The concept of primitive accumulation: Lenin's contribution', *Journal of Contemporary Asia*, no. 4, 1977

P. O'Brien, 'A critique of Latin American theories of dependency', in L. Oxaal, T. Barnett and D. Booth (eds), *Beyond the Sociology of Development*, Routledge & Kegan Paul, London, 1975

R. Owen and R. Sutcliffe (eds), *Studies in the Theory of Imperialism*, Longman, London, 1972

C. Palloix, *Les Firmes multinationales et le procès d'internationalisation*, Maspero, Paris, 1973

N. Poulantzas, *Political Power and Social Classes*, NLB, London, 1973

N. Poulantzas, *Classes in Contemporary Capitalism*, NLB, London, 1975

N. Poulantzas, *Crisis of the Dictatorships, Portugal, Spain and Greece*, NLB, London, 1976

H. Radice (ed.), *International Firms and Modern Imperialism*, Penguin, Harmondsworth, 1975

P. P. Rey, *Colonialisme, neo-colonialisme et transition au capitalisme*, Maspero, Paris, 1971

R. I. Rhodes (ed.), *Imperialism and Underdevelopment*, MRP, New York, 1970

S. Rolfe and W. Damm (eds), *The International Corporation*, Praeger, New York, 1970

W. Schoeller and W. Olle, *The World Market, National Reproduction of Capital and the Role of the Nation State*, Economics Research Bureau Paper, Dar es Salaam, 1976

W. Schoeller and W. Olle, *Weltmarkt und Reproduction des Capitals*, Europäische Verlagsanstalt, Berlin, 1976

K. K. Subrahamaniam, *Import of Capital and Technology*, New Delhi Press, 1972

C. Tugendhat, *The Multinationals*, Penguin, Harmondsworth, 1973

C. Vaitsos, *Income Distribution, Welfare Considerations and Transnational Enterprises*, Institute for Development Studies, Sussex, 1972

Bill Warren, 'Imperialism and capitalist industrialisation', *NLR*, no. 81, 1973

Carl Widstrand (ed.), *Multinational Firms in Africa*, Scandinavian Institute of African Studies, Uppsala, 1975

INDEX